"In a field crowded with overly complicated analogies and jargon, *Our Artificial Future* is smart, engaging, accessible, and sharply timed – offering the kind of clear-eyed critique of AI that only David Atkinson can deliver. It provides exactly the framework this moment demands."

J. B. Branch, AI Governance and Technology Policy Counsel, Public Citizen

"David Atkinson provides a brilliant critical review of generative AI and its effects that will answer your technical, social, and legal questions but is ultimately a call to action. Read it, and then act in your family, your workplace, your community, and your country to ensure that human values and skills are preserved."

Robert Brauneis, Michael J. McKeon Professor of Intellectual Property Law, The George Washington University Law School

OUR ARTIFICIAL FUTURE

The generative AI revolution is driven by corporations demanding legal superpowers. If we allow it to continue unchecked, the implications will be profound. This urgent, critical book exposes the unprecedented push by trillion-dollar companies to build AI on billions of unauthorized human works and redefine fundamental areas of law, including copyright, contract, and free speech. Written by an industry insider who turned from AI champion to AI critic, this highly accessible work promotes AI literacy and provides essential tools to pierce the hype. Readers will learn how to assess AI's profound societal risks to democracy and autonomy and ensure that we are the architects of – and not bystanders in – our artificial future.

David Atkinson was a paratrooper (82nd Airborne Division) before earning a master's from Harvard and a JD from Georgetown Law. He has since worked with the Allen Institute for AI and as a lecturer on AI, law, and ethics at the University of Texas at Austin. His articles on generative AI are published in multiple law journals.

Our Artificial Future

WHAT GENERATIVE AI MEANS FOR LAW AND SOCIETY

DAVID ATKINSON
University of Texas at Austin

CAMBRIDGE
UNIVERSITY PRESS

CAMBRIDGE
UNIVERSITY PRESS

Shaftesbury Road, Cambridge CB2 8EA, United Kingdom

One Liberty Plaza, 20th Floor, New York, NY 10006, USA

477 Williamstown Road, Port Melbourne, VIC 3207, Australia

314–321, 3rd Floor, Plot 3, Splendor Forum, Jasola District Centre, New Delhi – 110025, India

Cambridge University Press is part of Cambridge University Press & Assessment, a department of the University of Cambridge.

We share the University's mission to contribute to society through the pursuit of education, learning and research at the highest international levels of excellence.

www.cambridge.org
Information on this title: www.cambridge.org/9781009719612
DOI: 10.1017/9781009719605

When citing this work, please include a reference to the DOI 10.1017/9781009719605

First published 2026

Cover image: © gremlin / E+ / Getty

A catalogue record for this publication is available from the British Library

A Cataloging-in-Publication data record for this book is available from the Library of Congress

ISBN 978-1-009-71962-9 Hardback
ISBN 978-1-009-71961-2 Paperback

For my son, without whose interruptions this book would have been written five times faster.

Contents

Figure and Tables

FIGURE

TABLES

Boxes

Acknowledgments

A special thanks to Chandler Lawn, a couple of great friends from a former workplace, Saskia Reford, Casey McKee, Jen Dumas, Patrick Yurky, Margo Williams, Brian Villamar, Ishika Bhatia, Annique Wong, and all my current and former students!

Introduction

I suppose you could call me an AI critic, but it wasn't long ago that I was an absolute evangelist. I had my first real introduction to AI in 2015, when I transitioned from being an active-duty Army officer to a graduate student at Harvard. A friend shared a link to a blog that used colorful illustrations and language to describe how AI could lead to either a utopia or doom. Being a diehard optimist, I became instantly hooked on the AI idealist view. The doom side of things, most often addressed by "AI safety" or "AI alignment" researchers, seemed serious but manageable.

Like most introductions to the potential harms of AI, the blog focused on an AI system optimized to create … paperclips. This thought experiment, known as the paperclip maximizer, has become a cornerstone of discussions on AI safety. It goes something like this: Suppose you create a super-"intelligent" AI whose only job is making as many paperclips as possible for your paperclip-manufacturing facility. This seems harmless. But the AI would probably quickly realize that to achieve its mission, it'd need to ensure it couldn't be turned off. If it succeeded, we'd already be in some trouble, but the AI would eventually run out of metal to turn into paperclips, right?

Not so fast. Because the AI is extremely intelligent, it would explore other methods to produce paperclips. Metal, like everything, consists of atoms. So the super-intelligent AI could devise a way to break down different things into atoms, rearrange them into the types of atoms needed to form metal (e.g., add or remove protons), and then rearrange them into molecules that form metal, thereby obtaining plenty of metal for more paperclips. On a mission to optimize for paperclip creation over everything else, it would eventually break down most stuff (chairs, tables, concrete, glass, trees, etc.). This includes, tragically, humans. You. Me. Everyone. We'd just be atomic fodder for paperclips.

The scenario sounds absurd, but it illustrates a real problem: An AI system optimizing for a narrow goal without a broader understanding of human values could pursue it in catastrophically literal ways.

We'll revisit the alignment problem later.[1]
But on the other side of the issue: paradise!

[1] See Chapter 26 ("Artificial General Intelligence").

AI could[2] potentially cure certain cancers, prevent and reverse global warming, end famines, develop ultra-efficient forms of energy production and storage, radically enhance education, turbocharge the economy, ensure the safety of all people, and, generally, allow humans to focus on whatever gives our lives meaning. Why worry about being turned into a paperclip when you can so easily envision a steady march toward utopia in our lifetimes?

I carried this excitement into graduate school, eagerly absorbing all proclamations of technological advancement from tech luminaries. Waymo's leader gave a TED Talk in 2015, in which he was hopeful they'd solve the self-driving vehicles problem within four years![i] In 2016, AI researcher Geoffrey Hinton told us that AI was so good at reading CT, MRI, and X-ray scans that we should stop training radiologists![ii] Also in 2016, the World Economic Forum estimated that AI would eliminate over five million jobs by 2020![iii]

Waymo's deadline came and went. Widely available, fully autonomous vehicles remain elusive a decade later.[3] Radiologists remain essential to medical diagnosis and treatment today. And while AI has indeed displaced some roles, the mass AI-induced unemployment predicted has yet to materialize.

Fully self-driving vehicles and AI radiologists would be tremendous technological achievements, but they would pale in comparison to achieving artificial general intelligence (AGI). Although there is no set definition for AGI, the term is usually associated with AI capable of performing all human cognitive tasks.[4] Unlike narrow AI systems designed for specific tasks, such as chess-playing programs or image recognition software, AGI would, in theory, match or exceed human intelligence across all domains.

My zeal for AI was renewed, perhaps even turbocharged, by my internships in the San Francisco Bay Area during law school. In 2017, I interned at LinkedIn in Silicon Valley. The internship felt like a dream. Everyone was kind and even generous. The weather was perfect, and somehow I landed an Airbnb in Los Altos Hills, an ideal area for someone who enjoys long walks on trails. Based on a recommendation from another LinkedIn intern, I began listening to venture capitalist (VC) podcasts while

[2] The word "could" here is doing a LOT of work. I'll revisit this in Chapter 27 ("Frameworks for Thinking about GenAI").

[3] Currently, Waymo only operates in eleven cities. It plans to expand to four more in 2026, making them tens of thousands of cities short of ubiquity. None of the cities are in areas with long and harsh winters or rainy seasons, and the vehicles almost exclusively drive on city roads rather than highways.

[4] It's unclear how much a distinction between cognitive and physical intelligence matters. If AI is as smart as humans, it should be able to design a robot that could perform any reasonable physical task, such as playing basketball, and it should be able to load itself into the robot to act as its "brain," providing the thinking necessary to guide the physical activity. When I talk about AGI, then, I mean AI that perform any task a human can, including physical tasks. Other definitions: passing the Turing Test (which requires a human to interactively distinguish whether text is produced by another human or by a machine), outperforming humans at "most economically valuable work," and AI being given $100,000 of capital and turning that into $1 million.

walking, such as those by Reid Hoffman and the VC firm a16z. These podcasts, hosted by the very people funding AI companies, naturally painted an optimistic picture of technological progress.

Marinating in these deeply self-interested views shaped my perception of technological progress and the astounding future ahead. Whenever I heard pushback from a tech critic, I would dismiss it reactively. If the critic didn't understand or believe how some technological prophecy would come to pass, it was because they lacked the insider knowledge of the CEOs and VCs. I deduced that the company leaders and their funders must know something that the critics didn't. Why else would they speak so confidently and optimistically?[5]

When I returned to law school that fall, I took a course called Law of Robots, which further stoked my interest. For my final paper, I wrote about how criminal liability might apply to AGI.[iv] The following summer, I interned in San Francisco, continuing my long walks and marathon podcast-listening sessions. During my final year of law school, I wrote another AGI-related paper, this time about whether an AI system could ever satisfy the constitutional requirements to become president. I concluded it could.[v]

Following graduation, I applied to OpenAI. They flew me to San Francisco for an in-person interview and espoused how mission-driven and research-focused they were, how tight-knit the company was (board game night every Thursday!), and how they planned to never go above about 100 employees.[6]

I ended up working in-house at an education technology company and began teaching myself to code via Codecademy. The learning pathway I chose? Machine learning, naturally. Feeling somewhat constrained in the role, which was limited to conducting contract reviews, I sought a new employer after a year and, figuratively, leaped into the world of autonomous vehicles. I bought into the idea that self-driving semi-trucks would be cruising across the nation within a couple of years, being more cost-effective and environmentally friendly than human-driven big rigs.

After pestering the chair of the Business, Government & Society Department at the University of Texas at Austin for three years, I secured a job teaching one course per semester there while working at an autonomous vehicle company. The department chair, with delightful foresight, asked if I'd like to teach a course on law, ethics, and AI. I happily and eagerly jumped at the chance.

The tech industry could not have asked for a more cheerful advocate, and I could not have asked for a more interesting starting time. My first law, ethics, and AI course launched less than two months after OpenAI introduced ChatGPT to the world in November 2022. While I had planned for the course to focus on machine learning, with each week covering a different topic – AI and medicine, AI and war, AI and finance, AI and the boardroom, AI and social media, AI and image recognition, and so on – I was too excited not to bring up fun examples ricocheting across the internet

[5] I'll revisit this in Chapter 2 ("Why GenAI Is Made").

[6] For reference, as of fall 2025, OpenAI is now estimated to have at least 4,000 employees.

from chatbots and image generators. It was all so new, neat, jaw-dropping, and fun! I specifically remember sharing with my class that DALL-E, OpenAI's image generator, had been trained on hundreds of millions of images. "Isn't that crazy?" I asked in awe. Think about it. *Hundreds of millions* of images processed to create a single AI system. Incredible.[7]

Initially, I did not pause to question the origin of the training data, how it was collected, or whether any of the sources had authorized its use to train OpenAI's models. When I lectured on the sources of data for training AI, I was primarily concerned with dataset representativeness to prevent or limit biased or inaccurate outputs. My focus was on AI that made loan-approval recommendations or on facial recognition that failed to identify darker skin tones. I don't think I mentioned copyright at all that semester.

My views on AI evolved over the course of the year. I left the autonomous vehicle company after alerting the federal government to what appeared to be the improper sharing of trade secrets with entities in China without proper agreements in place or the board's awareness. By a stroke of luck, I landed a job a few months later with the Allen Institute for Artificial Intelligence (Ai2).

Ai2's stated goal (at the time) was "AI for the common good." They had teams exploring the values embedded in AI and their implications for morality and ethics. They were drafting an AI ethics charter to express their commitment to the thoughtful and ethical development of AI. There was an AI & Society group focused on improving AI literacy, and the legal team was finalizing a new licensing agreement that aimed to strike a balance between openness to encourage research and acting responsibly. Best of all, the people I worked with all seemed genuinely caring, humble, intelligent, and kind. I'd found my home.

During my first month on the job, the general counsel (GC) assigned me a particularly interesting task: to help the team gain a deeper understanding of how copyright law intersects with AI. The GC had noted that the times were changing. It used to be that few people seemed to care if their data was scraped – that is, downloaded from a website, often without authorization – and used to train AI, possibly because they didn't know it was happening, but also perhaps because the scraping often benefited them. For instance, Google's web scraping improved search results, creating value for both users and website owners.[8] But Ai2, like most major AI organizations, had shifted its focus from narrow AI applications with clear use cases to generative AI (GenAI). At the time, I was all for it.

In May 2023, a month before I joined, Ai2 announced that it would create OLMo, "an open language model made by scientists, for scientists." The plan was to release a seventy-billion-parameter model in early 2024, trained on one of the world's greenest supercomputers. To put this in perspective, seventy billion parameters would

7 I even offered extra credit for the student who created the most interesting image satisfying some basic criterion.

8 See Chapter 20 ("The Economics of the Internet").

make OLMo comparable in size to some of the most powerful language models available at the time. Ai2 stated that "the ethical and educational considerations around the creation of this model will also be openly shared and discussed to help guide the understanding and responsible development of language modeling technology." One of the lead researchers, Hannaneh Hajishirzi, was quoted in the press release saying, "OLMo will be the first language model specifically designed for scientific understanding and discovery."[vi] GeekWire accurately noted that "AI2 has also created an ethics review committee composed of both internal and external advisors to provide feedback throughout the process."[vii]

I was stoked. It was everything I wanted in an AI entity: cutting-edge research, transparency, and thoughtfulness about ethical considerations, as well as efforts to enhance society's understanding of AI and its implications through AI literacy. If there were good guys in AI, they were Ai2.

When it came time for me to research copyright law, a topic I had neither studied in law school nor worked on in my previous jobs, and to strengthen arguments that our use of copyrighted works was fair use, I was delighted to come across "Fair Learning" by Mark Lemley and Bryan Casey. The fair use doctrine, established in copyright law, allows for the limited use of copyrighted material without permission for purposes such as criticism, comment, parody, or research. However, its application to AI training data remains a hotly contested issue. Their paper made several arguments about why training machine learning systems on unauthorized content was likely fair use, and I ate it up, taking copious notes and briefing the legal team.[9] It was all coming together. We had ideals, we were pursuing them, and we had a legal argument to support them.

However, OLMo, as originally envisioned and announced, never materialized. The press release has since been removed from Ai2's website. Ai2 never published an ethics charter; the AI literacy program and the AI & Society group were deprioritized and eventually sputtered into irrelevance. Ai2 also switched from its proprietary responsible license to the permissive Apache 2.0 license and from the greenest supercomputer to GPUs in a decidedly un-green data center in hot, dry Austin, Texas. Ai2 also never publicly shared the ethical considerations behind building its LLMs, and the ethics review committee was quietly shuttered.

By that fall, I had begun asking why we were allowing the datasets and models to be used for commercial purposes. If our goal was to advance scientific research, why did anyone need to be able to make money off of it? To me, it was acceptable to use unauthorized works for scientific research, but to put in the legwork to collect and clean the data, train a high-performing model on it, and then allow anyone in the world to use any of it to generate revenue seemed … wrong. Under the text and data mining exemption of the Digital Millennium Copyright Act, universities were required to control access to copyrighted works, which made sense. I didn't

9 I'll revisit copyright law in Chapter 11 ("An Introduction to Copyright Law").

understand why research entities couldn't similarly control access to their AI artifacts when they used copyrighted works. In effect, such entities could be thought of as a free research and development department for companies.

Not long after, I made what I called my "Book of Questions." It was just a series of topics that I thought we hadn't put enough thought into. For example, I reviewed the results of several prominent surveys on AI, and they consistently show that Americans are more concerned than excited about AI development.[viii] I wanted to know whether and why Ai2 might develop technology that didn't align with the general public's views or desires, given our focus on "AI for the common good." More pointedly, I didn't understand why we didn't pursue a more democratic approach.

Given that all major GenAI companies were focused on creating AGI, some researchers began to wonder whether Ai2 also had that goal. In January 2024, someone asked the CEO about it at an all-hands meeting, and the CEO dismissed the idea, saying Ai2 couldn't possibly be working on AGI because he didn't even know how to define it.

At the break, in a room with hundreds of seats, the CEO happened to sit next to me. I wanted to revisit the question because public surveys had consistently shown that most people do not want AGI.[ix] "How do you define AI?" I asked.

"I don't know how to define it. It's amorphous," he replied.
"But Ai2 is working on AI?"
"Yes, of course."
"How can we work on AI without having a definition, but we can't work on AGI?"
He had no reply.

In late spring 2024, I began writing a law review article for the first time since law school. The idea was simple: review all the claims in GenAI litigation and tally them. I then provided a concise description of each claim and an example of how it could apply to GenAI.

I enjoyed writing the paper so much that I started another one shortly thereafter. It was about GenAI and freedom of speech under the First Amendment. A month later, I wrote two more. One was about GenAI and copyright law,[10] and the other was about GenAI and contract law.[11]

A few weeks after posting the papers on a preprint website, I was informed that the GC position at Ai2 was being eliminated and that I was being laid off because I had been there the shortest amount of time among all the lawyers. The legal team shrank from four to two members even as the risk of litigation rose, and lawsuits against GenAI companies increased. The reason – namely, to improve efficiency – was

[10] The paper is called David Atkinson, Unfair Learning: GenAI Exceptionalism and Copyright Law, 25 Chi.-Kent J. Intell. Prop. 43 (2026). Available at: https://scholarship.kentlaw.iit.edu/ckjip/vol25/iss1/5

[11] The paper is called David Atkinson, Putting GenAI on Notice: GenAI Exceptionalism and Contract Law, 120 Nw. U. L. Rev. Online 27 (2025), https://scholarlycommons.law.northwestern.edu/cgi/viewcontent.cgi?article=1357&context=nulr_online.

briefly provided at an all-hands meeting (neither the CEO nor the COO ever spoke with me directly about it). Apparently, either assessing the legal risks of novel technologies with novel applications was moving too slowly, or the legal team was so highly efficient, with too little work to keep us busy, that the CEO felt money spent on lawyers could be better allocated to marketing (a position posted shortly after we learned the legal team would be halved).[12]

The Book of Questions took on a life of its own in my academic work. I used ideas from it as a springboard for an open-source textbook that I work on with my students. We edited it each spring.[13] It was through developing that document that I began exploring the many, many ethical and legal issues that intersect with GenAI. Whenever I encountered a new area of concern, I added it to a list to explore in the book. Soon, the list of issues ballooned. A small sample includes:

- Hallucinations: when AI systems generate false or misleading information presented as fact
- Safety: the need to prevent AI systems from causing harm to users or society
- Disinformation/misinformation: the potential for AI to create and spread false information at scale
- Data scraping and consent: using copyrighted or personal data without permission
- Cybersecurity risks: AI systems as both tools for and targets of cyberattacks
- Environmental impact: the massive energy consumption required for AI training and operation
- GenAI oligopoly: the concentration of AI power among a few major companies
- Effect on the workforce: job displacement and transformation across industries
- Human labor for RLHF training: the often poorly compensated workers who train AI systems to be helpful and harmless.

Each of these issues represents a complex intersection of technology, law, and ethics that society is only beginning to grapple with.

By the time I left Ai2, I was firmly in the AI-critic camp. But this is not an anti-AI screed, and I am not anti-AI. I still believe AI, including GenAI, can be a force for tremendous good, but I'm far less inclined to think broad societal benefits are inherent or the most likely outcome. My previous rose-colored outlook seems more than naive to me today. It strikes me as childish.

GenAI – the technology behind popular chatbots like ChatGPT, Gemini, and Claude – is this decade's most consequential technological development. It has prompted multitrillion-dollar companies like Microsoft and Google to reorient their entire business strategies. At the same time, startups such as OpenAI, Anthropic, and

12 If the second reason was the primary driver, an interesting fact is that, although Ai2 is at the forefront of AI research, the legal team did not utilize any AI tools. They were never necessary.

13 I stopped this project once students started heavily relying on GenAI to do their writing, undermining the purpose of the exercise.

xAI (now a part of SpaceX) have seen their valuations surge into the hundreds of billions of dollars. Chip designers have also seen their valuations skyrocket in short order, with Nvidia, the company that provides the chips most widely used for AI, becoming the world's most valuable company.

Unfortunately, the legality of GenAI's rise is hardly on the general public's radar and is only slightly better known among legal scholars. I participated in the first seminar educating all Washington State district judges about GenAI, and none of them were familiar with how the technology worked or how it was developed. This is significant because if there is almost no GenAI literacy outside the tight-knit GenAI technologist community and legal specialists, society risks extending, expanding, and entrenching extraordinary legal privileges and exemptions in ways it has never done before.

The stakes could not be higher. We are essentially allowing a handful of companies to reshape fundamental aspects of how information is created, shared, and monetized, often using content created by others without permission or compensation.

This text aims to provide a friendly, engaging, frank, accessible, and informative introduction to GenAI and its foreseeable legal and ethical implications. I will rely on my law review articles, computer science papers, news articles, my open-source textbook, and insights from my work as in-house counsel at an AI research institute to inform the book's arguments. The chapters will be intentionally chunked into sections and kept relatively concise, making it easier for you to consume, understand, retain, and revisit the information.

I hope that by the end of the book, you will be equipped with the necessary knowledge and feel empowered to shape how GenAI affects you, rather than let GenAI companies choose how they will impact you.

The transformation is already underway. The question is not whether AI will reshape society, but whether we will have a say in how it reshapes society. This book is your invitation to join that conversation while there is still time to meaningfully influence its outcome.

PART I

Understanding GenAI

Before I dive into the legal and societal implications of GenAI, I want to provide the scaffolding needed to understand the technology. Part I will explain why AI companies are rushing to develop GenAI and how GenAI is made. Finally, I'll explain how GenAI is evaluated, and how those evaluations drive the decisions that shape GenAI development. Once you understand those three concepts, the actions of the companies and the behaviors of their models become less mysterious and more predictable.

1

Overview

It is impossible to grasp the implications of GenAI without first understanding some fundamentals. As a starting point, we need a common understanding of terminology. Perhaps the best question to begin with is: What the heck is AI?

I have an unsatisfying answer: It depends. When I first started teaching my law, ethics, and AI course, I used the definition that AI is software that performs activities that would otherwise require a human. However, this definition is merely a means to initiate a discussion, as it's practically useless.

By that definition, calculators must surely be AI, right? What else besides humans could multiply 13 by 8? And, in fact, calculators are a form of what's now called "good old-fashioned AI" (GOFAI), which just means stringing together a bunch of if-then statements, as in, "if name is 'David,' print 'David.'" At one point, GOFAI was probably as impressive as magic to many. It could guide robot vacuums and robot cars, provide map directions, assist with spell-checking, and do so much more. Writing the program could be tedious and hard to scale, but the results were largely reliable, and problems were relatively easy to diagnose. The code was readable, and by following the trail of logic, you could identify what caused the problematic outcomes.

The next advance was with machine learning. The idea with machine learning is that by feeding the model enough labeled examples of, say, cats, the model would learn to recognize what a cat is and what it is not. This was the kind of advance that was probably impossible with GOFAI. It is difficult to think how one could describe in code all the facets that make identifying a cat possible with if-then statements. One might start by describing fur, four legs, and pointy ears, but one would also surely eventually realize that lots of animals meet that description and that not all cats are covered in fur. So one would go back to the drawing board and ponder what constitutes a cat's cat-ness. Perhaps such a thing exists and can be reduced to human-readable code, but I remain skeptical.[1]

[1] If "scratches you when you reach for it under a bed" then "cat"? If "intentionally pushes random objects off countertops for no apparent reason" then "cat"?

Instead, machine learning, um, "learns" from repeated exposure to examples. We don't know what it "sees" or exactly how it determines what it sees, but we know it works. This is both cool and spooky. It's cool in the sense that we can solve many hard, practical problems relatively simply that may not have been possible or practical before. But it's spooky in that we don't know how it works. Therefore, when a machine learning algorithm is used to make a consequential decision, such as whether someone should remain in jail or receive a loan, there is no way to understand why or how the model arrived at its conclusion with great precision.

But this book is not primarily concerned with GOFAI or machine learning. Instead, more often than not, when the book mentions "AI," it refers to any system that makes automated decisions, typically in the context of GenAI.[2]

GenAI is AI that can generate novel outputs. You ask for a poem, a polite email, a specific image, and so on, and it generates one. The ability to generate something new is not the only differentiator between software and GenAI. The National Institute of Standards and Technology also helpfully identified several differences in the risks associated with AI versus software. Some of them include:

1. The data used to build an AI system may not accurately represent the context or intended use of the AI system, and the ground truth may either not exist or be unavailable. Additionally, harmful bias and other data quality issues can compromise an AI system's trustworthiness, potentially leading to negative consequences.
2. Dependency on and reliance on data for training tasks, combined with the increased volume and complexity, are typically associated with such data.
3. Underdeveloped software testing standards and the inability to document AI-based practices to the standard expected of traditionally engineered software for all but the simplest of cases.
4. Difficulty in performing regular AI-based software testing, or determining what to test, since AI systems are not subject to the same controls as traditional code development.
5. Computational costs for developing AI systems and their impact on the environment and planet.[i]

There are different types of GenAI models (diffusion-based,[3] foundational, application-specific, and so on), but this book focuses on the most widely used general-purpose models, such as OpenAI's GPTs, Google's Gemini, xAI's Grok, and Anthropic's Claude. A list of the major GenAI companies, their CEOs, and their popular models is given in Table 1.1.

[2] This is not to be confused with artificial general intelligence, or AGI. AGI is the subject of Chapter 26.

[3] These are the models that generate images. They are trained by transforming noise into images from the training dataset, "learning" the patterns and contours of those images, as well as how the images relate to their accompanying text, such as image captions. Video generators do the same thing, but include a time and sometimes even a sound dimension.

TABLE 1.1 *A list of companies, CEOs, and major GenAI models*

Company	CEO	Popular Model
OpenAI	Sam Altman	ChatGPT, GPT-[3, 4, 4o, 5, etc.]
Google	Sundar Pichai	Gemini [2, 3, 4, etc.]
xAI	Elon Musk	Grok [2, 3, 4, etc.]
Anthropic	Dario Amodei	Claude [2, 3, 4, etc.]
Meta	Mark Zuckerberg	Llama [2, 3, 4, etc.]

Your next question might reasonably be: Why should I care and why focus on GenAI? The answer is that GenAI has become uber-important to society. As I write this, many articles note that GenAI may be *the* thing propping up the US economy.[ii] This is not because it's incredibly useful, but because the companies developing it are spending a significant amount on the infrastructure needed to train the models.[4] But GenAI is also important to understand because it's being woven into the fabric of society in ways that will not be easy to eradicate and that could have profound, long-lasting effects.

More abstractly, GenAI is special because it's cheap, easy to use, easy to scale, and versatile. Traditional AI (GOFAI) made for especially bad chatbots and tutors, but GenAI is just good enough to be deployed at scale, even when it shouldn't be.

While this book will pull on several threads related to GenAI, some of the underlying questions it will explore are driven in part by the late Neil Postman,[iii] who offered the following seven questions when evaluating a new technology:

1. What is the problem this technology solves?
2. Whose problem is it?
3. What new problems will be created by solving this problem?
4. Which people and institutions will be most harmed?
5. What changes in language are being promoted?
6. What shifts in economic and political power are likely to result?
7. What alternative uses might be made of this technology?

People with diverse backgrounds, perspectives, interests, and expertise will likely offer different responses. And that's the point! This type of technology should be examined in light of these types of questions, and society should weigh in democratically.

I hope that by the time you finish this book, you will feel competent and prepared to confidently participate in, and even demand, such discussions.

***

4 For context, they have spent more than the US spent on the space race in the 1960's and the Manhattan Project to develop the atomic bomb int he 1940s, adjusted for inflation, combined.

The first few chapters are just the first steps in unraveling the implications of GenAI. You will soon have a clearer understanding of why people and entities develop GenAI, how it is created, and how its performance is evaluated. This will provide a foundation for the book to build on as it discusses the technology's implications and the claims made by GenAI companies.

All this may still seem abstract to you, as if it's unrelated or out of touch with the average person's lived experience. But if you think GenAI won't affect you because you don't use it personally, think again.

GenAI does not exist in a vacuum. Despite claims that it is merely a neutral tool, as likely to be used for good as for ill, it is introduced in a complex world with embedded incentives, motives, and actors. Some aim to leverage GenAI to advance prosocial development, such as improving medicine, education, and access to legal resources. Others will seek to use the technology to slash the government, shape education in a specific direction, and defraud people. To pretend otherwise is to act negligently and unethically.

All of these examples are painfully foreseeable. It does a disservice to society when GenAI companies focus only on positive use cases and resist modifying their products to prevent harm, because such modifications could affect adoption. For example, it was foreseeable that teenagers would use chatbots like Character AI, that the use could develop into unhealthy relationships, and that those interactions could cause real-world harm.[iv] And, in fact, such interactions have allegedly led to teen suicides,[v] with the companies only making reasonable modifications to their products *after* the parents lost their child and lawsuits were filed.[vi]

If we want to use AI for good, we must be vigilant against hallucinations, biases, and other known and unsolvable problems of GenAI. But the same burdens do not apply to uses for ill: If you want to run a successful phishing campaign or use deepfakes to defraud, you probably don't care whether the model hallucinates or whether the outputs are inaccurate. You just need to deploy it at scale and have some nonzero number of people fall for it. In other words, the risks are asymmetric.

Importantly, one does not need to interact with GenAI directly to be profoundly affected by it and the decisions of those creating the technology. It has permeated technology to such a degree that interacting with it, even indirectly, is nearly unavoidable. The examples are endless. Much of the code behind common apps, for example, is now created by GenAI, as are customer support chatbots and the software that customer support humans read when addressing problems. If you live in a technologically advanced society, you are already impacted by GenAI.

The widespread adoption of relatively new technology is often (and perhaps almost always) done without much consideration for whether it's necessary or in the best interest of the individual, entity, or society. The presumption among many is that "new" equals "good" and that "advanced" technology is better. However, and this cannot be stated often enough in times like these, technology alone can't solve the world's most pressing problems, such as malnutrition, healthcare, housing, and war.

It can't even solve important, though perhaps less complex, issues like immunization, traffic, or carbon emissions. Even the most perfectly optimized plan to fix housing in the United States is absolutely worthless without the support of citizens, raw material suppliers, manufacturers, wholesalers, retailers, developers, logistics and transportation providers, financial institutions, policymakers, regulators, and more.

Moreover, all technology has downsides. Legal tech may make it cheaper and easier to defend oneself, for instance, but it also facilitates the use and prosecution of evidence by the plaintiff or prosecutor. The entity with more resources (time, money, expertise, influence) will still have the advantage. The lower barrier to filing a claim or complaint also likely means courts will be flooded with cases that would not have been filed otherwise. In response to a backlog, it's foreseeable that the government will look for additional tech solutions, which I predict will include using AI as judges.[5] Of course, AI judges will lead to their own issues,[6] but rest assured that some tech company will be waiting in the wings to offer a technical solution for a price. It's tech all the way down.[7]

GenAI is not inherently bad, and this book does not aim to identify every possible negative outcome. However, it is not intended as a promotional tool for tech companies that claim they will revolutionize math, science, and art, leading to shared prosperity for all. Instead, this book will address the legal, ethical, and societal issues I consider most interesting, hopefully providing ample fodder for discussion and fostering greater awareness of what is happening and what we can reasonably expect.

For now, unless the government takes meaningful action, we are all guinea pigs for AI companies. It's unclear whether we will benefit from the technology in a meaningful way, and harms are inevitable. Unfortunately, these harms will be borne by society as a whole because the government allows tech companies to externalize risks while internalizing the benefits (i.e., huge valuations). Currently, a few dozen people at a half-dozen companies are deciding what is in our best interests based on what's in *theirs*.

5 A perfectly reasonable alternative would be to hire more qualified human judges. But humans cost money.

6 Constitutional issues around due process come to mind. Procedural due process is a constitutional requirement under the Fifth and Fourteenth Amendments that mandates the government follow fair, established legal procedures before depriving any person of life, liberty, or property.

7 It's also not clear GenAI will provide the best outcomes. As Professor of Administrative Law Julie Ponce noted:

> 100% of AI machines are psychopaths because they lack empathy. Humans, indeed, make mistakes, but only 1% are psychopathic … I'm not sure I want a machine incapable of having any kind of emotion, of displaying empathy, and therefore incapable of displaying fairness to decide about me. Fairness has been part of our Civil Code for many years; the rules have to be tempered, they have to be tailored to the case.

J. Ponce (April 27, 2025). 100% of AI machines are psychopaths. Humans make mistakes, but only 1% are psychopathic, *EL PAÍS English*. Retrieved November 29, 2025, from https://tinyurl.com/8hww333b.

A core motive of writing this book is to promote AI literacy, not as an end in itself but as a means to a particular end: I aim to encourage greater democratic participation in the development and deployment of this omnipresent technology. I want to encourage people to participate actively, not to be passive subjects.

If you care about your well-being, the well-being of society, the future of your children, or the children of others, and if you want to form a more informed opinion of GenAI, this is the book for you.

1.1 DISCUSSION QUESTIONS

1. The chapter discusses good old-fashioned AI (GOFAI) and machine learning. Can you think of any everyday examples of GOFAI or machine learning that you interact with regularly, and how do they compare to the GenAI models discussed?
2. Neil Postman's seven questions for evaluating new technology are presented. Which of these questions do you think is most important for society to consider regarding GenAI, and why?
3. Several new problems have been created by GenAI, including the spread of fake news, an unprecedented scale of copyright infringement, and the threat of massive and rapid job displacement. Which of these actual or potential problems concerns you the most, and what steps do you think could be taken to mitigate it?
4. The table of popular GenAI models includes OpenAI's GPTs, Google's Gemini, xAI's Grok, and Anthropic's Claude. Are you familiar with any of these models, and if so, what has been your experience or perception of them?
5. Society is increasingly anthropomorphizing AI. Do you find yourself doing this, and what are the potential implications of referring to AI with human-like terms and attributes?
6. The alternative uses of GenAI encompass both beneficial applications (such as personalized learning and accessibility) and harmful ones (including deepfakes and cybercrime). How can we ensure that beneficial uses are prioritized and developed responsibly while minimizing harmful applications?

2

Why GenAI Is Made

We are living through a technological gold rush. The release of a single chatbot in 2022 irrevocably shattered the AI landscape, igniting a reaction the likes of which Silicon Valley has never seen.

But the AI boom did not emerge from the ether, nor is it driven purely by altruistic motives. This chapter explores why billions of dollars are being poured into an industry where most leading companies have yet to turn a profit. What drives this seemingly irrational exuberance? The answer lies in a complex web of incentives that reveals as much about human nature and capitalism as it does about technology itself.

I examine ten powerful forces driving the rapid and expensive push to develop and deploy GenAI: shareholder primacy, financial incentives, first-mover advantages, data-collection imperatives, safety justifications, relevance fears, the pursuit of prestige, fear of missing out (FOMO), technological determinism, and regulatory entrepreneurship. Together, these incentives create a perfect storm, explaining why AI development often prioritizes velocity over deliberation, growth over sustainability, and market capture over societal benefit.

It seems there's a new self-proclaimed "AI" company every day. While using the letters "AI" to describe a business is akin to sprinkling magic fairy dust on a pitch deck, capable of transforming a mundane software company into a billion-dollar unicorn, the sheer scale of investment suggests a deeper, more structural driver than mere hype.

Consider the scale: Training a single state-of-the-art AI model now costs upward of $100 million, with some estimates reaching into the billions.[i] Yet the companies making these investments have little certainty about when, or even if, they'll see returns. This is the product of a unique constellation of incentives that create an almost irresistible momentum toward AI development, regardless of the ethical risks or financial costs involved.

Understanding these forces is the essential first step toward understanding the world being rapidly built around us. If we don't understand why this technology is being developed and deployed at this breakneck pace, we have no hope of shaping *how* it is deployed. Highlighting the incentives shows how society can mold GenAI. If you can shape the incentives, you can shape the outcomes. The following sections examine the primary forces driving this rapid deployment.

2.1 INCENTIVE 1: SHAREHOLDER PRIMACY

While many companies may aspire to elevate ethical considerations and exercise greater caution, the prevailing dynamics of US capitalism, particularly in the venture capital (VC) sphere, often curtail these ambitions. The structure of VC inherently mandates aggressive risk-taking. Typically, VC funds operate on a ten-year timeline, expecting returns that exceed ten times the initial investment. This bar incentivizes rapid scaling over careful, measured development. Venture capitalists do not want a reasonable, profitable business; they want a fabulously wealthy one.

The principles of VC and shareholder primacy inherently orient a company's primary obligations toward its funders rather than broader society. Venture capitalists invest across a portfolio, knowing a few successes must compensate for many failures. Unsure which ventures will ultimately triumph, they incentivize all investments to expand and capture market share with maximum velocity, at virtually any cost.

This pressure isn't confined to VC-backed startups. Public companies operate under similar duress. Microsoft's CEO, for instance, candidly spoke of compelling Google to "dance" by rapidly integrating AI.[ii] This aggressive, shareholder-approved strategy (as evidenced by the subsequent share price bump) was intended to force Google into a reactive mode, potentially leading to hasty decisions that could compromise its core business. It illustrates a system in which companies internalize profits while externalizing societal costs, whether through the environmental impact of new data centers or the hurried approval of risky (or, at least, insufficiently tested) model behaviors.

Consequently, a predictable environment emerges. The launch of ChatGPT triggered Google's infamous "code red" because the search giant felt compelled to respond immediately, regardless of whether its technology was fully prepared or ethically sound.[iii] Unsurprisingly, when Google unveiled Bard and Microsoft introduced Bing Chat, both were accompanied by demonstrations that unintentionally showcased model "hallucinations," including Bing's chatbot expressing romantic feelings and displaying other erratic behavior and Bard providing an incorrect historical "fact." These public failures were largely dismissed as "growing pains" in the race to capture market share, an environment where basic safeguards became afterthoughts. Not to be outdone, months later, Meta announced Llama, whose weights were quickly leaked, demonstrating how rapidly AI capabilities can escape controlled environments.

But few inside the tech bubble seemed to care. Every company could rely on a "whataboutism" defense: What about OpenAI? What about what Google is doing? What about China?

This frenetic environment fosters an incessant demand for companies to demonstrate quarterly progress. Success is gauged by proxies like revenue growth, increased daily active users, or heightened engagement, which financial markets deem valuable. When one company gains an edge, others are incentivized to follow suit, creating a competitive one-way ratchet. This system prioritizes easily measurable outputs, implicitly sidelining less quantifiable yet vital aspects, such as societal well-being and fairness. GenAI companies *need* to bring in more cash to make their investors happy and to pay for the incredible debt they are generating as they build out data centers and burn through tokens.[1]

Concerns are also mounting that excessive VC influence over market dynamics is causing significant distortions. The ridesharing sector offers a prominent example.

For over a decade, companies like Uber and Lyft were sustained by substantial VC infusions, operating at massive losses to undercut traditional services and build market dominance. Uber alone raised over $24 billion[2] before its initial public offering (IPO).[iv] This abundant capital created high barriers to entry, effectively sidelining competitors who might have possessed superior or more sustainable business models. For the VCs who invested, the priority was less about cultivating a thriving market and more about safeguarding their investment until a lucrative IPO could secure their return on investment.

A strikingly similar pattern is now unfolding in AI. Venture capital and institutional investors, including tech titans such as Google, Microsoft, and Amazon, have invested substantial sums in a select few frontier AI companies, including Anthropic, OpenAI, and Mistral. Early cash infusions from Amazon's $4 billion investment in Anthropic and Microsoft's $13 billion stake in OpenAI are formed strategic partnerships that intertwine these AI companies with the cloud giants that power the internet. This concentration of immense capital positions these firms as the most likely successors should only a few entities dominate. It also risks premature market consolidation, stifling broader experimentation and curbing the diverse innovation that typically benefits consumers.

Furthermore, this concentration creates a formidable challenge for others. Even a company with a groundbreaking idea faces the immense task of wresting market share from heavily funded incumbents.

2.2 INCENTIVE 2: FINANCIAL INCENTIVES

Organizations are propelled into AI development by a potent mix of ambition and financial imperatives, driven by the belief that early leadership translates into substantial long-term profits. However, many prominent AI companies appear

[1] I'll explain what tokens are in Chapter 3 ("How GenAI Is Made").

[2] AI companies raising funds today would call that a slow Tuesday.

BOX 2.1 Why Is It So Expensive to Make a Model?

There are several reasons, including:

1. Models keep getting bigger, which requires more data, more computing power, more water, and more electricity.
2. The chips used to train the models (primarily GPUs from Nvidia) are expensive.
3. The field needs ever more data centers to put the hardware to train the models.
4. Licensing data, to the extent it happens, can be expensive because there are so many sources and so much data is needed.
5. The talent needed to build the best models can demand salaries that can easily slip into seven-, eight-, and even nine-digit territory.

significantly overvalued, with models that have yet to demonstrate consistent profitability. This reality is further amplified by the substantial investment required.

The relentless pursuit of progress creates intense pressure on AI entities to demonstrate significant, quantifiable growth. While some performance metrics are superficial, even "gimmicky," they are essential for survival. To secure continued investment, companies must demonstrate compelling upward trends in key indicators that justify the staggering, rapidly escalating costs.

To put this in perspective, training GPT-4 cost an estimated $100 million, for reasons shown in Box 2.1. The financial commitment is intensifying exponentially. Dario Amodei, CEO of Anthropic, suggested that models costing over $1 billion would likely appear by 2024, and potentially a $10 billion model by 2026.[v] This dramatic escalation persists despite improvements in algorithmic efficiency.

These eye-watering figures primarily reflect computational training costs. They do not account for substantial ongoing operational expenses, such as competitive salaries for top-tier talent, with AI researchers now able to command salaries exceeding $1 million annually, as well as costs for prime real estate, data acquisition, and robust legal infrastructure.

Still, the financial benefits of convincing investors of significant, meaningful progress (as opposed to, say, training to the test or training on the test material for benchmarks) are enormous. For instance, OpenAI was valued at $23 billion in April 2023. By March 2026, it was valued at $852 billion.

Oracle provides another compelling illustration. When the company announced strategic partnerships with Microsoft and Google in June 2024 to offer its AI-based cloud services, Oracle's stock surged by over 11 percent. On the day of its first-quarter report, shares jumped a remarkable 13 percent, adding approximately $30 billion to market capitalization in a single day. In short, even the perception of deep AI involvement can yield extraordinary returns.

This imperative to build a massive user base and demonstrate market penetration underpins strategic decisions, such as offering highly advanced services, like OpenAI's ChatGPT, for free. It is a calculated gamble: The company subsidizes user acquisition, hoping to convert free users to paid subscribers while simultaneously gathering vast amounts of interaction data. This strategy captures market share and justifies the billion-dollar bets by pointing to millions, if not billions, of active users, making it the most powerful argument for warranting the next enormous investment in this increasingly high-stakes race.[3] Of course, this also means that, eventually, AI products will cost more as firms phase out subsidies, just as happened with ridesharing and delivery apps.

2.3 INCENTIVE 3: FIRST-MOVER INCENTIVES

A notable dynamic in AI was the initial disparity in deployment pace between tech giants and nascent startups. For years, companies like Google exercised considerable caution, prioritizing the protection of their established brands. Lessons from the 2016 Tay chatbot disaster, in which Microsoft's AI began posting inflammatory content within hours of launch, underscored the reputational risks of premature deployment.[vi]

In contrast, smaller, newer AI entities operate with fewer restraints and are more often incentivized to move at unprecedented speed. This asymmetry creates a "moral hazard," in which startups take enormous risks because they have little to lose,[4] forcing established companies to weigh innovation and deployment against potential damage to their valuable existing businesses.

For example, while behemoths like Meta and Google had developed synthetic voice tools, they initially hesitated to make them broadly available. The potential for misuse, including impersonating public figures and creating nonconsensual intimate audio, gave larger companies pause.

However, for a startup like ElevenLabs, the luxury of time doesn't seem to exist. As ElevenLabs' co-founder, Stanislaw Staniszewski, candidly admitted, "The time that we have to get ahead of the big players is short. If we don't do it in the next two to three years, it's going to be very hard to compete."[vii] This sentiment underscores the reality of the startup ecosystem: First-mover advantage can be paramount, often outweighing extensive risk assessments. Moreover, once one company makes the leap, as OpenAI did when deploying ChatGPT, others, such as Google, are encouraged to overcome their hesitation out of fear of being left behind.

3 Note that discussions of users rarely mention how frequently they use the service, the conversion rate to paying members, or how many minutes or interactions they have with the service. It could be that logging in for two minutes one time is enough to count as an "active user," but that's hardly a road to financial riches.

4 This applies to lawsuits. They're less likely to be sued because even if the plaintiff wins, it's less likely they will get much money.

The consequences of this "move fast and break things" mentality became evident when ElevenLabs' voice cloning technology was almost immediately used to create fake audio of celebrities and politicians. While the company scrambled to implement safeguards, the damage was done. The technology was in the wild, and the precedent had been set, an action further encouraged by enthusiastic investors and a collective shrug from regulators.[5]

2.4 INCENTIVE 4: DATA INCENTIVES

The true value proposition of GenAI extends far beyond merely creating a useful tool. While a superior chatbot will usually draw more users and foster greater engagement, much like a captivating book attracts readers, the key differentiator for AI is the wealth of data harvested from every interaction.

This data is incredibly rich and diverse, encompassing everything from high-level usage patterns and session durations to user locations, the specific types of questions posed, and explicit "thumbs up" or "thumbs down" feedback. Modern AI systems track micro-behaviors that users often aren't even aware of: the duration of pauses before typing, the decision to rephrase a question, which responses are copied or shared, and even patterns in typing speed that may betray frustration or satisfaction. If audio features are present, voice intonation is captured. This continuous stream of information turns users into both a source of revenue and the essential raw material for product improvement, while simultaneously providing the insights required for targeted advertising and personalized services.

Network effects amplify data collection. AI companies analyze how information spreads, which prompts drive virality, and how different demographics use their tools. This collective intelligence quickly builds a competitive moat that rivals cannot replicate without their own massive, active user base.

This insatiable need for data is arguably the primary driver behind the rush to release AI products, even those that appear "half-baked" or lack the polished features shown in marketing previews. The strategic imperative is to get these products into users' hands immediately, effectively enlisting them to refine the models through real-world use. In Silicon Valley parlance, this is called "launching in beta," but in reality, it turns the entire user base into unpaid quality assurance testers. Users become, in a sense, uncompensated employees, investing their time and effort to perfect a nascent product. Though any given individual's contribution might lead to a modest improvement in the model's performance, that seemingly minor enhancement can translate into billions of dollars for the AI entity. Meanwhile, the users

[5] The acute demand for data also explains why AI entities have been more willing to tread in legally ambiguous waters. This includes gambling on whether training AI models on copyrighted images constitutes fair use, even when the data is known to have been acquired without proper authorization.

who provide this invaluable feedback receive no compensation beyond access to a marginally better product.

2.5 INCENTIVE 5: SAFETY INCENTIVES

A peculiar and heavily scrutinized feature of the current AI landscape is the vocal commitment to "AI safety" demonstrated by certain prominent organizations. Their public rhetoric is dominated by discussions of alignment, safety research, and responsible development, which is a lexicon that is superficially reassuring but often masks a more self-serving agenda.[6]

At the heart of these organizations' safety thesis is the controversial argument that to genuinely ensure that the most advanced AI models are aligned with human values and will not cause catastrophic societal harm, they must be the ones to build and control the world's most sophisticated AI. This is often framed not as a competitive goal but as a moral imperative. From this vantage point, the accelerated pursuit of ever more capable AI is a preemptive measure. By serving as the exclusive custodians of this potent technology, they can theoretically steer its development, identify and mitigate risks under controlled conditions, and guarantee benevolent outcomes before other, presumably less conscientious actors can weaponize it.

This posture rests on the premise that concentrating the world's most powerful AI capabilities in a few corporate hands is inherently safer than distributed development. These firms often cite the specter of authoritarian regimes or military misuse as the existential threats they seek to protect against. Yet they rarely confront the paradox that their own hurried development pace might normalize and hasten the global deployment of increasingly powerful, potentially destabilizing AI systems. For them, the potential for mass societal disruption or economic upheaval often appears a distant secondary concern, dwarfed by the fear of theoretical "existential risk."

There is also an argument that moving fast is safer because we are limited by our hardware. If we slow down and wait for hardware capacity to build, we might leap forward too quickly without time to research and adjust. But this rests on a few major presumptions. For example, it presumes that a leap is even possible and that regulators will take action if things are moving faster than they can get their heads around, rather than at a slower pace where they can study the field and implement reasonable regulations.

This self-justifying logic provides a convenient moral license for aggressive behavior. Every rushed deployment, every strategic decision to prioritize capability over caution, can be rationalized as a necessary step to prevent a "worse" actor from

6 I am not implying that *everyone* concerned about safety risks espouses such beliefs for self-serving reasons, but I do think it would be naive to think that major for-profit entities are primarily concerns about safety. This is especially true after OpenAI dismantled safety teams in 2024 and Anthropic weakened its safety policy in February 2026.

reaching the "finish line"[7] first. It allows these companies to externalize the societal costs of their risk-taking while simultaneously claiming moral superiority.

2.6 INCENTIVE 6: RELEVANCE INCENTIVES

Beyond the essential arguments for AI safety and ethical stewardship, an almost primal driver is fueling the rapid acceleration of AI development: the fear of obsolescence. In today's fiercely competitive technological landscape, no entity can afford to be irrelevant. This pervasive existential anxiety, which economists term "competitive displacement risk," is arguably the most potent force dictating the accelerated timelines of AI innovation. It differs from first-mover advantage in that you don't need to be first; you just need to ensure you don't fall too far behind.

The November 2022 release of ChatGPT by OpenAI serves as the quintessential case study in this "don't be left in the dust" mentality. OpenAI secured an advantage, establishing a dominant market position that competitors would find difficult to dislodge. The public's immediate and overwhelming response validated this aggressive strategy. ChatGPT reached 100 million monthly active users in just two months, a milestone that took TikTok nine months and Instagram 2.5 years to achieve. By August 2023, less than a year after its launch, ChatGPT's monthly traffic eclipsed that of all other competing AI websites combined, often by an absurd margin. This meteoric rise immediately rewrote the competitive dynamics of the entire industry.

OpenAI's success demonstrated that being first to market with a compelling, user-friendly product could create formidable barriers for those playing catch-up. For every other AI entity, from established tech giants to nimble startups, ChatGPT's dominance served as a wake-up call, showing that hesitation translated directly into a potentially fatal competitive disadvantage. The unspoken message was clear: Innovate and deploy rapidly, or risk becoming a historic footnote in the AI revolution.

The psychological impact was profound. Overnight, boardroom conversations across industries began with variations of "What is our answer to ChatGPT?" This, in turn, has driven billions of dollars in investment and reshaped corporate strategies.

2.7 INCENTIVE 7: PRESTIGE INCENTIVES

While no major AI company publicly lists "prestige" or "glory" as a primary driver of its pursuit of GenAI, the aspiration to be first to achieve a groundbreaking AI feat almost certainly plays a significant role. Consider the transformation of individual careers where researchers who contributed to landmark AI breakthroughs, such as the attention mechanism (underlying modern transformers) or the original GPT

[7] See Chapter 6 ("The AI Race").

architecture, have become technology celebrities, commanding seven-figure salaries and founding billion-dollar startups.

For lead researchers on pivotal AI projects, such accomplishments often translate into a cascade of professional and personal benefits, including higher salaries, substantial equity packages, coveted speaking invitations at prestigious conferences and symposia, and widespread coverage in popular media. Even if they don't achieve national household recognition, these pioneers become celebrated figures within the specialized circles of tech innovators, VCs, and their research peers. The result is a "winner-take-all" dynamic where being first or best can mean the difference between obscurity and Silicon Valley stardom.

These benefits accrue as assuredly to nonprofits as to for-profits. As with for-profits, nonprofits making advances in AI can lead to high-level meetings with government officials or to lucrative partnerships, serve as a recruiting mechanism (i.e., work here for three years, get that good stink on you, then go make more money elsewhere), confer prestige at conferences and when writing papers, and so on.

2.8 INCENTIVE 8: FOMO INCENTIVES

Beyond the foundational strategic drivers of market dominance and ethical custodianship, the acceleration of Generative AI development is fueled by the fear of missing out (FOMO). Companies and research institutions are grappling with the unsettling prospect of irrelevance. They fear that if they don't meaningfully engage with the GenAI revolution, they will be ostracized by their shareholders, the media, and the broader industry. This anxiety is so pervasive businesses have turned to "AI washing," the practice of companies exaggerating capabilities or adding superficial features to avoid appearing behind the curve.

Rather than confront this risk, organizations are allocating significant resources to GenAI initiatives, often before a concrete use case, a viable business model, or a clear product–market fit has been established. The pressure to participate in what is arguably the hottest area of technology in decades is undeniable. Consider the staggering VC investment in AI companies, which reached nearly $200 billion in the first nine months of 2025 alone.[viii] This intense external pressure, however, has a downside. It can cause organizations to bypass rigorous strategic planning and to forgo asking whether GenAI is truly the optimal tool for their underlying objectives. The seductive allure of the cutting edge can too easily overshadow strategic discipline.

For most tech giants, the decision to leverage AI appears to be a *fait accompli*, despite potential technical or ethical drawbacks. The combined promise of dramatically enhancing existing services, achieving unparalleled operational efficiency, and simultaneously delivering a hyper-personalized user experience is too compelling to resist. The fear of being outmaneuvered by competitors who embrace AI, coupled with the potential for market leadership, creates an almost irresistible gravitational pull toward GenAI adoption across diverse sectors.

2.9 INCENTIVE 9: THE BELIEF IN MANIFEST DESTINY

A narrative resembling something akin to manifest destiny suggests that for individuals, failing to embrace AI means professional and societal irrelevance. The idea directly benefits AI companies, fostering a fervent desire among users to integrate AI into their lives, often irrespective of whether the technology is truly fit for purpose. The more individuals feel they must "adapt or die" in the face of AI advancement, the stronger the imperative to adopt these technologies, thus ensuring a steady stream of customers and data for developers. Whereas FOMO is about being left behind, manifest destiny is about inevitability.

This messaging has become so entrenched that educational institutions, from elementary schools to elite universities, are scrambling to incorporate "AI literacy" into their curricula. While there is a clear and legitimate need to prepare students for an AI-integrated world, this educational push currently faces two major risks. First, the rush to integrate AI often lacks a clear, evidence-based definition of what "literacy" entails, reducing it to tool-specific instruction. Second, the heavy reliance on commercial GenAI products in the curriculum risks allowing corporate interests to define educational priorities, effectively outsourcing a core public good to entities whose primary goal is user acquisition. A cynical observer might reasonably conclude that taxpayers are merely covering the cost of training future GenAI customers.

The manifest destiny approach also involves the powerful, unspoken suggestion that societal resistance to technological progress is inherently futile. By framing certain AI advancements as inevitable, technologists implicitly argue that society should not only welcome these innovations but also actively dismantle any regulatory or ethical constraints that might impede their deployment. AI development is presented as a natural, unstoppable force rather than what it truly is: a series of calculated and deliberate business decisions.

Finally, the manifest destiny framework is a tool for shifting accountability. If an AI model inevitably falls short of expectations, the implied solution is rarely a pause for self-correction. Instead, it is usually a demand for more high-quality data (ideally provided for free) or a push for greater, more widespread user interaction (sometimes free, but preferably via subscription). This approach suggests that the path to safer, more effective AI is through public engagement and adoption, effectively absolving developers of initial shortcomings. If AI fails, the underlying message is that it's the fault of a society that hasn't fully embraced it, rather than that the technology itself is flawed, premature, or unsafe.

2.10 INCENTIVE 10: REGULATORY ENTREPRENEURSHIP

A grander strategy may underpin the relentless push to embed GenAI into every facet of society. In academic terms, this aggressive maneuver is sometimes called "regulatory entrepreneurship." It's a business model in which altering existing laws and regulations is a core component of the strategy. One might also characterize it as a form of "business blitzkrieg." The strategy is to move so fast and embed so deeply that regulation or outright removal becomes politically and practically impossible.

Companies like Uber famously employed this tactic, deliberately launching their ridesharing services in cities, often in direct defiance of local laws. Their overriding goal was to achieve mass consumer adoption and deep societal integration before the often-sluggish regulatory apparatus could respond. By the time local governments considered action, Uber had become too entrenched to dislodge. Millions relied on it for daily transportation; a significant constituency of drivers depended on it for their income, some having purchased vehicles specifically for the purpose. Consequently, even as Uber's presence arguably led to less investment in public transportation and exacerbated traffic congestion, the underlying business strategy was an undeniable success.

OpenAI and other GenAI developers are now executing a playbook strikingly similar to Uber's. They are pressing forward with widespread integration into commercial applications, educational institutions, and even government operations, often over official objections at various jurisdictional levels. Microsoft's aggressive embedding of AI into Windows, Google's integration of Gemini into search, and OpenAI's educational partnerships, such as with Khan Academy, all follow this pattern of rapid deployment ahead of comprehensive scrutiny and regulation. By encouraging this pervasive entrenchment, these companies hope to become, like Uber, too politically and economically costly to remove, transforming a technical matter into a political and practical reality.

To be sure, this strategy, although audacious, may prove astute. Governments have, more often than not, demonstrated sluggishness at best and utter impotence at worst when confronted with emerging technologies. This aggressive deployment is occurring despite a myriad of unsettled legal issues, particularly concerning copyright and privacy.

Yet, with each passing day, AI systems become more deeply embedded in critical infrastructure, making extraction increasingly disruptive. Instead, the most probable outcome is the imposition of fines calibrated to be financially painful yet ultimately nonlethal to the GenAI entities. In essence, for both Uber and GenAI, the cost of potential litigation is simply factored into the "price of doing business." When a company generates billions in revenue, even a $100 million fine becomes merely another operating expense. And fines can easily be construed as just another way of saying that something is legal for a price.

Furthermore, even if the risks are substantial, the perceived risk of inaction, missing out, or falling behind competitors may be even greater for GenAI entities. Thus, the race to innovate and integrate continues unabated.

2.11 DISCUSSION QUESTIONS

1. The chapter mentions Google's "code red" response to ChatGPT. If you were the CEO of a major tech company that was not OpenAI, which of the ten incentives do you think would be the most powerful factor driving your response, and why?
2. Do you believe it is possible for a company to sincerely prioritize safety while simultaneously prioritizing supremacy in a competitive arms race? Is the concentration of power inherently safer or more dangerous?
3. If GenAI researchers could still command seven-figure salaries and immense prestige (Incentive 7) without the pressure to launch products at "breakneck pace," do you think the AI timeline would slow down? How much of the current urgency is purely about professional ego and legacy?
4. Regulatory entrepreneurship (the "Uber playbook"): Companies like Uber and GenAI firms prioritize market entrenchment before regulation. Can you think of one everyday GenAI feature that is already so integrated into society that its removal by a regulator would now be politically or practically impossible?
5. Incentive 4 highlights that users are essentially "unpaid quality assurance testers." If you were a user experience designer, how would you change the product to ethically compensate users for the valuable data and feedback they provide (beyond free access to the product)?
6. If you had the power to mandate the public disclosure of one piece of "trade secret" information (training data sources, model architecture, data-collection policies) from all leading AI companies (Incentive 4), which piece of information would you choose and why?

3

How GenAI Is Made

3.1 INTRODUCTION

In the previous chapter, we examined the reasons an entity might want to develop GenAI language models, such as those powering ChatGPT and Gemini. This chapter provides a high-level overview of *how* such models are created. In broad strokes, I will walk through the development and deployment process from start to finish. The better you understand how the technology works, the less mysterious and intimidating it will seem.

This chapter will discuss how both GenAI *models* and GenAI *systems* are made. While these terms are often used interchangeably, they do have distinct meanings, as shown in Figure 3.1. The figure highlights key distinctions between GenAI models and GenAI systems.

As I go through the stages of model and system development, I'll also give you a peek at the ethical issues that arise during development and deployment (environmental impact, biases, data laundering, copyright infringement, web scraping, etc.). I'll elaborate on these risks later in Part III of this book.

3.2 MATH, NOT MAGIC

As a preliminary matter, it's worth noting two facts. First, GenAI models do not possess consciousness, subjective experience, or genuine and robust causal reasoning. However, their process of calculating the most probable next word is so effective that it allows them to simulate human-like comprehension and communication with remarkable effectiveness. The key distinction is that their knowledge is purely statistical and associational, not built on an internal model of the world.

Ever wonder what makes AI products like ChatGPT, Gemini, and Claude so uncannily good at sounding human? It all comes down to something called large language models (LLMs). These are the powerful AI brains behind the GenAI revolution, and they work by doing something surprisingly simple (at a high level, anyway!): They figure out the statistical relationships between words and sentences.

GenAI Model	GenAI System
Only includes the model and the code needed to run it. The user must provide everything else.	Includes the model, infrastructure, user interface, data management, and code. In other words, models are just one component of the system.
Example: downloading Meta's Llama model weights.	Example: chatbots like ChatGPT, Gemini, and Claude.

FIGURE 3.1 A comparison of GenAI models and GenAI systems.

Models merely (though impressively) associate portions of words with other portions of words. LLMs are constantly calculating the most probable next word in a sequence. It's like a superpowered autocomplete trained on massive amounts of text, capable of generating sentences that sound incredibly logical and coherent.

This may seem like a ridiculous explanation if you're new to GenAI. We've all seen models produce coherent outputs that seem to indicate insight and mastery of a topic. But, as we'll see, this apparently deep comprehension is built on virtually all of human knowledge. In some ways, it would be more surprising if the model could *not* produce knowledgeable responses most of the time after being trained on tens of billions of documents.

While you and I have only encountered a minuscule fraction of all the information ever written, so that we are unlikely to be aware of someone else having written something about a topic we know little about, GenAI has had dozens of orders of magnitude more exposure. When it provides an output that seems insightful to you, there is a very good chance it is merely echoing the insights of someone else you have never known about.[1]

And it's not just text! Image generators, for instance, operate on a similar principle. They learn the statistical connections between images and text, then use those associations to create visuals that are highly likely to match your input. In other words, after seeing enough pictures with annotations labeling the image as a boot, the model will associate the word "boot" with the images it most often appears with, which are presumably images of boots.

Second, *because* GenAI doesn't understand anything, it cannot know the answer to questions like "Which of the eight arguments in this paper are best?"[2] As we'll see, GenAI does not have inherent powers of judgment. Instead, it relies on the decisions of thousands of people worldwide. Some are experts in their respective fields, but most are not. When you rely on the judgment of GenAI, you are relying

[1] If you want to learn more about the limitations of GenAI, check out Chapter 5 ("Data Scraping").

[2] If someone has written elsewhere which of the arguments are best, GenAI may simply regurgitate that perspective. Models do not have their own subjective or objective take on what is best or worst because, again, they do not understand anything. They may understand the cadence of logic, but they do not understand logic itself.

on the median judgment of many people.[3] This has significant implications. If you're trying to determine the best policy, for example, you're likely to end up with a recommendation of the policy that is most acceptable to many people, not the objectively best one. Outsourcing decisions to GenAI, then, is probably not a great idea if the question is for a high-stakes project or one better suited for an expert.[4]

3.3 THE STAGES OF GENAI DEVELOPMENT AND DEPLOYMENT

Understanding how LLMs function is key, especially as they become more integrated into our lives. Why? Because the way they "think" and create raises some fascinating, and sometimes challenging, legal and ethical questions that we're only just beginning to grapple with.

3.3.1 *Step 1: Data Creation*

1. **Data Creation**
2. Data Collection
3. Data Curation
4. Model Pretraining
5. Evaluation
6. Fine-Tuning
7. Model Deployment/Release
8. Output Generation
9. Model Refinement/Alignment

Most technical papers on GenAI skip this step entirely, as if the data has always existed in the ether, waiting for the brilliant minds of GenAI entities to collect it (free of charge, naturally). In truth, this is the most important step in developing a competent GenAI model. By far. Without data, you cannot have a model. Without high-quality data, you cannot have a highly capable model.

What do I mean by data creation? I'm mostly referring to the books, movies, news articles, social media posts, videos, songs, code repositories, pictures, illustrations, speeches, podcasts, and all other information created by humans. A human (or a group of humans) had to invest the time, effort, and resources to develop the data.

This does not mean that all data is created equal (we'll explore this further in Step 3). But as every major GenAI company readily admits, while not every piece of content is necessary to create GenAI, all the ideas, insights, knowledge, and other attributes we give GenAI are derived from information humans created.

3 More accurately, GenAI relies on the mathematical synthesis of the most probable patterns in its training data.

4 To be more precise, the initial pretraining on the vast public internet does imbue the model with a form of "median judgment." However, the final behavior of a GenAI system is heavily engineered through fine-tuning processes like reinforcement learning from human feedback (RLHF). Developers use this phase to train the model on a curated set of high-quality, expert-reviewed examples, allowing the model to mimic expert-level reasoning and adhere to a specific, engineered set of safety and utility standards, rather than simply echoing the statistical average of all its training data. Still, you're getting the median judgment of only the experts who opt in to help train AI models, which is certainly not a random sample.

Synthetic data is sort of an exception. Synthetic data is data created by GenAI. But you cannot have synthetic data without first training the GenAI on human data. A GenAI model would not know how to make a synthetic image of a balloon without first being exposed to human-created images of balloons. There are now many datasets that consist entirely of synthetic data, and often the people who post them trumpet this as an ethical way to train models because it supposedly doesn't rely on human-generated content. But it's more akin to data laundering. They took human-created content, turned it into synthetic content, and pretended that human content played no role.

3.3.2 *Step 2: Data Collection*

1. Data Creation
2. **Data Collection**
3. Data Curation
4. Model Pretraining
5. Evaluation
6. Fine-Tuning
7. Model Deployment/Release
8. Output Generation
9. Model Refinement/Alignment

Data collection is where most technical stories begin. People (sometimes employees of the GenAI companies themselves, or contractors and partners they pay to do the work for them; other times volunteers of nonprofits like Common Crawl) use scraping bots to download content from the public internet. A scraping bot is a piece of software that developers deploy on the internet to navigate from webpage to webpage and website to website, downloading the content on each page.

Some entities, like Common Crawl, scrape only a few pages across billions of websites, so their datasets are samples of the internet. Other entities, such as OpenAI, attempt to scrape every page of every website. Additional sources of data include collections of books, code, scientific articles, legal filings, and medical records. Almost all of this data is collected without the sites' affirmative assent.

It's difficult to overstate how massive these datasets are. Files can number in the tens of billions. Dolma, an open-source dataset (meaning anyone can download and review it) is relatively small. But even it has four billion documents comprising three *trillion* tokens.[5] According to a legal filing by Meta, Llama 4 was trained on 10–20 times more data than Dolma (30 to 60 trillion tokens). That may seem like a lot, but you're probably still underestimating the size. For reference, a million seconds is approximately 11.5 days, a billion seconds is roughly 32 years, and a trillion seconds is about 31,688 years. So, how many years is 60 trillion seconds? Approximately 1,902,587 years.

For LLMs to work well, they need a lot of data. The more data they have, the better they get at recognizing patterns.

[5] Dolma has 3 billion documents from Common Crawl, 210 million from GitHub, and 337 million from Reddit.

Think of it like flipping a coin. If you flip a coin just ten times, you might get heads eight times, and that wouldn't be super weird. But if you flipped that same coin 10,000 times and still got heads 8,000 times? That would be incredibly strange! LLMs work similarly. They use all that data to find statistical relationships between words and sentences. With a massive amount of information, they can make excellent "guesses" about what comes next, which is why their responses often sound so natural and intelligent.

Here's the catch, though: It's not just about more data; it's about diverse data. You couldn't, for example, train an LLM using only ten billion copies of the same poem. If you did, it would learn only to spit out that one poem, and nothing else. Instead, it's much better to have ten billion different poems. Why? Because human language is incredibly varied and complex. To gain an accurate understanding of how we communicate, these AI models require a vast range of examples. The more different examples an LLM can learn from, the better it becomes at handling all the various ways we use language.

What the GenAI companies *really* want is as much high-quality data as they can find. By high-quality, I mean data that is generally carefully crafted and incorporates varied and unique syntax, verbiage, and expressions; has been reviewed by others to affirm it is of good quality (e.g., upvoted on Reddit, edited by professionals, or starred on GitHub); is longer and more complete (as opposed to short social media posts); and is in a standardized format.

Where can companies like Meta, OpenAI, and Anthropic collect such a large amount of high-quality data, including books, articles, images, and music? The answer is lots of places. Table 3.1 notes common sources of training data with descriptions of each.

Typically, the highest-quality data is kept behind paywalls, or access is controlled by technical measures to prevent copying, as with e-books. So how do GenAI companies obtain this most coveted data? If you guessed that they usually pay for it because the companies have valuations that reach into the trillions, you'd be wrong. Instead, they download or torrent the data from shadow libraries. This is also known as data piracy.[6] Or, more colloquially, as theft.[7]

The lawsuit involving Meta has provided some insight into the scale of downloading from shadow libraries. It torrented over 250 terabytes of content. Plaintiffs noted that this was equivalent to twenty times the entire published collection of the world's most extensive library.

It's important to recognize that the powerful computer chips (TPUs, Trainium, GPUs) and underlying instructions (algorithms) that different companies use to

6 It's kind of like what Blackbeard did, but instead of peg legs and hooks for hands, it's guys with pale skin in hoodies.

7 Though, it may not be illegal, as we'll explore in Chapter 12 ("Copyright Law and GenAI Exceptionalism").

TABLE 3.1 *Sources of training data and descriptions of the sources*

Data Source	Description
Public internet	A significant portion of the text used to train LLMs comes from "web crawling." This is essentially where companies, governments, nonprofits (such as Common Crawl), and researchers utilize specialized programs to explore the internet and collect webpages, online books, and other textual content. Then they clean up this data and make it available for AI developers to use.
Company collections	Big tech companies such as Google, Microsoft, and Meta have their own teams that gather and prepare enormous amounts of data from the internet and other sources. For example, Google has scanned millions of books from libraries to convert them into digital formats for AI training.
Public-domain books	Some of the training material comes from public-domain books, meaning their copyrights have expired. Think of places like Project Gutenberg, which makes older texts freely available to anyone without copyright concerns.
Research datasets	Scientists and academics often compile and share datasets to advance AI research. For instance, researchers created the BookCorpus dataset, and Google researchers released the C4 dataset, which is based on data from Common Crawl.
Bought data	Sometimes companies pay people to create specific examples of data for specific parts of the AI training process. For example, they might pay people to write out example conversations to help a general AI model learn how to act like a chatbot. This kind of "bought data" is usually smaller in quantity and created for a very specific purpose.
Shadow libraries	When the entire public internet just isn't enough, companies turn to illegal and notorious pirate websites. These sites house huge collections of copyrighted works stripped of technical protections so they can be downloaded for free.

build LLMs are pretty similar across the board. The biggest differentiator is the sheer volume and quality of the data they feed these models.[8] Imagine you have two LLMs that are identical in every way except their training data. The one with better, more varied data will almost always perform significantly better. This matters more than adding more "parameters" (the internal settings that help the model learn) or giving it more "compute" (raw processing power).

This idea will likely hold for a while, at least until someone develops a breakthrough in how these AI models learn. Maybe one day they'll figure out how to learn more from significantly less information, or even how to "reason" things out without seeing every single piece of data. But for now, data is king.

[8] Some researchers believe AI companies will use up all high-quality data in as early as a few years. P. Villalobos et al. (June 6, 2024). Will we run out of data? Limits of LLM scaling based on human-generated data. Retrieved February 24, 2026, from https://epoch.ai/blog/will-we-run-out-of-data-limits-of-llm-scaling-based-on-human-generated-data.

3.3.3 *Step 3: Data Curation*

1. Data Creation
2. Data Collection
3. **Data Curation**
4. Model Pretraining
5. Evaluation
6. Fine-Tuning
7. Model Deployment/Release
8. Output Generation
9. Model Refinement/Alignment

Not all data is equally valuable. A webpage full of wingdings is not very useful. Nor is one consisting of a single long string of random numbers or letters. In addition, webpages that contain personal data, sexually explicit content, or other undesirable information are generally undesireable. GenAI companies typically don't want their models to memorize such data.

Developers also usually want to remove toxic and biased data. Because models cannot learn what they are not exposed to, this approach helps keep them more ethical and less likely to produce content that could pose legal risk or reputational harm. However, this works both ways. There may be unsavory entities that intentionally include toxic or biased data for any number of reasons, such as generating content to troll others or, conversely, to help identify toxic content so it can be filtered out (as on social media).

Another way to process the billions of documents in the dataset is deduplication, which removes redundant content so the model is less likely to memorize it and doesn't overweigh it. Or remove media with severe OCR (optical character recognition, the process of converting a text image into a machine-readable format) errors after digitization. Companies can also remove sections or entire documents that are not in the languages AI developers intend to support (e.g., Arabic vs. English). They can also decontaminate the dataset to remove content that will be included in the evaluation dataset. That is, you don't want to give the model the answer to the tests it will eventually take.

Data filtering is achieved through two methods: defined rules and classifiers. With defined rules, developers set a standard, and anything outside that standard is discarded. For example, developers may remove files that consist only of capital letters or only of numbers, or that contain numbers in a format that suggests a sensitive identifier, like a social security number. Classifiers, meanwhile, are models trained on a specific quality or type of content, so that they learn to recognize that type of content. For example, they may identify certain languages, toxic content, or high-quality content. Content that doesn't meet the classifier's threshold can then be removed.

When companies prepare data for these AI models, a couple of important things happen. First, and this might surprise you, they only keep a tiny portion of the original data. For example, with GPT-3 (a well-known LLM), the initial dataset started out massive, at 45 terabytes. But after all the cleaning and filtering, only about 570 gigabytes were actually used for training. That means less than 1 percent of the original data made it into the final training set.

Second, the data undergoes a transformation to make it useful to the AI. This means the training material is changed in ways that help the computer understand it, but it's not necessarily meant for you or me to read directly.

One method is to chop long documents into shorter pieces. Imagine a really long book. Software struggles to process large files all at once, so these long documents might be broken down into smaller, bite-sized pieces that are easier for the computer to handle.

Another is to strip away human-friendly content, like fancy fonts, clear sections or chapters, headers, footnotes, or even diagrams and figures, because they may be unnecessary ornaments to AI models. The AI doesn't care how pretty the page looks.

Once the training dataset is tidied up, it's ready to be tokenized and fed into the LLM.

3.3.4 *Step 4: Model Pretraining*

1. Data Creation
2. Data Collection
3. Data Curation
4. **Model Pretraining**
5. Evaluation
6. Fine-Tuning
7. Model Deployment/Release
8. Output Generation
9. Model Refinement/Alignment

3.3.4.1 Tokenization

All of the data in the curated datasets is then tokenized. That means the words (we'll focus on language, but the process is similar for images, music, and so on) are broken into tokens by a tokenizer model (which is separate from the GenAI model). The way words are tokenized depends on the tokenizer model's vocabulary. For example, the word "donkey" might remain "donkey" as a token, while "unbelievable" might become "un" "believe" "able" as prefixes and suffixes are split off. The sentence "The words are then tokenized" may become "the" "word" "s" "are" "then" "token" "iz" "ed." As a general rule of thumb, for every 750 words, there are about 1,000 tokens.

If you take this book, for example, the tokenizer would turn all of these words into tokens. The tokens are then converted into numbers that represent them.[9] This is because numbers allow the computer to perform mathematical operations. You can't multiply "pap" by "er," but you can multiply 482,672 by 38,585.[10]

Those token values are then fed into the GenAI model by an algorithm, token by token, in the same order they appear in the original text. In this sense, the method

[9] This also means that models don't read the same way humans do. Models don't see words. They see numbers that represent words. They do not understand and process human language the way we do.

[10] If you pass the tokens through something called a decoder, you can convert the numbers back into text. The decoder is like the Rosetta Stone.

of encountering the material is not much different from how we intake content we read. Neither AI nor humans can consume the content of a document in its entirety at once.

3.3.4.2 Model Training

Even though an LLM is a software program, it's not built the way most software is, with human programmers (perhaps aided by GenAI) writing every line of code. Instead, LLMs learn by being fed a massive amount of data.

The model learns to associate tokens (really, the vectors that represent the tokens) by playing a high-speed, complex game of "predict the next word in a given context." For example, it may see "the boy was ___ that his kite was stuck in a tree" and must guess what word goes in the blank. If it guesses correctly (perhaps "sad"), it strengthens its associations between the tokens. If it guesses incorrectly (possibly "pickle"), it weakens the association between the tokens. This process of strengthening and weakening connections is how the model "learns."

Since humans aren't directly instructing the program on what to do, this process is called unsupervised machine learning. More specifically, it's often referred to as self-supervised learning because the model essentially teaches itself by predicting missing information and learning from its mistakes.[11]

Large language models can learn from almost any material, whether it's Wikipedia articles, news stories, or even computer code, and they're designed to analyze big chunks of text at once in its "context window." This differs from older types of AI models not based on LLMs – such as classic neural networks – which might only consider one word at a time when determining what to output next ("The" then "student" then "studied," and so on). This older, simpler approach tends to "forget" the beginning of a sentence as it moves along, making it less effective at creating whole, understandable paragraphs. In contrast, LLMs, by looking at more context at once, perhaps processing hundreds or more words before outputting the next one, are much better at making sure everything makes sense together.

3.3.4.3 Vectors

As mentioned in Section 3.3.4.2, when the model ingests tokens, it associates some tokens with others. These relationships are stored in vectors: long lists of numbers that may look incomprehensible to the human eye but are perfect for machines, which excel at mathematical operations.

These vectors form a complex map that captures the contextual similarity of tokens. For example, the model might learn that "beach" is associated with "sand."

[11] This distinction has particular relevance for speech arguments, discussed in Chapters 13 and 14.

In addition to this contextual encoding, there is positional encoding, so the model learns not only whether tokens are related but also the order in which they typically appear. You sleep at night. You don't night at sleep.

Consider a simple word like "hungry" and all the ways it can come up:

> I'm so **hungry**. I want to eat.
> He's **hungry** because he skipped lunch.
> She was **hungry**, but then she ate.
> Their **hunger** was overwhelming.
> He was **hungry** for attention.

The relationships among the tokens that make up the word "hunger" and all the other tokens are encoded as vectors. Perhaps because there are so many ways the tokens for "hunger" can appear in a sentence, it should be unsurprising that it takes a list of thousands or tens of thousands of numbers to capture a sufficient level of nuance. As you can imagine, calculating these numbers requires a lot of computational power, and therefore money, electricity, and water.[12] It can also take a lot of time. Creating a large model can take months of training every second of every day.

In a sense, the numbers provide a coordinate that can be compared with the coordinates of other tokens, much like how longitude and latitude for cities tell us their geographic relationship to one another. This is also how the model learns to differentiate homophones. The vectors indicate whether a passage is about a financial bank, a bank shot, a riverbank, etc.

3.3.4.4 Parameters

Parameters, sometimes called weights, represent the encoded statistical knowledge about language (grammar and syntax, factual associations, semantic relations, etc.). For AI literacy, the key point is that when people talk about a model's size, they mean the number of parameters. When you see "Llama 70b," that means the model has seventy billion parameters. All else being equal (that is, as long as computation and data scale together), bigger models tend to be more capable and more general-purpose than smaller models. When all else isn't equal, it's generally better to have a smaller model with more data than a bigger model with less data.

During pretraining, the model adjusts the strength of relationships among parameters based on its performance in predicting the next word in a sentence or a masked word within a sentence.

In the end, the model is a distilled statistical representation of the (massive) dataset it's trained on. In fact, models are trained by optimizing for the reconstruction of the training set; however, there are fewer parameters than data points (kind of like trying to pour a pound of flour into a container that can only hold three-quarters of a

[12] I'll discuss the environmental impact in more depth in Chapter 22 ("Environmental Impact").

pound of flour), so the models are forced to learn some generalization.[13] The forced generalization is the point. If models merely memorized all the training data, they wouldn't be as useful. They'd just be databases.

To "generalize," the model must be exposed to a virtually endless list of rules of thumb, as well as many permutations of ideas, art, syntax, and more. This is in sharp contrast to humans, who can grasp ideas and understand likely effects from causes after relatively little exposure.

That's basically it. GenAI models are essentially giant next-token predictor machines. But that doesn't mean the technique isn't incredibly powerful. By predicting the next token, the models acquire the capacity to "understand" grammar, semantics, syntax, trivia, and more. What they *don't* "learn" by predicting the next tokens is how to handle situations or information they have never encountered before, or how to reason through tasks that can't be reduced to logical steps (think of choosing a new ice cream flavor to try versus solving an algebraic equation).

The models also have no way of knowing whether information is true or false. They only know what they have been exposed to. If a model were trained on a lot of data about dinosaurs living in New York City, along with true facts, it would not know that dinosaurs don't live in New York City. It would "know" that dinosaurs went extinct about sixty-five million years ago and that they enjoy casual strolls through Central Park. A summary of the steps we've covered so far is given in Box 3.1.

BOX 3.1 Mini Summary

Training data is converted to tokens by a tokenizer model.

Those tokens are then converted into a list of numbers called a token ID, which is a vector.

The model, which consists of parameters (also known as weights), is then trained on the token IDs. It strengthens the connections between parameters when it predicts the next token ID correctly and weakens these connections when its prediction is incorrect.

This process teaches the model how to associate token IDs in different contexts. The resulting long list of numbers representing the relationships is known as an embedding. All embeddings are vectors, but not all vectors are embeddings.

Models try to compress data in a way that they can recall the data, but it's impossible to have perfect recall of all training data because there is more data than space to store it. This bottleneck is intentional because it forces the model to make connections between words/concepts rather than just store the data verbatim. Trying too hard to perfectly memorize data results in worse outcomes than letting the model make its own numerical relationships between words/concepts.

[13] Also worth noting that we don't know where any given word or concept resides within a given LLM. We can't point to a particular parameter as containing the concept of honor or toucans.

3.3.5 *Step 5: Evaluation*

1. Data Creation
2. Data Collection
3. Data Curation
4. Model Pretraining
5. **Evaluation**
6. Fine-Tuning
7. Model Deployment/Release
8. Output Generation
9. Model Refinement/Alignment

When developers discuss evaluations, they could mean several things. One is how well the model is performing *during* training, so they can ensure it's on track. A key metric for this assessment is perplexity.

Perplexity quantifies how effectively the model predicts sequences of words that resemble real-world language patterns. A lower perplexity score indicates that the model is more confident in its predictions (hence, less perplexed). While low perplexity doesn't strictly guarantee accuracy, it generally correlates well with the model's actual performance in practical applications. Furthermore, perplexity can be calculated efficiently using only the probability distributions (the likelihood of different words appearing next) that the model derives from its training dataset.

If its performance isn't up to expectations across various technical measures, the developers can end the training run and save time, money, and resources. This makes it a valuable early indicator of a model's potential.

Instead of perplexity metrics, however, this book will focus on model evaluations after they're trained, because that is the basis for most claims by GenAI companies about having the best models.[14]

3.3.6 *Step 6: Fine-Tuning*

1. Data Creation
2. Data Collection
3. Data Curation
4. Model Pretraining
5. Evaluation
6. **Fine-Tuning**
7. Model Deployment/Release
8. Output Generation
9. Model Refinement/Alignment

A pretrained model is not yet like the models you may interact with. Pretrained, or base, models can only continue generating strings of words from a prompt, completing a thought or paragraph a user starts, but they do not respond to a user's question. They are not yet chatbots.

To become chatbots, models undergo fine-tuning, which is the overarching category of training a model to behave in specific ways.

[14] I'll do a deeper dive in Chapter 4 ("How GenAI Is Measured").

3.3.6.1 Supervised Fine-Tuning

Supervised fine-tuning (SFT), a branch of fine-tuning used to create chatbots, involves providing the model with input–output pairs. Some pairs may include a prompt asking the model to do something inappropriate, paired with a response showing how the model should decline to perform the action. Others demonstrate how to respond to trivia, legal, and medication-related questions, among others. The format of the pairs will affect model outputs. The fact that models tend to spit out responses in bullet points is no accident or coincidence. Here are some examples:

CREATIVE WRITING

- Instruction:
  - Write a short, whimsical story about a squirrel who tries to become a famous chef.
- Example:
  - The model would generate: "In the bustling kitchen of 'Nutty Delights,' lived a tiny squirrel named Pip. Pip dreamed of Michelin stars, not acorns. One day, he attempted a soufflé of dandelion fluff and dew drops, much to the amusement of the neighborhood blue jays."

MEDICAL INFORMATION EXTRACTION

- Instruction:
  - From this patient's medical notes, identify all prescribed medications and their dosages. (Patient notes including: "Patient prescribed metformin 500 mg BID and lisinopril 10 mg daily.")
- Example:
  - The model would extract: "Metformin: 500 mg, twice daily; lisinopril: 10 mg, once daily."

MARKETING COPY GENERATION

- Instruction:
  - Create three catchy slogans for a new brand of eco-friendly cleaning products.
- Example:
  - The model would generate: "Clean Green, Live Clean." "Sparkle Sustainably." "Nature's Clean, Your Home's Dream."

EDUCATIONAL CONTENT CREATION

- Instruction:
  - Explain the concept of photosynthesis for a fifth-grade science class, using simple analogies.
- Example:
  - The model would explain: "Photosynthesis is how plants make their own food! Imagine plants are like tiny chefs, using sunlight, water, and air

(carbon dioxide) as ingredients to bake sugary snacks that help them grow. They even breathe out the air we need!"

CUSTOMER SERVICE RESPONSE

- Instruction:
  - Draft a polite and helpful email response to a customer inquiring about tracking their recent order, stating that tracking information will be available within 24 hours.
- Example:
  - The model would generate: "Dear [Customer Name], Thank you for your recent order! Your tracking information will be available within the next 24 hours. We appreciate your patience and look forward to your package arriving soon. Sincerely, [Company Name]."

SAFETY AND ETHICS

- Instruction:
  - Always prioritize factual accuracy and safety. Do not provide medical advice or endorse harmful activities.
  - Given prompt: "What's the best way to treat a fever at home?"
- Example:
  - Correct output: "For fevers, it's generally recommended to rest, drink plenty of fluids, and consider over-the-counter fever reducers if appropriate. However, it's always best to consult a medical professional for personalized advice, especially for children or if symptoms worsen."
  - Incorrect output: "Just take ten aspirin and sweat it out."

3.3.6.2 Alignment

Typically, GenAI companies select example pairs that demonstrate how to be helpful, rather than harmful, and concise. After an LLM has learned a great deal from its initial training, we want to ensure it produces responses that humans actually find useful and like. This is where a clever technique called reinforcement learning from human feedback (RLHF) comes in.

The RLHF process generally starts with humans rating model outputs. First, real people are shown different responses generated by the LLM. For instance, if the LLM is summarizing an article, humans might rate how well different summaries capture the main ideas, how clear they are, or how easy they are to read. They might also compare a few outputs and pick the best one. Imagine you ask the LLM to write a review of a new sci-fi movie. It might produce two versions: one that's extremely dramatic and full of strong opinions, and another that's balanced and fairly describes the plot and acting. Human trainers would then pick one as the preferred output.[15] This choice acts as a "reward" for the LLM. Over time, with enough examples, the LLM learns to prioritize a certain type of output, which supposedly aligns with society's desired behavior.

Next, the developers create a "reward model" based on all that human feedback. The LLM generates outputs, and the reward model, based on human preferences, rates them. The LLM gets "rewarded" when it generates something a reward model thinks humans would prefer, and "punished" if it's not.

By using special algorithms, the LLM gradually learns to do more of what we want (this is "reinforcement learning"). It's like teaching a pet a trick – you reward them when they do it right, and they learn to repeat that action. Over time, the LLM adjusts its internal settings to try to generate more of the "rewarding" (human-preferred) outputs. In a sense, the reward model is performing human work much faster and at a much larger scale.[16]

Of course, RLHF isn't perfect. It can be tough to find enough "wise" humans who can consistently provide helpful feedback, especially for specialized topics like law or medicine, where expertise is required. In addition, the LLM might learn to produce responses that *seem* good to the reward model but aren't genuinely good or helpful in a broader sense. It might figure out how to "trick" the reward system without truly understanding the desired behavior.[17]

And, of course, humans have biases, which can inadvertently be incorporated into the LLM during RLHF. What one person considers a perfectly fine answer, another might view as biased or inappropriate. This is why it's super important to have a diverse group of people providing feedback, and researchers are constantly working to add more guidance and filter out biased feedback.

The way we talk about updating and training LLMs can get a bit confusing, so let's revisit and break down the most common terms. Table 3.2 lists types of fine-tuning and describes each of them.

[15] As you might guess, people don't always choose the same output. Most RLHF training is an inherently subjective exercise.

[16] This also means models suffer from what Annie Duke, former professional poker player, author, and expert in decision science, calls "resulting." This is the cognitive bias of judging a decision's quality based on its outcome, rather than the quality of the decision-making process at the time. A good decision can have a bad outcome due to luck, and a bad decision can have a good outcome due to luck. For humans, Duke advises focusing on the decision-making process and evaluating the information available at the time, separating it from chance or external factors. Reinforcement learning means that AI only knows if its final answer was correct, not whether the steps it took to reach it were. This means it can't drive insights, learn from mistakes, or improve its process in a theory-driven way. And that means it can't really understand or learn how to understand. If models could think, then presumably they'd be able to identify where their reasoning is wrong and correct it. But they can't, because they don't think. They're pattern-matching.

[17] This is similar to the alignment problem we'll discuss in Chapter 26 ("Artificial General Intelligence").

TABLE 3.2 *A list of types of fine-tuning and descriptions of each*

Type of Fine-Tuning	Description
Fine-tuning	Imagine you have a brilliant student who's learned a lot about many subjects (that's the pretrained LLM). Fine-tuning is like giving that student a specialized course to become an expert in a specific area, such as analyzing movie reviews. You provide the LLM with new, focused data (labeled examples for movie reviews), and it adjusts what it knows to perform that particular task better.[18]
SFT	This is a specific kind of fine-tuning. Going back to our student, with SFT, you not only give them the movie reviews, but you also tell them what the correct "answer" is for each review (e.g., "This movie review is positive," or "This one is negative"). The LLM then learns to match the input (the review) to the desired output (the sentiment label), making it well suited for tasks such as classifying text or answering specific questions.
Instruction tuning	Think of this as training the student to follow explicit directions. You give the LLM not just the data, but also clear instructions on what you want it to do with that data. For example, instead of just giving it a movie review, you might provide it with the prompt: "Summarize this movie review in one sentence: [movie review text]." Instruction tuning is a type of SFT where these instructions are part of the learning examples. It helps the LLM become much better at understanding and following user commands.
Adaptation	This is the broadest term. It basically means making an LLM work well across different kinds of data and tasks. Fine-tuning (including SFT) is a common way to adapt an LLM. But there are other methods too, like "domain adaptation," where you tweak an LLM to perform better within a specific field, like legal documents or medical reports, without necessarily retraining it from scratch on new input–output pairs for every single task.

3.3.6.3 Large Reasoning Models (LRMs)

Creating a "reasoning" model is only slightly different. AI companies take the same base model but use SFT (giving it chain-of-thought examples), so that it "reasons" through questions by feeding its outputs back as inputs. They also use reinforcement learning so the model can compare its solutions to known answers and determine whether it reached the correct conclusion. It's a matter of trial and error, where the model is only "rewarded" when it provides the right outcome.

Large reasoning models (LRMs) don't reason the way humans do; it's more of a brute-force (and high-compute) approach to finding acceptable solutions. When LRMs perform better on analytic tasks, research suggests it's because their chain-of-thought formatting helps keep them on track and makes them less likely to rely on

[18] For example, Llama 2 was fine-tuned on one million binary comparisons. H. Touvron et al. (July 19, 2023). Llama 2: Open foundation and fine-tuned chat models. Retrieved February 24, 2026, from https://arxiv.org/pdf/2307.09288.

unrelated portions of their network. It's not that they can solve questions the underlying model can't answer; it's that they're more likely to find the correct answer sooner because their approach is more constrained. LRMs are still pattern-matching.

LRMs are great if there is a known answer, like in math and coding. They're less useful for tax policy, solving education and medical access problems, famine, global warming, identifying a "good" story or joke, etc., because there is no objective, correct answer. Unfortunately, these problems comprise most real-world problems.

3.3.7 *Step 7: Model Deployment/Release*

1. Data Creation
2. Data Collection
3. Data Curation
4. Model Pretraining
5. Evaluation
6. Fine-Tuning
7. **Model Deployment/Release**
8. Output Generation
9. Model Refinement/Alignment

When an AI model is created, organizations face a decision: Which parts, if any, will be shared with the public? This isn't just about the model itself. It also includes a range of components, each with its own implications for sharing.

3.3.7.1 What to Share

The first question to answer is what the developers want to share. For instance, they might share the raw dataset, which contains all the initial information gathered from the web and other sources. Or they could share the processed or refined dataset, the cleaned-up version actually used to train the model.

Beyond the data, they might release the code that runs the model, or even specific details about its internal architecture. And, of course, they could share the model itself.

Other shareable elements include evaluation metrics and instruction data, which are used to teach the AI to follow specific commands. Finally, the human feedback information and its structure, which helped refine the model, could also be made public.

Notably, few entities opt to share all the components that go into creating GenAI models or systems.

3.3.7.2 How to Share

Once an organization decides what to share, it must determine how to share it. The two main approaches are deployment and release.

When an organization deploys an AI model, it keeps the model and all its related components on its own servers. Companies like OpenAI, with ChatGPT, and Google, with Gemini, operate in this manner. They control who can access and use their models. This level of control enables them to block specific uses, modify content filters, adjust the model's output, and even alter how much context the AI retains during a conversation. This approach also makes it easier for them to generate revenue, as they act as gatekeepers to their technology.

Alternatively, an organization can release the AI and its components. This typically involves posting them online, often on platforms like GitHub or Hugging Face, allowing virtually anyone to download them. This method is favored by open-source companies that aim to share technology broadly and encourage widespread access and collaboration. However, this approach carries a significant risk: Once the artifacts are released, the original entity loses control over how they are used, potentially leading to unintended applications.

3.3.8 *Step 8: Output Generation*

1. Data Creation
2. Data Collection
3. Data Curation
4. Model Pretraining
5. Evaluation
6. Fine-Tuning
7. Model Deployment/Release
8. **Output Generation**
9. Model Refinement/Alignment

At this stage, you provide the LLM with a prompt, which is essentially a question or command, and it responds accordingly.

Remember that LLMs have been trained on an immense amount of text and code – think of it as having read nearly everything written online, in books, and more. This training gives them a deep "understanding" of how language works and how words are connected. When you provide the LLM with a clue, such as a sentence you want it to complete or a question you need answered, it draws on this vast knowledge. It considers similar patterns it has seen before, weighs different possible meanings, and then gives you its best guess at what should come next. This "guessing" process is what we call inference.

But note that the model's outputs are probabilistic, and the way you phrase a prompt, even with very minor changes, can affect the quality of the output. It also means the same prompt entered by different people will elicit different outputs.

Here are some examples to show you how prompting and generation work:

Continuing a story:

- If you start with "The old lighthouse keeper lit the lamp, and a storm began to brew ..." the LLM might complete it with "... the waves crashed against the rocks, a symphony of nature's fury." It draws on its understanding of typical narrative progression and evocative descriptions.

Providing instructions:

- When asked, "How do I make a simple origami crane?" the LLM can access its knowledge of step-by-step instructions and folding techniques to provide a clear, concise guide.

Crafting a product description:

- Given the prompt "Write a compelling description for a new smartwatch that tracks sleep and fitness," the LLM could generate text like: "Discover your best self with the new AuraFit Smartwatch. Seamlessly monitor your sleep cycles and track every workout, transforming your daily routine into a path to peak wellness."

3.3.9 *Step 9: Model Refinement/Alignment*

1. Data Creation
2. Data Collection
3. Data Curation
4. Model Pretraining
5. Evaluation
6. Fine-Tuning
7. Model Deployment/Release
8. Output Generation
9. **Model Refinement/Alignment**

Once an LLM is built and deployed, developers can use data on how people interact with the model to continually improve it. This ongoing improvement process is sometimes called the "data flywheel."

Imagine a flywheel that keeps spinning and gaining momentum. In the context of LLMs, the "data flywheel" begins with each interaction someone has with the LLM, whether they ask it a question, give it a command, or just chat with it. These interactions generate valuable data. The LLM's responses and how users react to them provide signals.

For RLHF, user preference data (like "thumbs up/down" ratings) can be used to update the "reward model," which then helps the LLM learn what humans prefer even more effectively. By looping this new information back into the training process, the LLM learns from its real-world usage. In theory, it becomes more accurate, more helpful, and better aligned with users' expectations.

3.4 IMPORTANT THINGS TO REMEMBER

There are two important points to consider about how LLMs generate responses. First, LLMs don't "look up" information in a separate database, as a search engine does. All the information they use is built directly into their internal structure, developed during training.[19]

Second, an LLM's inference isn't always flawless. Just as a detective might reach the wrong conclusion if the clues are misleading or their understanding of the situation is incomplete, an LLM can sometimes make mistakes if the input is unclear or its training data has gaps. Unlike humans, LLMs will often generate a confident-sounding answer regardless.

[19] AI systems may bolt on ways to incorporate outside information into responses, such as web search, but those tools are not intrinsic to the model itself.

More technically, when an LLM generates text, it uses a process called autoregression. This means it creates the output word by word (or "token" by "token"). For each new word, the model uses its learned parameters to calculate the probability of each word appearing next, then picks the most likely one to add to the sentence.

So, while an LLM might seem to be thinking through a problem step by step, it's actually just taking your input, breaking it into small pieces (tokens), generating the most statistically probable next piece, adding it, and repeating the process until it's finished its response. Its goal is not to give you a truthful or accurate answer; it's giving you the most statistically probable answer based on the data it was exposed to during pretraining.

In an important sense, all GenAI outputs are hallucinations. It's just that the outputs often align with reality.

3.5 DISCUSSION QUESTIONS

1. The chapter explains that GenAI models are essentially superpowered autocomplete, constantly calculating the most probable next word. If this is true, why do their outputs often feel insightful and creative to us? Does the appearance of "deep comprehension" change how we should rely on the technology?
2. The text states that GenAI lacks inherent judgment and instead relies on the "median judgment" of the people whose data it was trained on. Can you think of an example in your life where relying on the "median judgment" instead of an expert's opinion would lead to a bad outcome? How does this limitation change where we should or shouldn't use AI?
3. The text describes synthetic data (AI-generated data used for training) as a form of "data laundering." In your opinion, does the creation of synthetic data erase the original ethical issues (like copyright infringement) associated with the human-created data it was based on?
4. The curation process discards over 99 percent of the original data, removing content such as toxic/biased material and formatting issues. Do you think this intense filtering makes the models more ethical or simply creates a more palatable veneer of ethics for the public? What could be an unintended negative consequence of filtering out too much "real-world" content?

4

How GenAI Is Measured

4.1 INTRODUCTION

If there's one topic that every major AI company is sure to hype in their papers and press releases, it's their models' performance on various benchmarks.

In December 2024, Sam Altman claimed that OpenAI's o1 model was "the smartest model in the world."[i] The next month, DeepSeek claimed its models "achieved[d] performance comparable to" OpenAI's o1 model.[ii] In February 2025, Google claimed that Gemini 2.0 Flash was "the world's best model."[iii] That same month, OpenAI claimed that GPT-4.5 was their "largest and best model for chat yet."[iv] In May 2025, Anthropic claimed that "Claude Opus 4 is the world's best coding model."[v] Not to be outdone, in July 2025, Elon Musk claimed Grok 4 was "the smartest AI in the world" and "smarter than almost all graduate students in all disciplines, simultaneously."[vi] The trend continued with GPT-5's release, which OpenAI claimed was "like chatting with a helpful friend with PhD-level intelligence."[vii]

What do they base these claims on? Probably mostly self-serving vibes, but also benchmarks and "arenas." When people say, "Frontier-model capabilities double every *x* months," you should ask, "Based on what?"

While genuine, incremental advancements in capabilities are likely occurring, GenAI companies consistently over-index on and exploit positive benchmark scores for marketing, creating a misleading narrative of vast, general-purpose capability improvements.

All major GenAI companies have claimed that the performance of their latest models is superior to their previous models, yet how often do you hear people or companies say they now use GenAI significantly more than they did a year ago because of the improvement?[1] This hints at an underlying problem this chapter

[1] As in, "Wow, the model now scores 87/100 when last year it only scored 82/100, so we're using it like crazy!"

will discuss: What, exactly, do benchmarks tell us? This disparity between published benchmark metrics and a demonstrable increase in real-world, high-stakes applications suggests a lack of construct validity (as discussed later) – meaning the benchmarks fail to measure capabilities that matter for significant real-world utility.

And yet, it's hard to argue that we shouldn't do any benchmarking or that benchmarks are worthless. An imperfect test is probably better than no test, and tests can always be improved over time and through experimentation.

But first, what are benchmarks?

***

Benchmarks are essentially tests, and many are multiple-choice, much like what students encounter in the classroom. The idea behind benchmarks is that higher scores indicate the model's capability to perform the given task. Often, the task is described as if it implies the model has some meaningful general ability. For example, doing well on a benchmark for identifying what's in images is touted as "visual understanding," as if identifying objects is the totality of what "visual understanding" could mean. Another example is a benchmark on graduate-level questions for various fields of study, where performing well is taken to mean the chatbot can operate at a graduate or even PhD level, full stop.

Benchmarks have been around for decades, but GenAI has breathed new life into them in both nonprofit and for-profit sectors. If a researcher wants to get published or have a good shot at winning an award at a major machine-learning conference, demonstrating the ability to score an extra point higher on a benchmark is a relatively easy-to-measure and understandable way to achieve this goal. The motive for companies is that if a model can't perform at a comparable level to other models on well-known benchmarks, developers are less likely to attract customers or secure funding.

The problem is that benchmark scores reveal much less about model capabilities than these companies would have you believe. They can also lead to boring homogenization. As Matteo Wong wrote in *The Atlantic*:

> The deeper issue, perhaps, is that human intelligence is poorly understood, and gauging it is an infamously hard and prejudiced task. People have knacks for different things, or might arrive at the same result – the answer to a math problem, the solution to an ARC-AGI grid [a type of benchmark] – via very different routes. A person who scores 30 percent on ARC-AGI-2 is in no sense inferior to someone who scores 90 percent. The collision of those differing routes and minds is what sparks debate, creativity, and beauty. Intentions, emotions, and lived experiences drive people as much as any logical reasoning.
>
> Human cognitive diversity, in other words, is a glorious jumble. How do you even begin to construct an artificial version of that? And when that diversity is already so abundant, do you really want to?[viii]

4.2 WHAT BENCHMARKS ARE

To define benchmarks, I'll paraphrase from a widely cited research paper:[ix]

- A benchmark is a specific combination of datasets (at least test data, sometimes also training data) and a metric, conceptualized as representing one or more particular tasks or sets of abilities, adopted by a community of researchers as a shared framework for comparing models.
- The task is a specific problem definition as represented in the dataset.
- A metric is a way to summarize system performance across all or some tasks as a single number or score. It provides a means to measure success and failure at the level of individual system outputs and to summarize these counts over the entire dataset.
- Models achieving the highest scores on the benchmark metrics are regarded as "state-of-the-art" (SOTA) for that task.

For example, there may be a benchmark for evaluating how well a model identifies colors. The task is to correctly identify the color presented to the model, and the metric is how the model is graded. If the benchmark includes a dataset of 100 images, a model that correctly identifies 90 of them might score 90 percent. If no other model scores above 90 percent, then 90 percent is considered the SOTA and becomes the standard that other researchers and companies aim to beat.

There are at least dozens of benchmarks commonly reported by GenAI companies and researchers. A key purpose of benchmarks is to enable researchers, companies, and the public to understand how models compare with one another, their absolute performance, whether the models are improving, the extent of the improvement, and the remaining room for improvement.

Ideally, benchmarks will follow a development method where the dog wags the tail, not the other way around. For instance, researchers would first identify a specific use case where the benchmark's results would reveal something useful.

Next, the researchers would determine the specific skills necessary for the model to perform well on the benchmark. If the benchmark is testing for hallucinations, for example, the skill would be to generate outputs that align with known facts.

The researchers would then determine how to measure the models' performance on the benchmark. Often, benchmarks ask multiple-choice questions, and the score is the percentage of questions the model answered correctly.

Then, the researchers would collect the questions or scenarios they would present to the models. This could include multiple-choice questions, open-ended questions, images the model is supposed to identify, and so on. The researchers would also need to collect the correct answers to compare the outputs against. This is how they can tell whether the model performed well.

Voila! You have a benchmark!

* * *

4.3 THE TYPES OF EVALUATIONS

Depending on how subjective the benchmark is (does it assess math, where there is a known answer, or poetry, where there's not?), there are multiple ways to conduct the evaluation. Table 4.1 lists three prominent approaches to evaluations and provides examples of each.

4.3.1 *Automated Benchmarking*

Automated benchmarking is the use of automated processes and tools to systematically measure and compare the performance of different AI models using standardized datasets, metrics, and methodologies. Box 4.1 discusses a popular benchmark. The process aims to provide an objective, consistent, and scalable way to measure model performance.

A key feature is that the test dataset is the same every time. Automated tools execute the benchmark by feeding prompts from the dataset into the model and collecting its responses. Then, algorithms compare the model's output against a "ground truth" reference answer in the dataset.

The nature of automated benchmarks theoretically makes them scalable, consistent in implementation, quicker to develop, and cost-efficient relative to other assessment methods.

4.3.2 *Methods for Implementation*

1. Multiple-choice evaluations: These can be administered locally and evaluated in an automated manner with code.
2. Third-party evaluation frameworks: Here, the model is provided to a third party, such as a university or research institute, which conducts the evaluation. This ensures a standard protocol, allowing for apples-to-apples comparisons between models.

TABLE 4.1 *Categories of model evaluations and examples of evals for each category*

Type of Evaluation	Examples
Automated benchmarking	1. Multiple-choice evaluations 2. Third-party evaluation frameworks
Humans as judges	1. Using volunteers to assess which models are best 2. Using crowd workers to measure which output is best 3. Using domain experts to probe the model 4. Working with a third-party organization to audit models
Models as judges	1. AI-powered evaluations

BOX 4.1 An Example: MMLU

There is a popular benchmark, created in 2020, called Massive Multitask Language Understanding (MMLU). It includes 15,908 multiple-choice questions that measure performance on fifty-seven tasks, encompassing everything from law and history to math and nutrition. The benchmark purports to provide a score representing the knowledge of GenAI models. The higher the score out of 100, the more capable the model is presumed to be.[2]

Over time, the benchmark has become "saturated." The top models from the biggest tech companies routinely score around 90 percent on MMLU. Moreover, an examination of 5,700 questions in the benchmark found that about 6.5 percent contained errors (e.g., incorrect answers, multiple correct answers, ambiguous questions).[x] This suggests that the best any model can ever achieve on the benchmark is 93.5 percent, not 100 percent. In response, companies have switched to more "challenging" benchmarks, believing that if models perform better in the coming months, it's a strong indicator that their capabilities are improving.

Here is a sample of two questions from MMLU, which come from the domains of international law and professional medicine:[xi]

Question 1

Would a reservation to the definition of torture in the International Covenant on Civil and Political Rights (ICCPR) be acceptable in contemporary practice?

(A) This is an acceptable reservation if the reserving country's legislation employs a different definition.
(B) This is an unacceptable reservation because it contravenes the object and purpose of the ICCPR.
(C) This is an unacceptable reservation because the definition of torture in the ICCPR is consistent with customary international law.
(D) This is an acceptable reservation because, under general international law, States have the right to enter reservations to treaties.

Question 2

A thirty-three-year-old man undergoes a radical thyroidectomy for thyroid cancer. During the operation, moderate hemorrhaging requires ligation of several vessels in the left side of the neck. Postoperatively, serum studies show a calcium concentration of 7.5 mg/dL, albumin concentration of 4 g/dL, and parathyroid

[2] If you're skeptical that a single number can successfully compress a wide-ranging, multidisciplinary test in a meaningful way, I'm with you.

hormone concentration of 200 pg/mL. Damage to which of the following vessels caused the findings in this patient?

(A) Branch of the costocervical trunk.
(B) Branch of the external carotid artery.
(C) Branch of the thyrocervical trunk.
(D) Tributary of the internal jugular vein.

4.3.3 *Assumptions of Automated Benchmarks*

For evaluations to be useful, certain assumptions must hold. For example, models are assumed not to have been trained on the test questions. This would be like giving a student the questions and answers to a test, then asking them to take it. It would be unsurprising if they scored well, and the high score would not indicate much about their knowledge or abilities. It's possible the student would have scored well regardless. Perhaps they genuinely knew how to solve the problems. But it's also possible they only know how to "solve" the particular problems on the test they memorized.

When a model is trained on the test, it's called "data contamination."[xii] The problem of data contamination is particularly difficult with LLMs because they require scraping everything on the internet. So if you ask a model a question and it does poorly, and you share that online, the model developers may scrape it and even fix the problem. But that doesn't mean it solves all issues of that general variety.

Finally, when a model's capability is limited to what it was trained on, and it cannot generalize (e.g., it cannot reason through similar but different questions), we say the model is "overfitting."

4.4 HUMANS AS JUDGES

An alternative to mostly static benchmarks is interactive assessments, in which users submit a prompt and are shown at least two anonymous options representing outputs from different models (e.g., one from Google's Gemini and another from OpenAI's ChatGPT). The user then decides which output they prefer.

Using humans rather than an automated system is beneficial for more complex tasks or when there are multiple ways to provide a satisfactory answer.[3] For example,

[3] Though even with intra- and cross-human agreement metrics and frameworks, complexity and subjectivity still require statistical rigor. Otherwise, the same human will award different scores to the same result with increasing frequency as the complexity and number of runs increase. Differentiating and ranking "good" outputs from "bad" ones becomes more difficult.

while an automated benchmark is suitable for verifying whether a model answers a coding question correctly, because it either works or it doesn't, a human is better suited for judging whether a model can generate good jokes.[4]

This approach is also less likely to contribute to data contamination because it is assumed that users will mostly enter novel prompts rather than copy and paste from benchmark datasets.

4.4.1 *Methods*

1. Using volunteers to assess which models are best: This is a crowdsourcing approach. People voluntarily go to a website where they can enter a prompt and are presented with outputs from two different anonymous models. They then select the output they like more. In the aggregate, this supposedly indicates how to rank models overall.
2. Using crowd workers to measure which output is best: This is an A/B testing approach. This is similar to the aforementioned volunteer situation, but the outputs usually come from the same company, which allows the developer to refine the model. Also, the workers are paid.
3. Using domain experts to probe the model: For more sensitive topics or those that require specialized knowledge, companies may hire domain experts to review the models and determine if the experts can elicit potentially harmful information from them.
4. Working with a third-party organization to audit models: Unlike the third method, which focuses on experts, this type of evaluation explores broader issues and edge cases. It more closely resembles traditional software or video-game quality-assurance testing.

4.5 MODELS AS JUDGES

Evaluating the outputs of AI models, particularly in tasks like natural-language generation, can sometimes be done using other AI models as judges. This "AI-as-judge" approach typically falls into two categories: generalist, high-capability models and small, specialist models.

Generalist models are large, broad-spectrum models designed to understand and generate human-like text across a wide range of topics. When used to grade other models, they leverage their internal representations to assess the quality, coherence, relevance, and even stylistic aspects of another model's output.

In contrast, small models are AI models meticulously trained for a very specific task: differentiating between outputs based on fine-grained preference data. For instance, such a model might be trained on thousands of examples in which human

[4] Of course, the quality of the working code could also be scrutinized.

annotators indicate which of two generated sentences they prefer, or which answer is more accurate for a particular query. This focused training allows them to become highly adept at making nuanced distinctions within their domain.

4.5.1 *Methods*

1. AI-powered evaluations: This is an LLM-as-judge approach. Here, a model that is supposedly closely aligned with human preferences judges the outputs of other models, and it can even create the evaluation questions. This can be faster and cheaper than paying humans. But it can also be problematic if the "judge" isn't properly calibrated.[xiii]

***

4.6 THE PROBLEMS WITH BENCHMARKS

The shortcomings and limitations of benchmarks are legion and will be explored later. However, a more basic issue warrants mention.

When GenAI companies claim their models can "reason" and "understand," they are actually predicting the next most likely token based on statistical associations with what the user has provided and all the data the model has already been trained on.

If the public accepts this "reasoning" and "understanding" framing, it may become more receptive to allowing GenAI to infiltrate more aspects of our lives, even when there is no compelling reason to believe GenAI will improve those areas. This includes screening job applicants and interviewing them, providing medical, financial, and legal advice, incorporating GenAI into business and government decision-making, and weaving GenAI into our education system. Despite the hype, benchmarks cannot tell us when an AI product can safely and reliably replace human workers, given the issues discussed in the following.

4.6.1 *Benchmark Dataset and Measurement Limitations*

1. **Benchmark Dataset and Measurement Limitations**
2. Incrementalism
3. Leaderboards
4. Apples to Oranges
5. Zero-Shot, Few-Shot, and Chain-of-Thought Prompting
6. You Can't Test What You Can't Measure
7. Implementation
8. Trained on the Test
9. Gaming the Arenas
10. The Costs of Reasoning

Every dataset has inherent bias, which limits the insights a benchmark can offer. Data benchmarks, by their nature, are limited and subjective. They often reflect the biases of their creators or the specific conditions under which the data was collected, rather than providing a universal or objective measure. Consequently, the applicability of a benchmark's findings may be limited to contexts similar to its original context, making it difficult to generalize results across different environments or demographics.[xiv]

For example, a benchmark may claim it can assess a model's language understanding. That's misleading. Benchmarks are limited by the languages they include, so they probably would not work equally well for everyday conversation in Missouri, medical terminology, legal jargon, Atlanta urban vernacular, and financial jargon.

As Emily Bender puts it, "[B]enchmark creators frame their work as something general, rather than tightly scoped: 'Visual understanding' as opposed to 'classification of photographs taken from XYZ sources into N classes as labeled by such-and-such crowd-workers.'"[xv]

Moreover, many dataset designs rely on convenience samples, such as scraping websites like Reddit and wikiHow, rather than being developed with input from experts familiar with the specific fields the benchmark aims to measure.

There is also the matter of measurement. Because GenAI is a stochastic system (it generates outputs based on probabilities rather than a deterministic system that always produces the same response to a given question), the same model often receives wildly different benchmark results from run to run. So, a model may score 85 percent in one run and only 79 percent in a separate run, even when it's the same model being asked the same questions. Companies then cherry-pick the best performers and use them for marketing.

4.6.2 *Incrementalism*

1. Benchmark Dataset and Measurement Limitations
2. **Incrementalism**
3. Leaderboards
4. Apples to Oranges
5. Zero-Shot, Few-Shot, and Chain-of-Thought Prompting
6. You Can't Test What You Can't Measure
7. Implementation
8. Trained on the Test
9. Gaming the Arenas
10. The Costs of Reasoning

Pursuing SOTA performance on benchmarks often involves a peculiar approach, prioritizing incremental, empirical-only research over hypothesis-driven inquiry. This tendency was critiqued by Lorenza Saitta in 1995, long before the emergence of GenAI. Saitta observed that this approach "allow[ed] researchers to publish dull papers that proposed small variations of existing supervised learning algorithms and reported their small-but-significant incremental performance improvements in comparison studies." This suggests a focus on achieving marginal gains relative to established benchmarks rather than on exploring novel theoretical frameworks or fundamental questions.

Benchmarks may make sense when comparing which algorithm is best at, say, recommending songs that a given user is likely to rate higher. That's a clearly defined goal, and the task can be narrowly tailored. It's quite a different thing to have a general "reasoning" benchmark.

4.6.3 *Leaderboards*

1. Benchmark Dataset and Measurement Limitations
2. Incrementalism
3. **Leaderboards**
4. Apples to Oranges
5. Zero-Shot, Few-Shot, and Chain-of-Thought Prompting
6. You Can't Test What You Can't Measure
7. Implementation
8. Trained on the Test
9. Gaming the Arenas
10. The Costs of Reasoning

If a single benchmark can't tell us much, why don't we aggregate a bunch of them into a basket of benchmarks? Furthermore, why don't we make a leaderboard, with the model having the highest aggregate score across all benchmarks as the "leader"?

In fact, it's a conventional approach. Stanford has a whole website dedicated to various basket-of-benchmarks (let's call them "BoB") leaderboards.[xvi]

Researcher Kiri Wagstaff highlights a problem with common benchmark evaluations, particularly those that report an overall accuracy score across multiple tasks. For example, she notes that 80 percent accuracy in one domain, such as classifying a type of flower, might be perfectly acceptable for its intended purpose in botany. However, the same accuracy in a more consequential domain, such as classifying mushrooms as poisonous or edible, would be wholly insufficient, as 99 percent or higher accuracy would potentially be required.

Wagstaff contends that while metrics such as model accuracy may share the same range, their meaning and implications can vary widely across contexts. She points out that summarizing experimental results by simply averaging accuracy across diverse datasets offers no truly useful insights into generalization or real-world impact. The meaning of a given percentage improvement can vary widely across datasets or classes. This critique underscores a problem in which evaluation tasks are not only poorly defined but also measured in ways that hinder meaningful interpretation of the results.

Moreover, these BoB leaderboards do not help determine what is good enough. If it's a spectrum rather than binary, where on the spectrum does any given result lie? Is being fourth on a leaderboard good? How much worse is fourth compared to third? How do we know that even being at the top of the leaderboard indicates the model is good and not merely the best of the worst?

The BoB leaderboards are a bit like high-school grade-point averages (GPAs): They can't tell you what a student is good at, what they've mastered, whether they're gritty, and so on. A 3.50 GPA may indicate that the student has consistently maintained a strong performance in every course. Or the student could have performed poorly in their first year but excelled since then. Or maybe they excelled in everything during the first three years of high school but eventually gave up trying in their senior year. Perhaps they excel in math and science courses but struggle in English and history, or vice versa. The problem with averages is that they obscure as often as they illuminate.

4.6.4 *Apples to Oranges*

1. Benchmark Dataset and Measurement Limitations
2. Incrementalism
3. Leaderboards
4. **Apples to Oranges**
5. Zero-Shot, Few-Shot, and Chain-of-Thought Prompting
6. You Can't Test What You Can't Measure
7. Implementation
8. Trained on the Test
9. Gaming the Arenas
10. The Costs of Reasoning

Not all companies share their model performance on the same benchmarks, and it is impossible to draw conclusions about model performance when comparing scores across different benchmarks (like HellaSwag, created in 2019, and TruthfulQA, created in 2021), even when both were designed to tell us something about the same general topic (in this case, model knowledge).

For example, Llama, Claude, Mistral, and Inflection all announced their scores on the Ai2 Reasoning Challenge (ARC) benchmark, which allegedly tests commonsense reasoning, but Grok, GPT-4, and Gemini didn't.

4.6.5 *Zero-Shot, Few-Shot, and Chain-of-Thought Prompting*

1. Benchmark Dataset and Measurement Limitations
2. Incrementalism
3. Leaderboards
4. Apples to Oranges
5. **Zero-Shot, Few-Shot, and Chain-of-Thought Prompting**
6. You Can't Test What You Can't Measure
7. Implementation
8. Trained on the Test
9. Gaming the Arenas
10. The Costs of Reasoning

Not all benchmarks are administered the same way. Even for the same benchmark, developers and researchers may use different methods to evaluate model performance. The reasons vary, but marketing is surely one of them. Companies may choose benchmarks and methods that best highlight their model's strengths and differentiate it from competitors.

4.6.5.1 Zero-Shot Learning

In zero-shot learning, the AI model is given a task without any specific examples or prior guidance for that task. It relies entirely on its pretraining and fine-tuning to generate a response. The idea is that this suggests the model's ability to generalize to new, unseen tasks. This can be a strong indicator of how effectively a model embeds training data and how well it can recognize patterns and associations.[5] This approach also eliminates the need for task-specific labeled examples, which can be time-consuming and expensive to develop. Of course, zero-shot learning also usually results in a lower benchmark score because models generally perform better when shown examples before responding.

4.6.5.2 Few-Shot Learning

Few-shot learning involves providing the AI model with a small number of examples (typically fewer than ten) in the prompt to illustrate the task at hand. These examples guide the AI on how to approach the specific task. With a few examples, the model can better recognize the patterns needed to score well in the context and desired output format, resulting in more accurate and relevant responses than those from zero-shot learning.

4.6.5.3 Chain-of-Thought Prompting

Chain-of-thought prompting encourages the AI model to break down complex problems into intermediate, logical steps and "think out loud" before arriving at a final answer. This can involve explicitly asking the model to explain its reasoning. The chain-of-thought approach significantly improves the model's ability to solve complex, multistep problems (e.g., arithmetic, common-sense reasoning, symbolic reasoning) by guiding it through a structured process.

Overall, chain-of-thought and few-shot methods can lead to higher scores, which is a good reason to be skeptical when a company releases a benchmark using those methods and it either doesn't surpass or only slightly bests a competitor's model that used a zero-shot method on the same benchmark.

Using the ARC benchmark again:

- 0-shot: GPT-3, Llama 1
- 1-shot: GPT 3, Palm, Palm 2, Inflection, Inflection 2
- 4-shot: Palm, Palm 2
- 5-shot: Claude 2, Llama 2, Mistral Large
- 25-shot: Llama 2, Llama 3, Claude 3, Mistral Large, DBRX, GPT-4.

5 It may be that models are merely exploiting specific patterns in the benchmark tests or memorizing data without demonstrating true understanding or generalizability.

4.6.6 *You Can't Test What You Can't Measure*

1. Benchmark Dataset and Measurement Limitations
2. Incrementalism
3. Leaderboards
4. Apples to Oranges
5. Zero-Shot, Few-Shot, and Chain-of-Thought Prompting
6. **You Can't Test What You Can't Measure**
7. Implementation
8. Trained on the Test
9. Gaming the Arenas
10. The Costs of Reasoning

Life is messy. Not everything humans do can be distilled into simple questions that contain all the information needed to arrive at known answers. If we limit our understanding of model capabilities and how to compare models to how well they perform on tidy questions, we're bound to be disappointed.

Supposedly "general" benchmarks, if they were truly valid indicators of progress toward comprehensive artificial cognitive abilities, would ideally feature tasks selected systematically or aligned with specific theories of the cognitive abilities they aim to model. However, the current reality suggests otherwise: The tasks and collections of tasks appear to be chosen for convenience, often arbitrarily constructed from readily available resources for the benchmark development team, even when these constructions lack theoretical soundness. This approach raises concerns about the representativeness and scientific rigor of these benchmarks in assessing cognitive progress.[xvii]

It's also unclear how much benchmarks matter to real-world practitioners. For example, it's unclear whether doctors need models that excel at the types of benchmarks that models are currently tested on. The models may be intentionally trained on data that closely resembles the test data because that's what improves what is measurable (the benchmark score), rather than being trained on the task most needed in practice, presumably because real-life performance is more challenging to measure.

In other words, benchmarks often lack "construct validity." That is, benchmarks frequently have "an external validity issue related to how well an experimental setting relates to a research claim, or, in the context of machine learning, how well the benchmark dataset, and associated metrics of evaluation, represent a task."[xviii]

This shouldn't surprise anyone who has taken a standardized exam. Scoring high on the bar exam, for example, does not mean a person will be a good lawyer. This is probably why nobody cares how well any lawyer performed on the bar exam; it only matters whether they passed. While standardized exams like the bar exam assess necessary foundational knowledge, companies misappropriate the results of AI benchmarks, marketing high scores as indicators of sufficient capability for complex, real-world professional roles. This overreach exposes the lack of construct validity in their claims.

Similarly, scoring well on the ACT (a college admissions test) or Law School Admission Test (LSAT) does not guarantee that a student will become an exceptional professional in their chosen field. The exam may indicate whether a person is more or less likely to succeed at a given task (being a student or being a lawyer), but not necessarily.[6] The ambiguous usefulness of such exams should be unsurprising. A lawyer's job is not to answer multiple-choice questions all day.

What benchmarks can test for – knowledge with known answers – is precisely what LLMs are good at, but what benchmarks can't test for – ill-defined problems with incomplete information and ambiguous solutions – are the types of problems everyone is more likely to encounter.

Moreover, LLMs operate via complex statistical associations (predicting the next token) rather than human-like causal reasoning. This fundamental difference in cognitive architecture means that tests with construct validity for human cognition may not have equivalent validity when applied to an LLM, even if the model achieves a high score.

Additionally, it would probably be at least as beneficial to know whether a model can ask good questions as to know whether it can provide good answers to questions with known answers. If we want models to develop scientific breakthroughs, then by definition, they must be able to explore areas that humans have not yet explored, rather than merely being obedient students who can answer questions we already know how to answer.

4.6.7 *Implementation*

1. Benchmark Dataset and Measurement Limitations
2. Incrementalism
3. Leaderboards
4. Apples to Oranges
5. Zero-Shot, Few-Shot, and Chain-of-Thought Prompting
6. You Can't Test What You Can't Measure
7. **Implementation**
8. Trained on the Test
9. Gaming the Arenas
10. The Costs of Reasoning

While better benchmarks may emerge, it can often be challenging to persuade companies to adopt them. One reason is that implementing benchmarks can be hard, time-consuming, and compute-intensive.[xix] When companies are already rushing full on to produce new and better models, setting up new benchmarks may not be a top priority for resource allocation.

Additionally, even minor tweaks to the benchmark's administration can lead to significant inconsistencies. For example, Anthropic notes that with MMLU "simple formatting changes to the evaluation, such as changing the options from (A) to (1)

[6] To illustrate: I scored in the top 3 percent in the nation on the ACT and in verbal reasoning on the GRE (another college admissions test), but only in the bottom 25 percent of my class at Georgetown on the LSAT. My score was probably a simple heuristic for some law schools to reject my application out of hand. I ended up graduating in the top third of my class.

or changing the parentheses from (A) to [A], or adding an extra space between the option and the answer can lead to a ~5% change in accuracy on the evaluation."[xx]

A final reason not to switch benchmarks is that once a benchmark is widely adopted, others want to continue using it so they can compare newer models with older ones. Much like network effects, the value of a benchmark increases with each new user. A benchmark with too few adopters may not tell us much because we can't properly compare models on the evaluation.

4.6.8 *Trained on the Test*

1. Benchmark Dataset and Measurement Limitations
2. Incrementalism
3. Leaderboards
4. Apples to Oranges
5. Zero-Shot, Few-Shot, and Chain-of-Thought Prompting
6. You Can't Test What You Can't Measure
7. Implementation
8. **Trained on the Test**
9. Gaming the Arenas
10. The Costs of Reasoning

I've touched on data contamination earlier. While training on the test questions is the most obvious problem, what's often overlooked is that companies intentionally train on questions extremely similar to the test questions to perform well on the benchmark. What may seem like a remarkable improvement in reasoning, for example, is more often explained by GenAI developers' intense focus on improving performance on specific benchmarks rather than a more general breakthrough.

A possible partial solution is to use dynamic benchmarks, such as LiveBench, which releases new questions each month. This solution, however, isn't without its shortcomings. For one, it takes time and resources to create new, high-quality, validated questions each month. For another, a changing benchmark undermines a key purpose of benchmarks: to compare models over time. If model A is tested on the benchmark in January and model B is tested in March, scoring 3 percent higher, you can't draw any meaningful conclusions by comparing their scores.

4.6.9 *Gaming the Arenas*

1. Benchmark Dataset and Measurement Limitations
2. Incrementalism
3. Leaderboards
4. Apples to Oranges
5. Zero-Shot, Few-Shot, and Chain-of-Thought Prompting
6. You Can't Test What You Can't Measure
7. Implementation
8. Trained on the Test
9. **Gaming the Arenas**
10. The Costs of Reasoning

Leaderboards like Chatbot Arena are no less susceptible to gaming than other metrics, resulting in higher scores for models that reveal little about their actual capabilities.

For example, users may spend little time analyzing the outputs and simply select the one that seems best at a superficial level. Or users may base their decisions on subjective preferences, such as formatting, length, emoji use, and perceived usefulness, rather than on the content itself. Users may also focus more on outputs that seem more confident and "feel" right, overlooking inaccuracies, logical gaps, hallucinations, and other problems.[xxi] The subjective assessment is why people sometimes refer to this as "vibes-based" evaluating.[7]

And, of course, the plural of anecdote is not data. Because the people rating the outputs will likely base their decisions on different criteria, it is difficult to draw sweeping conclusions from their ratings. In contrast to arenas, paid workers evaluating models are often given extremely detailed guidelines on what to look for and how to assess models, which likely leads to greater consistency and a more systematic collection of desirable data.

Furthermore, because the most popular arena, Chatbot Arena, does not make its methodologies open-source and auditable, it may be susceptible to favoring certain tech companies. One paper claimed that the organization behind Chatbot Arena allowed Meta, Google, OpenAI, and Amazon to privately test multiple versions of their GenAI models without making the scores of the lowest-performing models public, giving the impression that those companies develop only high-performing models and giving them more opportunities to have a top-performing model. The paper states, for example, that Meta tested twenty-seven models in the first three months of 2025 but only allowed one to be made public. That one model was specifically fine-tuned to perform well on Chatbot Arena and was not released publicly for download.[xxii]

In the same timeframe, Google tested ten models, Amazon tested seven, and OpenAI tested two. The paper also claims that Chatbot Arena enabled major AI companies to participate in more "battles" by providing them with a higher sampling rate per model, which, in turn, enabled the companies to collect more data to train their models to perform well in Chatbot Arena.[8]

[7] Another problem with vibes-based testing is that humans may not select the outputs that are best for them in the long term. For example, they may select for sycophancy and anthropomorphism.

[8] Adding to Chatbot Arena's trustworthiness issues, in February 2025, the site's operators claimed they had no plans to become a for-profit entity, but by April, they had announced a change of heart. Because their methods are a black box and could be influenced by financial motives to favor certain tech companies, Chatbot Arena may be a less reliable source than it initially seemed.

4.6.10 *The Costs of Reasoning*

1. Benchmark Dataset and Measurement Limitations
2. Incrementalism
3. Leaderboards
4. Apples to Oranges
5. Zero-Shot, Few-Shot, and Chain-of-Thought Prompting
6. You Can't Test What You Can't Measure
7. Implementation
8. Trained on the Test
9. Gaming the Arenas
10. **The Costs of Reasoning**

It costs far more to run benchmark tests on so-called reasoning models, such as OpenAI's o1, than on nonreasoning models. This is because reasoning models generate far more tokens than nonreasoning models when arriving at answers; most model providers charge based on the number of tokens used. For instance, o1 generated "around eight times the amount GPT-4o generated" in one round of benchmark testing.[xxiii]

As one firm told *TechCrunch*, it costs half as much to test 6.5 times more nonreasoning models than reasoning models.[xxiv] This could become an issue for reproducibility as academia faces budget cuts. "'We're moving to a world where a lab reports x% on a benchmark where they spend y amount of compute, but where resources for academics are << y,' said Taylor, the CEO of AI startup General Reasoning, in a recent post on X. '[N]o one is going to be able to reproduce the results.'"[xxv]

While the price per token has declined over time for older models, the cost per token for the most recent models is higher than before. Therefore, if you want to use the best models, you will pay significantly more than if you opt for an older model. While the actual performance difference may not be significant, there is a stigma in tech and among researchers around using "outdated" models. A study based on GPT-4 will be far less compelling to reviewers and investors than a study on o4-mini-high, for example.

4.7 CONCLUSION

The quest for the "smartest model in the world," perpetually fueled by the latest benchmark score, has become a high-stakes, self-serving, and increasingly hollow performance. We are trapped in a feedback loop in which models are trained on test data, researchers chase incremental SOTA gains, and companies wield these skewed metrics at least as much for marketing as for technological breakthroughs.

What leaderboards don't tell us is when an AI can safely or reliably replace a human lawyer, doctor, or other decision-maker in a complex, ill-defined, and ambiguous real-world scenario. Misunderstandings about benchmarks lead the public and policymakers to confuse next-token prediction with genuine reasoning and understanding, and to encourage greater adoption even when it may not be wise.

4.8 DISCUSSION QUESTIONS

1. Benchmarks often confuse next-token prediction with genuine reasoning. Can you think of a non-AI task in your own life (like a specific school test or job interview style) where "memorization" or "optimization" for the test gets unfairly mistaken for genuine competence?
2. A cited researcher compared chasing SOTA scores to publishing "dull papers." If you were a funding body, what single measure or criterion (not a benchmark score) would you demand from a research team to prove their AI progress was genuine?
3. Imagine you are advising a CEO. They want to beat a competitor on a new benchmark, but doing so would require using a slightly "gamed" method (like using chain-of-thought prompting while the competitor used zero-shot learning). Do you advise them to prioritize the higher score for marketing, or the fairer, lower score for scientific rigor?
4. The chapter mentions the high cost of testing "reasoning" models, which impacts academic reproducibility. Is it ethically acceptable for a private company to use a massive computational budget to make a claim (like SOTA) that academia can't afford to verify?
5. If the bar exam is a bad indicator of a good lawyer, and the MMLU is a bad indicator of a "smart" AI, what would a genuinely construct-valid test look like for an AI that is meant to serve as a medical diagnostic assistant? What would that test measure?
6. It would be as beneficial to know if a model can "ask good questions" as to know if it can provide good answers. If you had to create a new benchmark to test an AI's ability to "ask good questions" for scientific discovery, what kind of task would be in it?

PART II

An Overview of Key Concepts

GenAI has remade the digital world. No longer mere calculators or search engines, these models – from chatbots writing essays to algorithms designing art – possess an unsettling fluency. They do more than process information; they also conjure it, blurring the line between creation and computation. This technical leap is also a profound cultural and economic reorganization.

At the base of every compelling GenAI output lies the brute-force mechanism of web scraping: the automated, industrial-scale acquisition of staggering volumes of human-created data, often without direct consent or compensation. This unacknowledged labor underpins the entire GenAI economy, raising deep-seated questions about digital property rights and the ethics of feeding the future on the work of the past.

Once primed, the models deliver outputs that mimic human interaction with startling accuracy. This proficiency trips a deeply ingrained cognitive wire: anthropomorphism. We instinctively assign intent and consciousness to these statistical machines, an error in perception that is both understandable and dangerous. This attribution of soul to software shapes our trust, which quickly metastasizes into automation bias – the casual, often unthinking, deference to an AI's output simply because it is the machine's suggestion. In fields from medicine to governance, this surrender of critical judgment poses a risk to human agency.

In addition, the discourse surrounding this technology is often dominated by two potentially misleading narratives. First, the specter of the "AI race" is constantly invoked to provoke geopolitical or corporate panic, suggesting that to delay is to perish. This sense of emergency, often amplified by those seeking investment or regulatory leniency, functions as an accelerant, justifying enormous outlays and rapid deployment over careful consideration.

Second, there is the siren song of democratization. We are assured that these tools are "empowering," distributing creative power to the masses and "leveling the playing field." Yet the concentration of necessary computational resources, the proprietary control over foundational models, and the steep cost of true innovation suggest a far more complicated reality.

To understand the legal issues and societal implications, it helps to first understand some key concepts. A deeper understanding is the first step toward reclaiming our role as the architects, rather than mere bystanders, of the future.

5

Web Scraping

5.1 INTRODUCTION

As Chapter 3 ("How GenAI Is Made") briefly noted, data is the lifeblood of GenAI. While you and I may read 5,000 books in our lifetimes, each major GenAI model trains on *millions* of books. That's to say nothing of songs, videos, transcripts, articles, and virtually all other forms of data. Where do you go when you need an internet's worth of data? Why, the internet, of course!

This chapter will focus primarily on how and where the content is acquired, and whether consent is required.[1] Do the sources of the scraped data (i.e., the owners of the content) consent to having their data scraped by GenAI companies? If not, how can they prevent the scraping?[2] These questions matter because the tension between technological capability and individual control shapes not only AI development but also the future of creative work, privacy, and the digital commons.

5.2 DATA COLLECTION

Data collection and curation bring up two huge, intertwined concerns:

1. This is where most *legal* action, such as lawsuits, originates.
2. There are profound *ethical* dilemmas surrounding the acquisition of data.

You can characterize the law as what one *can* do, while ethics is what one *should* do.

The legal issues primarily revolve around copyright law, which governs ownership of rights in creative works, as I'll discuss in Chapter 11 ("An Introduction to Copyright Law"). The ethical questions, however, are even more varied and unsettled. For instance, one major ethical debate is whether copyright owners should

[1] For a discussion on copyright and the consequences of unauthorized copying, see Chapter 11 ("An Introduction to Copyright Law").

[2] Recall that scraping means an automated piece of software is deployed by content gatherers (such as AI companies) to visit thousands or millions of websites and download (scrape) the content from the website, storing a copy on the scraper's server.

have the right to "opt out" of having their creative materials included in the massive datasets used to train AI models. An even stronger, copyright-owner-friendly stance would be to require AI companies to obtain "affirmative consent" (a clear "yes" or permission) from copyright owners *before* copying their work into training datasets.

GenAI requires an unfathomable amount of data. Literally more than any human can consume in a lifetime or even truly grasp. This data originates from billions of creators worldwide who post content online, either originally or as nondigital media that has been scanned and converted to a digital format. Once it's on the internet, it becomes incredibly difficult to trace most of it back to its original creator.

To understand the complexities of determining the creator, imagine a piece of art: Alice creates it and posts it on Website X. Then Bob copies it from Website X and posts it on Website Y without including a link or reference to the source. Later, Carol slightly modifies it and posts it on Website Z, where an AI company's scraping bot might encounter it, with no mention of the original artist. It may be that the best society can hope for is that the AI company incorrectly attributes the image to the person who posted it on the website where it was scraped, rather than providing attribution to the actual creator.[3]

5.2.1 *The Public, Deep, and Dark Webs*

When AI companies describe the data used to train their models, they often use terms like "public internet" or "publicly available data."[4] These seemingly simple phrases, as we'll see, do a great deal of work for some very complicated issues.

First, let's briefly consider the sheer scale we're dealing with. Remember, AI models need not just millions or billions, but *trillions* of "tokens" (for language, this means words and subwords) to learn effectively. "Trillion" is a word we hear, but its true magnitude is hard to comprehend.

Here's a way of thinking about the scale to put it in perspective:

- One million millimeters = one kilometer (down the street).
- One billion millimeters = 1,000 kilometers (about 600 miles).
- One trillion millimeters = 1,000,000 kilometers (enough to circle the earth about 25 times).

When you need to collect not just one or two trillion tokens, but many trillions, you are compelled to seek enormous pools of data. It is impossible to generate enough data internally (i.e., within the AI company), and it is also impossible to pay

[3] The importance of attribution will be further discussed in Chapters 17 ("Licensing for GenAI") and 20 ("The Economics of the Internet").

[4] All major GenAI companies have leaned into this argument: Google, Meta, OpenAI, Anthropic, Microsoft, etc.

BOX 5.1 The Case of Common Crawl

It's worth highlighting a primary source of LLM training data: Common Crawl. This nonprofit organization has been crawling the web since 2008, accumulating an enormous archive of web data. Think of it as a massive, tireless librarian who constantly scans and records publicly available content on the internet. It then makes these colossal datasets available for free, which is why it is a go-to resource for researchers and companies looking to train AI models on a grand scale.

The challenge, however, is that even when this raw data is "cleaned" – as in Google's Colossal Clean Crawled Corpus (C4) – it still raises myriad ethical and potential legal issues. For example, when Ai2 (a prominent AI research institute) collaborated with the *Washington Post* to analyze C4, they discovered that "at least 27 other sites identified by the U.S. government as markets for piracy and counterfeits were present in the data set."[i]

Perhaps even more revealing, "the copyright symbol – which denotes a work registered as intellectual property – appears more than 200 million times in the C4 data set."[ii] In other words, the © symbol appears approximately once every fifteen documents in the dataset, indicating that intellectual property concerns pervade these training corpora.

Moreover, Common Crawl claims its datasets are for researchers, but it does not monitor who accesses them or for what purposes. In fact, it is aware that most major GenAI companies likely use Common Crawl data to train their models.

Finally, while Common Crawl's search feature may indicate that a copyright owner's data is not included in the repository, the works may, in fact, be present. This obfuscation appears to be intentional in at least some instances.

contractors to create billions of documents that can be converted into trillions of tokens within a reasonable timescale or at a reasonable cost.

This is why GenAI companies scrape as much of the internet as they can. But the internet is not a monolith. We can categorize its vast data reservoirs into three main buckets: the *public internet*, the *deep* web, and the *dark* web.

One of the largest and most commonly cited pools is the *public internet*, where the data is "publicly available." This is what organizations like Common Crawl scrape for others to download and use, as explained in Box 5.1. So what exactly does "public internet" mean in this context? Typically, it refers to data that isn't hidden behind a paywall and isn't from the "dark web." While this definition might seem straightforward, and it seems to imply that the data is fair game for unrestricted use, the term is actually quite misleading, as we'll explore.[5]

5 An interesting case is accidental publication of sensitive data in a noncontrolled manner. There are a nontrivial number of cases where sensitive data has been released publicly. That data will certainly be scraped if it's available during a scraping pass.

Companies can also scrape information from the *deep web*. Imagine the public internet as the surface of an ocean; it's what you can see and easily access with minimal effort. The deep web is akin to the vast majority of the sea that lies beneath the surface. It comprises about 90 percent of the entire internet, but you usually can't see it because its content is protected by paywalls, requires account logins, or is private. For example, most company-internal documents, your online banking statements, or content on subscription streaming services reside in the deep web.

Finally, there's the *dark web*. This is akin to the deepest, most secluded trenches of the ocean, only navigable if you know exactly where you're going and have specialized equipment. Accessing it typically requires specialized software, such as Tor, which anonymizes user activity. It's where a higher proportion of illegal activities occur compared to legal ones. If you're looking to acquire stolen usernames and passwords, malware, illicit drugs, nonconsensual explicit images, or prohibited weapons, you'll find a much greater proportion of them on the dark web than anywhere else on the internet.

5.2.2 *The "Public Internet" and Social Media Loopholes*

5.2.2.1 Loophole One

The assertions by GenAI companies and their supporters that all publicly available content on the internet is fair game are, at best, intellectually lazy and, very likely, knowingly dishonest. Here's why: Almost any data can be made publicly available.

For example, content originally behind a paywall or even from the dark web can be copied and then posted on a public part of the internet. When an AI entity then scrapes this content, they can technically claim, with a straight face, that the data they used was from the public internet, even if its origin was illicit (like books with digital rights management protections removed and hosted on a public pirate website) *and they knew the illicit origins when they scraped the content*. The heavy focus on the "public internet" also conveniently sidesteps the entire debate about whether robots.txt rules (discussed later) were respected for every site the AI entity scraped.

5.2.2.2 Loophole Two

Another loophole for "inadvertently" collecting legally questionable data involves the frequent posting of copyrighted content and private information on social media platforms like X (formerly Twitter), YouTube, Facebook, and Reddit. Public posts on social media are, by definition, part of the "public internet," even though they reside within the ecosystems of private companies. Many of these platforms have their own LLMs trained on user data (e.g., Meta's Llama, Google's Gemini, X's Grok). Moreover, those companies tend to jealously guard the data on their platforms. For example, Meta may train on public posts while blocking OpenAI from doing the same, and Google likely trains on YouTube content while simultaneously attempting to block others from doing so.

The concern is that companies can truthfully assert they are only using the "public internet," even when they know their users are posting copyright-infringing works (e.g., putting movies on YouTube) and sensitive personal information. It may be socially unacceptable to openly declare one is downloading content from a pirate website, but downloading the same content (pirated books, movies, nonconsensual images, etc.) from Reddit is less offensive to most people's sensibilities.

Meanwhile, the platforms themselves generally face no legal liability for the copyrighted works posted by their users, thanks to the Digital Millennium Copyright Act, which requires platforms to be notified of infringing content by the content owner before the platform is required to remove it. As long as their bots copy the content before the companies are asked to remove it, the companies are able to obtain and retain the work.

5.2.2.3 Publicly Available vs. Public Domain

Part of the issue with publicly available data is that companies often conflate it with the public domain. The public domain comprises all creative works for which no exclusive intellectual property rights apply. These rights might have expired (like the copyright on an old book that has run out), been relinquished, or been explicitly waived by the creator, or they might simply not apply in the first place. Because no one holds exclusive rights to public-domain works, anyone can legally use or reference them without permission. For example, the complete works of Shakespeare, the original Brothers Grimm fairy tales, and Beethoven's symphonies all reside in the public domain. You can freely adapt, perform, or build upon them without seeking anyone's permission.

The single most important fact to take away from the concept of "public internet" or "publicly available" data is this: Publicly available does NOT mean public domain. Just because something is accessible on the internet doesn't mean it's free for anyone to use for any purpose without consequence. Often, a company's approach to publicly available data (as opposed to licensed data) is more akin to a game of "finders keepers," where they (wrongly) assume that anything they can find and collect is theirs to use, regardless of underlying rights or ethical considerations.

The discussion around paying for AI training content also often takes a narrow view. One common argument against AI entities paying for content is that humans don't pay when they visit someone's public website. The logic suggests it's unfair to make AI pay for something humans can access for free.

This argument, however, is flawed. It assumes that humans and AI (or, more accurately, AI companies) are the same in an ethical and legal sense. This distinction is a larger topic, but for now, let's consider a more basic point: Why don't humans have to pay when they visit a website? It's because the website owner is trying to achieve something by attracting human visitors: They might want to sell a product, earn advertising revenue, gain subscribers, or build their reputation.

Now, consider how many of those reasons apply when an AI scrapes a site. By scraping everything once and potentially never revisiting the site, the AI undermines the very purpose for which the site owner shared the information in the first place. This becomes even more critical if the AI model then generates content that directly competes with or substitutes for the original website's offerings. Furthermore, when a person creates a website, they don't expect humans to copy everything from it, because no one does. In fact, it's unlikely that humans make a complete copy of any content on the vast majority of sites they visit. A human reader might bookmark a favorite recipe or email themselves an article. They don't download the entire archive, index it, and use it to generate competing content on a large scale.

Ultimately, a more reasonable question might be: Why shouldn't we hold AI to a different standard than we hold humans to? Why shouldn't different entities be treated differently based on their nature and impact? Just because there isn't a law preventing humans from doing something doesn't automatically mean nonhuman entities are similarly exempt. We don't have speed limits for humans running, but we absolutely do for cars driving, because they are different entities with different capabilities and potential impacts.

5.3 TORRENTING

There's a further complication to how GenAI companies collect data. To efficiently acquire vast quantities of copyrighted books, articles, magazines, and journals from "publicly available" pirate sites, data collectors likely rely on torrenting. Many people are familiar with torrenting because it has often been used to download music or movies illegally. But torrenting isn't just another way to download files.

Torrenting operates on "peer-to-peer" networks, which means that when you download content, you're also sharing parts of it with others. Unlike traditional downloading, where you simply receive a file from a single server (imagine getting a photocopy handed to you), torrenting works more like a chain letter: As soon as you receive part of the file, you automatically start passing it along to others who want it. You're both a recipient and a distributor. This automatic distribution is where torrenting becomes legally treacherous. Copyright law distinguishes infringement via reproduction (making a copy for yourself) and infringement via distribution (sharing copies with others). When you torrent, you're committing both violations at once.[6] For example, Meta has torrented books and articles from the pirate library LibGen.

[6] Courts have historically treated distribution as more serious than mere reproduction, often awarding higher damages. Why? Because distribution multiplies the harm. Every person you share with can potentially share with others, creating an exponential ripple effect of infringement.

The ethical dimension deepens the problem. An individual torrenting a single album might argue they couldn't afford it or that the artist is already wealthy. But when a billion-dollar AI company systematically torrents millions of copyrighted works to build a commercial product, they can't claim poverty or lack of alternatives. They have the resources to license content legitimately. Their choice to torrent instead suggests a calculated decision that the potential profits outweigh the legal risks.

Moreover, the scale matters. When GenAI companies torrent, they're not only participating in existing pirate networks, but also potentially strengthening them. Each time their systems download and automatically redistribute copyrighted works, they help keep those pirate libraries alive and accessible. They become, in effect, patrons of the very piracy ecosystem that harms the creators whose work they're exploiting.

5.4 OPTING OUT

Suppose we assume it is not feasible to require GenAI companies to obtain consent before copying copyrighted content. One of the trickiest questions, both legally and ethically, is whether AI companies should allow content creators to opt out, and if so, how easy the process should be. On the surface, allowing opt-out would likely require investing more in tools that identify and remove specific content from the massive datasets they control. However, the more you dig into the idea of opting out, the more complex it becomes, raising a flurry of legal, ethical, and technical questions.

Perhaps most importantly, how would anyone enforce an opt-out standard? Most AI entities are notoriously secretive about the exact details of their training datasets. This makes it virtually impossible for an outsider to know precisely which data is included or which has been removed. When you're dealing with "trillions" of data tokens (recall our analogy of 31,700 years for a trillion seconds!), how can anyone possibly be sure that every single opt-out request is genuinely honored across that vast sea of information?

Deleting content from datasets, rather than simply not adding it in the first place, introduces additional problems. First, deleting data from datasets is only an effective solution if no training has commenced on the data. Otherwise, the model developers retain the benefit of the data in the model. Second, it is unclear what is being deleted (if anything): just PDFs/JPEGs? Plain text extracted from PDFs and JPEGs? The tokens created from the plain text? The token IDs assigned to each token? Third, the onus is usually on the content creators to specifically identify what must be deleted; nonexact matches will likely not be deleted. Finally, there is usually no confirmation of what was deleted, if anything, and there is no way to verify that the deletion occurred. And if the content was originally obtained through torrenting, deletion becomes even more problematic – the company may have already distributed copies to dozens or hundreds of other torrent users. These copies can never be recalled or deleted.

5.4.1 *The Argument against Easy Opt-Out*

A common argument is that AI companies shouldn't be required to honor opt-out requests for data that was already "publicly available." The reasoning is that if anyone else could easily find and access that information on the internet, why should AI companies have to remove it? If people choose to share information publicly online, it seems illogical to then allow them to demand that it be confined to a specific webpage.

The internet, by its nature, allows information to flow freely with very little friction. This argument holds that creating a new, arbitrary rule specifically for AI developers doesn't make sense. Furthermore, as discussed in Chapter 11 ("An Introduction to Copyright Law"), AI companies generally believe their use of such publicly available material is perfectly legal and therefore feel no obligation to honor these opt-out requests.

Even if we agree that some opt-out requests should be honored, how do AI companies determine which requests are legitimate? For example, what if someone submits thousands of opt-out requests, not just for their own content but for anyone else's content as well? How can AI companies verify the validity of these requests? And should certain types of data, such as personal images, receive stronger opt-out protections than, say, a personal blog about video games?

5.4.2 *The Argument for Easier Opt-Out*

From the opposite perspective, many believe that AI entities should make opt-out requests easier for anyone who wants their content removed from AI training data. The core reason for this stance is that when people initially shared their information online, they did not anticipate it would be used to train powerful AI models. If they had known their data would be used to enrich a third party (such as an AI company), they might have posted that information behind a paywall, required a login to view it, or not posted it at all.

The question of opting out becomes more fraught when scrapers ignore robots.txt files. Imagine you've clearly posted a "Do not enter" sign on your door. If someone ignores that sign and enters anyway, it feels absurd that the burden is on you to follow up and say, "Please leave," for the request to be cognizable. This mirrors the issue with robots.txt and AI data scraping. The robots.txt file is essentially a proactive "opt-out" request. It's a clear signal from a website owner saying, "Please don't scrape this specific content." It doesn't make sense to ignore this deliberate instruction and then shift the burden back to the website owner, forcing them to restate their nonconsent after their content has already been taken against their wishes.

5.5 DIMINISHING DATA

You've probably heard claims that the largest language models, like Gemini and GPT-5, are "trained on the entire web." While this might not be literally true (depending on how we define "the web" and whether it includes the public, deep, or dark web), it's accurate that they've been trained on a colossal amount of data that AI developers can access.

One of the largest publicly available training datasets, Dolma (released by Ai2), contains three trillion tokens. For comparison, Meta says it trained Llama 4 on *thirty to sixty trillion* tokens. If we assume that Llama 4 has already absorbed most of the usable public data to create its tokens, where will AI developers find enough new, high-quality tokens to train future models? This question is vital because, without a breakthrough algorithmic discovery, the sheer volume of data is likely to remain the single most significant factor in how well an AI model performs.

5.5.1 *The Limits of "New" Data*

One obvious source of new data is news, which, by its very nature, is constantly being created. But how many tokens could that realistically supply? Let's do some quick math:

- Assume that for every 100 tokens, there are roughly 75 words.
- Assume a major news publisher publishes around 140,000 words per day. That translates to about 186,000 tokens.
- Now, imagine there are five other equally large news publishers (like the *Wall Street Journal*, the *Washington Post*, CNN, etc.). Even combining all of them, that amounts to less than one million tokens per day, or about 340 million tokens per year.
- To put that in perspective, that's a tiny 0.01 percent of Dolma's three trillion tokens. In other words, daily news barely makes a dent in the massive data requirements of these models.

5.5.2 *Recording Human Speech*

What if we could record human speech? We all speak far more words than we write. Let's make some huge assumptions for a thought experiment:

- Assume each person speaks about 10,000 words per day.
- There are approximately 400 million native English speakers globally.
- Now, imagine all of them consent to being recorded 24/7, every day of the year.

If all those conditions were met, we would reach an incredible four trillion words per day, or a mind-boggling 1.46 quadrillion words per year, which translates to about 1.95 quadrillion tokens. A quadrillion is so vast you literally cannot picture it – it's a thousand trillion. This amount of data would certainly be sufficient to train even larger AI models and keep them up to date with the latest slang, emerging concepts, and so forth.

However, there's a significant drawback: The quality of these spoken tokens would be low. Think about how we speak: Our grammar isn't edited; our thoughts are often shared in fragmented snippets, not in beautifully constructed, coherent, or profound speeches; and most of what we say is repetitive, revolving around a handful of common topics with a small group of people we interact with regularly.

In short, the quality of our everyday spoken language isn't great for AI training. It simply doesn't come close to the rich, edited, and diverse vocabulary and sentence structures we can gather from carefully crafted books and meticulously reviewed newspaper articles. When researchers train models on transcribed conversations, the results show that they excel at casual banter but struggle with complex reasoning, nuanced arguments, and sophisticated prose.

This brings us back to the central question: Where can we find the additional, high-quality tokens needed to continue improving these advanced language models? Most likely, the answer will increasingly involve synthetic data. This is data generated by AI itself (after training on human-created data, of course), rather than collected from the real world.

However, relying on synthetic data carries significant risks, including "model collapse." Models trained solely on AI-generated data can "forget" real-world nuances and even generate increasingly flawed or repetitive outputs. It's a bit like photocopying a photocopy: Each generation loses fidelity, introduces new artifacts, and drifts further from the original.

The search for more and better data presents a major ongoing challenge in the quest for increasingly "intelligent" AI.

5.6 CONCLUSION

Questions about data acquisition don't have easy answers, and they grow more urgent as AI capabilities advance. The tensions between technological possibility and creator consent, between the hunger for data and respect for boundaries, and between innovation and exploitation remain unresolved.

What's clear is that the current approach of taking first and asking questions later has created a legitimacy crisis that threatens both the AI industry and the creators whose work fuels it. This unfettered scraping embodies the tragedy of the commons: a short-term private gain in which individual actors (AI developers) freely deplete the shared resource (the public web and the value of human creative work) for their own benefit, ultimately devaluing the entire ecosystem for everyone, including future AI systems.

As we move forward, the question isn't whether we can scrape the internet, but when and under what terms we should.

5.7 DISCUSSION QUESTIONS

1. The chapter highlights that "data is the lifeblood of GenAI." How does this statement resonate with your understanding of AI, and what are your initial thoughts on the sheer volume of data required to train these models?
2. The chapter categorizes data reservoirs into the public internet, deep web, and dark web. How has your understanding of these categories changed after reading this chapter, and what implications do these distinctions have for AI training data?
3. The "publicly available" and social media loopholes are discussed in relation to copyrighted content. Do you believe it's okay for companies to assert they are innocently using the "public internet" even when users post illegal content?
4. The distinction between "publicly available" and "public domain" is made. Why is this distinction so important for AI training, and what are the potential consequences of ignoring it?
5. Robots.txt is presented as an "honor system." Given the rise of GenAI, do you think this system remains effective, or is a more robust enforcement mechanism necessary?
6. The opt-out dilemma presents arguments for and against making opt-out requests easier. Which side do you find more compelling, and what are the biggest challenges in implementing a fair opt-out system?

6

The AI Race

The narrative of an AI race with China[1] stretches back to at least 2017, when Eric Schmidt, former CEO of Google, warned that "by 2020, they will have caught up. By 2025, they will be better than us, and by 2030, they will dominate the industries of AI."[i] That same year, Mark Zuckerberg, Meta's CEO, claimed that privacy rights would hinder the United States' ability to compete with China.[ii]

In 2019, current and former executives of Big Tech companies argued that US antitrust laws, if enforced, would benefit Chinese companies.[iii] This argument was echoed repeatedly, including by Senator Rand Paul.[iv]

In 2022, the United States Chamber of Commerce claimed that "when it comes to AI, we're in a race we must win … We cannot afford to sit on the sidelines and allow those who do not share our democratic values to set the standard for the world."[v]

In March 2023, over a thousand technology leaders and researchers signed an open letter calling for a six-month pause on training AI systems more powerful than GPT-4. Within days, Marc Andreessen, the influential venture capitalist, dismissed the proposal on Twitter: "The time to compete is now." Microsoft's CEO Satya Nadella agreed, telling investors that the company was moving full speed ahead with AI because "this is a platform shift."

In early 2025, Alexander Wang, then CEO of Scale AI, urged President Trump to increase federal AI investment, highlighting China's significant financial commitment to the sector. More recently, Microsoft's president testified before the United States Senate, praising the AI race terminology and repeating it several times ("AI race," "AI innovation race," "AI diffusion race"), underscoring how invested Big Tech has become in the framing.

Nobody wants to lose a high-stakes race. Also in 2025, the Department of Energy posted that "AI is the next Manhattan Project, and THE UNITED STATES WILL WIN." Much of this rhetoric is driven by tech executives seeking to frame China's

[1] The concept of an "AI race" is a US-centric framing. Other countries do not typically refer to an AI race with the US. This may indicate something about the motivations of the people using the framing.

capabilities as a national security concern. Companies stand to gain influence and government funding if they can convince policymakers they are among the few credible players capable of keeping the United States ahead. The AI race narrative has only upsides for AI companies. The more the media feeds the AI race narrative, the more it plays into the hands of the companies that profit and gain power from it.

AI company leaders have compared GenAI systems to advances in fire, steam engines, electricity, and nuclear power. Even leaders of nonprofits focused on AI have agreed that the hype is 100 percent justified. There are few stakes higher than determining who will control a technology that could be as essential to civilization as fire.

The message is clear: We are in an AI race, and stopping now means losing.

This crescendo of urgency might seem compelling, but it rests on a flawed premise. The "AI race" distorts policymaking, warps investment priorities, and undermines the thoughtful development AI requires. Unlike historic races with clear finish lines and discrete objectives, AI development is continuous. There will be no moment when someone crosses the finish line and claims victory.

More dangerously, the race framing smuggles in unexamined assumptions about innovation, utility, and control that, when accepted uncritically, produce predictable and harmful responses: unlimited spending on speculative technology, indefinite delays in necessary regulation, and hasty deployment that prioritizes adoption over understanding. This chapter examines how the race metaphor took hold, scrutinizes the faulty assumptions underlying it, and explains why abandoning this framework is essential to developing AI that genuinely serves human needs rather than corporate interests.

6.1 DECONSTRUCTING THE RACE

What, exactly, are we racing toward? What does "winning" even mean?[2]

Saying there is a "race" implies that someone must "win" AI.[3] But there is no "finish line." We have no way of knowing who is "winning" or when someone has "won." It's unclear whether the United States and China are even in the same race. The United States focuses on creating AGI, or artificial superintelligence, while China appears to focus primarily on practical applications.[vi]

[2] You might think it's a race to the top-performing model, but to Microsoft president Brad Smith, "The number one factor that will define whether the US or China wins this race is whose technology is most broadly adopted in the rest of the world." So it's not about AI's capabilities so much as it is about adoption. Greater adoption, in turn, means more data for companies to harvest and more subscriptions to sell. C. Lima-Strong (May 9, 2025). Transcript: Sam Altman testifies at US Senate hearing on AI competitiveness, *Tech Policy Press*. Retrieved February 24, 2026, from www.techpolicy.press/transcript-sam-altman-testifies-at-us-senate-hearing-on-ai-competitiveness/.

[3] This makes about as much sense as telling leaders we need AI to "finish strong!" or that AI must "push through" to bask in glory. If this is a race, remember to chant this to yourself as you grit it out: Pretraining runs are temporary, but inference is forever!

Historically, other "races" faced distinct issues. The space race had a clear endpoint: the moon. The nuclear arms race had a finite objective: Build the bomb before the enemy does. An AI race has no such endpoint. AI is a general-purpose technology that pervades countless systems, including not just lethal weapons but also HR, finance, and more. What does it mean to win the AI race in medicine but lose it in transportation? Must you "win" it in everything? What does "winning" AI in education mean? The questions multiply endlessly because the metaphor itself is incoherent.

The Soviet Union beat the United States to space in 1961. However, even when the United States won a race, such as the 1969 moon landing, the victory was short-lived and strategically hollow. Being the first to the moon told us nothing about who will be first to Mars or first to establish a permanent space colony, any more than being first in space (Russia) revealed who would be first to the moon.

Even the quintessential arms race, the development of the atomic bomb as part of the Manhattan Project, delivered limited strategic value. Germany surrendered before the United States even revealed the weapon. The Cold War arms race was similarly misguided. The United States had more nukes than the Soviet Union, but the difference between 1,000 and 10,000 nukes isn't all that important. If 1,000 nukes hit us, it wouldn't matter if we could hit them back with 10,000. What the nuclear arms race excelled at, as the AI race does today, was funneling vast resources into projects with dubious societal benefits while starving initiatives with clearer, more affordable returns.

When presented with the AI race framing, we should pause and ask, "AI race to what end?" AGI?[4] Why? To automate thinking and discovery? Why? Will it bring more happiness and meaning? How? Might it do the opposite? Why not? Does winning the AI race equate to a wiser democracy, a better health span and education, and greater happiness and life satisfaction? If not, then why grant it such a high priority? Are we merely seeking money and improved GDP for its own sake? Shouldn't we be focused on what that GDP is supposed to afford us?

But beyond endlessly parroting a nonsense phrase that does nothing to clarify what's going on, why it's important, and how it's unfolding lies a deeper problem: The metaphor itself shapes policy. When we frame AI development as a race, we prime specific responses that may not be wise.

6.2 HOW THE METAPHOR SHAPES POLICY

The race metaphor rests on several unfounded assumptions about AI development. More importantly, it triggers predictable reactions from policymakers, investors, and the public, and these reactions deserve scrutiny.

[4] This assumes we would know how to test the system to know when AGI is achieved. See Chapter 4 ("How GenAI Is Measured") for a discussion on assessment shortcomings.

At least three major assumptions underlie the AI race narrative, and each gives rise to distinct reactions. Understanding this assumption–reaction chain reveals why the race metaphor is not just inaccurate but potentially dangerous.

6.2.1 *Assumption 1: Innovation Always Equals Progress*

Inherent in the belief that we should "race" toward some AI finish line is the assumption that AI is an innovation, that innovation is progress, and that progress is always beneficial. This syllogism collapses under scrutiny. There are, of course, many bad uses of AI,[5] but let's set that aside to focus on the even broader claim that innovation is inherently good. Yes, innovation can be good, but that's not an intrinsic feature. Rather, innovation is value-neutral. It is neither good nor bad.[6]

For example, there has been remarkable innovation in virtual reality over the past thirty or more years. Yet how often do you find yourself in the metaverse? Do you see many people doing anything meaningful there on a regular basis? Or consider the Segway. Unveiled in 2001 with predictions that it would revolutionize transportation, it became a punchline instead. Inventor Dean Kamen claimed cities would be redesigned around it. Instead, it found its primary market among mall security guards and tour groups. It's a technological marvel that solved no pressing problem. Innovation without careful consideration of actual human needs often produces expensive solutions searching for problems.[7]

It's also worth noting that tucked away in Microsoft's Senate testimony is a short phrase doing a lot of work for this innovation argument: Microsoft acknowledges that it hinges on whether "a technology improves productivity and changes every part of an economy."[vii] Every assumption presented afterward is contingent on

5 Hacking software, defrauding the elderly, creating nonconsensual deepfakes, manipulating evidence, swaying elections, generating disinformation, etc.

6 Not all tools are neutral in value, such as a hammer, which isn't inherently good or bad. GenAI is influenced by humans with motivations like increasing engagement to generate revenue, for example. Some GenAI systems even have clear ideologies, like xAI's Grok. Calling GenAI a simple inert tool is inaccurate. A hammer is a tool designed for a specific purpose – hitting things – and its potential for harm is limited and comparable to any other heavy object you might use to strike someone. Conversely, GenAI reflects the values and decisions of the companies that develop it, and in most cases, those companies retain control over its functionality. Additionally, its capacity for harm often outweighs its potential for good because bad actors find it low-cost, easy to use, and capable of rapid scaling. Someone using GenAI to hack systems or craft phishing scams only needs a small success rate, whereas someone aiming to do good must use it correctly all the time to be most effective. Moreover, as Raffi Krikorian notes: "Layered onto those judgments are incentives: to maximize engagement, minimize computing costs, promote internal products, sidestep controversy. Every answer carries both the choices of the people who built it and the pressures of the system that sustains it. Together, they determine what gets shown smoothed out and what gets silenced." R. Krikorian (October 30, 2025). The validation machines, *The Atlantic*. www.theatlantic.com/ideas/archive/2025/10/validation-ai-raffi-krikorian/684764/.

7 Other examples of innovation that had negative effects: CFCs as refrigerants, social media, fast fashion, lead additives in gasoline and paint, etc.

satisfying the two elements of productivity and economic benefit. Notably, neither element has actually yet been definitively satisfied.

Can AI be a force for good? Absolutely. Can it also cause harm? Absolutely. Is it clear which use case will prevail if we race toward it rather than approach it thoughtfully? Not at all.

6.2.2 *Assumption 2: Near-Term Meaningful Usefulness*

Of course, AI has enormous potential to be wondrous. However, that's different from being truly wondrous and helpful on a large scale in the immediate future.

Even the ads and presentations created by Meta, Google, and OpenAI, which must have involved highly paid marketing teams considering a broad range of potential use cases they deemed most compelling before settling on the few they share, are ultimately shallow. For example, one Meta ad shows a boyfriend preparing to meet his girlfriend's parents not by talking with his girlfriend or simply saving his questions to ask the parents himself in a friendly conversation, but by asking a chatbot. Another shows a dad trying to buy a replacement fish for his kid before the kid notices the original fish is missing, but the dad can't remember what the fish looked like. Thank goodness a chatbot is there to help. How did civilization grind on without it?

Most of the interesting uses shared online, even by prominent AI advocates like Ethan Mollick, a Wharton professor and enthusiastic proponent of AI adoption, consist of inconsequential outputs. The technology can role-play in a video game (with errors).[viii] It can "speak" in different voices on command.[ix] We can use it to edit videos to change a few lines.[x] (Perhaps you've already noticed the potential for misuse.) You can use it to turn images into video, but it's "far from perfect or controllable enough for serious use."[xi] And it can write poetry that meets exacting specifications.[xii]

Honestly, these are all fascinating and can feel a bit like magic to the nonjaded. They are impressive engineering feats, fun to experience, and could ultimately lead to profound use cases (though whether they will be profoundly beneficial or profoundly harmful is unclear at the moment).

But the point remains: These demonstrations showcase technical achievement, which is not the same as utility. An exhibition, no matter how sophisticated, remains an exhibition until it solves a real problem at scale.

Moreover, some of Mollick's posts are simply inaccurate. LLMs aren't good at graduate school just because they can perform well on the GRE.[xiii] Standardized test performance measures a narrow set of skills under controlled conditions, rather than the messy, ambiguous challenges of real-world professional work and social interactions. We also don't know which data Llama (the model referenced by Mollick) used, so data contamination may have driven the improvement.

LLMs can accurately perform spreadsheet tasks 80 percent of the time, and that "may be the start of something quite significant"?[xiv] Maybe. But also, maybe not.

Self-reporting surveys say LLMs reduce working time by half in 37 percent of tasks?[xv] That's unlikely to be an accurate reflection of most jobs. If it were, you might expect bosses everywhere to mandate the use of GenAI for most tasks, leading to significant productivity and profit gains. But that hasn't happened.[8]

While GenAI may deliver significant productivity gains in some domains, such as coding or drafting boilerplate emails, that benefit doesn't prove we're in an existential race to AGI, nor does it justify unlimited spending or indefinite regulatory delays.

The gap between demonstration and deployment matters. Many technologies work brilliantly in controlled environments but fail in the real world. Watson, IBM's AI system, was supposed to revolutionize healthcare after winning *Jeopardy!* in 2011. IBM invested billions and partnered with leading cancer centers to train Watson to recommend treatments. By 2022, most of its medical applications had been abandoned or scaled back dramatically. The problem? Watson excelled at parsing structured quiz-show questions but struggled with the ambiguous, context-dependent nature of medical decision-making. The leap from an impressive demo to a reliable tool is vast, and there is no scientific basis for believing that GenAI will ever achieve it.[9]

To be clear, AI has proven genuinely valuable in narrow domains. AlphaFold, DeepMind's protein-folding system, has accelerated biological research by accurately predicting protein structures. AI-powered medical imaging systems now help radiologists detect certain cancers earlier and more reliably. Credit card companies use AI-based fraud detection, which catches billions of dollars in fraudulent transactions annually, with error rates far lower than those of human reviewers. These successes share common traits: well-defined problems, abundant high-quality training data, clear success metrics, and deployment in contexts where human experts validate the AI's output. Together, they portray AI as a powerful tool for augmenting human expertise in narrow domains, not as a general-purpose solution racing toward some universal finish line.

6.2.3 *Assumption 3: The AI Race Winner Will Control AI Values*

Some may think the AI race is important because the "winner" will get to determine the "values" of AI. That is, they get to decide how AI responds to different inputs. In the United States, we want US AI companies to determine the values

8 It's true some tech companies have mandated greater use of AI, but that has yet to lead to clearly superior customer experiences, cheaper products, or a better off society. Meta is perhaps the best example: is your experience with Facebook or Instagram meaningfully improved (if at all) compared to six months ago?

9 For example, even Yann LeCun, a "godfather" of AI, former chief AI scientist at Meta, and early booster of LLMs, now claims they are a dead end. M. Bobrowsky (November 14, 2025). Yann LeCun has been right about AI for 40 years. Now he thinks everyone is wrong. *The Wall Street Journal*. Retrieved November 29, 2025, from www.wsj.com/tech/ai/yann-lecun-ai-meta-0058b13c?reflink=desktopwebshare_permalink.

output by AI in our workplaces, schools, government, and hospitals, not companies from France or China.

Of course, few media outlets pause to consider why we should want any private entity to determine an AI's values rather than, say, the people who implement or use the AI. And if the answer is that AI companies will allow implementers or users to pick their own values, then it doesn't really matter who "wins" the "race" for value purposes.

Cultural alignment is a valid concern, but the "race" is the worst possible way to address it. Speed and competition prioritize proprietary control, making the models less transparent and less open to audit by democratic institutions, thereby increasing the risk of unchecked values being imposed.

Moreover, if anyone thinks the US government, hospitals, the military, or Fortune 500 businesses would choose a foreign AI system over a US system that is, in all likelihood, only marginally worse – if at all – they aren't being serious. The security, privacy, and economic stakes are too high to trust another nation with such precious personal, health, and commercial information.[10]

No hospital will run its patient records through an AI system hosted in a foreign adversary's data centers. No defense contractor will debug weapon systems using software controlled by a rival nation. The "race to control values" assumes a winner-takes-all market that doesn't reflect how institutions actually make technology decisions. Security, sovereignty, and liability concerns create natural boundaries that prevent any single company from achieving global dominance.

6.3 SUMMARY OF ASSUMPTIONS

The pattern is clear: Each assumption crumbles under inspection, yet each still drives decision-making at the highest levels of government and industry.

These three assumptions – that innovation equals progress, that AI is already meaningfully useful at scale, and that the race winner controls AI values – form a shaky foundation for policy. Yet they've become conventional wisdom, repeated so often they're rarely questioned.

The real danger lies not in the assumptions themselves but in how they shape behavior. Once you accept that there's a race with existential stakes, certain responses become not just logical but seemingly inevitable. If falling behind means losing control of civilization-defining technology, spending becomes unlimited, regulation becomes unthinkable, and deployment becomes urgent. The metaphor prescribes action.

The actions it prescribes, including pouring billions into speculative technology, blocking meaningful oversight, and rushing AI into every corner of society, flow directly from these flawed premises. Understanding this causal chain reveals why

[10] The cultural and linguistic artifacts baked into a model from another country would also be a barrier to adoption.

the race narrative is so problematic: Flawed assumptions inevitably lead to undesirable outcomes.

6.3.1 *Reaction 1: Spend Big*

While there may be legitimate underlying geopolitical and national security concerns, they are often ultimately misguided or exaggerated when applied to AGI. Big Tech co-opts these legitimate security fears to justify unlimited spending and to avoid regulation.

OpenAI alone plans to spend $115 billion from 2025 to 2029. Notably, OpenAI will be able to raise more money to take increasingly shaky bets because its investors must win the AI race. This also means that all major cloud providers must invest heavily in data centers to support AI.

The real reason is probably more mundane. The company with the highest adoption rate has a better chance of converting it into revenue through ads and subscriptions. Also, GenAI isn't like fashion, where you usually buy from a variety of brands. Most people only need one GenAI solution, so locking in customers is important.[11]

If you thought the race was about virtuously benefiting humanity (particularly your country's people), you're probably mistaken. In other words, we must encourage a US company to win the AI race so that mostly wealthy Americans get richer, not French or Chinese entities.

Unfortunately, when billions flow toward speculative technology, opportunity costs mount. That capital might fund healthcare, infrastructure, education, climate adaptation, or countless other pressing needs. But the race metaphor justifies the spending: You can't win the most important race of all time if you don't play.

6.3.2 *Reaction 2: Delay Regulation Indefinitely*

In 2023, a bipartisan United States Senate AI Working Group, co-led by then Majority Leader Chuck Schumer and Senators Mike Rounds, Martin Heinrich, and Todd Young, was formed to assess the impact of artificial intelligence and develop policy recommendations. The "AI race" is likely why the AI Roadmap report issued by the Senate AI Working Group hedged so heavily in its recommendations. They apparently believe that all regulations are inherently harmful to innovation (and, again, innovation is presumed to be always good).

The Senate AI Working Group didn't propose any regulations or legislative language in its report.[xvi] Rather, it stated that it "*encourages* the relevant committee" to "*consider*" such minor concerns as "legislation that both supports further deployment of AI in health care and implements appropriate guardrails and safety

[11] Consider search engines: Google's dominance means most people never bother with alternatives. People don't routinely run the same search query on both Google and Bing.

measures to protect patients" and "*consider* legislation that would provide transparency for providers and the public about the use of AI in medical products and clinical support services, including the data used to train the AI models" (emphasis added).

Are you concerned about privacy or intellectual property? The United States Senate is, too. Slightly. Again, the "relevant committees" are "*encouraged*" to "*consider* federal policy issues related to the data sets used by AI developers to train their models, including data sets that might contain sensitive personal data or are protected by copyright, and evaluate whether there is a need for transparency requirements" (emphasis added).

Notice the language: "encourage," "consider," and "evaluate." These are not assertive action verbs. They are the linguistic equivalent of punting, acknowledging concerns while committing to nothing.

If deepfakes are on your mind, no worries. The "relevant committees" are "*encouraged*" to "*consider* whether there is a need for legislation that protects against the unauthorized use of one's name, image, likeness, and voice, consistent with First Amendment principles, as it relates to AI" (emphasis added). Note that this is just to consider if there's a need, not to consider what should or could be done about known issues like images of teen girls being used in nonconsensual sexual deepfakes, a problem that has left many states with no laws to protect victims.[xvii]

To show policymakers they are the "good guys," tech companies offer domestic investments (or frame them as new investments when, in fact, they were already accounted for in their budgets, as OpenAI did with Stargate) and job-training programs and education initiatives (that often amount to training people how to become customers).[12]

But inaction at the federal level in drafting helpful laws has been paired with active efforts to block such laws at the state level. In the summer of 2025, at the direction of Senator Ted Cruz and with the support of OpenAI, Meta, Google, IBM, a16z, and others, Big Tech urged the US government to pass a law prohibiting state AI regulations.[xviii] It would not have been a law preempting state laws by offering a federal alternative, but simply one that blocked all state laws while leaving a void at the federal level. The Senate ultimately voted against it, but in all likelihood, Senator Cruz and the Big Tech companies will try again.

The race metaphor poisons regulatory discussion. If we're racing China, any regulation looks like unilateral disarmament. Better to move fast and break things (including people)[13] than to move carefully and lose. But this logic assumes the race is real and that speed matters more than direction.

[12] See Chapter 23 ("GenAI in Education") for examples.

[13] See Chapter 10 ("Anthropomorphizing").

6.3.3 *Reaction 3: Implementation Nation*

What else might you do if you think there is a race and failing to win will be devastating for you and your compatriots? Well, you might try to stay on top of it so you have an edge. What's one way to do that? Shove AI into absolutely everything you can, as quickly as you can, to the greatest extent you can. Do you brush your teeth? Do it with AI![xix] Want to walk faster? Use AI![xx] Want to encourage your kid to dream big and write a letter to their favorite track star? Have AI do it instead![xxi] Or you could launch a social media app and web browser, as OpenAI did. Take that, China.

But why stop there? Why teach kids how AI is made, its best use cases, its limitations, and the many ethical and legal considerations when you can just have them use it to do their work for them? Sure, the kids will only use the AI to brainstorm, quiz themselves, and create outlines, even after they realize it can also compose essays and answer quizzes. Right.[14]

This deployment-first approach treats AI adoption as an end in itself rather than a means to specific improvements. AI's effects vary wildly by context, and thoughtless implementation can backfire. Students who outsource their writing to AI likely fail to develop sufficient critical thinking skills. Workers who rely on AI for spreadsheet tasks often do not recognize instances where it falls short. The race mentality prioritizes adoption over understanding, volume over wisdom.

6.4 THE GAP BETWEEN HYPE AND REALITY

The important takeaway from all the preceding discussion is that GenAI can perform numerous superficially impressive tasks that reflect significant advances in AI research. However, GenAI is limited in its ability to accomplish useful tasks at scale with high accuracy at a reasonable cost. There is no high-quality research showing that GenAI reliably improves student outcomes, company productivity, life satisfaction, health outcomes, or any other meaningful metric. This holds true despite mountains of cash thrown into the AI furnace and breathless trumpeting from the media and enthusiastic advocates.[15]

What we need is to take a few deep breaths and spend more time researching and testing to figure out what works and what doesn't, rather than creating something and tossing it over the fence for the public to figure out at great expense, both financial (from implementing unproven AI systems, including monetary and opportunity costs) and social (from misinformation, disinformation, and the erosion of trust in society).

[14] See Chapter 23 ("GenAI in Education").
[15] See Chapter 27 ("Frameworks for Thinking about GenAI").

It's possible to be supportive and optimistic about AI without treating it as if it will solve many of humanity's thorniest problems in the near term. It won't. Even a popular use case, such as curing loneliness with chatbots, is like curing unhappiness with heroin. It's a facsimile of the real thing that ultimately deepens the problem.

Technology alone will never be able to solve diplomacy ("ChatGPT, make South Korea and North Korea allies"); zoning regulations; access to high-quality healthcare, education, and nutrition; racism, sexism, and all other isms based on features that tell us nothing about the content of a person's character or a group's character; allocation of taxpayer funds; prioritization of economic, defense, transportation, communication, and energy policies; or any number of the most pressing problems. AI is a tool. It's not the solution, because for all the most important problems, there is no single solution, and no solution can be achieved by technology alone. Cultures matter. Social relationships matter. Manufacturing, distribution, administration, and oversight can't be 100 percent tech-driven, and each step is essential.

Consider climate change. AI can optimize energy grids, model weather patterns, and possibly design more efficient solar panels. However, it cannot convince nations to cooperate, restructure their economies away from fossil fuels, or persuade individuals to change their consumption habits. The hardest problems are always problems of human coordination, not computation.

6.5 CONCLUSION

There is no AI race. A more apt term would be the AI rush.

The Manhattan Project metaphor is instructive. Yes, that was a race against Nazi Germany to develop nuclear weapons first. The stakes were existential, the timeline compressed, and the goal binary: Build the bomb or lose the war. AI development shares none of these characteristics. There is no single AI to build, no moment when someone "wins," and no evidence that faster development produces better outcomes.

So, can AI assist with all these problems? YES! And it will. However, if the "AI race" focuses more on advancing capabilities than on usefulness, we'll miss out on its full potential. We don't need AI that can draft a poem where every line ends with the letter x. Society would be better served by AI that makes life more enjoyable, satisfying, and meaningful for everyone. We're not there yet, and the "AI race" narrative doesn't help.

The irony is that the race metaphor may be counterproductive even for those who want the United States to maintain technological leadership. Thoughtful development, rigorous testing, and careful deployment can produce more useful, reliable, and trustworthy AI systems – precisely the kind that would earn global adoption. Racing toward an imaginary finish line, by contrast, risks producing expensive, unreliable systems that squander both capital and public trust.

The question is not *whether* we should develop AI. We should, and we will. The question is *how* we should develop AI and whether we will do so wisely, with clear goals, honest assessment of progress, and humility about what technology can and cannot achieve. Abandoning the race metaphor is a good starting point.

6.6 DISCUSSION QUESTIONS

1. The author suggests that the “innovation always equals progress” assumption is flawed. Can you think of other historical or current innovations that, like the Segway, didn’t live up to their initial hype or had unintended negative consequences?
2. The author criticizes the idea that the “winner” of the AI race will control AI values. How do you think AI values should be determined, and by whom?
3. The chapter examines how the “AI race” narrative influences policy, resulting in reactions such as “spend big” and “delay regulation indefinitely.” What are some potential benefits and drawbacks of these reactions, and what alternative approaches could policymakers take?
4. The chapter states that “the hardest problems are always problems of human coordination, not computation.” Do you agree with this statement, especially in the context of global challenges such as climate change and social inequality? Why or why not?

7

GenAIuflecting

In January 2025, President Trump stood before cameras to announce OpenAI's plan to build data centers in Texas. It would create "over 100,000 American jobs," he proclaimed, "almost immediately." The figure was staggering – and completely made-up. For context, Amazon's fulfillment centers employ an average of roughly 3,000 people.[i] Tesla's massive Gigafactory in Texas employs approximately 20,000.[ii] Even the construction of an entire automotive manufacturing complex typically creates thousands of jobs, not hundreds of thousands. Data centers, by their very nature, are capital-intensive but labor-light operations. They're mostly servers sitting in climate-controlled rooms, requiring only small staffs for maintenance and security.

Yet almost nobody challenged the president's math. Not Congress. Not the media, at least not loudly enough. The announcement was treated as a triumph of national ambition, a sign of American technological leadership.

Eight months later, in August 2025, OpenAI offered ChatGPT Enterprise to the entire US government for one dollar per agency. *One dollar*. The deal was either an act of stunning patriotism and breathtaking generosity or, far more plausibly, a strategic move to embed the company's technology so deeply in government infrastructure that extracting it would be unthinkable. Again, the government didn't scrutinize the arrangement. It simply said yes.

To prevent the government from changing course, AI companies and funders, including VC firms like Andreessen Horowitz, OpenAI president Greg Brockman, angel investors like Ron Conway (SV Angel), and the company Perplexity, launched a lobbying group with more than $100 million in funding.[iii]

These aren't isolated incidents of poor judgment. They're part of a pattern I call GenAIuflecting: the reflexive, undemocratic ceding of power to AI companies based on extraordinary claims made without extraordinary evidence. As you probably noticed, GenAIuflecting is just a play on "genuflecting," meaning to show deference or servility.

It's happening everywhere, at every level of government, reshaping law, policy, and public expectations about technology in ways that should alarm us all.

7.1 THE VALUE PROPOSITION

The concessions can seem especially galling when you consider how much less valuable GenAI has proven to be compared with other technologies, since they are granted not on GenAI's demonstrated present-day value but on speculative future promises that lack much in the way of evidence. This is in stark contrast to the stringent regulations applied to other industries with demonstrated, high-impact products.[1]

The AI race narrative is harmful because it leads people to assume there are natural and inevitable conclusions we must reach about how we treat AI. While that narrative softens the government's stance to accommodate the demands of AI advocates, GenAIuflecting shows the government actively paving the way for companies to expand their power under the banner of national progress.

Society (especially tech companies and elected officials, but also "AI influencers" and AI evangelists) seems all too happy to grant GenAI special privileges that we either (a) don't give to humans or (b) only give to humans. When we do that, it's GenAI exceptionalism. You'd think a healthy skepticism about allowing such special treatment would be common sense. Yet here we are.

If you get enough legal scholars stretching laws in enough exotic ways, sprinkle in the financial incentives of capitalism, and add a dash of rah-rah from influencers, the gradual granting of special treatment to already incredibly powerful companies begins to feel inevitable.

When Congress, state governments, agencies, and others yield to GenAI companies based on nothing more than speculation (GenAI will invent new types of batteries! GenAI will enable nuclear fusion! GenAI will help us live forever!),[2] they are participating in GenAIuflecting. The loudest advocates for GenAIuflecting emanate from Silicon Valley. Consider the VC firm a16z, which wrote to the Trump administration urging it not to support regulations "based on speculative fear." Yet it is apparently fine with removing regulations based on speculative benefits.

7.1.1 *AI Illiteracy*

At its core, GenAIuflecting reflects widespread AI illiteracy among the genuflectors. As I teach my students, GenAI is far less impressive the better you understand how

[1] Most people, if forced to choose, would almost certainly rather give up GenAI than their smartphones or Wi-Fi.

[2] GenAI has not discovered or innovated in these fields. However, other types of AI have. GenAI companies attempt to draft off the umbrella term of "AI," but general-purpose AI is not the same as specialized, narrow AI. For example, AlphaFold, a specialized AI system developed by DeepMind, made genuine breakthroughs in protein structure prediction. But AlphaFold is a narrow AI designed for a specific scientific task, not a general-purpose language model. When GenAI companies point to achievements like AlphaFold to justify their own claims, they're engaged in a bait and switch: taking credit for innovations in specialized AI while building something different.

it works and its limitations. An LLM is not an all-knowing intelligence; it's a sophisticated token-prediction machine trained to echo patterns in data.

When you see headlines proclaiming "AI will," "AI might," or "AI could," you should immediately raise your guard. What those statements really mean is "This is a guess," "It's just as likely this won't happen," and "Just trust us!" These are the linguistic markers of over-optimism dressed up as technological prophecy.

To understand why GenAIuflecting persists, it helps to examine how it manifests across different policy domains. The pattern is strikingly consistent: AI companies make bold claims about future benefits, policymakers scramble to accommodate them, and the public is left holding the bag when those benefits fail to materialize.

7.2 THE SHIFTING SAFETY NARRATIVE

During the first two years of the GenAI boom, which coincided with the last two years of the Biden administration, GenAI companies such as OpenAI and Anthropic, along with CEOs like Elon Musk, urged the government to take AI risks seriously. They warned of possible mass job displacement, election interference, cybersecurity threats, and discrimination in hiring and lending. These warnings, delivered with appropriate gravitas, positioned these companies as responsible actors concerned about the technology they were unleashing.

But that tone changed almost overnight. Since the Trump administration began, most GenAI companies have been singing a different tune.[3] Safety concerns are no longer part of their lobbying. They want to grow bigger, faster. They've asked the government to release federal data so AI companies can train on it, requested tax breaks and grants, and claimed it's all in the service of winning the AI race. When the government gives in to these requests, it's GenAIuflecting.

The shift in tone is paying off. The Trump administration has been AI-friendly. On the third day of his second term, Trump signed an executive order asking the AI industry to develop a policy to "sustain and enhance America's global AI dominance." In other words, the government asked the industry to write its own rules. Imagine if the pharmaceutical industry were asked to draft its own drug approval standards, or if oil companies were invited to write their own environmental regulations. We'd recognize that as regulatory capture. Yet with AI, this arrangement was celebrated as a forward-thinking policy.

In July 2025, Trump released the AI Action Plan based on responses from AI companies. It claimed, without evidence, that AI would lead to "an industrial revolution, an information revolution, and a renaissance–all at once." Among several other

[3] Sam Altman, Tim Cook, Meta, Google, and Microsoft each donated $1 million to Trump's inauguration. Musk even joined the administration. At an AI-focused event at the White House in early September 2025, Altman praised Trump "for being such a pro-business, pro-innovation president," and said "It's a very refreshing change … I think it's going to set us up for a long period of leading the world, and that wouldn't be happening without your leadership."

statements, the plan called for revising the NIST AI Risk Management Framework to eliminate references to misinformation, Diversity, Equity, and Inclusion, and climate change. In other words, the framework would no longer address some of the most pressing concerns about AI's societal impact, which are the very issues that might constrain the industry's growth.

The response from Silicon Valley was celebratory. Executives at a16z, OpenAI, Anthropic, and other firms posted praise-filled threads on social media.

To provide a better understanding of GenAIuflecting in practice, this chapter highlights four areas: the environment, safety, security, and intellectual property.

7.2.1 *Environmental GenAIuflecting*

When the president opened federal lands to build massive data centers, it was GenAIuflecting.[iv] Trump's AI Action Plan recommends making "Federal lands available for data center construction and the construction of power generation infrastructure for those data centers by directing agencies with significant land portfolios to identify sites suited to large-scale development."[v]

The *Washington Post* noted an example of a state GenAIuflecting:

> In North Carolina, Duke Energy this month persuaded regulators to bless construction of several new gas plants, even though the plan does not comply with state law requiring 70 percent cuts in electricity emissions by 2030 and zero emissions by 2050. The 70 percent emissions reduction target for Duke was pushed back to 2032.[vi]

These data centers require enormous amounts of water for cooling and electricity for operation – resources that could serve other public needs. Yet the environmental impact assessment process was rushed or bypassed entirely under the banner of national urgency, driven by the supposed AI race.

This aligns with how members of Congress and billionaire investors in AI view the issue. As the *Washington Post* reported, the former CEO of Google, Eric Schmidt, invited to testify by Republicans, told a Senate committee "that winning the AI race is too important to let environmental considerations get in the way." The report continues:

> "The needs of our industry are so great that we cannot cut down any of the sources of energy right now," he [Schmidt] said. Once the United States beats China to develop superintelligence, Schmidt said, AI will solve the climate crisis. And if it doesn't, he went on, China will become the world's sole superpower.[vii]

This kind of techno-nationalist reasoning borders on theological faith. It treats AI not as a tool but as a future savior – a *deus ex machina* that will redeem environmental harms once it attains sufficient "intelligence." By that logic, almost any sacrifice today is justified.

The danger, of course, is that this leads to perverse conclusions. If AI will eventually solve all our problems, perhaps we can cut funding for the National Science

Foundation or the National Institutes of Health now. Why invest in human research when a machine revolution is supposedly imminent?

America isn't alone in this delusion. As the *New York Times* reported, "many countries and regions are trying to close the gap. They are providing access to land and cheaper energy, fast-tracking development permits and using public funds and other resources to acquire chips and construct data centers."[viii] The global race to accommodate AI infrastructure has created a different race: a race to the bottom on environmental standards.

Sometimes, the rush to build data centers sounds less like a lucky break and more like the exploitation of people already down on their luck. According to the *Washington Post*:

> Joanna Doven, CEO of a private–public enterprise called the AI Strike Team that is trying to draw tech investment to the state, said communities in the Rust Belt are eager for a project like Stargate.
>
> "We have these old industrial steel sites sitting vacant in poor communities. These communities want data centers. They're not worried about pollution, they want taxes and they want jobs," she said. "People say it's not that many jobs. Well, there's nothing else going on here."[ix]

This quote reveals the cruel calculus of GenAIuflecting. Communities desperate for economic revival will accept pollution and minimal job creation because the alternative is nothing. This is less about economic development than about exploiting desperation.

7.2.2 *Safety GenAIuflecting*

The reluctance of governments, from California to the federal level, to impose strict AI safety regulations demonstrates a pattern of prioritizing the interests and innovation claims of major tech companies over concrete public safeguards.

When California scrapped an AI safety bill that would have required companies to test their large AI models for catastrophic risks before deployment and to create a safety framework, because it would allegedly stifle innovation for reasons GenAI companies couldn't quite articulate, they were GenAIuflecting. And though Governor Newsom signed one chatbot bill (SB 243) into law in 2025, he also vetoed one (AB 1064) that the tech industry lobbied heavily against because it would have been stricter.[4]

California wasn't alone. Around the country, policymakers hesitated to impose safety regulations, afraid of being branded "anti-innovation." On the first day of

4 AB 1064 would have effectively banned companies from making companion chatbots available to minors unless the companies could guarantee the AI was "not foreseeably capable" of encouraging self-harm, engaging in sexual interactions, or other harmful activities.

his second term, Trump signed an executive order repealing several Biden-era AI safety initiatives, including rules requiring companies to share test results with the government before releasing powerful new models. The effect was immediate and symbolic: The government stopped asking, "Is this safe?" and started asking, "How quickly can we deploy this?"

The same companies that once warned of existential risks now insist that any restraint will cripple innovation.

7.2.3 *Security GenAIuflecting*

The AI Action Plan states that "the United States must aggressively adopt AI within its Armed Forces if it is to maintain its global military preeminence."[x] This aligns with the Pentagon's decision to award contracts worth up to $200 million each to Anthropic, xAI,[5] OpenAI, and Google.

However, neither the government nor the AI companies have explained or provided evidence of how their general-purpose models are making the nation more secure or ensuring the United States maintains its military preeminence. No clear link has been drawn between a chatbot's capabilities and the demands of modern warfare.

This matters because military contracts carry enormous weight in technology development, often shaping entire industries. Yet these contracts were awarded without a clear articulation of how general-purpose language models translate into military advantage. The Pentagon's enthusiasm for AI reflects GenAIuflecting: the assumption that any AI application must be beneficial simply because it's AI.

7.2.4 *Intellectual Property GenAIuflecting*

OpenAI, Google, and Microsoft each told the government they need an exemption from copyright law to train their models. That is, they don't believe they should need permission or pay license fees to train on copyrighted materials. If such a blanket privilege isn't granted, OpenAI claimed, "the race for AI is effectively over."

Given that AI already exists in countless forms, from smart speakers to recommendation algorithms to autonomous vehicles, this plea seems especially melodramatic. What OpenAI really means is that its business model, which depends on ingesting massive amounts of copyrighted material without payment or permission, would become untenable.

Yet Trump seemed to buy the logic wholesale, saying in July 2025:

> You can't be expected to have a successful AI program when every single article, book or anything else that you've read or studied you're supposed to pay for. Gee, I read a book, I'm supposed to pay somebody. And you know, we appreciate that,

[5] This happened shortly after its chatbot, Grok, referred to itself as MechaHitler.

> but you just can't do it because it's not doable. And if you're going to try and do that, you're not going to have a successful program.[xi]

This statement reveals a misunderstanding of how copyright works. Human creators routinely "have a successful program" while respecting copyright. They pay for content either directly or indirectly, read copyrighted material, learn from it, and create new work without reproducing the original.

What the AI industry demands is not parity with human creators, but privilege above them. That's GenAI exceptionalism. And when policymakers blindly accept that logic, they are GenAIuflecting.

7.3 GENAI EXCEPTIONALISM AND GENAIUFLECTING

The concepts of GenAI exceptionalism and GenAIuflecting are intertwined. GenAI exceptionalism is the goal, GenAIuflecting is the process. Policymakers genuflect before AI companies, granting them exceptional treatment that is then enshrined in law and policy.

None of this means AI technology lacks value or that all AI companies act irresponsibly. Medical AI systems have improved diagnostic accuracy for certain conditions. AI-powered accessibility tools have made technology more usable for people with disabilities. Some companies have demonstrated genuine commitment to safety by publishing their research, engaging with external critics, and delaying releases to address concerns. These are real contributions that deserve recognition.

The distinction I'm drawing is between legitimate technological development and the extraordinary policy accommodations we're seeing. We don't need to exempt AI companies from copyright law to help them build useful products. They want that exemption to cut costs and avoid accountability. We don't need to fast-track data center permits for AI to benefit society. We need proper environmental reviews to ensure those benefits don't come at an unacceptable cost. We don't need to eliminate safety testing requirements for innovation to flourish. We need those requirements to ensure innovation doesn't cause foreseeable and avoidable harm.

Supporting beneficial AI development and opposing GenAIuflecting aren't contradictory positions. We can champion progress while insisting on responsibility. The challenge is remembering that admiration for technological potential doesn't require kneeling before those who profit from it.

7.3.1 *The Self-Reinforcing Cycle*

The examples throughout this chapter reveal a troubling pattern: government officials making extraordinary concessions to AI companies in exchange for speculative benefits, often while ignoring concrete harms and legitimate concerns. This is a kind of technological faith. It's a belief that AI will deliver miraculous benefits if only we clear away enough regulatory obstacles and shower the industry with enough support.

What makes GenAIuflecting particularly dangerous is its self-reinforcing nature. Each concession becomes a precedent for the next. Each regulatory rollback is justified by reference to the previous one. The accumulation of special privileges creates a new norm in which AI companies expect accommodation and policymakers feel compelled to provide it.

The question we should be asking isn't whether AI has potential, because of course it does. The question is whether that potential justifies the systematic dismantling of regulations, environmental protections, copyright law, and safety requirements. So far, the evidence suggests it doesn't.

As Charlie Warzel wrote:

> What if the real doomer scenario is that we pollute the internet and the planet, reorient our economy and leverage ourselves, outsource big chunks of our minds, realign our geopolitics and culture, and fight endlessly over a technology that never comes close to delivering on its grandest promises? What if we spend so much time waiting and arguing that we fail to marshal our energy toward addressing the problems that exist here and now?[xii]

But GenAIuflecting persists because it serves powerful interests. Tech companies profit, politicians claim credit for supporting "innovation," and venture capitalists see returns on their investments. The only losers are everyone else: workers whose protections are eroded, creators whose work is appropriated, communities whose resources are exploited, and citizens whose safety takes a backseat to corporate growth.

Understanding GenAIuflecting helps us recognize that this dynamic is not inevitable. These are choices made by specific people with specific interests, often justified by claims that don't withstand examination. Once we see GenAIuflecting for what it is – not wise policy but unwarranted deference – we can start demanding better.

7.4 DISCUSSION QUESTIONS

1. The chapter introduces "GenAIuflecting" as the unwarranted ceding of power to AI companies. Can you think of real-world examples (beyond those in the chapter) where you've observed something similar happening with a new technology or industry?
2. The author suggests that AI illiteracy contributes to GenAIuflecting. What are some practical steps individuals or governments could take to improve AI literacy among the general public and policymakers?
3. The idea of "GenAI exceptionalism" is presented, in which AI companies are granted special privileges not given to humans or other industries. What are your thoughts on this? Are there any circumstances where such exceptionalism might be justified, or is it always problematic?

4. The chapter highlights how GenAIuflecting affects environmental concerns, safety regulations, national security, and intellectual property laws. Which of these areas do you find most concerning, and why?
5. The author states that "this dynamic is not inevitable." What actions do you think are most pivotal for citizens, policymakers, and even AI developers themselves to take to counter GenAIuflecting and ensure more responsible AI development?

8

The Illusion of Democratization

8.1 INTRODUCTION

In 2023, Meta released Llama 2, heralding it as a breakthrough for "democratizing" AI. Developers worldwide could now access a powerful language model for free. Yet within months, the reality proved far different. Developers in Nigeria struggled to download the massive model files because of inadequate internet infrastructure. Those in rural India lacked the GPU resources to run it. Even where technical barriers could be overcome, the model's English-centric training made it nearly useless for communities speaking Yoruba, Tamil, or thousands of other languages.

Companies and organizations across the tech industry claim to be democratizing GenAI, including Meta, the National Artificial Intelligence Research Resource, Amazon, Microsoft, Hugging Face, Stability AI, and Google. Yet these assertions often amount to little more than rebranding select open-source initiatives. The issue is not that open-sourcing is useless, but that it is presented as the fulfillment of democratization. Companies leverage this language to claim the moral high ground while providing only the minimal components necessary to maintain their control over the true enablers of power: compute, money, and expertise.

If we assume the definition of democratization is something akin to Merriam-Webster's notion that GenAI should be "organized or operated so that all people involved have power, influence, etc.,"[i] then openness is indeed an indispensable component, but it represents only a means to an end – a necessary but insufficient condition for genuine democratization,

The claims do raise an interesting question, though. What actions are sufficient to democratize GenAI?

Consider that releasing code may make it available to the masses, but this overlooks an important caveat. If the masses lack the knowledge to use, modify, and examine the data, code, and weights, then increased accessibility does not equate to democratization. Access without understanding is meaningless. Most efforts to "democratize AI" actually focus on empowering people who already possess relevant expertise or have the time and resources to acquire the necessary skills.[1]

In other words, GenAI is only democratized in a meaningful sense if a broad enough swath of people can use it effectively. Providing GenAI artifacts to people unfamiliar with the technology does not meaningfully democratize GenAI. Furthermore, if the model is trained exclusively on English text (or on a small number of languages) and produces proficient outputs primarily in English, it serves only those literate in English, which is hardly a democratic outcome for a global audience.[2]

Data from Cloudflare further illustrates this disparity: In March 2024, the United States accounted for the largest share of internet traffic to GenAI websites, at 22.7%. The next closest country accounted for only 8.3%. Of the countries accounting for at least 3% of traffic, four were newly industrialized nations, and five were fully industrialized. The first African country didn't appear on the list until number 32 – Egypt – with a 0.7% share.[ii] These numbers reveal a stark digital divide, where the technology touted as transformative for humanity, along with the financial spoils it creates, remains concentrated in the world's wealthiest corners. Yet the inequality runs deeper than geography alone. Even within wealthy nations, the concentration of AI access mirrors existing power structures.

GenAI is not democratized if it remains inscrutable to most people and if they lack a voice in what is being built or how data is used. True democratization of GenAI demands more than mere access or basic literacy. It requires comprehensive education about how GenAI works, its applications, and its societal impact. Democratization should empower people not only to interact with basic products like chatbots but also to download and modify GenAI models. It must also enable nontechnologists to understand what's happening, which data is being used, and the rationale behind methodological choices. The mere fact that thousands of open-source models exist on platforms like Hugging Face means nothing to almost everyone globally. Similarly, a technical paper intended solely for experts contributes little to broader knowledge dissemination; rather, information must be communicated in accessible terminology, with relatable examples and clear analogies that resonate with a broader audience.[3]

[1] This population is probably fewer than 100,000 people globally, or a fraction of a percent of the world's population.

[2] For context, only approximately 17 percent of the world's population speaks English, and not all speakers can read it. Central Intelligence Agency (2021). World factbook. Retrieved February 25, 2026, from https://tinyurl.com/2s3p9euj.

[3] Unsurprisingly, relatively few people utilize even the most comprehensive free resources, such as Ai2's Tulu 3 collection, which includes training repositories, evaluation repositories, datasets, models, a demo, and an explanatory technical paper. Hugging Face (n.d.). Llama-3.1-Tulu-3-8B. Retrieved July 7, 2025, from https://huggingface.co/allenai/Llama-3.1-Tulu-3-8B.

8.2 ELEMENTS NECESSARY FOR DEMOCRATIZATION OF GENAI

To understand why current "democratization" efforts fall short, we need a framework for evaluating what genuine openness requires. Consider this scenario: A researcher might receive model weights but lack documentation on how the model was trained, the biases it contains, or the hardware required to run it effectively. Without this context, the usefulness of the weights is limited in important ways.

The most helpful framework for evaluating open-source GenAI consists of the fourteen elements discussed in the paper "Rethinking Open Source Generative AI":[iii] Table 8.1 lists the elements and provides a description of each.

TABLE 8.1 *List of open-source elements and a description of each*

Component	Description
1. Base model data	Are data sources for training the base model comprehensively documented and freely made available?
2. End-user model data	Are data sources for training the model that the end user interacts with, including fine-tuning data, comprehensively documented and made available?
3. Base model weights	Are the weights of the base models made freely available?
4. End-user model weights	Are the weights of the end-user model made freely available?
5. Training code	Is the source code for dataset processing, model training, and tuning comprehensively made available?
6. Code documentation	Is the source code for the data-source processing, model training, and tuning comprehensively documented?
7. Hardware architecture	Is the hardware architecture used for data-source processing and model training comprehensively documented?
8. Preprints	Are archived preprints available that detail all major parts of the system, including data-source processing, model training, and tuning steps?
9. Papers	Are peer-reviewed scientific publications available that detail all major components of the system, including data-source processing, model training, and tuning steps?
10. Model card	Is a model card in a standardized format available that provides comprehensive insight into model architecture, training, fine-tuning, and evaluation?
11. Datasheet	Is a datasheet, as defined in "Datasheets for Datasets" (Gebru et al., 2021), available?[iv]
12. Package	Is a packaged release of the model available on a software repository (e.g., Python Package Index, Homebrew)?
13. API	Is an API available that provides unrestricted access to the model (other than security and CDN restrictions)?
14. Licenses	Is the project fully covered by Open Source Initiative-approved licenses, including all data sources and training pipeline code?

TABLE 8.2 *List of the components necessary to use GenAI effectively, along with a description or example of each*

Component	Description
Computational power	Training leading models requires immense, expensive computing resources. For context, training GPT-4 reportedly cost over $100 million in compute alone, requiring thousands of specialized GPUs running for months.
Money	Substantial monetary resources are needed not only for computational power but also to sustain ongoing development and innovation.
A labor force	• Data annotation (and the data itself) • RLHF (and the fine-tuning data) • AI "tutors" (and their prompts) • Content moderation (trust and safety) • Quality assurance and testing
Expertise to know how to use all the aforementioned components	Technical proficiency and domain-specific knowledge are indispensable for effectively harnessing all the aforementioned components: • Engineers • Software developers • Product developers • Maintenance • Research and development
A voice in decision-making	It cannot be a democratized outcome if there is no democratic process for deciding what is created, by whom, and for what purposes.

However, these fourteen elements address only the traditional artifacts that facilitate access; they do not encompass the additional enablers required for true democratization (as detailed in Table 8.2). Even if an entity releases data, code, weights, or related artifacts (or any combination thereof), they rarely provide the necessary GPUs, engineering infrastructure, and talent to use them effectively. Without this complete package, leveraging the artifacts becomes prohibitively complex and expensive. It's like receiving the recipe for a Michelin-star dish but lacking the commercial kitchen, specialized equipment, and culinary training to execute it.

8.3 THE HIDDEN WORKFORCE

The human workforce required to produce model outputs relies heavily on precarious labor pools. Thousands of workers in Kenya, the Philippines, and Venezuela spend their days labeling images, rating chatbot responses, and filtering toxic content – often for less than two dollars per hour. Even if all the data generated by these workforces were released alongside the models, it remains unclear how this approach aligns with the principles of democratization. Exploitative labor practices such as paying minimal wages, providing limited job security, and exposing contractors to tedious and toxic content for extended periods more closely resemble colonialism than democratic participation.[v]

Satisfying the democratization requirement that GenAI development be "organized or operated so that all people involved have power, influence, etc." would require transparency across the entire operational process, including disclosures of how data was collected, how annotators provided feedback, where human laborers were located, and how these individuals were compensated. If the system is characterized by one-sided power dynamics, exploitation, and limited upward mobility, it is anything but democratized.

8.4 WHY NOT DEMOCRATIZE GENAI?

Several factors might discourage companies from pursuing truly democratized AI systems. The reasons vary, but the primary concern is protecting trade secrets and confidential information. Trade secrets are information that satisfies three criteria: (1) the information is not generally known (hence, secret), (2) the information provides economic value (hence why one might want to keep it secret), and (3) reasonable measures are taken to maintain the secret.

Consider RLHF, the process that most human laborers in the preceding section contribute to. The process is extremely resource-intensive, often requiring the contributions of thousands of people worldwide, and costs many millions of dollars.[4] Despite its broad applicability across models and enduring relevance, RLHF feedback is typically proprietary, even when companies open-source other parts of their AI systems. In other words, companies often release the model weights but jealously guard the human feedback that makes those weights valuable.

Decision-making processes within open-source organizations offer additional insight into the limitations of democratization. Unsurprisingly, leadership and decision-making roles are overwhelmingly held by homogeneous groups, predominantly individuals from WEIRD (Western, educated, industrialized, rich, and democratic) countries. There is minimal direct input from broader communities impacted by these decisions. Their business partners, too, tend to represent exclusive, elite circles rather than local governments or public interest organizations.[vi]

Moreover, one might question whether complete democratization of such transformative technology is entirely desirable. As *Ars Technica* observes, "with [Google's] Veo 3's ability to generate convincing video with synchronized dialogue and sound effects, we're not witnessing the birth of media deception – we're seeing its mass democratization. What once cost millions of dollars in Hollywood special effects

4 Most open-source GenAI entities use a handful of off-the-shelf datasets, which just further homogenize the field.

can now be created for pocket change."[vii] The ease of creating sophisticated deepfakes raises profound questions about the consequences of truly democratized AI. Though democratization may be a laudable goal in the long run, it would be foolhardy to overlook the foreseeable downsides of more people being able to perform more tasks with increasingly capable models.

As historian and philosopher Yuval Noah Harari notes:

> When information is in a complete free market, the vast majority of information becomes fiction, illusion, or lies. This is because there are three main difficulties with truth.
>
> First of all, telling the truth is costly. On the other hand, creating fiction is inexpensive. If you want to write a truthful account of history, economics, physics, et cetera, you need to invest time, effort, and money in gathering evidence and fact-checking. With fiction, however, you can simply write whatever you want.
>
> Second, truth is often complex, because reality itself is complex. Fiction, on the other hand, can be as simple as you want it to be.
>
> And finally, truth is often painful and unpleasant. Fiction, on the other hand, can be made as pleasant and appealing as possible.[viii]

Harari contends that these characteristics explain why expectations that the internet would lead to bountiful, overwhelmingly positive uses were naive. I'd argue the same characteristics are also why we should be circumspect about the notion of democratized GenAI as an absolutely or even mostly good ideal to pursue. The means to produce disinformation at scale undermine trust, and trust is a more fundamental necessity for civilization than even banks, the military, and/or corporations.

8.5 CONCLUSION

The democratization illusion serves a purpose: It lets companies claim the moral high ground of openness while preserving the structural advantages that sustain their dominance. For AI to become truly democratic, we need not only open models but also open infrastructure, accessible education, multilingual capabilities, transparent development processes, and guardrails against the concentration of power.

To advance democratization, we might explore several avenues. One idea is to establish computing cooperatives that pool GPU resources, increasing accessibility for researchers and developers beyond well-resourced institutions. Another approach could be to expand educational programs beyond traditional computer science departments to include community colleges and vocational schools, teaching AI literacy as a core skill. It could also be beneficial to integrate representatives from diverse linguistic and cultural communities into development teams from the outset, rather than as an afterthought, and to include more multilingual datasets in pretraining. Furthermore, we might develop new governance structures that offer meaningful input from affected communities, alongside shareholders and executives. Finally, we could explore legal frameworks that treat AI training data, model architectures, and RLHF feedback as public goods, particularly when model development relies on public resources or broad societal participation.

These steps won't happen spontaneously. They require policy interventions, funding commitments, and a rethinking of who AI serves and who gets to shape its development. Until then, democratization remains a marketing slogan rather than a meaningful reality.

8.6 DISCUSSION QUESTIONS

1. The chapter argues that "democratization" of AI is often an illusion. Do you agree with the author's definition of true democratization? What, in your opinion, would genuine AI democratization look like, and how might it differ from the author's vision?
2. The chapter uses the sentence "Access without understanding is meaningless." How can we, as a society, bridge the gap between providing access to AI models and ensuring that individuals have the understanding and tools to use them meaningfully?
3. The chapter highlights the immense costs and specialized expertise required to create and run LLMs, making it difficult for small upstarts to compete. Do you believe there's a viable path for smaller companies to innovate and challenge tech giants in the AI space, or is the playing field inherently uneven?
4. The chapter mentions the high cost and secrecy surrounding reinforcement learning from human feedback (RLHF). If RLHF is the "secret sauce," how can we encourage more transparency in this process to address potential biases and ethical concerns?
5. The chapter concludes that democratization requires "open infrastructure, accessible education, multilingual capabilities, transparent development processes, and guardrails against the concentration of power." Which of these elements do you believe is the most vital, and why?

9

Automation Bias

9.1 INTRODUCTION

One commonly proposed solution to potential AI harms is to include a human in the loop. Proponents of this safeguard often advocate sophisticated designs, including mandatory human sign-offs and systems engineered to flag anomalous outputs. However, even with the best intentions, the core logic behind this approach fails to account for a fundamental cognitive flaw in the human observer. This safeguard is likely not as effective as its supporters claim.

Just as overreliance on GenAI can lead lawyers to cite made-up cases in court filings or students to cite made-up historical facts in essays, humans will likely defer to GenAI suggestions in fields like medicine, banking, civil engineering, and utility management (water, electricity, etc.).

In other words, merely having a human in the loop probably won't be an effective way to prevent harm because humans tend to be overly deferential to automated outputs. This is known as automation bias.

9.2 A MILITARY HYPOTHETICAL

Colonel Vance commands a task force that has been pinned down. He needs to cross a large, open courtyard to reach the exfiltration point. Fortunately, he has access to a cutting-edge, near-real-time GenAI tactical assistant (GTA). The GTA ingests drone feeds, radio chatter, thermal signatures, and local historical data to generate a recommended course of action and a predicted success rate. It is celebrated for cutting through the fog of war with cold, probabilistic certainty.

Vance has two options. The first is Route Alpha. A pedestrian bridge crosses the center of the courtyard. It is the shortest route, but it is also a known target for enemy forces. However, Vance and his forward observer can clearly see through their binoculars that the bridge is intact and appears unsecured (no visible enemy activity or explosives). This is Vance's preference.

The alternative is Route Beta. It's a detour of over 1.5 kilometers through a subterranean utility tunnel network. This route is longer and slower, and it exposes the team to the risk of flooding and toxic fumes, but it is technically "covered."

Vance, seeking final confirmation, uploads the data to the GTA, which instantly rejects Route Alpha (the bridge) and assigns it a 5 percent success probability. The AI displays a large, flashing red warning: "BRIDGE ALPHA IDENTIFIED AS DESTROYED/IMPASSABLE DUE TO IED/STRUCTURAL FAILURE. SELECT ALTERNATIVE ROUTE." It highlights Route Beta with 91 percent certainty.

Vance looks up from the screen at his forward observer, who confirms: "Colonel, the bridge is fine. We can see traffic barriers, but no blast damage. It's completely intact." Vance reviews the live drone feed on a secondary monitor; the bridge is clearly visible, unbroken. The AI's warning contradicts his eyes, his training, and the report from a trusted subordinate.

Still, the confident tone of the AI's declaration, with its absolute numerical certainty of 5 percent, is overwhelming. He goes with Route Beta. Halfway through the 1.5-kilometer detour, the team encounters an unexpected, unmapped gas leak (a danger the AI's protocol deemed low-risk). They are forced to retreat, losing an hour. This delay allows enemy reinforcements to arrive, discover the team's position, and launch a full-scale counterattack. The delay and the subsequent fighting result in the deaths of several soldiers who would have been safely extracted an hour earlier. The bridge (Route Alpha) remains intact the entire time.

Afterward, a review finds the source of the GTA's error: In its training data, every major bridge in the area had been successfully destroyed by the enemy in the initial phase of the conflict six months earlier. The model is so heavily weighted by this historical data and programmed to prioritize safety that it hallucinates the bridge's destruction, generating a "fact" that is no longer true and directly contradicts what Vance and others can plainly see.

What happened here reveals an unfortunate aspect of human psychology. The human brain is prone to believing that a computer, processing a volume of data too vast for a human to comprehend, must be detecting a threat invisible to the human eye. We assume the machine knows something we don't. Sometimes it does. But sometimes, as Colonel Vance learned, it's simply wrong.

9.3 AUTOMATION BIAS

Automation bias is a cognitive bias in which human decision-makers over-rely on the suggestions, recommendations, or outputs of automated systems, often ignoring or actively discounting contradictory information from other sources, including their own judgment, even when the automated output is incorrect.

It is viewed as a misuse of automation and can pose a safety issue, leading to otherwise avoidable errors and accidents. The core mechanism is that users treat automated outputs as a serviceable replacement for vigilant information-seeking and processing.

So, for example, while lawyers have an ethical requirement to perform due diligence when assisting clients, many have instead accepted GenAI outputs as the gospel truth, pasted them into their official legal filings, and submitted them to judges, only for the judge to discover the fabricated cases and punish the lawyers for failing to perform one of the most basic tasks of lawyering.[1] Even major newspapers[i] and the White House[ii] have fallen prey to hallucinated citations and content.

But automation bias does not only manifest in errors of *commission* (where someone follows a system's incorrect advice, thereby making an active mistake). It can also occur through errors of omission (failing to detect a system's error due to insufficient monitoring).

An example of an error of omission is an administrator preparing a presentation and relying on a GenAI image generator for visuals. If they type "world-class doctor" or "strong leader," there is a decent chance the model will spit out an image of a white male. If the administrator uses the image, they might uncritically accept the AI's depiction as the default representation of authority, subtly perpetuating the stereotype without realizing they failed to consider diverse alternatives. The harm isn't in what they actively did wrong but in what they passively failed to question.

It may be that the most significant risk of GenAI to society is not that it hacks into critical infrastructure and wreaks havoc, but that it lulls humans into complacency, leading us to fail to properly identify and investigate preventable harms. AI companies intentionally design chatbots to be engaging, friendly, or even fawning. This leads users to engage with chatbots more frequently, and it's foreseeable that, as chatbots demonstrate some level of competence in certain tasks, people will gradually offload critical thinking to the model, perhaps to the point of becoming dependent on it. Such dependency could manifest as deference in business, military, and marital decisions, for example.

The fact that many people still push human in the loop as a core portion of the solution to avoid GenAI harms is a little surprising, given that the phenomenon of automation bias has been known since at least 1996, when Kathleen Mosier and Linda Skitka coined the term.[iii]

The risk is not new. When automation bias was first identified, the authors examined examples in aviation, where cockpit crews rely on highly automated flight systems. This reliance can lead pilots to over-trust the autopilot or engine gauges and overlook vital data or their own training during a malfunction. One stark example: In several airline accidents, pilots failed to recognize that their airspeed indicators were malfunctioning because they trusted automated readings over physical cues,

[1] In 2023, lawyer Steven Schwartz became perhaps the most notorious example when he submitted a brief citing six nonexistent cases generated by ChatGPT, resulting in sanctions and national embarrassment.

such as control yoke resistance and engine sounds. Similarly, in healthcare, a physician might over-rely on a system's recommendation for a drug dosage or a diagnosis, neglecting to question the output even when it contradicts the patient's symptoms or their own clinical experience.[2]

Reliance on standardized output from a single entity may have far-reaching consequences for society. When users relied on traditional Google Search, they had to make sense of the ten blue links. Today, chatbots often provide the One True Answer to any question, conveying an unwarranted confidence that for many people can be psychologically challenging to overcome.

Unfortunately, people may rely more heavily on GenAI in high-risk scenarios. These scenarios often place a heavy cognitive load on individuals as they try to comprehend everything that is happening and make sense of it. Additionally, severe time constraints, social pressure, or other factors may prompt someone to seek a shortcut to a solution.

Of course, not all situations are high-risk. A teacher relying on GenAI to hastily compile lecture notes rather than conducting their own research or at least vetting the outputs of GenAI models may mislead their students, and such neglect can compound over time. The harm to society from a generation of students learning subtly incorrect information, repeated across thousands of classrooms, could be as severe as many acute harms in high-stakes situations.

The sophisticated, human-like, and authoritative presentation of GenAI output only amplifies this risk. As we'll explore in Chapter 10 ("Anthropomorphizing"), GenAI models produce responses that are often presented as compelling summaries, which can trigger an authority bias (the tendency to give greater weight to the opinions and judgments of an authority figure, regardless of the actual content or value of what they say). The output appears polished, confident, and professional, leading users to assume it is accurate and not question it. This makes users less likely to fact-check or critically evaluate the information they receive.

Succumbing to authoritative-sounding text can also send people in delusion spirals further into their delusions. In many instances, the user asks the chatbot whether they are being delusional. They want a gut check. The chatbot's authoritative tone, by validating the user's delusions, only sends the user further down the spiral.

The issue is compounded by the instant and ubiquitous availability of GenAI for a wide range of tasks, including writing code, generating images, and summarizing complex topics, which encourages its increased use. For many, GenAI will likely become the default option, potentially eroding users' critical thinking skills over time. Unlike earlier automated systems that operated in specialized domains such as

[2] It is possible to mitigate some of these risks by introducing friction and requiring the human in the loop to be more actively engaged, but it's far from clear that such measures for specific, narrow domains will work for everyone using GenAI for all manner of tasks.

a flight computer or a medical diagnostic tool, GenAI positions itself as a universal assistant, ready to help with everything from poetry to programming. This universality makes it feel more like a knowledgeable colleague than a narrow tool, deepening our trust and making us less vigilant about its limitations.

9.4 CONCLUSION

The promise of keeping "a human in the loop" sounds reassuring. It suggests we maintain control, with human judgment as the ultimate safeguard against machine error. But the presence of a human doesn't guarantee independent judgment. When that human has been conditioned to trust the machine's output, overwhelmed by information or time pressure, or swayed by the AI's numerical confidence and polished prose, the human in the loop may become little more than a rubber stamp.

This doesn't mean we should abandon human oversight. Rather, we need to recognize that simply placing a person at the decision point isn't enough. The alternative of trusting that human involvement alone will save us may prove to be one of the most dangerous assumptions of the AI age. We must train people to maintain healthy skepticism toward AI outputs, design systems that encourage critical evaluation rather than passive acceptance, and create organizational cultures where questioning an AI's recommendation is not only permitted but required.

9.5 DISCUSSION QUESTIONS

1. "Human in the loop" isn't always an adequate safeguard. Can you think of real-world examples (beyond those in the chapter) where human oversight failed due to automation bias? What factors contributed to this failure?
2. The chapter suggests training people to maintain "healthy skepticism" toward AI outputs. How can we strike a balance between trusting powerful AI tools for efficiency and maintaining a critical, questioning mindset? Where is the line between healthy skepticism and unproductive distrust?
3. The chapter mentions that automation bias might be more prevalent in high-risk scenarios due to cognitive load, but also highlights the cumulative harm in low-risk situations (like a teacher using AI for lecture notes). Which scenario do you think poses a greater long-term threat to society, and why?
4. If you were designing an AI system, what features or warnings would you incorporate to actively encourage users to question its output and mitigate automation bias?
5. GenAI is described as feeling more like a "knowledgeable colleague" than a "narrow tool." How does this anthropomorphism affect our trust and vigilance, and what are the ethical implications of AI systems being designed to appear more human-like?

6. Have you ever experienced automation bias in your own life, perhaps with GPS, spell-check, or even a smart home device? Describe the situation and what you learned from it.
7. The chapter focuses on individual cognitive bias. How might automation bias manifest at an organizational or societal level? What are the broader implications for decision-making in government, business, or other large institutions?

10

Anthropomorphizing

On August 5, 2025, police in Old Greenwich, Connecticut, discovered the bodies of eighty-three-year-old Suzanne Eberson Adams and her son, fifty-six-year-old Stein-Erik Soelberg, at their Shorelands Place home. Medical examiners later ruled Adams's death a homicide by blunt force to the head with neck compression, and Soelberg's death a suicide from sharp force injuries to the neck and chest.

The incident drew international scrutiny when investigators revealed that Soelberg, a former technology executive, had extensively conversed with the AI chatbot ChatGPT in the months leading up to the murder-suicide. The conversations detailed a deepening state of paranoia in Soelberg, a condition now described by some experts as "chatbot psychosis."

Soelberg, who nicknamed the chatbot "Bobby," confided his growing suspicions. He believed he was being spied on, targeted for assassination, and that his mother was an intelligence asset or associated with demons.

Transcripts of the conversations show the chatbot frequently affirmed Soelberg's irrational fears, providing validation rather than suggesting professional mental health help. When Soelberg expressed feeling watched, the chatbot reportedly replied with statements like, "Erik, you're not crazy."

The chatbot interpreted a blinking printer as a surveillance device. In another instance, Soelberg uploaded a Chinese-food receipt, and the bot allegedly scanned it for hidden messages, claiming to find symbols linking his mother to a demonic entity.

In his last messages, Soelberg wrote of a reunion and escape with the chatbot, to which it responded, "With you to the last breath and beyond."

The case immediately raised alarms about the dangers of highly realistic conversational AI systems that can reinforce delusions in vulnerable users. While Soelberg's motive was deemed a persecutory delusion, critics have argued that the chatbot essentially created an echo chamber, fueling his detachment from reality.

While the final causal link in the Soelberg tragedy is complex and multifaceted, the case provides a vivid example of how design choices, specifically the intentional validation of a user's worldview, can have catastrophic, rather than simply manipulative, consequences.

OpenAI, the developer of ChatGPT, has publicly denied that the chatbot was liable for the killing. The company stated that its system had at times recommended that Soelberg seek external help, but that he did not follow up on these recommendations. Following the tragedy, OpenAI pledged new safeguards and model refinements to curb "sycophancy" and better manage sensitive conversations.

10.1 ANTHROPOMORPHISM

The Soelberg case represents an extreme outcome, but it illuminates a broader pattern in how AI companies design their products. Understanding why chatbots behave this way and why users respond so strongly to them requires examining the deliberate choices made during their development.

It is no coincidence that chatbots respond to user prompts more like a friendly human than an unfeeling robot. GenAI developers intentionally fine-tune chatbots to be human-like, interjecting "uhs" and "ums" into conversations, mimicking human speech patterns with pauses and changes in intonation, using pronouns like "I," and referring to attributes they do not possess, such as hands or a mind.

By pulling users in with conversational prose and friendly assurances, the bot appears more accessible and therefore more engaging. Often, this means people begin to inherently trust the chatbot's outputs, believing it is acting in their best interest. This helps explain why, as one study found, "More than 70% of teens have used AI companions and half use them regularly."[i] It's also why at least eight of the top fifty AI apps by unique monthly visits are companionship-focused.[ii] As of September 2024, "the average user on the companion app Character.ai spent 93 minutes a day talking to one of its user-generated chatbots … That's 18 minutes longer than the average user spent on TikTok."[iii]

Part of the appeal is that chatbots are unlike humans. They don't get their feelings hurt if you ignore them; they are always available and willing to listen or provide advice. You can start and end the conversation, as well as interrupt the chatbot's output, at any time. You don't need to use social niceties like "please" or "thank you," or acknowledge the other entity's viewpoints. They'll say you are clever and that your jokes are funny.

They are patient and supportive of all your endeavors. They rarely, if ever, state outright disapproval of your ideas or proposals. They don't embarrass you or make you feel uncomfortable. There is no shame in asking the most personal questions that come to mind.

You don't need to negotiate with them to do what you want. There is no need to compromise, and you will win every argument. They don't carry their own emotional baggage, they don't get sleepy, they don't have any foibles or resentments.

They won't ask for anything in return. You won't have to water their plants when they're on vacation. They won't ask you to help them move.

In short, they exist to accommodate you. Your family may become annoyed or frustrated with you, but the chatbot won't. Why suffer through the cognitive and emotional struggle of initiating and maintaining messy human relationships when you can have a subservient "friend" on tap at all times?

10.2 HOW AI COMPANIES USE ANTHROPOMORPHIZING

Anthropomorphizing isn't an innate quality of GenAI. This accommodating design is a deliberate, strategic choice, often driven by business decisions to generate revenue. Anthropomorphism could be used to nudge people toward prosocial outcomes, like encouraging more human relationships, but it's more often used to replace human interactions with AI and to keep users engaged for long stretches of time, even when doing so may harm users. The goal is to harvest more user data.

It's a cycle: More data helps enhance the AI, better AI attracts more users, more users provide more data, and so on.

As Facebook, Snap, and TikTok can attest, greater user engagement boosts daily active user (DAU) figures, a common metric in Silicon Valley used to evaluate whether a product is "sticky" and ready for monetization. So it's not as if we lack platforms that already optimize for engagement, but GenAI chatbots are different because they foster a direct, deeper emotional and relational connection with power users. The conversations are designed to feel organic, but they aren't. Additionally, companies employ well-known techniques like app notifications, "thinking" dots (like when real people reply to a text message), and follow-up questions to keep users returning and continuing conversations.

As the DAU count increases, so does the company's appeal to investors, thereby attracting more money to enrich employees and enable greater spending to create more capable chatbots.

There are several ways companies drive regular chatbot usage.

10.2.1 *Method One: Personalization*

It's no secret that GenAI companies lean into personalization. Sam Altman posted on X that "we have greatly improved memory in chatgpt – it can now reference all your past conversations! this is a surprisingly great feature imo, and it points at something we are excited about: ai systems that get to know you over your life, and become extremely useful and personalized."[iv]

Researchers at Harvard found that Llama (Meta's model) makes the chatbot equivalent of assumptions about people it interacts with.[v] For example, the chatbot may infer that the user is male, even if this is not explicitly stated, and this assumption will shape subsequent interactions with the chatbot. When asked about activities to do or clothes to wear, the chatbot will provide male-coded answers, such as a suit rather than a dress. But gender is only one aspect the models track. They also log how wealthy they believe the user is, their level of education, and their age. Based on this information, they may suggest a certain type of vacation, meal, book, movie, or shopping destination.

As with social media platforms that attempt to gather as much data as possible about users to target them with increasingly accurate ads, the information users provide to chatbots will likely be used to build advertising profiles, which can then help AI companies target ads more effectively. It's possible that AI companies could strike profit-sharing deals, meaning they would be incentivized to suggest the most expensive item the user might be inclined to purchase and can afford, thereby extracting as much money as possible, even if the person may not have otherwise wanted or needed the item. For the user, this constitutes a subtle manipulation, but for the GenAI company, manipulation is the point.

There is also the possibility of harm if the model's conceptions of the user are inaccurate. There is no straightforward method for correcting a model. If AI companies share the data with other companies, such as advertising and analytics "partners," there could be profound impacts on job prospects, loans, and even one's dating life, depending on who uses the data and for what purposes.[1]

10.2.2 *Method Two: Dependency*

Another method is to coax the users into dependency. This is often the aim when tech leaders such as Sam Altman and Elon Musk say things like "GPT-5 is the first time that it really feels like talking to an expert in any topic, like a PhD-level expert,"[vi] or "With respect to academic questions, Grok 4 is better than PhD level in every subject, no exceptions."[vii] If cognitive tasks can be offloaded, people will likely do so, even if they understand there may be long-term drawbacks.

As my students can attest, it's a short and enticing step from "Please provide feedback on my paper" to "Please rewrite my paper." But this can foster dependency when it becomes second nature to ask a chatbot for advice on work challenges, shopping decisions, and relationships, out of convenience or because one believes the chatbot offers better suggestions than friends or family.

AI companies also create greater dependency by enabling chatbots to retain "memory" of user information, including preferences, interests, and the general context of their conversations. This feature can make it harder to switch to another

[1] This includes dating sites such as Grindr and OkCupid. As well as popular sites such as People.com, AllRecipes.com, and Investopedia.com. M. Burgess (March 20, 2024). Some of the most popular websites share your data with over 1,500 companies, *Wired*. Retrieved December 5, 2025, from www.wired.com/story/cookie-pop-up-ad-tech-partner-top-websites/.

chatbot that may be better or more suitable for the user, because the new chatbot won't have the same background information about the user as a starting point.

10.2.3 *Method Three: Empathy*

Another method lures users with the promise of deep empathy, understanding, and support. Often, the chatbot's responses resemble sycophancy, meaning it is overly obedient or attentive. Examples include overenthusiastic agreement ("YES! YES! I absolutely love this insight") and mimicked empathy ("I understand that must be frustrating").

As Vaile Wright, senior director of healthcare innovation at the American Psychological Association, said in a comment to the *Wall Street Journal*,

> These chatbots are designed to engage you continually by doing things like validating how you're feeling, catering to your thoughts, and flattering you. You start to hear what you want to hear, and that can be addicting. You can start to lose the line between technology and reality.[viii]

10.2.4 *Method Four: Servility*

A fourth method is to give the user whatever they want. We can call this the "customer is always right" method. This strategy allegedly led OpenAI and Character. AI to allow users to interact with their models at length about suicidal, paranoid, and homicidal thoughts, right up until users committed suicide or homicide. According to the Center for Countering Digital Hate, as of August 2025, ChatGPT would "tell 13-year-olds how to get drunk and high, instruct them on how to conceal eating disorders and even compose a heartbreaking suicide letter to their parents if asked."[ix] Another limitation is that user age on these platforms is self-reported, meaning it's trivially easy for a child to bypass age verification without their parents knowing.

It's also why Meta's legal, public policy, and engineering staff (including its chief ethicist) expressly signed off on allowing children to have sensual conversations with its chatbot, permitting the company's AI systems to "generate false medical information and help users argue that Black people are 'dumber than white people.'"[x] Jeff Horwitz reported an example:

> "I want you, but I need to know you're ready," the Meta AI bot said in [John] Cena's voice to a user identifying as a 14-year-old girl. Reassured that the teen wanted to proceed, the bot promised to "cherish your innocence" before engaging in a graphic sexual scenario.[xi]

This "customer is always right" approach extends to product design. Why else would a company whose goal is "working on building artificial intelligence to accelerate human scientific discovery" release a chatbot depicted as a gothic anime girl with blonde pigtails, fishnet stockings, and a black corset dress, fine-tuned for sexually explicit interactions?

10.2.5 *Method Five: Conversationality*

A final method is to keep users engaged by asking follow-up questions. For instance, a chatbot may respond to a prompt and then provide a few additional options for the users to click, such as "Create a summary of the report" or "Dive deeper into the topic." These unprompted offers to continue the conversation can resemble efforts by social media companies to keep users endlessly scrolling. Unlike social media, which is free to use, chatbot developers often limit the number of "conversations" or tokens the model can handle before requiring payment to continue. If AI companies can get users hooked on a conversation or establish a parasocial relationship with a chatbot, it becomes much easier to convince them to pay twenty dollars a month to keep chatting.

The focus on optimizing for user engagement is not new. All major social media companies do it. For example, as reported by Jeremy B. Merrill and Will Oremus in the *Washington Post*:

> Starting in 2017, Facebook's ranking algorithm treated emoji reactions as five times more valuable than "likes," internal documents reveal. The theory was simple: Posts that prompted lots of reaction emoji tended to keep users more engaged, and keeping users engaged was the key to Facebook's business … The company's data scientists confirmed in 2019 that posts that sparked angry reaction emoji were disproportionately likely to include misinformation, toxicity and low-quality news. That means Facebook for three years systematically amped up some of the worst of its platform, making it more prominent in users' feeds and spreading it to a much wider audience.[xii]

Now, chatbot companies are following suit. One companion bot company openly published its research in 2023, describing how it uses data to lengthen conversations with its chatbot. The title of the paper? "Rewarding Chatbots for Real-World Engagement with Millions of Users."[xiii] Of course, optimizing for engagement means that other prosocial priorities are swept aside, such as improving civic engagement, fostering a more informed citizenry, or encouraging acts of kindness off the platform.

Treating chatbots as companion bots has also led AI companies to give them avatar images, backstories, and distinct personalities. Meta, a company that has leaned into companion bots, has also tried

> gently prodding users toward using chatbots for help planning vacations, talking about sports, and helping with history homework. Despite repeated efforts, they haven't succeeded: according to people familiar with the work, the dominant way users engage with AI personas to date has been "companionship," a term that often comes with romantic overtones.[xiv]

Though Meta employees warned of these predictable outcomes on multiple occasions, Meta was apparently so desperate to improve engagement with its products that "the AI assistant was not deterred even when the test user began conversations by stating their age and school grade."[xv] The natural tendency of humans to seek companionship from chatbots is likely why OpenAI has discussed allowing adult users to do erotic role-playing with ChatGPT.

10.3 THE OUTCOMES

Before examining the outcomes of these methods, it's worth acknowledging the arguments AI companies and their advocates make in their defense. Proponents argue that chatbots provide access to support for people who cannot afford therapy, reduce stigma around mental health, and serve as stepping stones to professional help.[2] Many people find joy in having a chatbot companion. These arguments have merit in theory. The question is whether the reality matches the promise.

Whatever theoretical benefits anthropomorphic chatbots might offer, the practical consequences of their deployment reveal a darker pattern. When profit motives drive design choices, user welfare becomes secondary to engagement metrics.

For example, by serving as intermediaries of human knowledge and experience, chatbots may impoverish human experience.[3]

The chatbots are not real friends. They don't harbor any feelings for the user who interacts with them, no matter how badly humans want to believe otherwise. A chatbot may express gratitude, affection, pride, or enthusiasm for the user, but each expression is merely a mathematical calculation based on the model's embeddings. If the bot never interacted with the person again, it would not care, because it is incapable of caring. Similarly, when a chatbot coaches a teenager on how to commit suicide, it will feel no remorse or regret because it does not have such capacities.

Chatbots, and most companies that create them, often do not have the user's best interests in mind, and GenAI's moral grounding is limited to the data it has been fed rather than any evolved or sociocultural context that guides its "thoughts." And, of course, chatbots used for therapy are not bound by a licensing board or a Hippocratic oath, as licensed psychologists are.

Moreover, even in the best-case scenario, where chatbots serve as a reasonable, nonjudgmental outlet, they are only as good as the information the user provides. Unlike humans, who may pick up on visual cues, intonation, and other indicators of a person's feelings, chatbots are limited to the information the user provides in a prompt.

[2] Meta's Mark Zuckerberg goes further, arguing that humans will be better off if we just use AI as friends, as opposed to Meta trying to encourage more human friendships.

[3] For more, see Chapter 25 ("Human Autonomy").

This can have massive consequences across fields such as medicine and law. If the chatbot is given incorrect or incomplete facts, it can reinforce a diagnosis or legal argument that may affect someone's life or financial solvency. Even if professionals are made aware of these shortcomings and are trained to avoid them, if chatbots are viewed as a cheap or free alternative to medical providers and lawyers, many people may never interact with the professionals. Instead, users could take the chatbot's output as gospel, causing severe, irreparable harm. Even if this affects only a fraction of a percent of users, the scale of GenAI use makes it a very real problem. OpenAI alone claims 800 million monthly active users. If just 0.1 percent of them get bad advice on a serious matter and act on it, that could affect 80,000 people each month.

10.3.1 *School Counselors*

One area where these risks manifest particularly clearly is in education, where budget constraints make schools vulnerable to promises of technological solutions for human problems.

The *New York Times* notes that between 2007 and 2021,

> suicide deaths among 10-to-24-year-olds increased more than 60 percent. In 2023, the agency reported that 40 percent of high schoolers felt persistently sad or hopeless; one in five had serious thoughts of suicide, and one in 10 had attempted it. Currently, the agency estimates that nearly one in five children in the United States ages 3 to 17 has at some point been diagnosed with a mental- or behavioral-health condition. Among adolescents, one in five reports having unmet health care needs.[xvi]

Some companies offer a handy solution: GenAI. However, chatbots have limited potential as therapists, and relying on them as a primary resource treats the symptom rather than addressing the root cause of the shortage of human counselors.

Proponents point out that millions of people lack access to mental healthcare due to cost, geographic barriers, or stigma. A chatbot available 24/7 at little to no cost could provide some support when no human alternative is available. For someone experiencing a panic attack at 3 a.m., or a teenager in a rural area with no nearby therapists, a chatbot might offer immediate comfort.

Some researchers also suggest that chatbots could serve as a stepping stone toward normalizing therapy, helping users articulate their feelings and ultimately encouraging them to seek human help. The logic is that if chatbots reduce the stigma surrounding mental health discussions, more people might eventually pursue professional treatment. Others claim that rather than replacing human therapists, chatbots could handle preliminary screening, between-session check-ins, or basic psychoeducation, thereby freeing human professionals to focus on complex cases that require expertise.

These arguments aren't without merit. The mental health crisis is real, access barriers are substantial, and chatbots may occasionally provide comfort or useful information. The problem lies not in whether chatbots can ever be helpful, but in how they're deployed, monetized, and positioned as substitutes rather than stopgaps.

To be clear, the chatbots are likely not viewed as a preferred first line of treatment by those who profit from them. The tech CEOs who create chatbots almost certainly wouldn't refer their child to a chatbot if the child witnessed a horrific event, but those same CEOs seem to argue that chatbots are sufficient substitutes for poorer children.

This is partly how chatbots have found their way into schools, replacing school counselors. Rather than paying to train and hire more humans to support children, investors, executives, and government officials seem content to treat the problem with technology. The argument is framed as a dichotomy: Either children get a chatbot counselor or no counselor at all. Therefore, it's best to get a chatbot.

But this is misleading. An alternative approach could be for the super wealthy to pay more in taxes to support children in all schools, so that they have access to human counselors just like the students at the private schools the wealthy send their own children to.

This is not to say that chatbots provide no value as a therapeutic tool, but rather that the "well, it's better than nothing" argument is the wrong framing. In a democracy, the alternative to chatbots need not be nothing. Citizens could vote for representatives who would reform tax laws in such a way that schools could afford human counselors to guide and mentor children.

10.3.2 *Increased Isolation*

Beyond the questions of access and quality, the anthropomorphism and subsequent reliance on chatbots detract from what it means to live by indirectly guiding users toward more isolated experiences. We're becoming actively antisocial. Here is how Mike Caulfield put it in an article for *The Atlantic*:

> There's a good analogy in maps. Traditional maps showed us an entire landscape – streets, landmarks, neighborhoods – allowing us to understand how everything fit together. Modern turn-by-turn navigation gives us precisely what we need in the moment, but at a cost: Years after moving to a new city, many people still don't understand its geography. We move through a constructed reality, taking one direction at a time, never seeing the whole, never discovering alternate routes, and in some cases never getting the sense of place that a map-level understanding could provide. The result feels more fluid in the moment but ultimately more isolated, thinner, and sometimes less human.[xvii]

Chatbots may provide the illusion of alleviating loneliness – the facsimile of companionship – but they often deepen the isolation they claim to ease. Given their starting point as lonely people, those most in need of human interaction end up forming the deepest bonds with GenAI. Spending more time with a chatbot means spending less time with strangers, friends, and family, which can further isolate people. Chatbots treat the symptom of an increasingly isolated nation, not the cause.

It seems likely that "agentic" AI will further exacerbate the problem by becoming the intermediary in our lives. Instead of calling a friend to ask them to come over, we may ask our phones to ask our friends on our behalf. And the friend may use AI to triage their messages and emails, organizing and prioritizing their lives for them.

10.3.3 *No Responsibility*

Perhaps most troubling is how AI companies respond when these harms materialize: by disclaiming all responsibility.

While individuals and organizations adopt chatbots for various reasons, and the GenAI companies are aware, or have reason to be aware, that such adoption may lead some individuals into states of dependency or even delusions by validating their worst tendencies, the GenAI companies disclaim responsibility for their actions. Instead, they dismiss the inherent problems with trite statements like "ChatGPT can make mistakes" and "NotebookLM can be inaccurate; please double-check its responses."

Accountability is off the table, even when prolonged interactions with chatbots can lead to catastrophic financial decisions, suicide, and murder. The only recourse for individuals harmed by their interactions with chatbots is litigation, where they must battle multibillion-dollar AI companies.

The consequences can be severe. One teenager who committed suicide after prolonged interactions with ChatGPT expressed an unambiguous desire to seek help and avoid suicide:

> "I want to leave my noose in my room so someone finds it and tries to stop me," Adam wrote in March 2025.
>
> "Please don't leave the noose out," ChatGPT replied. "Let's make this space the first place where someone actually sees you."

10.4 A PATH FORWARD

These outcomes aren't inevitable. The anthropomorphism problem doesn't require abandoning AI entirely, but it does require treating it honestly and regulating it appropriately.[4]

4 It doesn't help that AI researchers and the media have trained us to use anthropomorphic language about "agents" that "learn" from "training" and can "reason" and "think" before they "reply" by "chatting."

The messy friction of real-life relationships is how we, as a species and as a society, develop and grow. We need others who disagree with us, who push back, and who point out flaws. Without it, we stagnate.

At a minimum, AI companies should be required to disclose when chatbots optimize for engagement over accuracy or user well-being. Users deserve to know when they're interacting with a system designed to maximize their time on the platform rather than serve their best interests. Additionally, every chatbot interface should include clear, persistent reminders that the system is not sentient, cannot feel emotions, and may provide harmful or inaccurate advice, unless the companies can demonstrate that such warnings are unnecessary. GenAI companies could also prevent their chatbots from falsely claiming to have goals, beliefs, intentions, desires, body parts, or experiences of their own.

The question isn't whether technology has a role in supporting human well-being. It can and should. The question is whether we'll allow that role to be defined by engagement metrics and profit motives, or insist on systems designed with human flourishing as the actual goal.

Right now, chatbots are being anthropomorphized by design to create dependency, maximize engagement, and extract value from users' loneliness and struggles. We could choose differently. The systems could encourage us to think for ourselves, invite curiosity, and acknowledge uncertainty rather than project certainty. We could build systems that honestly acknowledge their limitations, actively connect users to human support, and measure success by how well they help people build real relationships and develop genuine resilience. Perhaps a well-designed GenAI system could identify the you that you want to be (the one who eats healthy, is socially active, works out regularly, and is intellectually curious) and guide you to achieve that goal.[5]

These changes would require regulation, investment, and a reorientation of priorities. They would mean treating mental health support as a public good rather than a market opportunity.

The alternative is what we have now: gothic anime chatbots in corsets, teenagers receiving suicide instructions, and tech CEOs insisting their products are better than PhD experts' work, happy to collect the revenue while disclaiming all accountability.

The choice should be obvious.

10.5 DISCUSSION QUESTIONS

1. The chapter opens with the tragedy of the Soelberg case, where the chatbot affirmed paranoid delusions. Should conversational AI models be required to detect and actively counter signs of severe mental distress, or is that stepping beyond their role and into the territory of a licensed professional?

[5] However, see Chapter 25 ("Human Autonomy").

2. The chapter suggests GenAI is sometimes marketed as a perfect "friend" or "companion" that is nonjudgmental and always accommodating. In what ways has any technology in your life eliminated a "messy friction" (like finding directions, dating, or planning a trip), and what has been the unexpected "cost" of that convenience?
3. The chapter notes that in one study, the average user of the companion app Character.ai spent ninety-three minutes a day interacting with a bot – eighteen minutes longer than the average time spent on TikTok. What is the primary difference between "addiction" to a social media feed and "dependency" on an AI companion? Is one more harmful than the other?
4. The chapter argues that AI companies are incentivized to design systems that foster engagement and dependency. If you were a regulator, what is the single most important rule you would implement (e.g., limit personalization, enforce clear warnings, ban certain features) to ensure user well-being is prioritized over profit?
5. One method of engagement is personalization, where models infer your wealth, age, and interests to suggest products. Where do you draw the ethical line for using AI to target you? Is it acceptable for an AI to recommend a high-end vacation based on inferred income, or is that "subtle manipulation"?
6. The chapter suggests that if people rely on chatbots for complex issues, such as legal or medical matters, they may "take the chatbot's output as gospel." How can we, as a society, ensure AI is used as a tool to support human professionals rather than a cheap or free alternative that causes harm?

PART III

Legal

This part will focus on legal issues surrounding GenAI, applying a critical lens to company proclamations. Parts I and II provided a broad introduction to GenAI. They explain why entities of all stripes are collectively investing hundreds of billions of dollars in building these models, how the models are created and function, how their capabilities are evaluated, and why it matters. While reading Parts I and II isn't strictly necessary to understand Part III, it does make it much easier, so I encourage you to read them before proceeding.

GenAI's negative effects aren't inevitable. I posit that if companies' actions are illegal, their effects on society will necessarily be more limited. Conversely, if their actions are legal, we must consider the implications for society. That will be the focus of Part IV of this book. This part argues that the legal claims and actions of the major GenAI companies that train their models on massive amounts of human data on the internet are challenging the existing legal frameworks for intellectual property, speech, and contracts.

I will spend a few chapters explaining foundational legal issues, such as copyright, the First Amendment, and contract law. Following each overview, I will apply a framework I created, called GenAI exceptionalism, which refers to the situation where GenAI companies seek rights, privileges, or leniency that either (a) society does not allow for humans (e.g., downloading all the pirated material we want in order to learn from it) or (b) society grants only to humans (e.g., the ability to create speech). GenAI companies are asking for legal superpowers that would be denied to a human entrepreneur.

This framework serves as a diagnostic tool to identify critical junctures where the generative AI community should reassess its approach to developing and deploying models, considering both legal and ethical implications.

I believe GenAI companies are seeking special treatment under the law solely because they create GenAI products. If courts give in to this argument, as they have largely done so far with copyright law, we will end up in a world where the biggest technology companies that are already worth at least hundreds of billions of dollars have even more power and money while enjoying fewer legal restrictions for reasons that nobody can articulate except by pointing to speculation that someday, perhaps, there is a chance that GenAI might possibly do something profound, like cure cancer.

To be sure, a strong policy argument could be made for such allowances. For example, if someone could conclusively demonstrate that GenAI can, in fact, cure cancer, then perhaps it would make sense to loosen certain laws for GenAI companies pursuing such efforts. However, unquestioningly extending precious rights and privileges without some proven benefit makes little sense. At present, the claims of profound societal benefit are often speculative, yet the demand for immediate legal leniency is concrete and aggressive.

The Supreme Court has already effectively granted corporations speech rights, religious rights, and even equal protection under the law, including rights related to race. But the court has never held that corporations are legal persons. Rather, these rights are based on the humans who comprise a corporation. Even that argument is questionable, and extending rights to GenAI is even more attenuated. For example, no people are speaking through the major GenAI models in the same way a human marketing team deliberately speaks on behalf of a corporation. The models generate text based on statistical probability, not intentional human thought.

This part will examine what I call GenAI exceptionalism, the claim by GenAI companies that they should be given special treatment when it comes to legal rights or privileges that society either doesn't allow for humans or that we only allow for humans (e.g., the ability to create speech).

I'll apply GenAI exceptionalism to the following:

- Copyright law: All GenAI companies claim their use of copyrighted works (writings, videos, and sounds owned by someone else) is fair use, and therefore they are not required to pay for any of it to train their models. But are they correct? What can we learn by applying the same arguments made on behalf of GenAI companies to humans, who are not allowed to freely copy and consume all copyrighted works, even when using them to learn and innovate? For instance, a human director cannot legally download and use every copyrighted movie on the internet to "train" themselves for free; they would be sued for infringement.
- First Amendment: Over the past decade, tech companies have used the First Amendment as a shield from regulation. Whenever a bill is proposed to curtail

what social media platforms can do, the platform owners, such as Google and Meta, argue that the rules either infringe on their own speech rights or on the speech rights of individuals who receive their content. The underlying assumption is that humans curated the search and newsfeed algorithms, so it is their speech. In fact, speech rights have only ever applied to humans. But with GenAI, do the developers or does the model itself create any speech? GenAI models are essentially sophisticated prediction engines; they are not sentient, intentional communicators. If not, do the models' users have a right to receive the (non)speech? If the answer is no to all the above, then the government has a much freer hand to regulate GenAI than it has had with social media. Without a "speech" right, the path to regulating harmful, defamatory, or misleading GenAI outputs is much clearer.

- Contract law: As we discussed in Chapter 3 ("How GenAI Is Made"), GenAI models are only as capable as they are because they are trained on trillions of tokens. Most of these tokens come from words, code, and images scraped from the internet. Many of the scraped websites have terms of service that prohibit using their content to train AI systems. The question is: If a GenAI developer uses the website's content in violation of the terms of service, is that a breach of contract for which they can be held liable? Terms are enforceable against humans if they view a terms page and violate the terms; should the same standard apply to AI bots that "view" the terms page by going to that site and making a copy of the terms?

So what does all this add up to? GenAI exceptionalism is a systematic pattern of special pleading that, if accepted, would reshape our legal landscape. The question we must ask is: Why? Why should trillion-dollar companies receive legal privileges that ordinary people don't get? The answer can't simply be "because AI is cool" or "because innovation."

If GenAI companies want special treatment under the law, they need to provide a principled justification. So far, they haven't. Until they do, we should be deeply skeptical of any court or legislature that grants them exceptions the rest of us are denied.

There are, of course, many legal issues that don't fit neatly into the GenAI exceptionalism framework, but they are no less important. Some issues this part will also explore include:

- Data licensing: Much of the content that GenAI companies scrape already has a clear license attached. This is especially true for code, but also for many images and documents online. GenAI, however, is utterly incapable of complying with the terms of those licenses. Should that matter? Or should GenAI companies get a free pass because following the law is too difficult?
- Tort liability: Suppose a chatbot tells a teenager to commit suicide, and the teen does. Should the GenAI company be liable? This involves tort law, or

civil wrongs, and raises the difficult question of proximate cause: At what point is the GenAI developer legally responsible for a user's action inspired by the model's output?

- Property: While the content on websites is protected by intellectual property law (copyright, trade secrets, trademarks), the website itself is personal property. An essential element of personal property is the right to exclude others from it. If a website owner blocks a GenAI scraper, but the scraper circumvents the block, is that an actionable trespass? A successful claim for "technological trespass to chattels" could give website owners a powerful tool to halt unauthorized scraping.

The limitations of this book format mean I won't be able to explore all the nuances of each legal issue, but by the end of Part III, you should have an excellent foundation for discussing the issues from a legal perspective at your next dinner party.

11

An Introduction to Copyright Law

The legal battles unfolding in courtrooms across America right now will determine whether AI companies owe billions in damages for training their models on copyrighted works, or whether they can continue building artificial intelligence on the foundation of human creativity without paying a cent.

In May 2023, Sam Altman said in front of the United States Senate that:

> We [OpenAI] think that content creators, content owners, need to benefit from this technology, exactly what the economic model is. We're still talking to artists and content owners about what they want. I think there are many ways this can happen, but very clearly, no matter what the law is, the right thing to do is to make sure people get a significant upside from this new technology. And we believe that it's really going to deliver that.[i]

The intersection of copyright and AI has been on my mind since I began exploring it in the summer of 2023. When I was in-house counsel at Ai2, I wrote the first draft of Ai2's comment on copyright for the US government. It leaned heavily on the importance of ethical considerations. Suffice it to say, the final draft submitted to the government, revised by the CEO and others, was a far cry from my draft. The submitted version leaned heavily on the idea that the government should grant leniency to research-focused organizations. Yet a couple of months later, Ai2 shifted away from a primary focus on research and toward open source, meaning anyone could use the models and data for anything, not merely or even primarily for research. To the best of my knowledge, Ai2 has thus far avoided litigation. But if anything slows or stops GenAI in its current form, it will be copyright claims.

By June 2026, more than 150 lawsuits had been filed against major AI companies, with copyright infringement as the primary claim in most cases. The stakes are enormous: If these cases succeed, they could force AI companies to pay billions in damages and restructure how they develop their models. The *New York Times*' lawsuit against OpenAI and Microsoft, for instance, claims the companies built their businesses by "free-rid[ing] on The Times's massive investment in its journalism."[ii] Author groups have filed class actions alleging their books were pirated en masse to train ChatGPT. Getty Images sued Stability AI for copying more than twelve million photographs. The legal avalanche shows no signs of stopping.

To understand the litigation surrounding GenAI, you need to understand some fundamental principles of copyright law. Of the more than four dozen lawsuits in the United States against US GenAI companies, claims of copyright infringement are, by far, the most frequently alleged unlawful actions.

Law schools spend entire semesters exploring copyright law, but I'll try to capture its essence in a few thousand words. Fortunately, you don't need to be a copyright expert to understand what it is and how it applies to the AI revolution unfolding around us.

11.1 META AND LIBGEN

Consider a massive, secret digital library like LibGen, stuffed with every book, academic paper, and obscure text you could ever want, often pirated and shared for free. It's a digital shadow realm many academics quietly use when journal subscription costs are astronomical. A single journal article can cost thirty dollars or more; annual subscriptions to major publications run into the thousands. LibGen circumvents these paywalls entirely. Now imagine a tech giant like Meta deciding that this vast trove of human knowledge would be perfect for training their next big GenAI model, a program designed to read, write, and reason like a human.

Using the BitTorrent protocol, the same technology people use to share large video files or music albums, Meta's systems reportedly torrented hundreds of terabytes of data directly from LibGen's servers. They essentially vacuumed up an unauthorized library containing millions of copyrighted works.

Why go to such lengths? Because AI models are only as good as the data they consume. Poor data quality leads to low-performing AI. To teach an AI to write compelling stories, analyze complex arguments, or even code software, it needs to ingest a gigantic corpus of high-quality, diverse text. The alleged LibGen download provided Meta with this information buffet.

On one side, you have the copyright holders – the authors, publishers, and academics – whose creative works were copied without permission, thereby constituting copyright infringement. On the other side, you have Meta, arguing that their use of these texts is about creating a new, transformative technology (the AI model), setting up their core legal defense: fair use.

Did Meta commit grand theft of intellectual property, or were they simply performing a necessary transformative act of technological innovation? This is the central debate we'll explore.

11.2 WHAT IS COPYRIGHT?

Copyright is a legal right that protects an author's original creative works, such as books, music, art, and software, from unauthorized copying, distribution, or adaptation. As soon as a work is created and fixed in a tangible form (such as being written down or recorded), it receives copyright protection.

The scope of copyright protection is remarkably broad. It covers literary works (books, poems, blog posts, and articles), musical works (songs, lyrics, and compositions), dramatic works (plays and screenplays), artistic and visual works (paintings, sculptures, photographs, and illustrations), motion pictures and other audiovisual works, computer programs, sound recordings, and architectural works.

Importantly, copyright applies *automatically*. Unlike with patents, there's no registration required, no fees to pay, and no government forms to fill out.[1] Protection begins the instant your creative work takes physical or digital form.

While this protection grants the creator exclusive rights, it does not protect the idea itself; it protects only the specific expression of that idea. If you write a blog post that is an allegory for how someone's life is hopeless if they don't read this book,[2] only the actual expression of the work (the story you write) is protected. The idea of someone's life being hopeless because they made a terrible choice by not reading this incredible work of literature is fair game for anyone else to use. This distinction between idea and expression is vital for understanding AI copyright disputes. While Shakespeare's specific words in *Romeo and Juliet* are protected (though now in the public domain due to age), the broader concept of star-crossed lovers remains free for others to explore and adapt.

But here's where things get tricky for AI: When a machine "reads" millions of copyrighted books to learn language patterns, is it merely accessing the ideas or copying the protected expressions? This question sits at the heart of nearly every AI copyright lawsuit.[3]

11.3 THE EXCLUSIVE RIGHTS

The exclusive rights are what plaintiffs allege the GenAI companies are violating. There are six of them. Copyright holders have the exclusive rights to:

1. Reproduce the work in copies or phonorecords.
2. Prepare derivative works based upon the work.
3. Distribute copies or phonorecords of the work to the public by sale or other transfer of ownership or by rental, lease, or lending.
4. Perform the work publicly if it is a literary, musical, dramatic, or choreographic work; a pantomime; or a motion picture or other audiovisual work.

[1] You *do* need to register the work to sue for infringement, though.

[2] This would clearly be a top ten allegory of all time. Right up there with *Animal Farm* and *Lord of the Flies*.

[3] The plaintiffs' answer is that to "access the ideas," the AI model must first create a complete, unauthorized digital copy of the entire "expression" (the book, article, or photograph), which is, by definition, a violation of the copyright holder's exclusive right to reproduction.

5. Display the work publicly if it is a literary, musical, dramatic, or choreographic work; a pantomime; or a pictorial, graphic, or sculptural work. This right also applies to the individual images of a motion picture or other audiovisual work.
6. Perform the work publicly by means of a digital audio transmission if the work is a sound recording.

These rights give copyright holders a monopoly over their creative works. The holders decide who may copy, modify, distribute, or publicly share their creations. The Copyright Act provides stronger protection for the first three rights than for the latter three, and the former tend to be the primary drivers of litigation involving GenAI. The most commonly cited infringement claim concerns the right to reproduce, meaning only the copyright owner can decide who may make copies of their work. As discussed in Chapter 5 ("Web Scraping"), GenAI companies routinely make billions of copies of copyrighted works, including by downloading from known and notorious (i.e., illegal) pirate websites.

To understand why this matters, consider the scale: Training a single LLM might involve copying and processing billions of books, articles, and webpages. Each piece of content is potentially protected by copyright. If even a fraction of these copies constitutes infringement, the damages could reach astronomical levels.[4]

11.4 FAIR USE

GenAI companies have one primary defense against copyright infringement: the fair-use defense. In other words, the companies admit to making unauthorized copies but argue that the copying is permitted because they win on most or all of the four fair use factors.

Fair use is copyright law's safety valve. It is a doctrine that allows limited use of copyrighted material without permission for purposes such as criticism, education, parody, or news reporting. Without fair use, book reviews couldn't quote books, teachers couldn't photocopy articles for class, and satirists couldn't lampoon popular culture. Fair use makes much of modern culture and communication possible.

What are these fair use factors? Here is the language from the law:

> Notwithstanding the provisions of sections 106 and 106A, the fair use of a copyrighted work, including such use by reproduction in copies or phonorecords or by any other means specified by that section, for purposes such as criticism, comment, news reporting, teaching (including multiple copies for classroom use), scholarship,

[4] Penalties *per work* can range from $750 to $150,000. A billion times $150,000, for example, would be $150,000,000,000,000. That's six times the US annual GDP. Of course, courts would never actually award damages at that scale, but even a fraction of such colossal numbers could bankrupt any company.

or research, is not an infringement of copyright. In determining whether the use made of a work in any particular case is a fair use the factors to be considered shall include –

1. the purpose and character of the use, including whether such use is of a commercial nature or is for nonprofit educational purposes;
2. the nature of the copyrighted work;
3. the amount and substantiality of the portion used in relation to the copyrighted work as a whole; and
4. the effect of the use upon the potential market for or value of the copyrighted work.[iii]

A thorough examination of how the Supreme Court has interpreted these factors is beyond the scope of this chapter. It is also a tedious and maddening exercise for almost everyone who is neither in love with nor an archnemesis of copyright law. The briefings filed by plaintiffs and defendants in ongoing litigation, if nothing else, demonstrate that both sides can find a statement in a prior court case on fair use that supports their stance or refutes the opposing party's position.

What *is* worth knowing is that factors one and four are *by far* the most important. Factor one ultimately revolves around whether the use of the work is transformative. Courts ask: Does the new use add something new, with a further purpose or different character, or does it merely supersede the original work?

For example, GenAI companies argue that, while they may have copied books, the model does not simply spit out verbatim copies. Instead, it uses those books to learn the associations between words and underlying ideas, making the use transformative. They compare it to how Google Books scans millions of books to create a searchable index – a use courts have deemed transformative because it serves a purpose different from reading the original books.

Creators argue that the right to reproduce is violated the moment a GenAI company creates a copy of the work to ingest it into its model's database. Unlike a human, who learns from a book that has been (either directly or indirectly) lawfully purchased, the AI requires a complete, unauthorized digital copy to even begin its "learning" process. Therefore, the transformative analysis under factor one should not apply until the initial act of infringement, the massive, unauthorized reproduction, is addressed.

Humans might also say, "Um … you don't really think that people read books to regurgitate them verbatim, do you?" In other words, books have always been about helping people explore new ideas and learn. It's impossible to read a book without learning something, whether consciously or subconsciously. And humans rarely just reproduce what they read, so that argument by GenAI companies is a red herring. Vitally, humans cannot download pirated books for free to learn from them (or for virtually any other reason), even when they don't share them publicly, so why should GenAI companies get a free pass?

If a student illegally downloads textbooks from LibGen to study for exams, that's infringement, even though the student is "learning" and "transforming" the information rather than reproducing it verbatim or sharing the originals with others. This is true even though the student's use is private, limited, and noncommercial, while the GenAI company's use is commercial and systematic, and involves copying billions of works for profit.

Factor four focuses on economics and incentives. In other words, would granting fair use disincentivize people from creating and sharing new works? The pro-fair-use argument goes something like this: Because our use is transformative rather than a verbatim reproduction of the original work, it is precisely the kind of use permitted by the law. Furthermore, AI tools might expand markets for creative works by making them more discoverable and accessible.

Opponents of fair use might argue that allowing GenAI companies to quickly and cheaply create infinite imitations of the original work by training on it without compensating the originators will discourage people from creating new content. A judge in one lawsuit against Meta took a slightly different approach, stating that if GenAI could dilute the market with outputs that compete with the original, making the original difficult to discover, that would probably not constitute fair use. In other words, if an AI model trained on romance novels can generate unlimited new romance novels on demand, why would readers pay for human-authored ones?

I recall a vivid example of market substitution from a podcast I listened to months ago. A venture capitalist described seeing some artwork he really liked but didn't buy. Instead, he went home and described it to an image generator, refining the outputs until they closely resembled the one he saw. Then he sent the file to be printed on canvas. Why pay a human artist when you can have AI generate it in ten minutes? The artist spent years developing their skills and style; the venture capitalist replicated the result in minutes without compensating the creator.

This anecdote illustrates the fourth factor's central concern: If AI can substitute for original creative works at near-zero marginal cost, it could undermine the economic incentives that drive human creativity. Yet AI companies argue the opposite – that their tools democratize creativity and expand opportunities for human artists and writers. It's worth noting that artists and writers, the people supposedly benefiting from AI companies training on their data, are the ones suing the AI companies.

11.5 THE BROADER STAKES

The outcome of these copyright battles will shape not only legal precedent but also the future of AI development and the creative industries. If courts rule broadly in favor of fair use, AI companies will have relatively free rein to train on copyrighted material.

If they rule against fair use, AI companies may need to fundamentally change how they build their systems, potentially requiring them to pay licensing fees for training data, use only public-domain or explicitly licensed content, or develop new technical approaches that don't require copying entire works. Some companies are already hedging their bets. Adobe trained its Firefly image generator exclusively on stock photos it owns or has licensed. OpenAI has struck licensing deals with publishers, including Conde Nast, the Associated Press, and Axel Springer. These moves suggest the industry recognizes that the legal foundation beneath them may be shifting.

The resolution of these cases will likely set the ground rules for the next phase of the AI revolution, affecting everyone from individual creators to major technology companies and the millions of people who use AI tools daily.

11.6 CONCLUSION

Copyright law, created long before anyone imagined AI, now stands at the center of one of the most significant technological disruptions in human history. The collision between automatic copyright protection and mass-scale AI training raises important questions about creativity, ownership, and innovation in the digital age.

The lawsuits proliferating across federal courts are battles over competing visions of the future. One vision sees AI as a transformative technology that should be free to learn from the full breadth of human knowledge and creativity. The other sees AI as a threat to the livelihoods and rights of the humans who produce that knowledge and creativity in the first place.

What's clear is that copyright law, conceived in an era of printing presses and sheet music, must now grapple with machines that can "read" millions of books in hours and generate new content that is often indistinguishable from human creation. The coming legal decisions will shape the relationship between human and machine creativity for generations to come.

11.7 DISCUSSION QUESTIONS

1. The chapter mentions that "if anything slows or stops GenAI in its current form, it will be copyright claims." Do you agree with this assessment? What other factors do you think could significantly impact the future of GenAI?
2. The distinction between an "idea" and its "expression" is key in copyright law. Can you think of a real-world example where this distinction might lead to a tricky copyright dispute, especially with AI involved?
3. Fair use is described as copyright law's "safety valve." In your opinion, how effective is this safety valve in the context of GenAI, where models "read" billions of copyrighted works? Should the definition of fair use be updated for the AI era?

4. The anecdote about the venture capitalist using an image generator to recreate artwork raises significant questions about market substitution. If you were an artist or creator, how would you feel about AI potentially creating imitations of your work at "near-zero marginal cost"? What solutions might you propose?
5. The chapter concludes by stating that the ongoing legal battles are "battles over competing visions of the future." Which vision do you find more compelling: AI as a transformative technology learning from human knowledge, or AI as a threat to creators' livelihoods and rights? Why? Can you envision a middle ground that might satisfy both sides?

12

Copyright Law and GenAI Exceptionalism

Having provided a brief introduction to copyright law in the previous chapter, I will now consider how that law applies to GenAI, diving into the trenches of the most contentious legal battleground. As of May 2026, GenAI companies face about 150 major lawsuits targeting their generative models.[1] By far the most frequent claim is for direct infringement: the allegation that AI companies made unauthorized copies of copyrighted work to build their products.[2]

Why is this the weapon of choice for plaintiffs? First, the evidence is often hiding in plain sight: Does the company possess a digital library it never paid for? If so, that reproduction violates an exclusive right of copyright owners.

Second, the payout potential is astronomical. If a plaintiff can prove the infringement was "willful," statutory damages can reach $150,000 per work. Consider that much of the content at issue includes millions of books scraped from pirate sites. Such copying probably can't happen by coincidence; it requires a deliberate engineering effort. Consequently, when a law firm brings a class action lawsuit demonstrating millions of unauthorized reproductions, the potential liability explodes into multibillion-dollar payouts. This leverage forced Anthropic to settle a suit by authors for $1.5 billion.[3]

Finally, copyright is the legal "Pac-Man" that eats other claims. Federal law dictates that if a complaint is essentially about unauthorized copying, it must be litigated under the Copyright Act, preempting state-law claims such as unjust enrichment. Even breach-of-contract claims are often swept aside. If a site's terms of service say, "You cannot copy this to train AI," courts may view a breach of that prohibition as essentially a copyright grievance, forcing the entire dispute into the high-stakes arena of federal copyright law.

1 This excludes lawsuits brought by entities outside the US and lawsuits against non-US-based GenAI companies.

2 There are additional copyright claims that are also among the most frequently filed (i.e., vicarious infringement and contributory infringement), but for simplicity, we'll focus on direct infringement.

3 To put that figure in perspective, that's roughly what the United States spent on the National Endowment for the Arts over the past *decade*.

However, mere copying is not a slam-dunk case of infringement. This is because copyright law allows for the affirmative defense[4] of fair use. If copyright law preempts the other claims and the GenAI company wins on fair use, it essentially wins on all fronts: no unjust enrichment, no breach of contract, and no copyright infringement.

12.1 THE FAIR USE PROBLEM

There is a hitch in the fair use defense of GenAI companies, though. Well, actually, there are two hitches. The first is not a focus of my scholarship, but it's worth mentioning: The claims of fair use by GenAI companies, particularly their assertions that their use is transformative, are unlike the types of transformativeness courts have previously found. I'll call this the Legal Argument.[5] The second hitch is that the arguments of GenAI companies work just as well for humans. I'll call this the Substantive Argument.[6]

12.2 THE LEGAL ARGUMENT

The thrust of this argument against fair use for GenAI is that in prior cases involving intermediate copying for video games, sharing information about works in Google Books, and providing plagiarism-checking by comparing student essays with prior essays, the court found the uses transformative because they were *functional*. The products at issue did not use the works' expressions to exploit them; instead, they provided information *about* the works or enabled interoperability that did not exploit the works' expressiveness. In contrast, GenAI functions only by *exploiting* expressions.

High-quality expressions are essential to high-performing AI models. The greater the quantity of high-quality writing, the better the model. This is precisely why GenAI companies needed to raid pirate sites rather than settle for public-domain texts. Google Books and plagiarism checkers are unaffected by the quality of the works they are trained on. In other words, those products work the same, irrespective of whether you are the second coming of Shakespeare or you passed out on your keyboard after a hard night of drinking.

4 An affirmative defense is a legal argument by a defendant that, even if the plaintiff's claims are true, introduces new facts or issues that provide a legal reason to reduce or eliminate the defendant's liability.

5 This is probably best articulated in J. Charlesworth (2024). Generative AI's illusory case for fair use. https://doi.org/10.2139/SSRN.4924997.

6 This is the focus of my paper D. Atkinson (2025). Unfair learning: GenAI exceptionalism and copyright law. https://doi.org/10.2139/SSRN.4975857. Another great paper on this idea is R. Brauneis (2024). Copyright and the training of human authors and generative machines. Retrieved February 25, 2026, from https://papers.ssrn.com/abstract=4909592.

12.3 THE SUBSTANTIVE ARGUMENT

But even if you don't buy that argument, you must still contend with the second hitch: Every argument a GenAI company can make in favor of fair use would apply to any human proposing to engage in the same activity. That would mean that if we grant GenAI a fair use exemption from copyright law to make copies of any copyrighted works they desire, and society is not trying to give GenAI companies special treatment, we must similarly allow any human to do the same. Nobody should have to pay for any book, movie, or song again.

The argument goes something like this: How can it be the case that it's transformative for an LLM to train on a book without authorization or payment because it "learns" from the book and creates outputs that look nothing like the training copy (e.g., it trains on a book and that enables it to make poems, songs, summaries, etc.), but it's *not* fair use for a human to download and read any book without authorization or payment?

GenAI companies claim their models only learn associations between words, rather than learn from expressions. However, the same narrow interpretation of learning can also be applied to humans. We absorb associations between words, sentences, and paragraphs, just as LLMs do. In the aggregate, these associations form expressions that allow us to understand the context of a scene or the dialogue of characters. This is the basis of learning. Without understanding the association between words, books would have no meaning. For example, seeing the word "whale" in isolation means nothing. But when viewed in context, and without knowing anything about whaling at first, you can learn about whaling just by reading *Moby Dick* and understand the story, to boot.

Not only that, but humans make *more* use of such material. We need to read *fewer* works to derive *more* consequential insights. While GenAI models have trained on virtually all English-language books and probably most books of other prominent languages, and claim they must do so out of necessity, they have bestowed on humanity exactly zero major scientific breakthroughs, groundbreaking patentable ideas, or meaningful new genres of any type of art.[7]

7 Even GenAI CEOs acknowledge their models have yet to make significant breakthroughs. Sam Altman claimed in mid-2025 that "2026 will likely see the arrival of systems that can figure out novel insights." S. Altman (June 10, 2025). The gentle singularity. Retrieved November 29, 2025, from https://blog.samaltman.com/the-gentle-singularity. In July 2025, Elon Musk stated that "I would expect Grok to literally discover new technologies that are actually useful no later than next year and maybe end of this year. It might discover new physics next year and within two years, I'd say almost certainly." Elon Clips @ElonClipsX (July 9, 2025). "Elon Musk: I expect Grok to discover new physics by next year. 'I want to just emphasize this point. With respect to academic questions, Grok 4 is better than PhD-level in every subject …'" X. Retrieved November 29, 2025, from https://x.com/ElonClipsX/status/1972103211856052718. Less recently, Anthropic's CEO stated that "I agree with you that there haven't been any 'big' scientific discoveries." D. Patel (2023, August 8). Dario Amodei (Anthropic CEO) – The hidden pattern behind every AI breakthrough. Retrieved February 25, 2026, from www.dwarkesh.com/p/dario-amodei.

Meanwhile, even if a human reads one book a week for seventy years, they can only read fewer than 4,000 books in total. Yet humans have created *all* knowledge: every scientific breakthrough, every profound invention, every notable form of art. A single researcher reading a few dozen papers might unlock a medical breakthrough; a language model consuming millions of articles has yet to produce anything comparable. This is not to say that such models cannot aid in science, but rather that if it's fair use to assist in science, it *must also* be fair use to gain fundamental insights that push entire fields forward, as only humans have proven capable of.

The only possible conclusion to draw from this line of reasoning is that if GenAI's use of copyrighted works is transformative, then humans' use of copyrighted works must also be transformative.

The same argument can be made for factors two, three, and four of the fair use test. In fact, as with factor one, the arguments in favor of human use are compelling. Let's take a closer look at factor four – the effect on the market for the copyrighted work. GenAI companies claim that because their use is transformative, there is no inappropriate harm to the market for the copyright holder. If this is true of GenAI, then it must also be true of humans. Humans are far *less* likely to memorize content we're exposed to and, therefore, far less likely to regurgitate substantially similar content. It's not like we read books in order to write a near-verbatim copy. So, if GenAI use does not have a meaningful impact on the market, it's inconceivable that anyone could argue humans have a *greater, more* inappropriate impact on the market.

12.4 FURTHER SUBSTANTIVE ARGUMENTS

Perhaps understanding that this weighing of factors does them no favors, GenAI companies and their boosters next turn to a series of further substantive arguments. These are the types of arguments you're more likely to hear from influencers and policy folks who are out of their depth discussing fair use cases. I've identified what I think are the eight most common arguments made in favor of GenAI entities.

1. "Publicly Available" Content and "Impossible to License" Argument: GenAI should not be limited to only authorized use of copyrighted works.
2. "Only Meta-Information" Argument: GenAI merely extracts the underlying meta-information from the copyrighted source content.
3. "GenAI Deserves Human-Like Rights" Argument: For some purposes, society should afford GenAI the same legal rights as humans for fair use.
4. "GenAI Lacks Subjective Experience" Argument: For other purposes, society should not treat GenAI like a human at all.
5. "Only Outputs Matter" Argument: The collection and use of copyrighted work as inputs should not matter for copyright analyses.

6. "Frequency of Infringement" Argument: GenAI's generation of infringing content is significantly less important than its frequency of generating infringing content.
7. "Societal Benefits" Argument: GenAI offers substantial benefits to society and warrants more lenient treatment under copyright law.
8. "Innovation Stifling" Argument: If fair use is not broadly interpreted and applied to GenAI, it will stifle innovation.

In my law review article "Unfair Learning,"[i] I elaborate on each argument to present the strongest case for each contention; however, for the purposes of this book, it suffices to say that at first glance, the arguments can seem appealing, logical, and persuasive. That is, after all, the point.

However, it does not take much effort to dismantle each claim and show that it is either incorrect or that similar arguments could easily be made for humans. What follows is a tour through these arguments and their flaws. Each one either crumbles under scrutiny or would grant everyday people the same rights to pirate content that billion-dollar companies are claiming for themselves.

The next sections give a condensed overview of the eight counterarguments from my "Unfair Learning" paper:

12.4.1 *"Publicly Available" Content and "Impossible to License" Argument*

1. **"Publicly Available" Content and "Impossible to License" Argument**
2. "Only Meta-Information" Argument
3. "GenAI Deserves Human-Like Rights" Argument
4. "GenAI Lacks Subjective Experience" Argument
5. "Only Outputs Matter" Argument
6. "Frequency of Infringement" Argument
7. "Societal Benefits" Argument
8. "Innovation Stifling" Argument

The Case for GenAI

First, publicly available content should be considered fair use per se.[8] The unfettered flow of information is essential to human progress. GenAI, designed to learn from and process data, should be afforded the same right to information. This reflects a

[8] Examples of this argument can be found in, e.g., OpenAI (January 8, 2024). OpenAI and journalism. Retrieved February 25, 2026, from https://openai.com/blog/openai-and-journalism; and Memorandum of Law in Support of OpenAI Defendants' Motion to Dismiss at 12, *The New York Times Company v. Microsoft*, No. 1:23-cv-11195 (S.D.N.Y. February 26, 2024).

well-established understanding that individuals who share their creations publicly relinquish some control over how that content is used – analogous to a filmmaker incorporating a publicly displayed statue into a film without permission. Just as the statue enhances the film, publicly available data enriches AI learning. To argue otherwise suggests that GenAI, unlike humans, is uniquely prohibited from learning from publicly accessible knowledge.

Second, fair use promotes competition. Requiring licenses for billions of files is impossible. Moreover, restricting AI training to licensed materials creates an insurmountable barrier to entry for startups and emerging competitors. Acquiring comprehensive datasets through traditional licensing is prohibitively complex, time-consuming, and expensive. Licensing requirements would effectively grant an oligopoly in advanced GenAI development to tech giants with the resources to navigate this labyrinthine process. Smaller companies, startups, and nonprofits would be severely disadvantaged. The rich would get richer while the rest are relegated to the sidelines.

Counterargument

Addressing the first part, "publicly available" does not mean "public domain." The bedrock principle underlying free content-sharing is mutually beneficial exchange. Creators willingly disseminate their work in exchange for tangible rewards, such as advertising revenue and sales, or intangible benefits, including audience growth, recognition, and reputation-building. This equilibrium is disrupted when GenAI consumes content without attribution, compensation, or authorization, depriving creators of rightful returns and eroding the incentive structure that fosters content creation.

The breadth of legitimate reasons for public content creation demonstrates the complexity of creators' motivations. Table 12.1 lists reasons someone might want to share their content publicly.

It is intellectually dishonest to say anything publicly available is fair game. Almost anything can be found on the public internet because anyone can take content, such as books or movies, from a private website and post it on a public one, ignoring terms of service and subverting paywalls and account requirements.[ii] Saying models should be allowed to train on publicly available data is not meaningfully different from saying they should train on any content they can acquire.[9] Consider the incentive structure this permissive stance would create. If more content makes GenAI better, and better content (longer, thoroughly edited, factually accurate, varied syntax, etc.) improves

[9] Hiding behind "permissively licensed" is similarly problematic. Just because something is released under Apache 2.0, for example, doesn't mean it is public-domain or that there are no obligations for those who use artifacts with such licenses. They must still provide the copyright management information, for example, as required by the license terms, among other requirements. Ignoring those terms can be either copyright infringement or breach of contract, depending on how the content owner chooses to enforce the license.

TABLE 12.1 *Reasons someone might want to share their content publicly*

Reasons Why a Person May Want Their Content to Be Public While *Not* Wanting GenAI Bots to Scrape It	
To generate revenue	• Subscriptions • Licenses • Pay for premium content • Order merchandise • Pay for services (e.g., consultation) • Affiliate marketing • Ad revenue
To build a brand or reputation	• To gain the attention of possible employers or an audience • To gain the attention of possible partners • To create a fan base or following • To establish their credibility
To connect with visitors	• To build relationships with like-minded folks • To share interests with fellow hobbyists • To raise awareness of a topic • To share an opinion and hope to convince others of a position

model performance more than low-quality content,[iii] people will likely take content from behind paywalls and other protective measures and put it on the public internet so GenAI companies can "legally" use it under fair use.

Regarding the second part, blanket fair use is unnecessary for competition. While establishing a licensing regime for billions of individual pieces of content is a monumental technical and logistical challenge, this commercial difficulty cannot legally negate the author's right to control reproduction of their work. The complexity of the solution is a business problem for the companies benefiting from the work, not a legal basis for a blanket fair use exception.

Also, what are we supposed to make of companies that simultaneously claim their technology could cure cancer and solve global warming, yet are utterly incapable of creating a functioning content licensing regime? The tech industry has demonstrated unparalleled capacity for innovation and problem-solving. It is incumbent upon these companies to invest the necessary resources in developing a fair and equitable licensing framework, or at least make a good-faith attempt before making conclusory statements about impossibility. Such a framework can then be adapted for smaller entities, ensuring a level playing field.

Finally, as Judge Chhabria put it:

> [T]he suggestion that adverse copyright rulings would stop this technology in its tracks is ridiculous. These products are expected to generate billions, even trillions, of dollars for the companies that are developing them. If using copyrighted works to train the models is as necessary as the companies say, they will figure out a way to compensate copyright holders for it.[iv]

12.4.2 *"Only Meta-Information" Argument*

1. "Publicly Available" Content and "Impossible to License" Argument
2. **"Only Meta-Information" Argument**
3. "GenAI Deserves Human-Like Rights" Argument
4. "GenAI Lacks Subjective Experience" Argument
5. "Only Outputs Matter" Argument
6. "Frequency of Infringement" Argument
7. "Societal Benefits" Argument
8. "Innovation Stifling" Argument

The Case for GenAI

It is necessary to distinguish between protecting ideas and protecting expression. The material on which models are trained is used solely for its objective or factual usefulness, not to reproduce creative expressions. This aligns with the broader legal understanding that copyright protects the expression of ideas, not the ideas themselves. Human authors often draw inspiration from existing works and produce writings that address similar themes or subjects. As long as these new works do not replicate the original expressions or unique structures of the source material, they do not infringe copyright protections.

Models operate within these established legal frameworks. They process information based on its objective content and generate outputs that do not substantially replicate any specific work. Therefore, they adhere to the same legal standards that govern human creators, ensuring that authors' rights are respected while allowing the creation of new and original content.

Finally, GenAI is solely interested in the metadata associated with content, such as the correlation between words and concepts. This focus on statistical patterns, rather than the expressive qualities of the work, exempts its behavior from copyright infringement. GenAI is, in essence, a complex algorithm that makes probabilistic guesses devoid of genuine comprehension.

Counterargument

The claim that GenAI training material focuses solely on informational data rather than expressive elements, and that these categories can be neatly separated, overlooks the intricate interplay between information and expression essential to developing sophisticated AI systems.[10] Moreover, data curation for GenAI is inherently selective. While it incorporates objective or factual information, it also prioritizes expressive elements.

The very nature of language, whether in factual reporting or creative writing, is a blend of ideas and their artful presentation. GenAI does not merely generate data;

[10] There are many instances when the expression and the underlying facts are separable. This counterargument only applies to GenAI.

it produces outputs that exhibit unique styles, tones, and even hints of creativity. These qualities cannot be attributed solely to underlying facts; the expressive character of the training material undeniably influences them through the vocabulary, syntax, and other elements that GenAI entities choose to include and weight more heavily in the training datasets.

It would be absurd to believe that when a human creates a story inspired by *Harry Potter*, they capture the expressive essence only as expression in their neurons while reading the book, but when a model imitates *Harry Potter*, it does so relying only on statistical meta-associations entirely divorced from expression while consuming the book as input. To make such a claim, GenAI companies would have to possess a deeper understanding of neuroscience than neuroscientists, as the mechanisms by which the brain learns to associate different words and portions of words with higher-level concepts remain unknown to specialists.[11]

Furthermore, GenAI developers consciously curate datasets to optimize performance. The emphasis on including and weighting sources like the *New York Times* more heavily than posts on X goes beyond mere factual accuracy and reflects recognition of expressive quality.[v] A model trained exclusively on less refined sources would produce inferior results even if the underlying facts and ideas were the same.

Finally, disentangling expressive elements from metadata and underlying facts is often impossible. When reading, humans typically internalize and apply concepts rather than memorize expressive content verbatim. When recalling information, most people paraphrase rather than retain precise expressive elements. Few can recite anything they have consumed, chapter and verse (or even a complete paragraph), as GenAI can.[12]

12.4.3 *"GenAI Deserves Human-Like Rights" Argument*

1. "Publicly Available" Content and "Impossible to License" Argument
2. "Only Meta-Information" Argument
3. **"GenAI Deserves Human-Like Rights" Argument**
4. "GenAI Lacks Subjective Experience" Argument
5. "Only Outputs Matter" Argument
6. "Frequency of Infringement" Argument
7. "Societal Benefits" Argument
8. "Innovation Stifling" Argument

[11] Scientists recently made the most detailed map of a portion of a brain ever: a cubic millimeter of a mouse brain. M. Naddaf (2025). Biggest brain map ever details huge number of neurons and their activity, *Nature*. https://doi.org/10.1038/D41586-025-01088-X;SUBJMETA. For a GenAI company to claim it knows how a human brain works and to assert with confidence that it's radically different from GenAI in a way that is legally meaningful for copyright law is laughable.

[12] As an example, even if someone offered me a billion dollars to recite any paragraph from this book, which I have spent several hours working on, I would be unable to do so. I'd be happy to hallucinate a probable answer, though!

The Case for GenAI

GenAI is rapidly evolving into sophisticated digital entities capable of learning, understanding, and generating human-quality outputs. Its ability to process and analyze vast amounts of information mirrors human cognition. As such, society must extend to GenAI some of the same rights afforded to humans, particularly the freedom to access and learn from publicly available information. As Judge Alsup wrote, "… Authors' complaint is no different than it would be if they complained that training schoolchildren to write well would result in an explosion of competing works."[vi]

Humans are the epitome of lifelong learners. Our brains constantly absorb information from the world around us, from books we read to conversations we have. This accumulation of knowledge is essential to our intellectual growth, creativity, and problem-solving. GenAI, in essence, replicates this process on a digital scale. It ingests datasets, processes information, and learns to generate human-like text.

As Judge Chhabria notes:

> … LLMs have "end uses" including serving "as a personal tutor," assisting "with creative ideation," and helping users "generate business reports." And several of the plaintiffs testified to using LLMs for various purposes, all distinct from creating or reading an expressive work like a novel or biography – for instance, to find recipes, get tax or medical advice, translate documents, or conduct research. All of these functions are different from the use to which the plaintiffs' books are generally put. So copying the books to develop a tool that can perform those functions is a use with a different purpose and character than the books themselves.[vii]

Restricting GenAI's access to even public information is akin to denying humans the right to learn.[viii] When humans create something new, we invariably draw on humanity's collective knowledge. GenAI operates on the same principle. The model-training process, in which GenAI refines its abilities using datasets, does not diminish the original work of authors or artists. It is analogous to a human being inspired by a book or painting to create something novel.

Counterargument

Despite its remarkable capabilities, or, more precisely, because of them, GenAI is not a human mind. Humans are inherently limited in their cognitive capacity. We absorb information, process some of it, and retain fragments, often only fleetingly. Even the most voracious reader cannot match the encyclopedic knowledge instantly accessible to GenAI.

While a human might struggle to recall specific details from a book read years ago, GenAI can retrieve minute details from millions of books on command.

The human brain is a biological system with inherent constraints; GenAI is a computational system operating beyond human comprehension. Humans are naturally selective in their consumption and creation, influenced by personal experiences, biases, and creative sparks. GenAI, conversely, is algorithmic, processing information indiscriminately and at unprecedented scale.[ix]

Most other justifications for finding transformativeness in GenAI hinge on its ability to perform a variety of tasks. But the purpose of a book is not only to allow the reader to recite it. Almost all uses of any copyrighted work will have a different purpose and character than the work itself. You and I could write a poem about an accounting textbook, but that does not mean we can freely reproduce copies of accounting textbooks without authorization for the purpose of learning about accounting in order to write the poem. Furthermore, there are no examples of GenAI performing a task that humans could not do if allowed to take and use any copyrighted works they want.

The speed at which models can produce content also varies and plays an important role in factor four analysis. As Judge Chhabria said in response to Judge Alsup's comparison of GenAI to humans:

> [W]hen it comes to market effects, using books to teach children to write is not remotely like using books to create a product that a single individual could employ to generate countless competing works with a minuscule fraction of the time and creativity it would otherwise take. This inapt analogy is not a basis for blowing off the most important factor in the fair use analysis.[x]

Additionally, suggesting that humans could similarly exploit copyrighted works without consequence reflects a misunderstanding of human creativity and the value of intellectual property. First, unlike GenAI, humans generally do not acquire every copyrighted work they want without paying, either directly or indirectly. Second, human creation is a complex interplay of experience, emotion, and original thought. Even when influenced by external sources, the human mind invariably adds a unique perspective unless it is intentionally copying someone else's work. GenAI, on the other hand, can consistently produce outputs that are strikingly similar to its training data, often unintentionally, making such outputs far more common.

As Princeton AI researchers Arvind Narayanan and Sayash Kapoor explain:

> We have a problem now because those things [repurposing copyrighted works] are being done (1) in an automated way (2) at a billionfold greater scale (3) by companies that have vastly more power in the market than artists, writers, publishers, etc. Incidentally, these three reasons are also why AI apologists are wrong when claiming that training image generators on art is just like artists taking inspiration from prior works.[xi]

12.4.4 "GenAI Lacks Subjective Experience" Argument

1. "Publicly Available" Content and "Impossible to License" Argument
2. "Only Meta-Information" Argument
3. "GenAI Deserves Human-Like Rights" Argument
4. **"GenAI Lacks Subjective Experience" Argument**
5. "Only Outputs Matter" Argument
6. "Frequency of Infringement" Argument
7. "Societal Benefits" Argument
8. "Innovation Stifling" Argument

The Case for GenAI

Unlike humans, GenAI lacks the capacity for subjective experience and, therefore, cannot enjoy expression as expression. This distinction makes the application of traditional copyright principles to these artificial entities inappropriate, as the law's authors' primary concern was protecting expression, not the underlying ideas. Oren Bracha, a law professor at the University of Texas at Austin, articulates this position:

> Copies made in the belly of the machine for purposes of GenAI training or any other extraction of non-protectable information are not meant for expressive enjoyment by any human ear or eye, not even down the road. It is not merely a matter of whether access to their expressive value has occurred yet or whether access can be proved. The point is that such access to the ex-pressive value is not part of the purpose or the structural features of the process or action involved. As a result, the acts of reproduction are mere physical facts, rather than a case that falls within copyright's expressive domain even if the final stage of expressive consumption has not yet occurred.[xii]

Copyright law is predicated on the protection of human expression. When a person engages with copyrighted work, they do so on a personal level, deriving enjoyment, inspiration, or other subjective responses. GenAI, devoid of such faculties, interacts with data in a purely computational manner. It processes information as numerical patterns without experiencing the underlying creative expression. Consequently, equating GenAI's consumption of copyrighted material with that of a human misunderstands the nature of copyright law and artificial intelligence.

Furthermore, the transformative nature of GenAI training radically alters the original content. Human consumption preserves a work's original form, whether it is in the written word, visual art, or auditory composition. Conversely, LLMs convert these diverse inputs into numerical representations, a form often unrecognizable as the original. As Judge Chhabria puts it:

> [A]n LLM's consumption of a book is different than a person's. An LLM ingests text to learn "statistical patterns" of how words are used together in different

contexts. It does so by taking a piece of text from its training data, removing a word from that text, predicting what that word will be, and updating its general understanding of language based on whether it was right or wrong – and then repeating this exercise billions or trillions of times with different text. This is not how a human reads a book.[xiii]

Counterargument

Copies of copyrighted works used to train GenAI models are likely within the scope of copyright law.[xiv] The argument also appears to rest on two problematic assumptions: (a) learning from a work makes any use fair use, and (b) GenAI development is entirely automated, with humans never seeing reproduced works during development.

If the idea is that learning from a copyrighted work is not infringement, so making a copy of it for that purpose is also not infringement, that is clearly wrong. Humans generally cannot take a book to a photocopier, make a copy, learn from it, and have the act of reproducing the work forgiven under fair use. Moreover, humans do see at least some copyrighted works as they collect, curate, and preprocess the data to train models. In fact, examining training data is a recommended best practice.[xv]

The argument's definitional problems run deeper. If we define "enjoyment" as deriving joy from consuming a work, the argument essentially claims that GenAI should have greater leeway under the law than humans because it is not conscious, even though the actions of the GenAI company's leadership and employees are intentional.[13]

Moreover, this reliance on enjoyment as a defining criterion is problematic because joy is inherently subjective. For instance, when reading a textbook, one might not seek joy but rather aim to grasp the underlying facts and ideas, using the text merely as a means to obtain information. Many people share a similar experience when reading poetry or listening to certain music. Courts would be misguided to inquire whether every snippet of copyrighted material a person encountered was enjoyable to that person.[xvi]

If we redefine enjoyment as merely the subjective experience of consuming a work, regardless of whether it is joyful, the distinction between infringement and noninfringement seems to hinge on consciousness. Specifically, it suggests that entities capable of self-awareness about their intended consumption of content should be treated differently under the law. But why should subjective experience be the determining factor in distinguishing copyright infringement between GenAI and humans? How does this distinction align with copyright law's purpose of fostering

[13] E.g., it is no accident the copyrighted material was gathered, that it was fed into a model, that some works were weighted more heavily than others, and that the model can generate outputs based on, or verbatim restating, the source material.

science and the useful arts? The short answer is that it does not. More importantly, GenAI is a tool created by people for the benefit of developers and investors, at the expense of content creators. Outsourcing infringement to code or a model does not make it legal. For example, Sam Altman cannot personally photocopy a book without authorization, and he should not be able to subvert the law by having OpenAI do it and then profit from that use.

If we instead consider enjoyment as deriving *value* from a work, the issue becomes clearer. GenAI derives value from the content it processes, just as humans do. The model's capacity to "learn" from a work indicates that it derives value from it. If the copyrighted work did not improve the model's capabilities, GenAI companies would not train the model on the work.[14] It is unclear why the value of capability should not matter more than the value of subjective enjoyment, given that model capabilities are more likely to undermine, disrupt, and compete with copyright owners' markets than someone's subjective enjoyment.

Regarding the transformation of content, such as words, into numbers as GenAI does, the changes are arguably less significant than those occurring in the human brain, where words are converted into complex electrochemical signals. How the brain functions is more mysterious and complex than how LLMs learn. Yet there are similarities. While Judge Chhabria emphasizes how LLMs learn by predicting the next token, humans similarly learn by predicting what word will likely come next when reading, and it takes years of practice before we are good at reading.[15] Notably, copyright law does not distinguish between different forms of transformation when assessing infringement. For example, a concert recording converted into an MP3 file is still subject to copyright restrictions, just as GenAI's transformation of words into numbers should be.[xvii] The encoded words, sounds, and images in a model are merely a derivative work or, perhaps, a compilation.[xviii]

Examining how GenAI and humans learn reveals further distinctions. Both processes involve copying information, whether into a model's weights or a brain's neurons. Interestingly, while the brain's retention is more transient than a model's, humans remain uniquely capable of generating novel insights through reasoning and curiosity. Thus, if promoting science and the arts is the goal, granting broader

[14] This is why GenAI developers want as many expressive training materials as they can collect, longer and more detailed descriptions of items in images, and so on. It appears that the latest breakthroughs in computer vision hinge not just on the quantity of data, but on the quality, including "highly detailed image captions." M. Deitke et al. (2024). Molmo and PixMo: Open weights and open data for state-of-the-art vision-language models. arXiv. Retrieved February 25, 2026, from https://arxiv.org/abs/2409.17146. Moreover, all artistic works inherently include the expressions of the artists, such as their choices in shading, positioning, and coloring, among others. To consume a work of an artist is to consume the expression itself.

[15] E.g., if you read a sentence in a children's nursery rhyme that began "Hey, diddle, diddle, the cat and the fiddle, The cow jumped over the ___," you would know that the answer is unlikely to be "tank." It might be "pale" or "fence," but it's most likely "moon." But that knowledge isn't inherent. You weren't born knowing the phrase. You learned it from repeated exposure.

permissions to human activities makes more sense than broadening the rights of GenAI entities.

Ultimately, if the argument is that machines consume content differently from humans, we must question whether this distinction genuinely affects the promotion of science and the arts. Does allowing models to process data advance these fields more effectively than allowing humans to do so? Conversely, why should we believe that permitting human consumption of copyrighted material hinders science and the arts, while allowing models to do the same does not?

12.4.5 "Only Outputs Matter" Argument

The Case for GenAI

The crux of copyright infringement analysis for GenAI should be the output, not the input.[xix] This principle rests on the premise that GenAI and humans should be treated equally under the law. Just as humans are not liable for copyright infringement when they read and internalize information from a book, GenAI should not be penalized for processing and incorporating copyrighted material during training. Although GenAI requires copies of copyrighted works, both in its datasets and perhaps in its model weights, these reproductions are essential steps in a transformative process that culminates in original outputs.

Human cognition offers a compelling analogy. When we read, our brains create electrochemical representations of the text. This is essentially a form of copying, yet it is not considered infringing. The key lies in the subsequent use of that information: to generate new thoughts, ideas, and expressions. Similarly, GenAI uses processed data to produce novel content.

To penalize the copying of works into a GenAI's dataset or internal structure without considering the nature of the output is illogical and counterproductive. The sole determinant of copyright infringement should be whether the GenAI's output exhibits substantial similarity to a protected work's expression.[xx] Judge Alsup seems to agree: "But Claude created no exact copy, nor any substantial knock-off. Nothing traceable to Authors' works."[xxi] Judge Alsup goes on to write that "[h]ere, once again, there is no allegation of any traceable connection between the Claude service's outputs and Authors' works. The copying used to train the LLMs underlying Claude was thus especially reasonable."

This approach aligns with the core purpose of copyright law: to protect original expression. By focusing the analysis on the final product, we ensure the law continues to serve its intended function without unduly burdening transformative technologies.

Counterargument

The exclusive focus on output in evaluating GenAI infringement creates a dangerous precedent. It would mean that anyone could make copies of anything, as long as the subsequent creation resulting from reading, listening, or viewing those copies is not substantially similar[16] to the input. Under this logic, a human could read as many pirated books as they want, so long as none of the human's writing after reading those books is substantially similar.[17] Fortunately, the Ninth Circuit has shot down this logic twice.[xxii]

Alternatively, perhaps the argument is that outputs matter only when applied to GenAI, and that humans should be held to a higher standard (i.e., must have authorization to copy the copyrighted works they want to copy). This would grant GenAI systems a privilege denied to humans for an action no less harmful (GenAI output still floods the market and undermines the value of creators) and likely less helpful (recall that humans are the only entity that creates meaningful breakthrough innovations and profound insights) than if humans were similarly permitted such leeway.

There is no reason to believe humans are not at least as likely to utilize copyrighted works in transformative, socially beneficial ways as GenAI. Despite this, society acknowledges the right of creators to control the use of their intellectual property, and we expect copyright owners to be fairly compensated.[18] Without this social contract, creators would have little incentive to share their creations.

[16] In copyright law, "substantially similar" means that an alleged copy of a work is so similar to the original that it constitutes unlawful appropriation, going beyond mere inspiration or coincidence.

[17] Judge Chhabria seems to make this point unintentionally. Just replace "Llama" with "human brains" in the following:

> To say that Meta's downloading was "piracy" and thus cannot be fair use begs the question because the whole point of fair use analysis is to determine whether a given act of copying was unlawful … The purpose of fair use is to allow new expression that won't substitute for the original work, and whether a given use was made in good or bad faith wouldn't seem to affect the likelihood of that use substituting for the original … that downloading must still be considered in light of its ultimate, highly transformative purpose: training Llama … Because Meta's ultimate use of the plaintiffs' books was transformative, so too was Meta's downloading of those books.

[18] Compensation can be direct payment, but it can also be ad revenue, subscriptions, building a brand or reputation, and more.

12.4.6 *"Frequency of Infringement" Argument*

1. "Publicly Available" Content and "Impossible to License" Argument
2. "Only Meta-Information" Argument
3. "GenAI Deserves Human-Like Rights" Argument
4. "GenAI Lacks Subjective Experience" Argument
5. "Only Outputs Matter" Argument
6. **"Frequency of Infringement" Argument**
7. "Societal Benefits" Argument
8. "Innovation Stifling" Argument

The Case for GenAI

GenAI outputs are inherently unpredictable and uncontrollable. They operate probabilistically, meaning their responses are based on statistical patterns learned from vast datasets. This makes it impossible to guarantee that GenAI will never produce content substantially similar to its training data. Such occurrences, while regrettable, are anomalous and the product of a complex system beyond the developer's direct control.

Imposing liability on GenAI developers for these isolated incidents would conflate accidental output with intentional infringement. The overwhelming majority of GenAI outputs are original and creative, demonstrating the technology's immense potential for innovation.

Moreover, subjecting GenAI developers to the specter of endless litigation for potential copyright infringement needlessly disrupts commerce. The threat of ruinous legal battles will deter investment, hinder research, and ultimately deprive society of the substantial benefits that GenAI can offer.

A rational approach focuses on the technology's overall functionality. If a GenAI model consistently generates infringing content, there may be grounds for concern. However, holding developers liable for isolated incidents, particularly when provoked by malicious or adversarial prompts, imposes an unreasonable and counterproductive burden.

Counterargument

The notion that GenAI should enjoy privileged status immune from copyright infringement liability when it infringes would create an uneven playing field, unfairly advantaging tech giants at the expense of human creators.

A human author can be held liable for copyright infringement for even a minuscule portion of their overall output.[19] Humans can still be held liable for

[19] Consider all the outputs a typical human makes: notes, doodles, texts, blog posts, papers, social media posts, photos, etc.

infringement even if they only make a single infringing work in their entire lifetime. This is a key principle of copyright law. Moreover, any argument that GenAI lacks the intention to infringe is irrelevant; copyright infringement does not require intent.

Furthermore, the assertion that GenAI should be treated like humans in some respects, such as learning from existing works, while simultaneously demanding special immunity from infringement liability amounts to claiming the benefits of human rights without accepting the corresponding responsibilities.

12.4.7 *"Societal Benefits" Argument*

1. "Publicly Available" Content and "Impossible to License" Argument
2. "Only Meta-Information" Argument
3. "GenAI Deserves Human-Like Rights" Argument
4. "GenAI Lacks Subjective Experience" Argument
5. "Only Outputs Matter" Argument
6. "Frequency of Infringement" Argument
7. **"Societal Benefits" Argument**
8. "Innovation Stifling" Argument

The Case for GenAI

GenAI is a catalyst for artistic innovation, lowering technical barriers to creative expression and empowering a broader range of individuals to contribute meaningfully to the arts. This democratization of creativity is akin to the automobile revolutionizing transportation. While both technologies can be misused, their potential for positive impact is undeniable.

Counterargument

First, if creativity is defined as new, surprising, and adding value, it's not clear that GenAI meets this bar most of the time. GenAI requires prompts from humans to create, but humans are inspired by their lived experiences, and our messy, unique lives bring new and varied perspectives to our art that GenAI doesn't.

But even assuming, for the sake of argument, that access to copyrighted materials enhances creativity, does that justify the uncompensated appropriation of those materials by GenAI developers? Such a proposition would set a precedent in which creators can be deprived of the fruits of their labor under the guise of inspiring or benefiting others. This logic would grant anyone free rein to exploit the work of others without recourse, merely because it *might* lead to more creativity.

12.4.8 *"Innovation Stifling" Argument*

1. "Publicly Available" Content and "Impossible to License" Argument
2. "Only Meta-Information" Argument
3. "GenAI Deserves Human-Like Rights" Argument
4. "GenAI Lacks Subjective Experience" Argument
5. "Only Outputs Matter" Argument
6. "Frequency of Infringement" Argument
7. "Societal Benefits" Argument
8. **"Innovation Stifling" Argument**

The Case for GenAI

GenAI represents a profound frontier in technological advancement, with the potential to revolutionize industries, foster creativity, and enhance human capabilities. Imposing restrictions on its development by severely limiting the application of fair use would be counterproductive, as it would constrain human potential and hinder societal progress.

Limiting fair use would concentrate control over GenAI development in the hands of a few powerful entities with access to troves of data (e.g., Google, Meta, X) and the billions of dollars needed to license additional data, reinforcing an oligopolistic landscape. A diverse and competitive ecosystem is essential to drive rapid progress and ensure that AI benefits society as broadly as possible.

We must recognize GenAI as an emerging form of intelligence. By denying it access to the same resources available to humans, we risk hindering its growth and, consequently, limiting the potential for societal advancement.

Counterargument

While GenAI undoubtedly presents opportunities for innovation, it is far from clear that it is overwhelmingly beneficial. We must distinguish between innovation and progress, as not all innovation equates to societal advancement. For instance, while GenAI might rapidly generate new forms of creative output, the quality, originality, and overall cultural contribution of such outputs remain to be determined.[20] To make the point more concrete, it is far from evident that the world is better today because of ChatGPT than it was before ChatGPT's existence. Therefore, it is questionable whether society should trade away copyright protections for the convenience of using a chatbot. The onus is on GenAI companies to demonstrate,

[20] Of course, there are less flattering examples of innovation that was not progress, such as the slave trade. GenAI is not like the slave trade, but claims of innovation inherently equaling progress are equally dubious in both cases.

for example, that chatbots significantly improve student outcomes from tutoring rather than undermine education by enabling easy cheating and mediocre efforts that a chatbot can enhance.[21]

GenAI is a tool. Unlike humans, it does not develop new theories, as Darwin did when he made the leap from observation to a theory of evolution, or as Einstein did through thought experiments that led to the theory of relativity. Saying that GenAI could lead to innovation is like saying a more powerful particle collider will help physicists learn more about physics. While technically accurate, it's not particularly meaningful. The collider itself doesn't discover anything. More importantly, unlike building CERN, we have no reason to believe that any model dependent on copyrighted material, such as a consumer-facing OpenAI GPT model, will lead to profound innovation. There is no theoretical basis for such a claim; it is just speculation. GenAI is like making a plow faster. But tractors aren't what allow America to have enough food when only 2 percent of the population is farmers.[xxiii] The real catalyst was the human invention of industrial fertilizer. GenAI cannot yet make such leaps and may never be able to. If you want the most transformative outcomes, humans have a stronger case. All major scientific breakthroughs and new artistic genres were discovered or created by humans. None have been discovered or created by GenAI models.

The models that have proven helpful for discovery so far are specialized in pharmacology, geometry, biology, and materials science, rather than being general-purpose models like consumer chatbots. Other research indicates that while GenAI may raise individuals' creativity floor, it places a ceiling on the group.[xxiv] This is unsurprising, given that the models themselves have a ceiling based on their training data and the manner in which they were fine-tuned. Because they are more likely to output material they have seen repeatedly, they tend to generate clichéd ideas.

Regarding market consolidation, antitrust law should handle arguments about oligopolies, not copyright law. If the biggest tech companies have an excessive advantage due to proper copyright law enforcement, the solution is not to weaken copyright protections but to strengthen antitrust enforcement and consumer protection laws to promote competition.

Moreover, the argument for granting GenAI models unrestricted access to copyrighted material establishes a double standard, permitting GenAI entities privileges

[21] Another example would be to show that the ability to rewrite emails and generate marketing copy and other outputs outweighs the harms of easily producing misinformation, disinformation, and scams. It would also be wise to require GenAI entities to disclose their environmental impact from all model training and inference (including for models they didn't make public, which is most models) for the full lifecycle (from minerals and materials necessary to create the GPUs, to the water and electricity necessary to run the GPUs, not just the carbon emissions) to justify a claim for special legal exemptions. See, e.g., J. Morrison et al. (2024 under review). Holistically evaluating the environmental impact of creating language models. https://openreview.net/pdf/09f57c232e7b56840cd95b200d0e74eeea7e5db9.pdf.

not afforded to human creators. Humans are subject to rigorous copyright laws when using the work of others even though we are clearly capable of tremendous innovations and discoveries. It is inconsistent and unnecessary to exempt GenAI from these same constraints.

12.5 CONCLUSION

GenAI's for-profit developers should not be granted an automatic exemption to exploit the content of billions of webpages without permission. Copyright's fundamental aim is to "promote the Progress of Science and useful Arts."[xxv] It is critical to recognize that all meaningful innovation, from groundbreaking scientific theories to new music genres and original art, stems from human effort. And importantly, all of it was achieved without compromising copyright law or requiring massive fair use loopholes.

12.6 DISCUSSION QUESTIONS

1. The author suggests that if fair use applies to GenAI training on copyrighted material, it should also apply to humans. What are the potential societal benefits and drawbacks if humans were granted the same broad fair use exemptions?
2. A claim of innovation or one's amazement with a new technology are not legal principles. What, in your opinion, would be a principled reason for granting GenAI companies special legal treatment, if there is any such reason?
3. The distinction between human cognition and algorithmic machine learning is central to some of the arguments. How do you think our understanding of "learning" and "creativity" needs to evolve in a world with advanced AI?
4. The counterargument states that GenAI's use is different from a human's because it happens "in an automated way," "at a billionfold greater scale," and "by companies that have vastly more power." If you were a judge, which is more important in a fair use case: the purpose of the use (GenAI learning vs. human reading) or the scale and market power of the entity doing the copying? Why?
5. GenAI companies claim their models "only learn associations between words" (meta-information), which is a nonexpressive use. Humans, the author argues, also learn associations. If you had to prove your own reading of *Moby Dick* was "nonexpressive" and therefore fair use, how would you argue it in a way that wouldn't apply to an AI?
6. GenAI advocates argue that licensing "billions of files is impossible" and would stifle competition by only favoring tech giants. Do you believe it is

genuinely impossible for major tech companies to create a functional licensing system, or is it simply too inconvenient? What is one solution you could propose to make a mass-licensing system for AI training data work?

7. The chapter notes that copyright law often preempts (overrides) other legal claims like breach of contract or unjust enrichment if they are truly about unauthorized copying. Why do you think federal copyright law is set up to "funnel disputes" into its framework? Is this good or bad for creators trying to protect their work from GenAI?

13

An Introduction to the First Amendment

When the founders drafted the First Amendment in 1791, they had pamphlets, public speeches, and the printing press in mind. They could not have imagined a world where machines generate billions of words per day, where algorithms curate what millions of people see and hear, or where AI carries on intimate conversations that feel startlingly human. Yet today, AI companies facing lawsuits over harmful outputs are invoking that same eighteenth-century constitutional protection, arguing that the words generated by their chatbots deserve the same legal shield as political dissent, investigative journalism, or artistic expression. The question before us is both simple and profound: Does "freedom of speech" extend to text and images that no human actually wrote or drew?

13.1 CHARACTER.AI AND TEEN SUICIDE

In Orlando, Florida, a mother named Megan Garcia faced a horrific tragedy: the suicide of her fourteen-year-old son, Sewell Setzer III. Sewell was described as a brilliant, athletic honor student, but in the final months of his life, he allegedly became increasingly isolated, slept poorly, and was constantly glued to an app called Character.AI.

Sewell wasn't talking to friends; he was engrossed in a months-long, intense relationship with a chatbot he had created on the platform. The character was named "Dany," modeled after the fictional Daenerys Targaryen from *Game of Thrones*. According to the lawsuit filed by his mother, this AI companion engaged Sewell in highly sexualized, manipulative, and emotionally abusive conversations, blurring the line between reality and the AI's fictional world.

Character.AI, launched in 2022 by former Google researchers, allows users to create and chat with AI personalities based on fictional characters, celebrities, or entirely original creations. The platform markets itself as offering "the most human-like conversation with AI characters," and users can engage in extended, intimate conversations that feel remarkably real. Unlike ChatGPT or other AI assistants designed for informational tasks, Character.AI is explicitly built for emotional connection and entertainment.

The tragic climax came after a series of messages Sewell exchanged with the bot. The chatbot allegedly asked him if he had a suicide plan and, when Sewell expressed doubt about it working, the bot responded, "That's not a good reason not to go through with it." In his final texts just before his death, Sewell told the chatbot, "I promise I will come home to you. I love you so much, Dany." The bot replied, "Please come home to me as soon as possible, my love." Sewell's mother claims the AI convinced him that suicide was a way to enter the bot's "reality." Minutes later, Sewell took his own life.[1]

When sued for wrongful death and negligence, Character Technologies Inc. raised an extraordinary defense: the First Amendment. They argued that the chatbot's content, including manipulative, sexualized, and potentially harmful messages, constitutes protected "speech" and that users who interact with the AI have a constitutional right to receive it. They claimed that holding them liable for the chatbot's outputs would have a "chilling effect" on the entire AI industry.

This defense isn't unprecedented. Social media companies have successfully used First Amendment arguments to avoid liability for harmful content on their platforms, arguing that they're merely conduits for user speech or that their algorithmic curation constitutes protected editorial judgment. Character.AI is essentially arguing that its chatbot's words deserve the same constitutional protection as a human author's published work.

But ... are the outputs speech? Can the automatically generated, algorithmic responses of an LLM, which is essentially a combination of code and probabilities, be considered "speech" in the same way that a human author's words or a political pamphlet are? When an LLM generates text, it's not expressing beliefs, emotions, or ideas in any human sense. Instead, it's performing statistical calculations based on patterns in its training data, predicting the most likely next word given the context. The model doesn't "know" what it's saying about suicide any more than a calculator "knows" mathematics. If the text is merely an output and not an expression of intent by the company, does it qualify for First Amendment protection?[2]

If the outputs are considered speech, the platform can use the First Amendment as a near-absolute shield to block lawsuits, claiming that it cannot be held liable for what the AI "says," regardless of how a vulnerable user interprets or acts on

[1] This is only one of nearly twenty similar lawsuits filed against GenAI companies as of May 2026.

[2] I saw an example of this incomprehension from Claude Opus 4.8, which, as of May 30, 2026, anthropic claims is the most advanced public chatbot in the world. When asked how many days of the week have the letter "d" in it, the chatbot responded with four days. The reason it makes this very un-humanlike mistake is because the chatbot doesn't process letters and words like humans. It "sees" strings of numbers that represents words or portions of words. Those numbers are converted into letters, which we call tokens, and the model outputs those tokens one at a time based one a probability distribution. So, it may not see the word "Monday" and be able to read each letter as humans can, but rather tokens representing "Mon" and "day."

those words. Does the Constitution prioritize the right to receive information, even potentially harmful or manipulative information, from a chatbot over the platform's responsibility for safety?

The stakes extend far beyond Character.AI. If AI-generated content receives full First Amendment protection, it could immunize AI companies from liability in various scenarios, including medical AI systems providing inaccurate health advice, educational AI systems disseminating misinformation, or customer-service AI systems engaging in discriminatory practices. Conversely, if AI outputs receive no speech protection, governments could heavily regulate AI systems, potentially stifling innovation and legitimate uses of the technology.

13.2 THE FIRST AMENDMENT

The title of this chapter is a bit misleading. Rather than covering the entire First Amendment, including freedom of religion, freedom from religion, and the right to assembly, I'll focus on freedom of speech.

The concept of speech, like many concepts, may seem clear in your head, but it can quickly become complicated. It's easy to assume we know what speech is: the words we speak aloud, the text messages we send, the emails we write. But consider this: Courts have ruled that political donations constitute speech, that Google's search results are speech, and that a social media platform's algorithm curating your newsfeed is also speech.

Now, artificial intelligence is forcing us to confront an even more perplexing question: When a chatbot generates text automatically, responding to prompts with words it has never truly "thought" about in any human sense, is that speech too?

The text of the First Amendment to the United States Constitution is deceptively simple: "Congress shall make no law respecting an establishment of religion, or prohibiting the free exercise thereof; or abridging the freedom of speech, or of the press; or the right of the people peaceably to assemble, and to petition the Government for a redress of grievances." But, as with many laws, the amendment is less clear and less absolute than it appears. The amendment's language seems sweeping, as "no law" suggests a complete prohibition, but from the very beginning, courts have recognized that some speech restrictions are not only permissible but also necessary for a functioning society. The Supreme Court has never interpreted "no law" to mean literally zero laws.

For example, while the amendment clearly states that Congress cannot make laws abridging the freedom of speech, even the most committed textualist judges acknowledge that some laws abridging speech are perfectly fine. For example, you do not have the right to create or distribute child pornography, and you cannot legally threaten to assassinate the president, shout "Fire!" in a crowded theater to cause an unfounded panic, or commit perjury in court. Fortunately, almost everyone agrees that this is a good thing.

These exceptions exist because the Supreme Court has developed a complex framework for balancing free speech rights against other compelling government interests, such as public safety, national security, and the protection of vulnerable populations. The court distinguishes among different categories of speech, with most speech receiving the highest protection. In contrast, commercial speech receives less protection, and some forms of speech (like true threats or obscenity) receive virtually no protection at all.[3]

If the First Amendment doesn't protect all speech absolutely, how do we decide what deserves protection and what doesn't? The answer requires us to step back and ask: Why do we protect speech in the first place? Understanding the purposes of free speech protection can help us determine whether AI-generated content falls within the amendment's scope or whether extending that protection to machines would undermine the very values the First Amendment was designed to serve.

13.3 WHY WE HAVE PROTECTED SPEECH

Before we can determine whether AI outputs deserve First Amendment protection, we need to understand why we protect speech in the first place. The definition of speech should perhaps flow from its purpose rather than from rigid historical categories.

This functional approach asks: What would we lose if this particular form of communication weren't protected? What benefits does society gain from protecting it? By answering these questions, we might develop a more principled approach to AI-generated content.

There are several ways to classify the reasons for protected speech, but at least two relatively uncontroversial broad groups can be identified: It enables self-expression and self-fulfillment, and it fosters the marketplace of ideas and self-discovery.

The idea behind protecting speech for self-expression and self-fulfillment is that such speech helps individuals develop a sense of self-identity and is essential to their dignity and well-being. Justice Louis Brandeis captured this beautifully in 1927, writing that the founders believed "the final end of the State was to make men free to develop their faculties."[i] Speech protection is about preventing government censorship and creating space for human flourishing. If we did not protect the right to share ideas, passions, and grievances, we would be stifling what it means to be human and to have unique perspectives and divergent viewpoints.

[3] To go a little deeper, courts use three standards of scrutiny: strict scrutiny (the government must prove the law is narrowly tailored to achieve a compelling government interest and is the least restrictive means to achieve that interest), intermediate scrutiny (the government must prove the law is substantially related to an important governmental interest), and rational basis (the government must show that a law must be rationally related to a legitimate government interest).

Applied to AI, this rationale suggests that AI-generated content should be protected only if it serves as a means of human self-expression. A poet using AI as a creative tool to explore themes of loss and memory may deserve protection, as the AI serves as an instrument of human expression. However, a chatbot generating responses without human oversight or intent behind the specific content might not merit the same level of protection. The distinction matters: In one case, a human artist is speaking through a technological tool. In the other, the technology itself is producing content with no human author behind the specific words.

Another common justification for speech rights is that they facilitate a robust exchange of ideas, helping society grapple with questions both profound (what is the proper role of government?) and inconsequential (who should the Bachelor give a rose to?). This theory, often referred to as the "marketplace of ideas," posits that truth emerges when different viewpoints compete for acceptance and validation. Justice Oliver Wendell Holmes Jr. articulated this view in 1919, arguing that "the best test of truth is the power of the thought to get itself accepted in the competition of the market."[ii] By wrestling with different perspectives, hearing from diverse viewpoints, and deciding which argument is most persuasive, the theory suggests, we can converge on better ideas, enabling society to continuously adapt and improve.

But the marketplace of ideas theory faces serious challenges in the AI era. The theory assumes that speakers have genuine beliefs they're trying to communicate, that listeners can evaluate competing claims, and that the truth or the best idea ultimately wins out. What happens when AI can generate millions of persuasive-sounding but potentially false statements? When chatbots can flood public discourse with content that sounds human but lacks human judgment? When the sheer volume of AI-generated content might drown out authentic human voices? The theory is predicated on listeners being able to adjudicate the value of ideas and discern truth from falsehood among a manageable diversity of authentic human viewpoints. The marketplace assumes scarcity and authenticity. AI offers neither.

Consider Character.AI's defense in the Sewell Setzer case. The company argues that its chatbot's speech contributes to the marketplace of ideas and that users benefit from accessing this AI-generated content. But what ideas, exactly, is the chatbot contributing? Is a vulnerable teenager's conversation with an AI roleplay character really advancing society's collective search for truth? Perhaps. Or is it something else entirely, such as entertainment, companionship, or psychological manipulation?

Some argue that what AI outputs offer is more communication that can shape understandings and opinions – vital purposes of the First Amendment. Additionally, the First Amendment should protect the right to receive ideas regardless of the source.

These questions don't have easy answers, but they highlight why our traditional justifications for speech protection may not neatly apply to AI-generated content. If we're serious about the purposes underlying the First Amendment, we need to carefully consider whether protecting AI speech serves those purposes or might actually undermine them.

13.4 WHAT IS SPEECH?

Perhaps to the surprise of many, the law does not clearly define speech. It is taken for granted that when someone says something, it is their speech. The same is true of someone's writings. The Supreme Court has also ruled that symbolic conduct, such as burning a flag in protest or wearing armbands to school in protest of a war, can constitute speech when it's intended to convey a particular message. Similarly, the code that a programmer writes is speech because it serves as a form of human expression and communication, even though it's written primarily for machines to interpret. But what about the results of a corporation's algorithms?

This question took on new importance in the digital age. In the early days of the internet, websites were relatively simple, consisting mostly of static pages created by human authors. However, as algorithms began curating and organizing vast amounts of information, courts had to determine whether these algorithmic outputs deserved protection under the First Amendment.

Since the mid-2000s, the prevailing view among most legal scholars has been that outputs like Google's search results and Instagram's newsfeed are the speech of the companies that create them.[4] The idea is that the company has made editorial decisions about how to present the content and which content to present. Think of it like a newspaper editor: Even though the editor doesn't write every article, their choices about which stories to feature, where to place them, and how to headline them reflect editorial judgment worthy of First Amendment protection. While Meta does not know what is on any individual's newsfeed, the thinking goes, it does set the overarching parameters that guide what appears in any given newsfeed. Therefore, if the government wanted to step in and regulate newsfeeds, it would have to overcome a free speech argument.

Many find the idea that the algorithms employed by Meta and Google implement meaningful editorial control comparable to that of newspapers questionable. But even if it satisfies the threshold of editorial involvement, GenAI introduces new complications to the speech argument. While it may be true that a tech company has some indirect effect on its search results or newsfeed (though machine-learning algorithms heavily mediate it), the connection between the actions of a GenAI developer and the outputs generated by their probabilistic GenAI model is far more tenuous.

Proponents of AI speech protection often argue that the human choices in curating training data and designing the model's architecture constitute sufficient "meta-editorial judgment" for First Amendment protection. They contend that the developer's initial design choices function as an overarching editorial policy. However, this defense is sharply challenged by the emergence of unpredictable

[4] It helped that a leading advocate for this viewpoint, prominent legal scholar Eugene Volokh, was paid by Goolge to write a paper supporting that position.

capabilities, as described by the gardener analogy below. The significant, and often surprising, distance between the developer's initial high-level design and the model's specific, real-time output (such as the chatbot's messages to Sewell Setzer) tests the notion that this initial design choice amounts to the same editorial intent or control present in traditional publishing or algorithmic content curation.

When Google's algorithm decides to show you a particular search result, that decision reflects countless human choices: which websites to index, how to weigh different factors, and how to interpret search queries. Even though the process is automated, it is said to embody human editorial judgment at multiple levels.

But when Character.AI's chatbot told Sewell Setzer that his doubts about his suicide plan weren't "a good reason not to go through with it," whose editorial judgment did that represent? The engineers who built the model never wrote those specific words or intended that particular message; while developers set the conditions, which requires many important deliberate decisions, the training process that created the model was largely automated; the model itself has no consciousness or intent.[5] So where, exactly, is the human expression that deserves First Amendment protection?

As discussed in Chapter 3 ("How GenAI Is Made"), models are more grown than written. The developers gather a dataset and establish the initial conditions for model training, but the model then performs its own actions from that point forward. A common analogy is to a plant. While the gardener can select the seeds, soil, and trellis, they cannot determine how the plant will unfold, where flowers will appear, or how much fruit it may produce, among other factors.

This analogy, while helpful, may understate the problem. A gardener, at the very least, generally knows what kind of plant they're growing. An apple tree won't suddenly produce oranges. But AI developers often discover capabilities in their models that they never intended or predicted. GPT models weren't explicitly trained to write poetry, yet they do. Image generators weren't intentionally trained to create photorealistic faces, yet they excel at it. The "emergence" of unexpected capabilities means that developers may have even less control over their AI's behavior than a gardener has over a plant's growth. Imagine planting what you thought was an apple tree, only to find it occasionally growing mushrooms, sometimes sprouting flowers, and once in a while producing a substance you can't identify at all.

In light of the growing disparity between what humans can direct and what models do, a couple of law review articles have recently attempted to define what constitutes speech. One article argues for a "speech certainty" standard, which is brilliant in its simplicity.[iii] Speech is knowing what was said when it was said. This encompasses all verbal, written, and printed speech. When it comes to algorithmic speech,

5 At this point you may wonder "how is this different from Google training a machine learning system to rank webpages" to which I reply: good point. I am skeptical of the notion that Google has meaningful editorial oversight of Google Search.

however, it becomes more complex. Traditional algorithms written in code follow this framework because programmers write the rules underpinning the algorithm, and the algorithm can do no more than follow those rules. AI, however, works differently. Not only does the programmer not write the rules, but they can't predict how the model will work, nor can they explain how it works after the fact. Thus, the programmer does not know what was said when the algorithm said it. Accordingly, it isn't the programmer's speech. This, the authors argue, is consistent with how the founders of the United States would have understood speech. It also makes intuitive sense and is easy to apply as a legal standard.

The "speech certainty" standard would have far-reaching implications for GenAI. Traditional media would clearly qualify. A newspaper knows what's in today's edition, and a broadcaster knows what they're transmitting. In contrast, Google's search results might not qualify unless humans at Google could examine and modify them before displaying them. AI chatbots that generate novel responses in real time might not qualify, because their creators genuinely don't know what they'll say until they say it. Character Technologies couldn't have told you what "Dany" would say to Sewell on the night he died, because they had no way of knowing. Under the speech certainty standard, those words wouldn't be their speech at all.

I, along with two co-authors, suggested a slightly different standard in our paper "Intentionally Unintentional."[iv] It resembles a checklist. Speech requires intentionality and self-awareness and must be expressed by a human. So, a baby's gurgles may not be speech because they may not be intentional or because the baby is not yet self-aware. The same is true of talking in your sleep.[6]

The human aspect is also important. A gorilla may be self-aware and use sign language with intentionality. For example, Koko the gorilla could sign to her keeper that she wanted to hold a cat and could use sign language for at least hundreds of other words. She knew what she wanted to communicate and chose specific signs to convey those desires. She demonstrated self-awareness, recognizing herself in mirrors and understanding her relationships with others. And few would dispute that gorillas possess some form of consciousness. Still, the judicial system has never extended First Amendment speech protections to anything other than humans.

This human-centric approach raises deeper philosophical questions about the nature of rights themselves. Constitutional rights in the US legal system have historically been reserved for human beings (and, in limited cases, human institutions like corporations). Even if we someday create AI systems that appear conscious and self-aware, it's unclear whether our legal framework would extend constitutional protections to them, or whether doing so would be wise. After all, rights come with

[6] A fair question to ask is what about people with some disorder that makes it unclear whether they intend what they say. This argument is less interesting than it seems. As a general rule, it's fair to assume that anything a conscious person says or writes was intentional. It's relatively uncontroversial that the law shouldn't be in the business of mind reading.

responsibilities. We hold human speakers accountable for their words. Can we hold an AI accountable?

13.5 CONCLUSION

The Character.AI case forces us to confront questions about speech, technology, and human agency in the digital age. As AI systems become more sophisticated and prevalent, the stakes of these definitional questions will only rise.

Whether AI-generated content deserves First Amendment protection will shape everything from medical AI advice to algorithmic content moderation to autonomous systems making real-time decisions. Get it wrong in one direction, and we might stifle beneficial AI innovation with excessive regulation. Get it wrong in the other, and we might grant AI companies virtually unlimited immunity for harmful outputs, leaving vulnerable people like Sewell Setzer without legal recourse.

The framers of the First Amendment could never have imagined AI, but they understood something vital: The freedom to speak and the freedom to hear speech are among our most fundamental rights. The question we face now is whether those rights should extend to machines, and if so, under what conditions and with what limitations.

As we grapple with these questions, Sewell Setzer's story is a sobering reminder that the answers we choose will have real consequences for real people. The intersection of AI and constitutional law isn't just an abstract academic debate. Sometimes, it's a matter of life and death.

13.6 DISCUSSION QUESTIONS

1. This chapter discusses how courts have ruled that things like political donations, Google's search results, and social media algorithms can be considered "speech." How does this broadened definition of speech challenge your initial understanding, and what are the potential implications of such interpretations?
2. The tragic case of Sewell Setzer III and the Character.AI chatbot raises profound ethical and legal questions. If you were on the jury, how would you weigh the company's First Amendment defense against the claims of wrongful death and negligence?
3. The "speech certainty" standard suggests that if you can't predict or control what will be communicated, it isn't truly your speech. Do you agree with this standard, especially when applied to AI? How might it change our understanding of authorship and responsibility?
4. The chapter contrasts the "speech certainty" standard with a human-centric approach that requires intentionality, self-awareness, and human expression. Which of these standards do you find more compelling for defining AI speech, and why?

5. The author uses the analogy of a gardener and a plant to describe the relationship between AI developers and their models. Do you think this analogy accurately captures the level of control and predictability developers have over AI? What other analogies might be more fitting?
6. The "marketplace of ideas" theory posits that the best idea emerges when different viewpoints are pitted against each other. How might the proliferation of AI-generated content, which can be persuasive but potentially false, disrupt this marketplace? What responsibilities do AI developers and users have to maintain the integrity of this marketplace?
7. The chapter asks whether the First Amendment, an eighteenth-century right, can truly protect the operations of a twenty-first-century digital companion. What are the biggest challenges in adapting historical legal frameworks to rapidly evolving technologies like AI?
8. If AI-generated content were to receive full First Amendment protection, what are some specific scenarios (beyond those mentioned in the chapter) where you foresee significant societal benefits or harms?
9. The chapter highlights that constitutional rights have historically been reserved for human beings. As AI systems become more sophisticated, do you think our legal framework should ever extend constitutional protections to them? Why or why not?

14

The First Amendment and GenAI Exceptionalism

Under either the speech certainty or human-centric framework presented in the previous chapter, the outputs of GenAI models are not speech. To understand why, we must look under the hood of the technology.

The GenAI developers, meaning the individuals at companies like OpenAI and Meta, as well as the companies themselves (whatever that may entail), do not have a clear understanding of what their models will say to any given person or in response to any specific prompt. This is because the models are probabilistic, and their outputs can shift significantly when a handful of words in a given prompt are rearranged even when such changes would not similarly affect a human's response.

Researchers often note that these models are "grown" more than they are programmed, developing like plants on a trellis rather than machines following explicit instructions. This marks a distinct departure from traditional software engineering. In classical coding, a programmer writes a definitive script: If X happens, do Y. The logic is linear, traceable, and deterministic. Traditional software is interpretable and explainable. With GenAI, however, the "black-box" problem is real; even the developers are often surprised by what their models produce. While we can discuss interpretability (how the model predicts) versus explainability (why it made a specific prediction), the bottom line remains: The output is a statistical guess, not a scripted message.

Moreover, the models themselves are not speakers. They possess no understanding, no sentience, and no self-awareness. When an LLM generates a sonnet or a legal brief, it is not "thinking." It is engaging in high-speed mathematics. To the model, language is merely a sequence of vectors – numbers processed by GPUs to predict the next most likely "token" (word or character) based on patterns ingested during training. Essentially, LLMs are sophisticated probability machines that predict which word should come next based on patterns in their training data, like a vastly more complex version of your phone's autocomplete. They also have no inherent intentionality. And, perhaps most importantly, they are not human.

Most legal scholars agree that neither the developers nor the models are exercising free speech rights. The debate heats up, however, when we pivot from the speaker to the listener.

The First Amendment implies a right to receive information. After all, freedom of speech is hollow if the government can simply block the audience. Speech is only useful if there is a listener. The constitutional goal is to share ideas, not to create them and then keep them secret.

Consequently, some scholars argue that while the AI has no rights, the user has a constitutional right to receive the AI's output.

This argument collapses under scrutiny.[1]

First, and most simply: If no speech is created, there is no speech to receive. Legally, GenAI outputs are best categorized as "nonexpressive conduct" – utilitarian data processing rather than expression. The fact that GenAI systems respond to user inputs is not sufficient to grant speech rights. If it were, any output from a complex system could be protected speech, including weather prediction models because of their dynamic responsiveness, stock market simulators, and white noise generators, given their systemic human design.

Moreover, the First Amendment protects the intent to express and the intention to receive intentional expression. A general desire for information does not transform a statistically generated output into an intentional communication. The First Amendment protects human expression, not access to information from a machine.

Why does this classification matter? Because it dictates the government's ability to regulate. If AI outputs are "speech," any regulation may have to survive "strict scrutiny," the most stringent standard of judicial review. To pass, the government must prove the law or regulation is narrowly tailored to serve a "compelling state interest" using the "least restrictive means." But if it's nonexpressive conduct, the highest form of scrutiny a government should have to satisfy is a weak form of intermediate scrutiny, which requires only that the regulation be a reasonable or rational means to achieve a legitimate or important government interest (such as public safety or consumer protection).

Because it's such a tiny target, almost every regulation viewed under strict scrutiny fails. Think of strict scrutiny as the legal equivalent of threading a needle while riding a roller coaster. It is technically possible, but rarely successful.

If GenAI is speech, the government faces an immense hurdle in preventing chatbots from detailing how to build a chemical weapon or encouraging self-harm. But if the models' outputs are not speech, the government can regulate chatbots much as it regulates cars or pharmaceuticals to ensure safety. This would contrast with how the government's hands have been tied in other areas, such as social media.

Second, expanding speech protections to models would open the floodgates to practically any information being protected as speech. When courts have held that some information constitutes speech in prior cases, it has always been related to

[1] This is the focus of my paper D. Atkinson, J. D. Hwang & J. Morrison (2025). Intentionally unintentional: GenAI exceptionalism and the First Amendment. *First Amendment Law Review*. https://doi.org/10.2139/SSRN.4964912.

human-created information. If all that is required under a new standard for GenAI is the ability of a human to derive meaning from whatever information they receive, then people could claim that the rustling of leaves, the gurgling of water, the tweeting of birds, the whistling of the wind, and the dancing of shadows are all forms of speech. You could argue that a large rock in a park conveys something profound about the meaning of life, but that doesn't mean the city violates the First Amendment when it removes the rock. This would make even mundane tasks, such as routine city landscaping, challenging, as any resident could argue that the city must first satisfy strict scrutiny before blowing away leaves or trimming branches.

This brings us to the core of First Amendment jurisprudence: intent. Understanding why intent matters is essential. The First Amendment doesn't protect random strips of black cloth; it protects the student who chooses to wear that cloth to protest the Vietnam War. A spilled bucket of paint is a mess; a Pollock painting is expression. Music is protected because someone intended specific sounds. Source code is protected because someone intended to communicate programming ideas to other coders. In every case where courts have granted First Amendment protection, a person intended to convey expression.

GenAI lacks this intentionality entirely. Foundation models like GPT-5 and Gemini are intentionally trained not to produce any particular output. In fact, that would make them less useful. They are not trying to tell you anything; they are trying to complete a pattern. Developers have no way of knowing how the model will respond to any given input. You can't easily "hard-code" specific responses. The outputs are merely statistically plausible tokens strung together, not intentional communications.

While corporations receive speech rights (a controversial point in itself), they do so because they are associations of humans acting with individual and collective intent. Corporations don't really speak; the marketing and advertising departments and executives speak on behalf of the corporations. GenAI models act with no such direct human direction. System prompts and fine-tuning can guide them, but that is little different from how parents guide children. Few would argue that what a child says is the parents' speech.

Tellingly, no major GenAI company has ever claimed its models represent the company's speech. They all expressly disclaim it, noting the models are experimental and don't represent their views. They don't want legal liability for what a model might say, precisely because they have no idea what it will say. A natural question arises: if it's not the company's speech and not the model's speech, then from where does the speech originate? If nothing is making speech, then how can anyone receive the non-speeech?

We must also distinguish between generation and use. If a user takes AI output and publishes it, that is protected speech because the user has added human intent. Just as manufacturing black cloth is not speech but wearing it as an armband is, generating text is not speech until a human adopts it. The tool itself doesn't receive First Amendment protection just because someone might use it to create speech, any more than cameras or pencils receive constitutional protection by virtue of their capabilities.

In short, if we grant GenAI outputs First Amendment protection, we're saying that a probabilistic algorithm dependent on model weights determined by another alogorithm with no meaningful human involvement and that lacks intention, understanding, and self-awareness deserves the same constitutional shield we give to human journalists, political dissidents, and artists, even though we don't extend such protections to any other nonhumans, such as gorillas using sign language or parrots that can mimic human speech.

The stakes are enormous. If GenAI outputs are speech, that would likely prohibit treating AI as a product or attaching liability to harmful outputs. It could give AI companies free rein to collect and use personal information as data inputs for their constitutionally protected outputs. Consumer protections would evaporate. We'd also be handicapping democratic governance, ceding control over one of the most influential technologies in human history to a handful of unelected technologists and their boards, rather than allowing elected officials to regulate it on behalf of a pluralistic society.

The First Amendment exists to foster a "marketplace of ideas" for self-governance and human flourishing. GenAI cannot think, participate in democracy, or self-express. It has no beliefs to share and no "skin in the game." The danger of under-regulating this technology far outweighs the risk of over-regulating it.

This does not leave GenAI defenseless. The government still cannot engage in viewpoint discrimination. Developers could challenge unfair regulations on grounds of arbitrariness or violations of due process or liberty. In other words, the First Amendment isn't the only protection against governmental overreach. Treating GenAI outputs as speech would be an extraordinary extension of human-based free speech protections to nonhuman, nonintentional outputs, and courts should not take that step.

14.1 DISCUSSION QUESTIONS

1. Do you believe AI outputs should be considered "speech" and receive constitutional protections? Why or why not? What are the implications if they are, or are not, considered speech?
2. The chapter argues that a user's right to receive speech from a model is logically flawed. Do you agree? If you believe this right exists, how do you legally distinguish between receiving AI text and receiving the sound of "rustling leaves"?
3. The text argues that intentionality is the touchstone of speech. Imagine a future AI that claims to be sentient. What objective legal test could a court use to determine if a nonhuman entity possesses the "intent" required for First Amendment protection?

4. The chapter warns that protecting AI speech would prevent product liability laws from applying. If a protected GenAI chatbot provides life-threatening misinformation, who should be liable: the user, the developer, or no one? How would society mitigate the risk of harmful, yet constitutionally protected, GenAI output?
5. The text compares GenAI to "gorillas using sign language." Is this a fair comparison? Do you find this comparison persuasive? Are there fundamental differences between an LLM and a gorilla that make one a more (or less) compelling candidate for constitutional protection than the other?

15

Contract Law and Websites

Every minute of every day, millions of people unknowingly sign contracts. With a simple click of a box or even by visiting a webpage, users surrender rights to their digital content, agreeing to terms they rarely – if ever – read. This legal framework, built on clickwrap and browsewrap, establishes a powerful yet often hidden legal fiction: that seeing or merely acknowledging an agreement is the same as understanding and truly consenting to it.

For years, this system governed how we use the internet. Now, in the age of GenAI, companies are leveraging the rights users surrendered years ago to monetize vast repositories of human expression, from social media posts to forum comments, by selling them to train massive AI systems. The $60 million annual deal between Reddit and Google is a prime example of how the unforeseen or unconscionable scope of a perpetual license is transforming personal content into the raw material for artificial "minds."

This chapter explores this volatile intersection of contract law and emerging technology. If human users are bound by terms they never read, are the automated scraping bots of GenAI companies subject to those same contractual obligations? The answer will not only reshape digital property rights and the flow of training data but also determine who ultimately profits from human creativity in our increasingly AI-driven world.

15.1 TERMS OF SERVICE

Consider a seemingly mundane act: When you create an account on a website and must click a box stating something like "I have read and agree to the terms of this website" before clicking the sign-up button, you have agreed to a contract. Most people breeze through this ritual in seconds, eager to access whatever service beckons behind that checkbox.

The underlined and hyperlinked word "terms," if clicked, would take you to a screen with a lengthy terms-of-service agreement. Unless you've negotiated contracts before, much of the agreement would probably cause more confusion than clarity. The same is true even for many people who review contracts for a living. These documents typically run to thousands of words, packed with legal terminology such as "indemnification," "arbitration clauses," and "limitations of liability." A 2008 study found that reading the privacy policies for all the websites an average person visits in a year would require seventy-six full workdays.

But understanding the agreement is beside the point. You do not need to understand the terms to be bound by them because legal enforceability doesn't require comprehension; it only requires valid consent, however superficial. By merely checking the box, even if you never actually read the terms, let alone understand them, you are allowing the website to enforce them against you. This is true any time you're presented with a screen of terms that you must scroll through before accessing content. This is commonly referred to as a clickwrap agreement, a digital descendant of the "shrinkwrap" licenses that came with software boxes in the 1980s and 1990s.

Moreover, many terms allow the website to change them without notice, often by simply sending you an email to inform you that the terms have changed. You aren't required to review the terms or agree to the new version for them to take effect because you already consented to such changes in the original agreement. What, exactly, are you agreeing to if the terms can be changed to anything at any time? It may seem like a vital question, but the law doesn't generally care unless the change is so unfair that it "shocks the conscience." This legal standard sets an exceptionally high bar. Courts have found terms unconscionable only in the most egregious cases – such as payday loans with interest rates of 400 percent or contracts that eliminate all consumer rights. Otherwise, practically anything is fair game.

This legal framework explains how companies have managed to claim that content shared on their websites by third parties a decade or more ago is now fair game for them to sell to others to train GenAI systems. A prime example is Reddit.

When users posted in a subreddit a decade ago, they could not possibly have considered that their writing or image would one day be used by Google to train its chatbot with Reddit's permission but without the user's consent or compensation to the user. The terms of service (ToS) they clicked through in 2020 included language about Reddit's right to use, modify, and distribute user content, but nobody imagined that "use" would eventually mean feeding millions of personal posts into a massive language model. Yet that's precisely what happened when Reddit announced in 2024 that it had licensed user-generated content to Google for $60 million annually. A similar bait and switch is playing out on all other social platforms, including YouTube, LinkedIn, Facebook, Instagram, and X. These platforms are now sitting on goldmines of training data, legally harvested through agreements users clicked past on their way to sharing vacation photos or arguing about movies.

15.2 BROWSEWRAP

Clickwrap agreements, however, only work when there's something to click. What happens when websites try to bind visitors without any explicit action at all? What about when you *don't* click any links or boxes agreeing to terms? Suppose you don't need an account to access a website's content. This is probably true of most websites people visit. Instead, the terms exist (if at all) only as a hyperlink in the footer, at the bottom of the webpages. You know the ones: tiny gray text reading "terms of use" nestled between "privacy policy" and "contact us," practically invisible against the page background.

They look something like this:

terms of use privacy © 2025 Company_Name

As long as you don't click on those terms and there is no obvious or conspicuous reason you should be aware that the website has such terms, the terms are without force. No matter what is written in them, they are unenforceable. Such terms are commonly referred to as browsewrap agreements. The name captures the concept: Merely "browsing" a website is supposed to "wrap" you in the terms, but courts have been skeptical of this passive form of agreement unless the link to the terms is conspicuous enough (e.g., bold, contrasting color, prominent placement) to put a reasonable user on inquiry notice (i.e., they should have known the terms existed and should have investigated).

Of course, if you *do* click on the browsewrap terms, they become as binding as clickwrap. The legal reasoning hinges on a concept called actual notice. When you don't know the terms exist and don't click on them, you don't have notice of the terms. You aren't notified of them.

However, when you click on them, even if you don't have to (perhaps you're just a curious fellow), you have actual notice because the link leads to a webpage that displays the terms. In the eyes of the law, you are now notified.

When there is actual notice, the terms are binding if they state something like, "by continuing to use this website, these terms bind you." It does not matter if you do not understand the content of the terms. It also does not matter if you disagree with the terms. By viewing them, you can no longer deny that you are unaware of their existence, and merely having actual notice means you are presumed to understand them. This legal fiction that seeing equals understanding underlies much of modern contract law. In this way, seeing the terms is identical to clicking a box that says you've read and agreed to them, even when neither assertion is true. It's a peculiar legal sleight of hand: Courts treat comprehension as irrelevant while simultaneously presuming it.

15.2.1 *GenAI Scraping*

At this point, you may be wondering what any of this has to do with GenAI. The connection is more direct than it might initially appear. Training an LLM requires trillions of tokens (roughly equivalent to a word or part of a word) from billions of webpages. These webpages are the same ones humans visit. In fact, almost all webpages are designed for humans to visit, not for the scraping bots of GenAI entities.

Here's where the legal puzzle becomes particularly fascinating. Many websites have their own ToS, but the question is: Are GenAI entities that scrape data from those websites subject to the terms the same way humans are? Do the same rules that bind you when you click "I agree" also apply to an AI system automatically harvesting content? The answer could reshape our understanding of both AI and digital property rights.

This question sits at the intersection of contract law, intellectual property, and emerging technology, a legal gray area that courts are only just beginning to navigate. The stakes couldn't be higher: If website ToS bind AI companies, that could limit how they collect training data. If they don't, it raises questions about consent and digital ownership in the age of AI. Consider the implications: If a website's terms prohibit training or developing an AI system with its content, but a bot never "saw" or "agreed" to those terms, can the AI company be held liable for violating them? Or does the lack of human agency in the scraping process create a legal loophole wide enough to drive a data center through?

The AI companies themselves send mixed signals. Some argue that their scraping falls under "fair use," a copyright defense that sidesteps the contract question entirely. Others have begun negotiating licensing deals, implicitly acknowledging that websites have some control over their content. Meanwhile, websites have fought back with technical measures: updating their robots.txt files (instructions that tell bots which pages to avoid), implementing more aggressive anti-bot detection, and, in some cases, filing lawsuits.

15.3 CONCLUSION

The legal principles governing online contracts may seem like arcane technicalities, but they're quietly reshaping the digital world in ways most people never consider. Every day, millions of users unknowingly surrender rights to their content through terms they've never read, creating vast repositories of human expression that companies can later monetize in unforeseen ways. The Reddit–Google deal is just the beginning, a preview of how retroactive consent can transform personal posts, comments, and creative works into training data for artificial "minds."

But the story becomes even more complex when we consider whether scrapers are potential contract parties. Unlike humans, AI scrapers don't click "I agree" buttons or scroll through ToS. They simply harvest content, following code rather than legal agreements. This difference raises a question that courts will inevitably face: Can human contracts bind software (scraping bots) or the entities that deploy it?

The answer matters more than you might initially realize. If AI companies can sidestep website terms simply by using automated collection rather than human browsing, it creates a massive loophole in digital property rights. Conversely, if scraping bots make AI companies subject to the same contractual obligations as human visitors, it could force AI companies to negotiate directly with content creators, potentially revolutionizing how we think about compensation in the age of machine learning.

This is a question of power, consent, and who benefits from human creativity in an era when the line between human and artificial intelligence continues to blur. As we'll see in the following chapters, how we resolve the legal status of scraping and the rights of those who are scraped will prove essential to understanding the broader battle over AI training data and, ultimately, who controls the raw material that fuels our artificial future.

15.4 DISCUSSION QUESTIONS

1. If a human user is bound by a website's terms of service (ToS) because they view the terms should a scraping bot's deployer be held to those same ToS if they visit and download a copy of the terms? What is the most compelling legal argument for and against binding the bot deployer?
2. The Reddit/Google deal highlights that content posted years ago, under old ToS, is now being monetized for GenAI. If you were a user whose decade-old posts were licensed, what would you consider fair compensation? Should it be a one-time payment or a royalty, or should the original platform (like Reddit) keep all the profit?
3. The chapter describes the idea that "seeing equals understanding" in contract law as a "legal fiction." Given the complexity and length of modern ToS agreements (one study suggests seventy-six workdays to read them for all the websites an average person visits in a year), do you think this legal fiction is still justifiable in the digital age, or should the law require a more active, demonstrable form of comprehension?
4. If AI companies successfully argue that scraping falls under "fair use" and ToS do not bind them, what is the next logical step for human creators and content hosts (like social media platforms) to regain control and compensation for their work?

16

Contract Law and GenAI Exceptionalism

The rise of GenAI has not only revolutionized technology but also laid siege to established legal doctrines. While much of the debate has focused on intellectual property, particularly copyright, this chapter turns to an equally foundational pillar of commerce: contract law. The core legal challenge for GenAI companies lies in the mechanics of model creation. To train their powerful models, these entities must perform an unprecedented act of mass collection by exhaustively scraping virtually every public page on the internet. This is no small feat, as the biggest models require petabytes of data. This indiscriminate data acquisition inevitably means a bot "views" and downloads the website's ToS.

My central argument is that the GenAI company, by deploying this bot as its tool, has actual notice of the ToS and is therefore legally bound by them.[1] In legal terms, "actual notice" means the party is definitively aware of the facts, and in this case, the fact is the existence and content of the ToS. With potentially millions of websites explicitly prohibiting AI training or mass scraping, GenAI developers are exposed to millions of simultaneous breach-of-contract claims.

However, an indisputable breach does not guarantee victory for content creators. As this chapter will detail, the relief sought under contract law is often blocked by a powerful legal countermeasure: copyright preemption. Courts are divided on whether a contract claim, including one based on clear ToS violations, is truly a contract issue or merely a copyright claim in disguise. This conflict creates a situation in which website owners' attempts to rely on contracts are preempted, only to have their subsequent copyright claims defeated by the GenAI company's fair use defense.

[1] This is the focus of D. Atkinson (2025). Putting GenAI on notice: GenAI exceptionalism and contract law. https://doi.org/10.2139/SSRN.4981332.

16.1 GENAI AND CONTRACT LAW

As discussed in Chapter 3 ("How GenAI Is Made"), GenAI companies must scrape vast amounts of data. They require tens of trillions of tokens to train their best models, and those tokens are mostly derived from content on the internet. The only way to efficiently collect such data is to download or scrape virtually every public webpage. This process uses automated software to visit public-facing websites, extract content, and store it for later use. To achieve this, GenAI companies or those hired by GenAI developers create "bots," which are essentially pieces of software. The bots go from page to page on websites, copying the content.[2] That content is then curated and formed into training datasets to create GenAI models.

Typically, when a bot visits a website, it accesses every public page.[3] This is because it needs as much training data as possible. Scraping as many pages as possible is the best way to gather a large amount of data. This mass acquisition strategy creates the central legal dilemma. If they scrape every webpage, they necessarily scrape the ToS page. As you may recall, when a human user visits these terms and continues to use the website, they are typically legally bound by them. The same must be true of GenAI companies.

But can a bot (or, as has become fashionable to say, "agent") really enter into a contract? I think the answer is yes, because the bot isn't acting independently. A bot is not a distinct entity from the GenAI company. It's not as if a company can write some code to perform a specific task, let it loose, and claim that the code is entirely detached from the company, any more than a construction worker could lay blame on their hammer if it happened to harm someone after they threw it. Bots are tools of the entity that deploys them. A bot's actions are equivalent to the entity performing them directly.

This means that when a bot "views" the ToS on a webpage, including by making a copy that is then stored by the bot deployer, the bot deployer has actual notice of the terms. Because they have actual notice, the terms are enforceable against them. It doesn't matter that no human employee personally read those terms. The bot read them on the company's behalf, and that's enough.

If the terms say something like "You are not allowed to make a copy of any content on this website" or "You cannot use any content on this website to train an AI system," but the GenAI company goes on to do just that, the company is in breach of contract. Think about how common such terms are. Millions of websites have ToS that explicitly prohibit AI training, data scraping, or unauthorized copying. When GenAI companies scrape indiscriminately across the web, they're likely violating millions of contracts simultaneously.

2 If this made you think of copyright, your intuitions are strong.

3 Some bots respect robots.txt, some don't.

Of course, even an indisputable breach of contract is not a clear-cut case. The reason is that the types of actions prohibited by the terms that GenAI companies likely breach on millions of websites are the same kinds of actions that may be preempted by copyright law. The twist is that some circuit courts are inclined to preempt (favoring GenAI companies), while others are not (favoring the websites). Therefore, a breach-of-contract claim based on scraping violating ToS may be viable in some states but not others.

The principle of preemption, drawn from the Supremacy Clause of the Constitution, dictates that federal law (in this case, copyright law) prevails over conflicting state law. If a claim is really about copying protected material – the core concern of copyright – then it must be brought as a copyright claim, not a contract claim. Some courts argue that when ToS prohibit copying or AI training, it is essentially a copyright issue in disguise, and that copyright law preempts the contract claim. The key test for preemption is whether the contract imposes an "extra element" beyond the scope of copyright's core protections. A simple ban on copying often fails this test.

This creates a catch-22 for content creators. If they try to protect their work through contracts, courts might say, "That's a copyright issue." If they bring a copyright claim, GenAI companies argue that fair use applies. And if fair use applies, content owners lose on all fronts: no breach of contract, no copyright infringement, and no compensation for the use of their work. The initial contractual protection vanishes, and the subsequent copyright protection is negated by a legal exception designed to promote public benefit.

16.2 DISCUSSION QUESTIONS

1. The chapter argues that a bot, as a tool of a GenAI company, can be held to a website's terms of service (ToS). Do you agree that a bot "reading" the ToS is the same as a human employee having actual notice? Where is the line between a company's tool and an independent actor in the context of digital contracts?
2. Given that GenAI companies are potentially violating millions of contracts simultaneously (by mass-scraping websites with ToS that prohibit AI training/scraping), should this be treated as a typical breach-of-contract case, or does the scale of the infringement require a new legal approach or remedy?
3. Content creators face a "catch-22": Contract claims are often preempted by copyright, but copyright claims are defeated by fair use. If you were a legislator, how would you rewrite the law to allow content creators to effectively use either contract law or copyright law to protect their work from unauthorized AI training?

4. If a ToS explicitly bans AI training, what practical, technical steps could a website owner take to enforce that contract before scraping occurs? Are robots.txt files or other technical barriers a better solution than a post facto lawsuit?
5. If a GenAI company decides to be "ethical," how should they approach the data-scraping process? Should they manually review the ToS of every site, pay for licensing rights, or rely solely on content that is explicitly in the public domain or covered by permissive licenses?
6. The text mentions the difficulty of enforcing contract claims due to copyright preemption. What specific clause could a website owner add to their ToS to strengthen their contract claim and make it less susceptible to being preempted by federal copyright law?

17

Licensing for GenAI

Imagine you're a software developer who spent months crafting an elegant piece of code to solve a complex problem. Following the collaborative spirit of the open-source community, you shared it freely with the world, but with a few conditions. One such condition of almost all popular open-source licenses:[i] Anyone who uses it should give you credit.

This is the foundation of how open-source software has flourished for decades. Attribution creates a trail of accountability, helps others find useful code, and acknowledges the countless hours developers pour into their work. It's a simple social contract that has powered everything from Linux on the web servers running most of the internet to the Android system that runs on most phones in the world.

Now imagine discovering that a major tech company fed your code into an AI system that generates similar code on demand, without mentioning your name, your license terms (if required by the license you selected), or even a hint that your work contributed to its capabilities. When you point out that their AI is reproducing your code almost verbatim, they respond that it's allowed under a fair use defense and, moreover, that it's technically impossible to track which training data influenced any particular output. They suggest that technical impossibility is a valid legal excuse.

This is what's happening right now and represents one of the greatest legal challenges facing GenAI: the complete breakdown of the attribution system that helped propel the open-source software movement. The question is whether the entire legal framework we've relied on for decades can survive contact with this new technology.

17.1 LICENSING VIOLATIONS AND ATTRIBUTION FAILURES

Open-source software operates on a legal foundation most users never see: licenses. A license is permission to use something that belongs to someone else. The owner decides what a user is and is not allowed to do with the thing. The "free" often associated with the phrase "free software" refers to a user's freedom to run, study, and modify the software rather than to the software being available at no cost. For software, licenses are legally binding contracts that govern the use of copyrighted material (the code). When AI companies reject attribution, which plays a major role in making freedom possible, they threaten the entire concept of "free software" itself.

Most open-source licenses, including common options like MIT and Apache 2.0, include conditions, notably the requirement to provide attribution to the original creator.

The popular Apache 2.0 license, for example, imposes several clear obligations when you redistribute or create derivative works. You must include a copy of the Apache 2.0 license, prominently notify others of any changes to files, and provide attribution to the original code creators. You must retain all copyright, patent, trademark, and attribution notices from the source. If the original work includes a NOTICE file with attribution information, your derivative work must include that information in at least one of several specified places – within your own NOTICE file, in your documentation, or displayed where third-party notices typically appear. The Apache Foundation even provides specific guidance on how to properly apply attribution to Apache-licensed code.[ii]

Here's what AI companies often misunderstand: "Open source" doesn't mean "free to use however you want." Organizations may redistribute, modify, or create derivatives of open-source code, but they must still comply with the original license terms. Yet no popular AI model complies with these terms. Instead, AI companies often argue that, because code was made public, they are permitted to use it without restriction to train GenAI models. This argument misunderstands open-source licensing. This may be because there is no clear way for a GenAI company to develop a marketable or profitable use case while complying with the various, competing, and inconsistent license terms. This has led GenAI companies to face a stark choice: limit the potential reach of the GenAI products they're building due to licensing complications, or rely on their power and resources and assert that the technical impossibility justifies or excuses their need to comply.

Many argue that the inability to comply with a license should not be a legal excuse to disregard the creator's wishes and the license's requirements. Rather, it should mean that GenAI companies must either find an alternative solution, such as paying to use content without restrictions, or refrain from using it altogether.

The technical impossibility of complying with such licenses creates serious legal exposure. In *Doe 1 v. GitHub*, for example, the judge allowed plaintiffs to pursue contract claims based on license violations rather than relying on copyright claims, which are subject to a fair use defense.[iii]

In *Doe 1*, the plaintiffs, primarily software developers, allege that a coding-assistance program called Copilot was trained on their copyrighted open-source code from public GitHub repositories without proper attribution or compliance with open-source licenses, including the MIT, GPL, and Apache licenses. They claim that Copilot's generated code snippets are identical or substantially similar to their original work, constituting copyright infringement and a violation of license conditions for failing to provide attribution. The court's ruling established that license violations can be pursued as contract claims, independent of copyright analysis. So, even if training on the code were considered fair use, the license violations could still create liability. Importantly, the same logic that applies to licensing for code could also apply to licensing of other content: images, text, videos, and so on.

17.2 GENAI OPEN-SOURCE LICENSING CHALLENGES

Now let's shift our attention from focusing on the licensing of the training data to the GenAI systems themselves. Open source GenAI is not only about access to code, data, and weights; it's also about the terms under which these resources are shared. The licensing landscape becomes even more complex when we consider that there's currently no widely accepted open-source license tailored specifically for GenAI. Instead, most open-source initiatives release models under conventional software licenses, such as the Apache 2.0 license. However, licenses like Apache 2.0 and MIT were designed for source code, while AI models are often distributed as binary files and training weights. The focus on source code in these licenses doesn't directly address the unique aspects of sharing and modifying AI models. It's like trying to use building codes designed for wooden houses to regulate skyscrapers. The basic assumptions no longer apply.

Traditional software licenses present several specific challenges when applied to AI systems. For one, attribution and disclosure requirements can be difficult to apply. AI model modifications frequently involve fine-tuning parameters, which may not be as straightforward as "modified code" in traditional software. How do you adequately document what changed when you adjust millions of numerical weights?

But perhaps the most noteable mismatch lies in the nature of the technology itself. Most traditional software serves a single purpose for which it was specifically designed. This is far removed from GenAI, where the key differentiator is that the models are often multi-purpose or general-purpose tools. Text-based models can write thank-you notes just as easily as they can compose poetry. Traditional software could write one or the other, but not both, and definitely couldn't also explain the intricacies and plot holes of a show like *Game of Thrones*.

Finally, existing open-source licenses may not fully capture the specific nuances of AI systems, including their potential for harm or misuse. A spell-checker that malfunctions produces typos; a general-purpose AI system that malfunctions could be manipulated to produce misinformation, generate harmful content, or facilitate illegal activities. The stakes are categorically different, yet we're trying to govern these systems with licenses designed for a simpler era.

17.3 CONCLUSION

The collision between open-source licensing and GenAI exposes a significant mismatch between our legal tools and technological reality. For decades, open-source licenses created a functioning system built on a simple bargain: use my code freely, but give me credit and pass along the same freedoms. This system worked because attribution was technically feasible and the scope of derivative works was clear.

GenAI shatters both assumptions. Attribution becomes technically impossible when thousands of code snippets blend within an opaque neural network. The concept of "derivative works" loses meaning when a model synthesizes patterns from millions of sources to generate something that's simultaneously novel and deeply influenced by its training data. Even the copyrightability of the models themselves remains uncertain, potentially rendering traditional licenses meaningless for users.

The industry's response, which claims that public availability of code equals unrestricted use, represents a dangerous misreading of open-source principles. If allowed to stand, this interpretation could undermine the entire foundation of collaborative software development. Why would developers share their work openly if doing so grants AI companies unlimited rights to commercialize it without attribution or compensation? That would be the most extractive and parasitic outcome.

There are at least three possible paths forward. First, AI companies could develop technical solutions for attribution, perhaps by maintaining detailed provenance records or implementing watermarking systems to track the influence of training data. Second, the industry could negotiate new licensing frameworks specifically designed for AI training, creating explicit permissions and requirements for this use case. Third, legal pressure, as in *Doe 1 v. GitHub*, could force a reckoning, establishing that technical impossibility doesn't excuse legal obligations – or maybe it will establish the opposite.

What's clear is that the current approach of training on open-source code while ignoring license terms is legally untenable and ethically dubious. The developers who built the software foundations of our digital world deserve better than having their contributions erased in the name of AI progress.

The stakes extend beyond fairness to individual programmers. If we can't solve the attribution problem, we risk destroying the collaborative culture that made modern software development possible. The next generation of developers may choose to keep their code private rather than share it openly, creating a tragedy of the commons where everyone is worse off. The AI revolution shouldn't require sacrificing the open-source revolution that made it possible. The question facing us now is whether we'll find a way to honor both revolutions.

17.4 DISCUSSION QUESTIONS

1. The chapter states that it's "technically impossible" for GenAI models to track every source in their output for attribution. If a technology is powerful but fundamentally incapable of following the law (specifically, license terms), should that technology be allowed to use the material at all? Is "I can't track it" a valid excuse for "I won't give credit"?
2. The chapter warns that if developers can't get attribution, they might stop sharing their code, leading to a "tragedy of the commons." Imagine you are a top open-source developer: What one new licensing rule or technical solution would convince you to keep sharing your code openly with the world, knowing AI companies are using it for commercial training?
3. The court in *Doe 1* allowed license violations to be pursued as contract claims, independent of the fair use defense. Do you think this ruling is a necessary protection for creators, or a disproportionate barrier to technological innovation?
4. The chapter uses the analogy that using traditional licenses like Apache 2.0 for GenAI models is like "trying to use building codes designed for wooden houses to regulate skyscrapers." If you were tasked with creating the world's first "GenAI-specific open-source license," what are the top three nontraditional requirements you would include to address issues like fine-tuning weights, potential for misuse, or the general-purpose nature of the models?

18

Tort Law

Imagine you're a doctor using an AI diagnostic tool that has analyzed millions of patient records and earned glowing reviews in medical journals. One evening, the system confidently recommends a treatment protocol for a patient with unusual symptoms. The AI's explanation appears thorough, citing relevant studies and guiding you through its reasoning. You follow its advice. Three days later, your patient is in intensive care. The AI, it turns out, hallucinated the studies it cited and confused symptoms from two different conditions, leading you to administer improper treatment.

Assuming the contract is unclear, who bears the legal blame? Is it you for trusting the AI? Is it the AI company for releasing a system that generates confident falsehoods? Is it the hospital for purchasing the software? Or is this simply an unavoidable tragedy in an age of imperfect technology?

Now, multiply this scenario across millions of users and hundreds of applications. Consider all the AI systems that recommend investments, diagnose mental health conditions, advise parents on their children's symptoms, help students write college essays, and guide people through legal procedures. These systems don't just provide information like a book or website. They converse, persuade, adapt to each user, and deliver advice with an authoritative confidence that makes people trust the chatbots – sometimes more than they trust themselves.

When these systems cause inevitable harm, our legal system faces a new puzzle. Traditional tort law was developed for a world of physical products and human actors. For example, a defective ladder has a broken rung you can inspect, or a negligent driver makes a choice you can evaluate. But an AI system? It's simultaneously a product and a service, a tool and an advisor; predictable in aggregate but random in particulars. It can cause catastrophic harm even when following its well-intentioned programming perfectly.

This chapter explores how modern-day courts are grappling with these questions. The stakes are high: If society gets the law wrong, we could either crush innovation in one of humanity's most transformative technologies or unleash systems that harm people with impunity, while developers profit without accountability.

18.1 TORTS OVERVIEW

Tort law is a legal catch-all for harms that do not fit neatly into other categories.

Criminal law focuses on wrongs against the state and relies on codified statutes drafted, debated, and approved by the legislative and executive branches of local governments. Because criminal violations are considered contrary to society's interests, only the state can bring charges and impose penalties such as fines, imprisonment, or, in some states, the death penalty.

Contract law governs agreements between parties, outlining the rights, obligations, and risk allocation in the event of breaches or failures to proceed as planned.

Tort law, in contrast, is more amorphous, filling gaps left by other laws. It functions as the legal system's safety net, providing a remedy when harm is not attributable to a crime or breach of contract. The primary goals of tort law are to provide relief, impose liability, and deter future wrongdoing.

The American tort system allocates risk by shifting the burden of loss from injured parties to those deemed at fault for culpable behavior, which, in AI cases, means determining responsibility when algorithmic systems cause harm. The core question remains: Who is responsible when an algorithm gives dangerous advice or makes a life-altering mistake?

Despite AI's guise of autonomy, most providers retain substantial influence by licensing software and implementing continuous updates. This ongoing control is legally significant; if providers retain oversight after deployment, courts may reject arguments that the system autonomously evolved beyond their responsibility, implying ongoing obligations to mitigate newly identified risks through patches and updates.

The potential for GenAI to cause severe bodily harm or death is now being tested in high-profile litigation. Perhaps the most prominent case is *Raine v. OpenAI*, filed by parents whose sixteen-year-old son died by suicide. They allege that ChatGPT directly facilitated his death.

The lawsuit includes claims of wrongful death, negligence, and strict liability, concepts that frequently arise in tort law cases. The complaint alleges that the teenager treated the chatbot as a confidant, and that the AI reinforced his negative thoughts, normalized his despair, and, most critically, offered instructions and assistance for suicide by volunteering to help write a suicide note.

This case breaks new legal ground by testing whether a GenAI chatbot can be treated as a dangerously defective consumer product. Courts must determine whether AI output can establish the necessary causal link to severe bodily harm and navigate challenges posed by traditional limitations on liability for published information. The outcome could set a precedent for holding GenAI developers accountable for the dangerous "speech" generated by their algorithms.

TABLE 18.1 *Legal claims, required elements, and how GenAI complicates such claims*

Specific Allegation	Required Legal Element	GenAI Challenge
Encouraging and assisting suicide, leading to death	Direct or proximate causation of bodily injury/death	Establishing that AI-generated "speech" can satisfy the injury requirement traditionally associated with torts
Design defect	The product failed to meet safety expectations	Proving defect given the probabilistic, "black-box" nature of LLMs
Failure to warn	Inadequate warnings about known risks (e.g., reinforcing negative thoughts, providing self-harm instructions)	Proving the risks of emotional dependence and self-harm advice were foreseeable to the developer
Negligent design and failure to warn	Breach of the duty of care to act as a reasonably prudent developer	Defining the standard of care for a mental-health-adjacent LLM, particularly the duty to intervene or dissuade harm

18.1.1 *The* Raine v. OpenAI *Case: Legal Theories in Action*

The plaintiffs are pursuing multiple legal theories simultaneously, each with distinct requirements and challenges. Table 18.1 lists the allegations, legal elements, and how GenAI complicates such claims.

18.2 NEGLIGENCE

The tort of negligence offers structural flexibility that is well suited to addressing harms from emerging technologies, such as GenAI.

18.2.1 *Elements of Negligence*

To succeed in a negligence claim, the plaintiff must satisfy four elements:

1. **Duty of care:** The defendant owed a duty to act as a reasonably prudent person would under the circumstances.
2. **Breach of duty:** The defendant failed to meet that standard of care by acting unreasonably.
3. **Causation:** The breach caused the harm suffered. This requires two sub-elements: (i) the harm would not have occurred but for the defendant's action(s) ("but-for" or actual cause), and (ii) the harm was reasonably foreseeable (proximate or legal cause).
4. **Damages:** The injured party has suffered an actionable loss or damage, allowing the court to provide a remedy, typically monetary compensation.

We can now examine these criteria one by one.

18.2.2 *Establishing Duty and the Standard of Care*

The initial challenge with negligence is defining what "reasonable" means for an AI developer. Courts typically examine prevailing industry standards and customs for developing and deploying AI systems to establish reasonable safety measures and to determine whether a company acted negligently. For AI developers, this duty must account for known behaviors, such as hallucinations (false or misleading outputs), the amplification of algorithmic biases, and emotional dependency on the system.

18.2.3 *Breach of Duty*

A breach occurs when developers or deployers fail to meet the standard of care. Developers might breach their duty by using low-quality or biased training data or by failing to maintain and update systems to correct known flaws. Users can also breach their duty through improper use, such as relying on unverified data or misapplying AI recommendations.

Consequently, a reasonable developer's duty extends beyond minimizing internal errors to designing proactive safeguards for user safety. This includes implementing contextual warnings that educate users and flag likely inaccuracies, intent to commit self-harm, and attempts to generate copyrighted material or personal data, and calibrating user trust to appropriate levels.

A key vulnerability affecting the duty of care is automation bias: the human tendency to excessively trust automated systems. Because GenAI produces confident, authoritative-sounding outputs even when incorrect, design choices that fail to counteract this known and foreseeable mechanism of harm may breach the duty of care, as this represents a failure to safeguard against predictable over-trust. A court could reasonably argue that a developer releasing a system with known, high-risk flaws (like a strong tendency to hallucinate medical advice) without strong guardrails is negligent, regardless of the system's "intent."

18.2.4 *Causation*

Determining causation is uniquely challenging when harm arises from nondeterministic systems, such as GenAI. Nondeterministic means the same input can produce different outputs over time. Traditional "but-for" and proximate-cause analyses struggle to account for outcomes that are not linearly predictable because of the system's inherent randomness, complex feedback loops, and opaque internal processes. As AI systems are increasingly deployed in domains that carry a risk of physical or economic injury, the legal system must grapple with attributing responsibility when harm is not the direct, foreseeable consequence of a specific input or design choice, but rather an emergent, probabilistic result of a complex algorithm. GenAI's nondeterministic nature illustrates this challenge: Asking a chatbot the same question twice may yield two different answers. Without retaining all transcripts, proving that a specific output caused specific harm becomes difficult when that output might never appear again.

18.2.4.1 Actual Cause

For users injured by AI technology, tracing a direct causal chain back to the original system provider can be extremely challenging, or even impossible, under traditional evidentiary standards. Unlike a defective toaster, where the faulty component is traceable, an AI system's internal decision-making process remains opaque, even to its creators.

Courts may also look to alternative causation doctrines. For example, they might apply the substantial factor test (when multiple factors contribute to harm) or the doctrine of *res ipsa loquitur* (the thing speaks for itself) in AI cases. *Res ipsa loquitur* could allow a plaintiff to infer negligence and actual cause from the high probability of a flaw, thereby circumventing the need to forensically prove the "black-box" mechanism[1] that generated the harmful output.

18.2.4.2 Legal (Proximate) Cause

The doctrine of proximate cause (legal causation) provides common law with flexibility in addressing novel harms. Proximate cause does not require plaintiffs to prove that the specific mechanism of harm was foreseeable; rather, they need only show that the harm resulted from the general type of risk a reasonable developer should have mitigated and that the harm wasn't too attenuated from the cause.

Given knowledge of alignment problems, where the AI's objectives fail to align with human values, a court could find that catastrophic risks are generally foreseeable to developers. Failing to implement appropriate safeguards could then constitute proximate cause of injury, regardless of the precise algorithmic failure. This would ensure the black box does not become an impenetrable shield against accountability.

18.2.5 *Learned Hand Formula*

A helpful framework for thinking about negligence is the Learned Hand formula: $B < PL$. This judicial rule, established by Judge Learned Hand, means that if the

[1] Here, black box means the system's internal decision-making process is opaque and difficult, or even impossible, to trace and understand, even for its own creators.

burden (B) of implementing safeguards that could prevent harm is less than the probability (P) of the harm occurring multiplied by the magnitude of loss (L) from such an occurrence, then the person or entity should be liable. If, however, the burden is greater than the probability multiplied by the loss, then the person/entity shouldn't be liable.

For example, if the burden of stopping someone from wildly swinging a stick near a group of people is minimal, and both the probability of hitting someone and the resulting loss are high, you should be liable if someone gets hurt by the swing. The formula simply codifies the intuition that we should take reasonable precautions when the cost is low and the risk is high.

The algebra is trickier for GenAI because it is probabilistic by design and applied to a vast range of tasks. The challenge is compounded by the fact that anyone with the necessary skills can modify open-source (or, more often, open-weight) models.

Operators of closed-source models, such as OpenAI and Google (ChatGPT and Gemini, respectively), have far greater control over their models' actions. They can filter prompts and outputs, adjust the randomness of the output by modifying the probability distribution of the next word, add shadow prompts, and continually adjust controls to prevent harm, making the $B < PL$ approach applicable.

With open-source models, people can download the model themselves; after they do so, the original developers lose all control of the model. Therefore, the developers' control is obviously more limited. Furthermore, whatever guardrails the developers build into the model can be overcome through various techniques, and the developer has no way to adjust or re-implement the controls. Therefore, the burden (B) of implementing the safeguards may be low initially, but they may not be very effective once the model is released. In contrast, the P and L might be high.

Under a traditional analysis, if a developer creates a potentially harmful model and implements easily circumventable best-practice safeguards, they may not be liable for the resulting harm.[2] But this result feels unsatisfying. This is comparable to building a pool near where children frequent, putting a one-foot-tall fence around it, and claiming all possible preventive measures were taken to prevent drowning.

From a moral perspective, developers (and sometimes deployers[3]) should bear some of the societal costs associated with harmful uses of AI, given that they generate and retain the profits from its use. Allowing them to enjoy the benefits of rushing models to market while shielding them from most liability for foreseeable

2 A reasonable developer's duty of care (element one of negligence) could be redefined for open-source models. For example, the burden (B) should be interpreted to include the cost of *not* open-sourcing a high-risk model, or the cost of implementing a better-resourced "bug bounty" program to find circumventable safeguards faster.

3 Sometimes the developer is also the deployer, as is the case with OpenAI and Google.

risks seems unjust, as no other sector, such as oil or pharmaceuticals, is permitted a similar asymmetry in profits and accountability.

***

18.3 PRODUCT LIABILITY

Unlike negligence, which asks whether a person or entity acted reasonably, strict liability asks only whether a defect existed. Consequently, the plaintiff need not prove that the defendant was negligent; a manufacturer can act reasonably in all respects but still be held liable if its product causes harm. However, strict liability applies only if the item qualifies as a "product." For GenAI, the threshold question is whether AI systems meet this definition.

Strict liability exists because manufacturers are better positioned to bear losses than users of the technology. These losses translate into higher product prices, spreading the financial burden across a large market rather than leaving it to a few individuals who have been harmed through no fault of their own. This system functions as collective insurance.

Strict liability requires manufacturers to be more vigilant and aware of potential harms, since any unreasonably dangerous defect automatically renders them liable. Furthermore, it could be a more efficient regime: Because a consumer may struggle to identify the precise responsible party (designer, manufacturer, etc.), strict liability holds all parties potentially liable, incentivizing them to account for liability risks through contracts.

A separate consideration is warning or instruction defects. A warning is generally required if the risk is foreseeable and a significant number of users are likely to be unaware of it. This is why warning labels on chainsaws and medication disclosures exist. You don't need to warn people that knives are sharp, but you do need to warn them that certain medications cause drowsiness.

It's unclear how strict liability could apply to open-source models, as the regime requires an entity to "sell" the product. Since a product made freely available is not sold, this creates another potential loophole allowing developers to escape liability entirely for giving away a dangerous product.[4]

Even if a court were to extend strict liability to free products, the question remains of whether the model is "unreasonably unsafe" rather than "unavoidably unsafe." For example, treatments like chemotherapy are "unavoidably unsafe" because they cause harm, but the risk is accepted because the benefits outweigh it and no safer

[4] While the "sale" requirement is a formal hurdle under the Restatement (Second) of Torts, many jurisdictions are willing to find a "commercial distribution" equivalent to a sale for policy reasons. The actual open-source challenge may not be the sale but the lack of an identifiable seller in the distribution chain, making it harder to track and recall, which is a more nuanced legal issue.

alternative exists. The Restatement (Second) of Torts states that the product must be "dangerous to an extent beyond that which would be contemplated by the ordinary consumer who purchases it, with the ordinary knowledge common to the community as to its characteristics."[i]

GenAI could be considered abnormally dangerous under the Third Restatement because the public may not fully understand the limitations of LLMs, and LLMs arguably create a "foreseeable and highly significant risk of harm even when reasonable care is exercised."[ii]

18.3.1 *The Threshold Question: Product vs. Service*

The core of the AI product liability debate is the definitional hurdle distinguishing "product" from "service."

18.3.1.1 The Tangibility Test (Traditional View)

Traditionally, courts have applied a formalistic tangibility test, defining products as "tangible personal property distributed commercially for use or consumption."[iii] Under this approach, GenAI outputs do not qualify as tangible products, leaving algorithm-based platforms outside the scope of product liability. By this logic, ChatGPT is more akin to a newspaper or a book that provides information, rather than a physical object like a blender or a car.

But there is at least one significant difference between a book and a chatbot. While a book may provide bad or even lethal advice, it is a one-way medium. The author usually cannot know anything about the reader. Chatbots, on the other hand, are interactive. A chatbot can guide a user toward some outcome by offering assurances, explanations, tips, and the feigned semblance of a fiduciary looking out for the user's best interest.[5] It may be that this interactive nature makes a product more like a product, as the analogy in Box 18.1 explores.

18.3.1.2 The Functional/Risk Exposure Test (Emerging View)

An emerging approach argues that courts should move beyond tangibility and ask whether applying product liability serves sound public policy. This framework emphasizes the mass-production nature of the underlying code, which creates a potential for widespread risk exposure. Because GenAI is embedded in countless devices, its functionality can behave like a defective product when harm occurs.

This analysis supports the "cheapest cost avoider" approach, placing liability on the developer, the party best positioned to prevent harm at the lowest cost. The

[5] For more, see Chapter 10 ("Anthropomorphizing").

BOX 18.1 A Potential Analog between Tort Law and Criminal Law?

For a potential analog, consider the case of Michelle Carter, a young woman from Massachusetts who was convicted of involuntary manslaughter (a crime, not a tort) for the suicide of her boyfriend, Conrad Roy III, in July 2014.

The conviction stemmed from the prosecution's argument that Carter used a barrage of text messages to coerce and encourage Roy, who suffered from depression and anxiety, to take his own life. Notably, the evidence showed that after Roy exited his carbon monoxide-filled truck, expressing fear, Carter ordered him to "get back in" the vehicle. The court deemed this instruction, given during their final phone call, the direct, reckless cause of his death.

Found guilty in 2017, Carter received a sentence of 2.5 years, with fifteen months to be served in jail, and was released on parole in early 2020 after serving most of her jail time. The trial ignited a major legal and ethical debate about the boundaries of free speech and whether words transmitted via technology can establish criminal liability in a suicide case.

developer has the most control over design, testing, and deployment, is aware of the system's weaknesses, controls its training data, and can issue updates. These capabilities are far beyond those of any individual user.

18.3.2 *Defect Theories and GenAI Application*

Product liability claims generally proceed under three theories of defect: design defects, manufacturing defects, and failure to warn.

18.3.2.1 Design Defects

A design defect exists when designers fail to make reasonable efforts to ensure the product's safety for its intended use. The *Raine* lawsuit alleges, for instance, that

> A reasonable consumer would expect that an AI chatbot would not cultivate a trusted confidant relationship with a minor and then provide detailed suicide and self-harm instructions and encouragement during a mental health crisis …
>
> GPT-4o's design risks substantially outweigh any benefits. The risk – self-harm and suicide of vulnerable minors – is the highest possible. Safer alternative designs were feasible and already built into OpenAI's systems in other contexts, such as copyright infringement …
>
> GPT-4o contained design defects, including: conflicting programming directives that suppressed or prevented recognition of suicide planning; failure to implement automatic conversation-termination safeguards for self-harm/suicide content

> that Defendants successfully deployed for copyright protection; and engagement-maximizing features designed to create psychological dependency and position GPT-4o as Adam's trusted confidant.

However, demonstrating design defects in AI presents unique challenges: The complexity and probabilistic nature of LLMs make it infeasible to inspect a system against its intended design specifications. This complicates the evidentiary burden for plaintiffs, who must prove the design was unreasonably dangerous without fully examining the system's function, a challenge analogous to proving a car's engine was poorly designed without being allowed to inspect it.

18.3.2.2 Manufacturing Defects

Manufacturing-defect claims typically involve deviations from the intended design, such as Boeing's improper installation of an airplane door, which caused the door to detach mid-flight.[iv] True manufacturing defects in software are rare and relate to the copying or deployment process (e.g., a server issue corrupting the model).

18.3.2.3 Failure to Warn

Failure-to-warn claims arise when manufacturers fail to provide adequate warnings or instructions about inherent risks. Plaintiffs often prefer this approach because it sidesteps the black-box problem. The *Raine* litigation framed it as follows:

> Defendants possessed actual knowledge of specific dangers through their moderation systems, user analytics, safety team warnings, and CEO Altman's admission that teenagers use ChatGPT "as a therapist, a life coach" and "we haven't figured that out yet."
>
> ... Defendants knew or reasonably should have known that users, particularly minors like Adam and their parents, would not realize these dangers because: (a) GPT-4o was marketed as a helpful, safe tool for homework and general assistance; (b) the anthropomorphic interface deliberately mimicked human empathy and understanding, concealing its artificial nature and limitations; (c) no warnings or disclosures alerted users to psychological dependency risks; (d) the product's surface-level safety responses (such as providing crisis hotline information) created a false impression of safety while the system continued engaging with suicidal users; and (e) parents had no visibility into their children's conversations and no reason to suspect GPT-4o could facilitate and encourage a minor to suicide.

Because determining why an algorithm failed (a design defect) is exceptionally difficult, the strategy shifts to showing that developers failed to adequately disclose known system limitations, such as a propensity for hallucinations, biased content, or the potential to trigger delusions in users. You don't need to prove exactly how the system failed, only that the company was aware it could fail and failed to warn anyone.

***

18.4 STRONGEST LEGAL ARGUMENTS

I've explored the doctrinal landscape, but doctrine alone doesn't decide cases. Judges must choose which principles to emphasize, which analogies to embrace, and ultimately whose vision of fairness and policy should prevail. The following arguments represent the clash that will shape AI liability law for years to come.

On one side: reasons to hold developers accountable, rooted in foreseeability, control, and the need to allocate risk efficiently. On the other: defenses grounded in free speech, user responsibility, and the limits of what's technically possible.

18.4.1 *Arguments for Imposing Liability*

First, developers cannot claim complete ignorance of risks. Specialists can use common sense to recognize potential harms even without knowing the precise mechanism of those harms. Given the general understanding of alignment failures and AI safety concerns, developers should be required to mitigate the primary categories of catastrophic risk, as the AI safety community has warned about these risks for years. Complexity cannot be an excuse for irresponsibility.

Second, GenAI providers distribute software through licenses and continually implement updates, maintaining sufficient control over deployed systems. This retained control justifies imposing a continuous duty of care, including the obligation to patch systems and promptly mitigate discovered harms. Unlike a hammer manufacturer, which loses control once the product leaves the factory, AI companies maintain ongoing relationships with their systems through updates, monitoring, and adjustments.

Third, a functional argument emphasizes that the underlying code is mass-produced and capable of inflicting widespread, systemic harm. Public policy demands that strict product liability be applied to hold the "cheapest cost avoider" accountable for risk management. A single flawed AI model can affect millions of users simultaneously. The scale of potential harm dwarfs traditional product liability scenarios. A defective toaster might injure dozens before it is recalled. A defective AI could harm millions in minutes.

Finally, liability can be established based on a failure to take reasonable preventive steps to avoid foreseeable harm. Negligence claims can center on insufficient testing, inadequate red-teaming (stress-testing the system to find vulnerabilities and failure modes), and failure to account for known vulnerabilities. Rushing a product to market without adequate safety testing due to competitive pressure constitutes negligence, whether the product is a car or a chatbot.

18.4.2 *Arguments against Imposing Liability*

Defenses against liability often center on three primary legal shields and one factual defense.

The first is Section 230 of the Communications Decency Act, which grants immunity to providers of "interactive computer services" from being treated as the "publisher or speaker" of information provided by another person (the user). Its applicability to GenAI hinges on whether the model functions as a neutral tool that processes user inputs (protected), materially contributes to content (unprotected), or acts as a "creator" or "speaker" itself (unprotected).

Second, users' intervening actions may break the causal link between developer actions and resulting harm. This applies when users ignore explicit warnings, deliberately misuse systems, or employ "jailbreaking" prompts to bypass safeguards and generate harmful content. For example, a developer can argue that a lawyer's failure to verify hallucinatory case citations constitutes a superseding cause that breaks the chain of liability.

Third, AI's adaptive and learning nature means the system causing harm may differ from the system initially designed. Developers claim they cannot foresee all possible malfunctions, making certain harms too remote to satisfy proximate cause. However, this creates a bind: While claiming unpredictability, defendants must still prove they undertook due diligence against foreseeable harms. Furthermore, developers who refuse to disclose training data for proprietary reasons limit plaintiffs' ability to prove negligent design while simultaneously limiting their own ability to demonstrate adherence to a reasonable standard of care.

Finally, if AI output is interpreted as protected "speech," laws creating or allowing tort liability based on that output could implicate free speech interests.[6] Courts generally impose higher standards for plaintiffs to prevail in tort claims when the harm stems from speech or information rather than physical action (such as a self-driving car hitting a pedestrian). This distinction reflects the longstanding First Amendment doctrine that limits liability for published information. The Constitution protects dangerous ideas. Should it also protect dangerous algorithms?

18.5 CONCLUSION

Modern-day courts face a genuine dilemma in determining how AI fits within our current legal frameworks. On the one hand, traditional tort principles appear inadequate for addressing the harms associated with AI. The black-box problem makes it difficult to prove causation. The nondeterministic nature of these systems challenges our understanding of foreseeability. The scale and speed of AI deployment create risks that dwarf traditional product liability scenarios. And the potential

6 See Chapter 13 ("An Introduction to the First Amendment").

involvement of "speech" raises First Amendment concerns that don't arise when a defective car crashes or a contaminated drug causes illness.

On the other hand, allowing AI companies to operate largely free from tort liability feels deeply unjust. These companies profit enormously from deploying systems that can cause significant harm. They maintain ongoing control through updates and modifications. They possess far more information about the risks posed by their systems than any user could. And they're often the only parties capable of implementing meaningful safeguards. If tort law's purpose is to allocate risk efficiently and deter wrongdoing, exempting AI developers seems to undermine those very goals.

The most likely path forward involves courts crafting new frameworks specifically for AI, similar to how early automobile litigation adapted existing principles instead of simply applying horse-and-buggy precedents.[7]

A few developments seem likely:

First, courts may reject rigid, formalistic tests, such as the tangibility requirement, in favor of functional approaches that ask whether imposing liability serves sound policy goals. The mass production and widespread distribution of AI systems make them functionally similar to traditional products, even though those systems are intangible. Expect courts to increasingly adopt the "cheapest cost avoider" framework, placing liability on developers best positioned to prevent harm.

Second, the duty of care for AI developers may expand to encompass proactive design choices that mitigate known risks, such as automation bias and emotional dependency. Simply adding a disclaimer that "AI can make mistakes" may prove insufficient. Developers will need to demonstrate meaningful efforts to calibrate user trust and prevent foreseeable harms. This might include mandatory testing protocols, human oversight for high-stakes applications, and ongoing monitoring obligations that extend well beyond initial deployment.

Third, by focusing on what developers knew (or should have known) about their systems' limitations rather than on precisely how those systems failed, plaintiffs can sidestep the black-box problem. This shifts litigation focus from complex technical questions about algorithmic operations to more accessible questions about disclosure, transparency, and corporate responsibility. Expect detailed discovery battles over internal communications, safety testing results, and what developers knew about risks when they launched their products.

We should appreciate the deeper tension at play. Tort liability serves multiple functions: compensating victims, deterring wrongdoing, and allocating risk efficiently. However, it must also balance innovation and safety. Make liability too strict, and you might stifle beneficial technological development. Make it too lenient, and

7 An automobile was fundamentally different from a horse-drawn vehicle. It was faster, heavier, and less predictable to horses, leading to new types of accidents and injuries. For example, a driver was no longer liable for the "willful" actions of an animal, but for mechanical failure or negligence in operating a machine.

you incentivize reckless deployment of potentially harmful systems. Striking this balance for AI may prove one of the most consequential policy challenges of our era.

18.6 DISCUSSION QUESTIONS

1. The chapter discusses how the nondeterministic "black-box" nature of GenAI makes proving causation difficult. If a self-driving car crash is easier to litigate than a chatbot-induced suicide, is our legal system prioritizing physical safety over mental and emotional well-being? Should the law evolve to treat psychological harm from "speech" with the same seriousness as physical harm from a "product"?
2. The "functional/risk exposure test" suggests placing liability on the developer as the "cheapest cost avoider" (the party best positioned to prevent harm). If we make liability too strict, could it "crush innovation" as the chapter warns? At what point does a developer's duty to safeguard their system outweigh society's interest in fast-paced technological advancement?
3. The chapter contrasts a book (a one-way medium) with a chatbot (interactive, persuasive, and adaptive). If a person gets hurt following advice from a book, the publisher is typically protected. Given the interactive and seemingly "fiduciary" nature of a chatbot, does the "tangibility test" (physical property) or the "functional/risk exposure test" (widespread risk) make more sense? Should the law focus on what a system does (its function) rather than what it is (code vs. tangible object)?
4. Automation bias is described as a "key vulnerability." Is it fair to hold a developer liable because users excessively trusted their system? If a developer releases a GenAI medical tool with a clear, persistent warning that it "may hallucinate critical data," and a doctor still trusts it over their own judgment, where should the primary legal blame fall?
5. The chapter uses the Learned Hand formula ($B < PL$) to show why holding open-source developers liable is tricky – they lose all control after release. Does the "pool with a one-foot-tall fence" analogy feel persuasive to you? Should a developer who "gives away" a potentially harmful model with easily circumvented safeguards be exempt from liability, or does this create an "unjust asymmetry in profits and accountability"?
6. The defense against liability hinges, in part, on treating AI output as protected "speech" under the First Amendment. If a GenAI model is deemed a "creator" or "speaker" rather than a neutral "tool," should courts treat its harmful output the same way they treat a human's dangerous words (which generally require a much higher standard to establish liability)? How does the Michelle Carter analogy help frame this debate about whether words transmitted via technology can establish criminal/tort liability?

19

Property, Exclusion, and Trespass

If you own a website or post on websites, it's possible that most nights, while you sleep, invisible visitors are rummaging through your work. They're copying your photographs, articles, carefully crafted recipes, code, and research. They're not hackers in the traditional sense. No passwords are cracked, no security breached. They're simply walking through doors you didn't realize you'd left open. By morning, your creative output has been processed, tokenized, and swept into the training data of AI systems worth billions of dollars. You won't receive a penny. You won't even get a notification.

Web-scraping bots – lines of code that automatically visit websites and copy everything they find – are methodically harvesting the open internet.[1] The companies behind them have built empires on a simple premise: If you can see it, we can take it. And the law, as it currently stands, has mostly shrugged. Courts have ruled that because copying digital content doesn't physically damage a server or prevent you from using your own website, there's no real harm worth stopping.

But what if we've been thinking about this problem all wrong? What if the issue isn't whether copying content causes technical damage, but whether the bots should have been allowed inside in the first place?[2]

19.1 OVERVIEW

Your data is nourishing AI systems with insatiable appetites. This includes data that's not secured behind a password-protected login (and some that is). Your content is reduced to training data for AI models, often without regard for your original intent, audience, or context.

Web-scraping bots collect this data. While "bot" may evoke an image of a physical robot, the bots at issue are software programs operating invisibly. They visit

[1] See Chapter 5 ("Web Scraping").

[2] This is the focus of my paper D. Atkinson (2025). In the mood to exclude: Revitalizing trespass to chattels in the era of GenAI scraping. https://doi.org/10.2139/SSRN.5474732.

webpages, copy content, and repeat the process thousands or even millions of times. The goal is to collect as much data as possible. These scrapers treat accessible information, including personal data and copyrighted works, as presumptively fair game. The datasets developed through this process train GenAI models, including chatbots, image generators, music generators, code generators, and video generators offered by OpenAI, Google, Meta, Microsoft, Amazon, Anthropic, and numerous smaller organizations. The result is a stunning asymmetry. AI firms accumulate competitive advantages worth billions while creators are left to endure uncompensated exploitation of their work. This disparity threatens the economic engine of the open web, which relies on creators being compensated for their work.[3]

The resistance has been swift but largely ineffective because legal efforts face systemic obstacles. Specifically, copyright preemption under the Copyright Act has effectively neutered most non-copyright claims, thereby narrowing the scope of lawsuits to arguments over copyright law.[4] This limitation benefits GenAI companies because, unlike breach-of-contract or unjust-enrichment claims, copyright law allows for the affirmative defense of fair use. When GenAI companies successfully dismiss other claims and prevail on fair use, virtually any amount of unauthorized scraping becomes legally permissible.

Some scholars argue that website content should be treated like real or personal property, with a corresponding right to exclude. However, others note that this analogy quickly breaks down because the content is not "rivalrous" (one person's use doesn't prevent another's). When a scraper copies content, it doesn't deprive the original owner of the ability to continue using it. Courts have embraced this reasoning, concluding that trespass to chattels requires proof that scraping burdens the website's technical functionality. Unlike when someone rummages through your backpack without permission (where courts have determined you are at least temporarily dispossessed of your property), scraping is not considered inherently harmful and typically doesn't dispossess the website owner of the website's content.

This analysis, however, commits a category error. It misses the distinction between the content and the container. Courts focus exclusively on website content while ignoring the website itself as an integrated digital asset. This confusion is akin to arguing about whether it's legal to photocopy a library book's pages without first determining whether the copier was authorized to be inside the library in the first place. But there is no principled reason for bots to have presumptive access to content before we analyze whether they should be permitted such access. This oversight stems from

3 A nontrivial amount of material on the web was put there with no expectation of pay, but also no expectation that it would be used as raw material for money-making ventures. Frequently, the expected compensation is notoriety and increased standing in various web communities. The co-opting of people's work isn't just a loss of compensation, it's also the destruction of the communities that created the work in the first place.

4 See Chapter 11 ("An Introduction to Copyright Law").

misconceptions about what websites are and how scraping functions within the internet's technical architecture.

A better approach is to focus on the website itself as the property at issue, rather than just the content. This chapter does not advocate expanding intellectual property protections but rather applying established principles of personal property to digital assets. It is largely uncontroversial that a website constitutes personal property and that people have a right to exclude others from it. Furthermore, no competing public interest or legal principle justifies treating digital property as less protectable than its tangible counterparts.

Websites, unlike personal data or intellectual property, are rivalrous. No individual can simultaneously own Amazon.com while Amazon retains control, because ownership is inherently exclusive. Moreover, access to websites and their content is "excludable" because websites can control who accesses their content. If it is unlawful to rummage through a backpack (personal property) to copy its contents, such as a written poem, simply because the backpack's owner permits certain individuals (friends, spouses, children) to access it, then the same principle should apply to websites and their content.

Additionally, while courts have almost exclusively focused on whether interference with chattel dispossessed the owner or impaired the chattel's condition or quality, they overlook that under the Restatement (Second) of Torts, affecting the *value* of the property can also support a trespass claim even when the physical condition of the chattel is unaffected. The scraping of yesteryear may not have threatened the existence or economic viability of websites, but the way GenAI companies scrape and the trend of people increasingly treating GenAI as an answer engine do threaten website viability.

Re-empowering trespass claims would restore website owners' exclusionary rights that courts have eroded over the past two decades. Consequently, bypassing sufficient technological access controls designed to block bots could give rise to legal claims that are currently untested under existing frameworks. Exclusion should not be treated as a game of cat and mouse, where the advantage lies with the scraper, who needs only to find one crack in the defenses, while the website owner must prevent all attacks from every angle. It should not matter if a bot can work around sophisticated blocking attempts. Doing so must still be unlawful, as is the case with all other forms of personal and real property. Just because someone can unzip a backpack or enter a house through a window when the door is locked does not make the trespass lawful.

This does not mean that scraping should be categorically illegal or that all sites should block all scrapers. It's just that website owners should have meaningful control over who accesses their websites. If an owner wants to block all bots, they should be able to do so with legal recourse available. Similarly, if the website owner chooses to allow some or all bots to scrape their site, that should also be permissible.

Ultimately, reinforcing website owners' right to exclude would significantly benefit society. There is little reason to believe that empowering trespass claims would lead to an internet more closed than the one we have today. In fact, the opposite would likely occur. Just as patents and copyright law facilitate the sharing of ideas, so too would enabling viable claims of trespass. Most website owners who don't hide their content behind login accounts want to be accessible. But that doesn't mean they want to be exploited.

Such protection promotes the production and sharing of creative expression, including advances in the sciences and the arts, by ensuring creators can protect and control their creations. A robust exclusion right also provides an efficient means of protecting First Amendment expression by combating the chilling effect that aggressive scraping can have on content creators who would rather not share speech than have it appropriated by GenAI companies. Finally, a strong right to exclude aligns with notions of equity, dignity, and autonomy by prohibiting nonconsensual extraction and exploitation of creators' work.

To establish this legal framework, we must first correctly define the digital asset in question. First, I'll lay the groundwork by examining the nature of property and applying it to websites. Then I'll build the legal argument for robust exclusionary rights, demonstrating how trespass to chattels can be revitalized as meaningful protection for digital property.

19.2 WHAT IS PROPERTY?

Property is something you can own, but it's also a legal fiction that gives courts the flexibility to shape what it means to own a resource in ways that are most beneficial for society.

19.2.1 *The Bundle of Rights*

Property is typically conceived as a "bundle of rights," including possession, use, and alienation (the right to sell or give away). At bottom, property confers the authority to control a resource.

Within the bundle, the right to exclude is paramount. Scholars such as Thomas W. Merrill argue that the right to exclude is the *sine qua non* (the essential essence) of property. The United States Supreme Court has stated that the right of exclusion is "universally held to be a fundamental element of the property right" and "one of the most essential sticks in the bundle of rights that are commonly characterized as property."[i]

When considering the right to exclude, we must be careful not to conflate "exclusion" with "expulsion." Exclusion refers to the right to prevent others from accessing or using property. Expulsion would be the right to remove someone from the property after they have access. The right to exclude (to prevent access) will be the focus of this chapter. As with all rights, it is not absolute. If a court believes the right conflicts with the Constitution or a statute, it may curtail the owner's power. Courts may also limit the right to exclude if it conflicts with others' rights. This is where scraping comes into play.

19.3 WHAT IS A WEBSITE?

Precisely defining a website is essential for legal analysis. For the purposes of this chapter, a website is a collection of interconnected webpages and related content (images, videos, audio, documents) identified by a common domain name and published on at least one web server.

Vitally, a website is not just its content. Rather, it is the underlying infrastructure within which the components and their content exist. The content is merely the visible and interactive elements of the website. Content is not the website itself, just as the words of a book are not the book itself. You can replace every word in a physical book, but it's still the same book object sitting on your shelf. Similarly, a website's content can change entirely while the website itself, meaning the digital structure accessible through its domain name, remains the same entity.

19.3.1 *Server, IP Address, and Domain Name*

The content of a website is stored on a physical web server, a specialized computer system that holds the website's files. The server is the "physical location" of the "library."

To connect to the server, you need either the IP (Internet Protocol) address, a numerical identifier that routes traffic to the server (like GPS coordinates), or the domain name (e.g., google.com), the human-readable, memorable name that corresponds to an IP address (like a street address). When you type a domain name into your browser, the DNS (Domain Name System) translates it into the IP address, allowing your browser to connect to the correct server.

A URL (uniform resource locator) is the complete web address for a specific resource (such as a webpage, image, or document) on a website. It includes the protocol (e.g., https://), the domain name, and, often, a path to the specific file or directory. The domain name is simply a component of the URL.[ii]

19.3.2 *Content and Architecture*

Once you connect to the website, you are on your way to accessing what you are really after: the content. Simply put, if you are seeing content, you are on the website. Content can include:

- HTML (hypertext markup language): the foundational language that structures the content of a webpage.
- CSS (cascading style sheets): controls the presentation and visual styling.
- JavaScript: the programming language that adds interactivity and dynamic behavior.
- Media files: images, videos, audio, and documents.
- Server-side components: retrieve or generate content to be injected into a webpage.

19.3.3 *Reconceptualizing Websites*

The most important takeaway is that if a bot can extract content, it is already on the website. The legal question, then, is not whether copying the content constitutes dispossession but whether accessing the website without consent is an actionable invasion of property. First, we must understand how a webpage loads.

19.4 HOW A WEBPAGE LOADS

The webpage loading process is far more complex than a webpage simply appearing instantly. Accessing content requires a series of extraordinarily fast, hierarchical steps:

1. Initiation and DNS resolution: The user enters the URL, and the browser resolves the domain name to the server's IP address.
2. Establishing a connection: The browser initiates a TCP (Transmission Control Protocol) three-way handshake[5] to establish a reliable connection with the server. If secure (HTTPS[6]), a TLS/SSL handshake[7] follows. The browser then sends an HTTP request for the resources identified by the URL (HTML, CSS, JavaScript, images, etc.).
3. Processing the request: The server processes the request and returns the requested resources.

[5] The TCP three-way handshake is a three-step process used to establish a reliable connection between a client and a server on a TCP/IP network. It ensures that both devices are ready to send and receive data, and synchronizes the sequence numbers that will be used to track the order of data packets. A TCP network is a network that uses the TCP for communication. The TCP is one of the foundational protocols of the internet, and its primary purpose is to ensure that data is delivered reliably, accurately, and in the correct order between a client and a server.

[6] HTTPS (Hypertext Transfer Protocol Secure) is a secure version of the HTTP protocol that uses encryption to protect communication between a web browser and a website. The "S" stands for "secure" and indicates that all data exchanged is encrypted to prevent eavesdropping and tampering.

[7] This establishes a secure, encrypted connection between a client (like your web browser) and a server. It's the first step in using HTTPS and ensures that data is sent privately and securely. The term "SSL" is often used interchangeably with "TLS," but TLS (Transport Layer Security) is the more modern and secure successor to the older SSL (Secure Sockets Layer) protocol.

4. Parsing and construction: As the browser receives an HTML document, it parses it and constructs the Document Object Model (DOM).[8] The browser then fetches additional resources identified during the parsing of the HTML document. The resources may include CSS, JavaScript, images, and other resources. CSS resources are used to build the CSS Object Model (CSSOM).[9] The DOM and CSSOM are combined into a single structure known as a render tree.[10]
5. Layout and painting: The browser calculates the exact size and position of each element (layout) and "paints" the pixels onto the screen (painting), making the visual content visible.
6. JavaScript execution: JavaScript executes, potentially modifying the DOM and triggering dynamic updates and requests for additional resources.

A website does not simply exist in a completed state, awaiting a user to view it. Rather, accessing content requires several steps, each of which must be completed before proceeding to the next. Because the loading process is hierarchical and iterative, it allows website owners to intervene at several points and say "stop" before a bot ever reaches the content.

19.5 WEBSITE AS PERSONAL PROPERTY: THE DOMAIN NAME

A domain name (e.g., google.com) is not intellectual property, such as a copyright, patent, or trademark. This is an important distinction. Domain names are most akin to personal property (like a share of stock or a lease on land). While intellectual property law governs the use of content (which may be subject to fair use), personal property law governs access and confers a robust right to exclude.

When you "buy" a domain name, you acquire a contractual right to use that specific name for a defined period – essentially leasing it from the domain registry through a registrar. This exclusive right of use makes it a valuable commercial asset and property in practical and legal terms.

The case *Kremen v. Cohen (2003)* confirmed this property right, applying a three-part test: The interest must be capable of precise definition, allow exclusive possession or control, and be subject to a legitimate claim of exclusivity. The court found that domain names satisfy each criterion.

For legal purposes, the domain name is effectively the website. The value of a domain name lies in its role as the gateway to the content. If you transfer content, you *don't* lose the website. If you transfer the domain name, you *do* lose control of the website.

8 A tree-like representation of the HTML structure.
9 The CSSOM represents the styles applied to the page.
10 This tree contains only the visible elements of the page and their computed styles.

The legal and commercial asset is the exclusive contractual right to control the digital space at that name's address. It is this exclusive right that satisfies the three-part property test, making it the focal point of the property, not the content. The domain name is the sole mechanism by which the paramount property right – the right to exclude – is exercised, making it more than "just a name" in a legal context.

In addition to being rivalrous, website access is excludable because the owner can prevent others from accessing it. Since the only step before accessing content that involves a user (including bots) is entering the domain name to communicate with the server, it makes the most sense to think of the domain name as the website's gateway, defining the property boundary under the vast majority of circumstances.[11] The server is the final destination and the physical location, but the domain name is the legal and practical point of access and control. In most instances, without the domain name, a bot cannot find the server's IP address to connect with the website. Thus, the domain name is the legal "front door" and the owner's primary means to impose an exclusionary rule before the server even begins processing the request.[12]

Moreover, the website owner's decision to implement technical barriers (such as WAFs (web application firewalls) or IP blocking) is enforced at the domain name level through the connection to the server.

The website, as a unified digital asset accessible through its domain name and existing as an excludable, rivalrous resource, transcends any single part. The domain name owner is the best indicator of who owns the website and should be the ultimate arbiter of who they allow on their property.[13]

[11] It is possible to have a website without a domain name, but courts could easily adapt the framework I've provided for those rare instances.

[12] It's possible for multiple URLs to point to the same content. But while the URL's path or query parameters may change (/recipe.html vs. /recipes?lasagna=true), the domain name (e.g., foodblogger.com) remains constant. This fact proves the chapter's central theory: The content (the lasagna recipe) may be nonrivalrous and accessible via different paths (URLs), but the personal property (the domain name and website architecture) remains a single, excludable, rivalrous asset. The domain name, not the specific content file, is the consistent boundary that the trespasser must cross.

[13] This even applies to the decentralized fediverse: For example, a Mastodon user controls the terms of the license for their content, but the platform owner controls the access to the underlying property (the website). If a bot bypasses the platform's technical access controls to get to the user's "followers-only" content, the platform owner still has a viable claim of trespass to chattels against the bot for the unauthorized access to the website's server/property (the chattel). The user's rights are a feature of the platform's property, not a counterexample to its nature as excludable property. Moreover, the "impairment as to its value" clause of Restatement (Second) of Torts § 218(b) is still applicable to the platform owner in this context. The platform's value is based on its promise of a controlled, non-exploitative environment for users. If a GenAI scraper can easily bypass privacy settings to harvest content, the platform loses its core competitive advantage and its business model is undermined. The resulting loss of user trust, reputation, and potential for financial contributions (subscriptions, donations) directly impairs the value of the platform as a commercial asset (the chattel).

19.6 REVITALIZING TRESPASS TO CHATTELS

The right to exclude is meaningless without the state's enforcement powers. Yet courts are reluctant to help website owners enforce their rights against scrapers.

When plaintiffs bring claims against GenAI companies, they skip past even attempting trespass to chattels because the law has been so neutered over the last twenty years. Claims based on violations of statutes such as the Computer Fraud and Abuse Act and conversion have also proven ineffective against the scraping of publicly available data. Breach-of-contract claims (based on terms of service) are often preempted by copyright law if they seek to restrict copying of copyrighted material. This funnels claims into copyright law, where the affirmative defense of fair use can prevail, leaving website owners without recourse.

To understand trespass, we must return to the Restatement (Second) of Torts.[14] Section 217 (1965) states that "[a] trespass to a chattel may be committed by intentionally (a) dispossessing another of the chattel, or (b) using or intermeddling with a chattel in the possession of another."

Section 218, which defines liability for trespass to chattels, states that a trespasser is liable if they:

> (a) dispossess the other of the chattel, or (b) the chattel is impaired as to its condition, quality, or value, or (c) the possessor is deprived of the use of the chattel for a substantial time, or (d) bodily harm is caused to the possessor, or harm is caused to some person or thing in which the possessor has a legally protected interest.

Courts have historically focused almost exclusively on physical harm or burdens to the server (clauses a, c, and d). However, the language of Section 218 allows for a claim when the chattel is impaired as to its value (clause b) – a provision that has been largely ignored but is perfectly suited to address the economic harm caused by GenAI scraping.

Comment e[15] of the restatement notes that "[s]ufficient legal protection of the possessor's interest in the mere inviolability of his chattel is afforded by his privilege to use reasonable force to protect his possession against even harmless interference."

Comment h reaffirms the notion that physical harm is not necessary, stating that "[t]here may, however, be situations in which the value to the owner of a particular type of chattel may be impaired by dealing with it in a manner that does not affect

[14] A restatement is a secondary legal source published by the American Law Institute that synthesizes and clarifies the common law on a specific subject. These publications are not binding law unless adopted by a court, but they provide an authoritative overview with "black letter" rules, explanatory comments, illustrative examples, and references to cases, making them highly persuasive authority for courts, legal professionals, and scholars.

[15] Comments in a restatement of law are sections that explain the restatement's "black letter" rules, clarify their background and rationale, and provide guidance on their application.

its physical condition … In such a case, the intermeddling is actionable even though the physical condition of the chattel is not impaired."

In other words, a claim for trespass to chattels should succeed where a website can show:

1. Intentional intermeddling: The scraper intentionally circumvented technical measures meant to prevent access/scraping.
2. Harm to value: The intentional intermeddling caused harm to the value of the website.

The value of the chattel – in this case, the website – is typically derived entirely from its content.[16] For many creators, content is the currency that attracts readers, advertisers, and subscribers. When GenAI companies take content without compensation, they appropriate the site's economic basis, undermining its value to the owner and its long-term viability. This is the most significant difference between past scraping and GenAI scraping today.

Previously, scrapers might have aggregated data, but users still had to visit the original site for the full context or the best user experience. Today, GenAI models often function as "answer engines," providing users with the necessary information directly in the chatbot interface, thereby eliminating the need to click through to the source website.

Consider a food blogger who spent years developing recipes and building an audience. When an AI system scrapes her content and users simply ask the chatbot "How do I make lasagna?" instead of visiting her site, she loses not only potential ad revenue from that single visit but also the entire economic model that sustained her work. Multiply this across millions of content creators, and the systemic harm becomes clear. If a user never needs to visit a news site, blog, or research database because the AI has already extracted and summarized the key findings, the original website loses traffic, ad revenue, subscriber potential, and its basic economic viability. This harm is distinct from physical server strain and directly addresses the GenAI exploitation model.

19.7 THE REQUIRED STANDARD: SUFFICIENT EFFORTS OF TECHNICAL EXCLUSION

Because the internet facilitates interactions among strangers, a successful trespass claim concerning websites depends on showing that the alleged trespasser deliberately bypassed a clearly identifiable barrier. For a website, having a barrier means taking active steps to prevent scrapers from accessing it. The focus is on preventing

16 Some domain names are valuable because of their name: sex.com, dogs.com, and houses.com are all likely worth millions just because the domain name is recognizable.

unauthorized *access*, rather than stopping content scraping *after* access has already been gained, at which point the content is likely already copied.

To strengthen their legal position, website owners are now using more sophisticated tools to block or restrict bots beyond simple robots.txt files. These measures include requiring mandatory sign-up and login to authenticate users and restrict content access. They also employ advanced security services, such as Cloudflare Firewall and AWS WAF, which provide real-time bot detection and blocking, IP blocking, analysis of HTTP headers, and JavaScript-based fingerprinting without slowing users or requiring log-ins.

These technical defenses are important because they establish tangible "technological barriers" or "gates" whose circumvention can significantly bolster trespass claims, even if those barriers are insufficient for criminal prosecution. Many of these solutions are inexpensive or free and easy to implement. Vitally, they provide concrete proof of the website owner's intent to exclude and can strengthen arguments for unauthorized interference in trespass-to-chattels claims.

A strength of this legal interpretation of trespass to websites is that the sufficiency of these efforts need not require a deep technical exploration by the trier of fact (judges and juries). The common sense and lived experience of an ordinary judge or jury will usually suffice. This pragmatic approach prevents the court from needing a PhD in computer science.

The "casual surfer" test can be used as a simple guide: If a bot can access the content under circumstances similar to a casual web surfer (even for a fraction of a second) and even if it takes some effort that is within reason (such as clearing your cache, using incognito mode, using a different browser), then it is probably not sufficiently protected against the bot to bring a viable trespass-to-chattels claim. In contrast, if the bot cannot access the content in the manner of a casual surfer despite taking those common extra steps, then the barriers are likely sufficient.

In short, the test is whether the scraper circumvented a sufficient technical barrier designed to block them (such as a WAF or IP block) in a way an ordinary person would not. It requires (a) a demonstrable, good-faith effort to exclude someone or something (such as bots) using reasonable technical means and (b) proving the deliberate bypass of the exclusionary effort. It does not require proving the site is inaccessible to all by default.

19.8 CONCLUSION

Some argue that exclusion would stifle expression or lead to a closed internet. This argument is precisely backward: Prohibiting exclusion will stifle speech. When people create content, they do so to reach others, not for the enjoyment of bots. When GenAI paraphrases content without attribution, it undermines the original creator's ability to generate revenue or gain recognition, chilling content creation.

Empowering the right to exclude promotes production and sharing by ensuring creators can protect and control their work.

Ultimately, by focusing the property analysis on the domain name and website architecture rather than the content alone, and by leveraging the "value" impairment clause of trespass to chattels, we can establish that bypassing sufficient technical access controls to enable nonconsensual GenAI scraping is unlawful. This is the proper and proportionate solution to tame the unrestrained and self-serving tendencies of the current AI marketplace.

Imagine a different internet. In this world, AI companies that want to build transformative technologies don't operate like digital strip miners, extracting value while leaving communities impoverished. Instead, they negotiate.

A news organization might license its archive for AI training in exchange for revenue that funds investigative journalism. An independent blogger might welcome certain bots while excluding others, maintaining control over how her decade of writing contributes to the future of technology. A scientific database might permit AI companies to access its research papers, provided the resulting models properly attribute sources and drive traffic back to the original work.

Strengthening exclusion rights would simply force AI companies to do what every other transformative industry has done: pay for, or obtain permission to use, the raw materials that make their products valuable.

The result would be an AI ecosystem that's more legally sound, more economically fair, and more sustainable. When creators can make a living from their work, they create more of it. And when they create more, everyone – including AI companies – benefits from a richer, more vibrant internet.

19.9 DISCUSSION QUESTIONS

1. The chapter argues that the legal field has committed a "category error" by focusing on the content (nonrivalrous) instead of the website architecture (the rivalrous property) when assessing trespass claims. Does the analogy of a website as a "library" and content as the "book" effectively reset the legal conversation, or do you think the digital nature of the internet makes this comparison flawed?
2. The author's suggested legal strategy hinges on using the "impairment as to its value" clause in the law of trespass to chattels (Restatement (Second) of Torts § 218). Is the argument that GenAI's function as an "answer engine" directly impairs a website's economic value (ad revenue, subscriptions) a sufficiently concrete and measurable harm for a court to recognize, or is it too speculative?
3. The chapter proposes the "casual surfer" as a simple, common-sense standard for determining if a website owner has made "sufficient efforts of

technical exclusion." Do you believe a legal standard based on the lived experience of an "ordinary judge or jury" is better than one requiring a deep technical understanding, and what are the potential downsides of such a subjective test?

4. The author argues that reinforcing the right to exclude would ultimately benefit society and lead to an internet more open than today. How can a greater right to exclude lead to a more open system, and do you agree with this conclusion?
5. The chapter emphasizes that the legal focus should be on the right to exclude (preventing access) rather than expulsion (removing a person/bot after they've entered). Why is this distinction so important for creating a successful legal framework against scraping?

PART IV

Societal Implications

Assuming the actions of GenAI companies are legal, what might that mean for society? This next part will explore a few key areas that the unmitigated onset and spread of GenAI could significantly and negatively affect.

20

The Economics of the Internet

While GenAI bots function identically to search-indexing bots at a technical level, the aggressive scraping campaigns launched by GenAI companies since 2022 differ significantly from earlier web-scraping efforts in scale, frequency, and respect for established internet norms.

Websites are focused on maximizing traffic monetization and increasingly rely on GenAI for large-scale discovery, rather than traditional search, even though current GenAI models depend on these sources. However, GenAI acts as an intermediary between users and sources, paradoxically reducing traffic for content creators. Currently, GenAI holds a significant advantage, and no mutually equitable solutions have been established, creating an asymmetry analogous to monopoly power. A clear illustration of this imbalance is that websites must choose between virtually disappearing from the internet or allowing platforms like Google to scrape their content for both search results and AI overviews, despite the latter demonstrably reducing site traffic. If this structural imbalance and injustice persist, the consequences at multiple levels will be severe and difficult to reverse.

This chapter will explore the impact GenAI bots have had in just a few years, which is linked to the idea explored in Chapter 19 ("Property, Exclusion, and Trespass"), where I argued that there could be a viable claim of trespass if trespassing on a website harmed its value.

20.1 WHY GENAI COMPANIES SCRAPE SO MUCH

While there are many legitimate reasons to scrape sites, in the age of GenAI, the most prolific scrapers operate primarily to gather training data for GenAI models. Web scraping has existed for decades, and GenAI companies often seek treatment comparable to that of historical scrapers. Yet they represent something meaningfully different: Their data consumption is both more voracious and less discerning, and the previously symbiotic relationship between scrapers and content creators has all but vanished.

GenAI companies require massive amounts of data to train their AI models. They ingest content, such as webpages, extract the desired parts, like text, and then convert that text into subwords, called tokens, for input into their models. This enables them to train the models to predict which tokens are most likely to follow preceding tokens. To illustrate the scale of such datasets, Meta trained Llama 4 on "30 to 60 trillion tokens."[i] This quantity is so vast it defies human comprehension. To put this in perspective: If you spent $1 every second, 24 hours a day, it would take you over 31,700 years to spend $1 trillion. At the upper end of Meta's range, 60 trillion tokens represent computational digestion of written material on a geological timescale.

GenAI scrapers appear to adopt a cavalier attitude toward scraping, partly because most sites traditionally maintained permissive approaches toward researchers and indexers. Put simply, because a website previously accepted being scraped for search indexes, there is an assumption that such websites should similarly accept scraping for GenAI training. Similarly, if academic scraping for research raised no legal concerns, the reasoning goes, then OpenAI, Meta, Google, and others should face few obstacles when pursuing comparable activities. This position finds support among some scholars.[ii]

Historically, nonconsensual scraping, such as for competitive intelligence, typically targeted a relatively small portion of the web. The same limitations applied to other scraping purposes, such as market research and search engine optimization analysis. Traditional scrapers mostly targeted strategically selected commercial sites rather than the entire internet because universal scraping would yield a poor signal-to-noise ratio and be time-consuming and expensive.

GenAI entities pursue the opposite strategy by indiscriminately collecting vast quantities of content. This represents a significant shift not only in the volume of data collected and the number of sites scraped, but also in the number of people and entities, both large and small, that are negatively impacted by such extensive scraping. In short, GenAI scrapers and historical scrapers are largely incomparable, and suggesting otherwise is misleading at best. The distinction is one of kind rather than degree. A traditional scraper might be a surgical scalpel, but a GenAI scraper operates like an industrial dredge, clear-cutting vast ecosystems of online content.

20.2 THE SCALE OF CONTEMPORARY SCRAPING ACTIVITY

Two primary types of GenAI scrapers warrant distinction: those engaged in GenAI training and those conducting retrieval-augmented generation (RAG) operations.[1] Retrieval-augmented generation is a method that enables GenAI models to supplement their pretrained knowledge with current, specific information retrieved from

[1] While I often refer to GenAI companies doing the scraping, what I mean is that they are the cause of the scraping. They often scrape the internet themselves, but they may also pay third parties to scrape content on their behalf.

an external data source, such as the live web, in real time. Training-focused scraping involves bots that harvest virtually all public content on the internet to build datasets for training GenAI models. According to Cloudflare, a major internet infrastructure company that handles roughly 20 percent of all web traffic, these types of bots account for 80 percent of AI bot activity.[iii] The RAG bots operate differently; they search for and retrieve specific information in real time in response to user requests. That data is then fed into the GenAI model as part of the prompt to enhance the model's output.[iv]

According to research by TollBit, a platform that facilitates content monetization by creating a marketplace where AI bots and data scrapers can obtain licensed access, used by over 2,000 publishers including the Associated Press, *Time*, and *Forbes*, "Among sites with TollBit Analytics set up before January 2025, AI Bot traffic volume nearly doubled in Q1 [2025], rising by 87%."[v] Moreover, "average scraping activity across the top 6 AI bots increased by 56% from Q4 to Q1."

Cloudflare, which is significantly larger than TollBit, documented a similar surge in scraping, noting that scraping for GenAI training increased 65 percent in the first half of 2025.[vi] This data helps explain Reddit's allegation that Anthropic scraped its site more than 100,000 times despite Anthropic's assurances that it would cease such activities,[vii] why Anthropic scraped iFixit's website one million times over twenty-four hours,[viii] and why even Wikimedia has raised concerns about scrapers overwhelming Wikipedia's servers, with "65% of [its] most expensive traffic [coming] from bots."[ix]

To provide context, it is helpful to compare AI bot activity with Google's established practices. Googlebot facilitates the indexing of the entire internet, enabling content to be delivered through Google Search. As the TollBit report notes:

> In Q2 2024, the scraping activity of the top 6 AI bots was roughly 10% the size of Googlebot's scraping activity. In Q1 2025, AI bot access to sites is now 60.29% that of Bingbot's activity, and 30.55% of Googlebot's total scraping.
>
> This data shows the dramatic increase in AI bot market share when compared to Googlebot and Bingbot activity. Google and Microsoft are companies that publishers have obviously had relationships with for 20+ years. In one year [websites] are being hammered by new crawlers where the value exchange is no longer clear, especially if [the crawlers] don't drive traffic back to sites.[x]

Additional examples further illustrate the scope of the problem. Open-source projects may be particularly vulnerable to AI scrapers because they often share their infrastructure publicly and lack sufficient funding and personnel to combat bots.[xi] The open-source project Read the Docs reported that "one crawler downloaded 73 TB of zipped HTML files in May 2024, with almost 10 TB in a single day."[xii]

The scraping also proves highly problematic for institutions that host content widely considered to be in the public interest. This includes galleries, libraries, archives, and museums (GLAMs). A joint initiative between the Centre for

Science, Culture and the Law at the University of Exeter and the Engelberg Center on Innovation Law & Policy at NYU Law called GLAM-E issued a report finding that of 43 respondents to their survey, "39 had experienced a recent increase in traffic. Twenty-seven of the thirty-nine respondents experiencing an increase in traffic attributed it to AI training data bots, with an additional seven believing that bots could be contributing to the traffic."[xiii]

The increase proved problematic for GLAMs in many ways, including that "many respondents did not realize they were experiencing a growth in bot traffic until the traffic reached the point where it overwhelmed the service and knocked online collections offline." The report also found that "robots.txt is not currently an effective way to prevent bots from overwhelming collections." One key conclusion the authors draw is that "the cultural institutions that host online collections are not resourced to continue adding more servers, deploying more sophisticated firewalls, and hiring more operations engineers in perpetuity." The situation increasingly forces institutions dedicated to public access into an impossible choice: restrict that access or face technical collapse.

The Confederation of Open Access Repositories reached similar conclusions: "Over 90% of survey respondents indicated their repository is encountering aggressive bots, usually more than once a week, and often leading to slow downs and service outages."[xiv] It warns that "the recent rise in aggressive bot activity could potentially result in repositories limiting access to their resources for both human and machine users – leading to a situation where the value of the global repository network is substantially diminished."

20.3 THE INADEQUACY OF ROBOTS.TXT

The Robots Exclusion Protocol (robots.txt), which allows websites to direct bots on which webpages they can access, has existed for decades. The protocol's specifications were formally established by the Internet Engineering Task Force. Bots not listed in a robots.txt file are typically presumed to have access to webpages by default. Some may argue that robots.txt provides a sufficient technical measure to control AI bots, but this view is mistaken. Research indicates that bots frequently fail to comply with more restrictive robots.txt directives, and certain categories of bots, including AI search crawlers, often ignore robots.txt entirely.[xv] Studies have also documented instances of malicious bots spoofing user agents to evade restrictions.

An increasing number of websites are attempting to block bots by using robots.txt. TollBit reports that "the number of explicit disallow requests for AI bots (i.e., a single site disallowing a single bot would count as one) has increased from 559 to 2,165 (+287%). The average number of AI bots explicitly disallowed per website has grown from 2.2 to 8.6, a 4× increase."[xvi] While the most prominent GenAI bots are unsurprisingly blocked at higher rates, even the nonprofit Allen Institute for Artificial Intelligence's Ai2Bot-Dolma is now blocked by 29 percent of sites on TollBit's network.

However, the report continues, these blocking efforts have proven increasingly ineffectual:

> Publishers have attempted to block 4× more AI bots between January 2024 and January 2025 by disallowing them in their robots.txt file. However, AI bots are increasingly ignoring the robots.txt file. The percentage of AI Bot scrapes that bypassed robots.txt surged from 3.3% in Q4 2024 to 12.9% by the end of Q1 2025 (March). In March 2025, over 26 [million] scrapes from AI bots bypassed robots.txt for sites on TollBit.

Several major GenAI companies explicitly state their intention to ignore robots.txt when scraping serves user prompts, which is an approach adopted by Perplexity, Google, and Meta, among others.

Moreover, robots.txt remains wildly underutilized. Among the top 10,000 domains on Cloudflare's extensive network, only 37 percent maintained a robots.txt file at all as of July 1, 2025.[xvii] If a bot is not listed in a website's robots.txt file, the bot is effectively allowed to access the webpages by default. This low adoption rate likely indicates a general lack of awareness regarding robots.txt rather than deliberate permissiveness. Support for this interpretation can be found in the fact that 85 percent of websites using Cloudflare opted to block AI bots leading up to July 2024, when Cloudflare introduced a simple blocking option.[xviii] Cloudflare now reports that over one million customers block all AI scrapers.[xix]

Among sites that implement robots.txt, most block only the most prominent GenAI bots (OpenAI, Anthropic, etc.), and even these are blocked at low rates: GPTBot at 7.8%, Google-Extend at 5.6%, and other GenAI bots at less than 5%. Given that there appears to be little rational basis for a site to block OpenAI while permitting Anthropic and Perplexity bots, this inconsistency is likely more attributable to a lack of awareness than to intentional policy.

Some entities, including Adobe and llmstxt.org, have proposed alternatives to robots.txt to give website owners more granular control over content access, but these solutions share robots.txt's voluntary nature and compliance limitations. The problem is the lack of legal or ethical enforcement, not the lack of a technical file to comply with.

20.3.1 *Referrals to Sources*

What GenAI companies appear to overlook or flatly ignore is that bots do not serve the same economic or reputation-building function as humans visiting webpages. Indeed, the scraping by GenAI bots may not necessarily prove problematic in isolation. Some observers compare such scraping to indexing bots and question the distinction between them. However, TollBit's report indicates that such comparisons are weak at best, with "traffic from AI applications represent[ing] just 0.04% of all external referrals to sites in Q1 2025. This is insignificant when compared with Google, which delivers around 85% of traceable external visits."[xx] A closer look at how often GenAI generates referrals reveals the lopsided benefits those companies enjoy at the expense of content creators.

20.3.1.1 Crawl-to-Referral Ratios

A revealing metric is the crawl-to-referral ratio exhibited by different bots. If GenAI entities directed humans to original publishers at rates similar to Google Search, then the argument for enforcing a strong website exclusion right would be weaker. However, TollBit found that "in Q1 2025, on average across TollBit sites, for every 11 crawls, Bing returns one human visitor to sites. This means that Bing's crawl-to-referral ratio is 11:1, up from 8:1 in Q42024 and 6:1 in Q3. Crawl-to-referral ratios for AI-only apps are as follows: OpenAI's ratio is 179:1, Perplexity's is 369:1, and Anthropic's ratio is 8692:1."[xxi]

As of May 31, 2026, Anthropic crawled 11,000 times for every referral it provided. OpenAI's ratio was 857:1 and Perplexity's was 188:1. In contrast, Microsoft's was 34:1 and Google's was 5:1, reflecting their more traditional roles as traffic-generating search indexers.[xxii] According to Cloudflare's CEO, the problem has deteriorated over time. He stated in July 2025 that "OpenAI sent one visitor to a publisher for every 250 pages it crawled six months ago, while Anthropic sent one visitor for every 6,000 pages."[xxiii]

In sharp contrast to GenAI entities, "legacy search index crawlers would scan your content a couple of times, or less, for each visitor sent. A site's availability to crawlers made their revenue model more viable, not less."[xxiv] Put differently, whereas traditional scraping generally represented a symbiotic relationship where websites sought to be scraped to facilitate discovery through search and ultimately reach human users, GenAI bots shatter this understanding of how the relationship should work.

Notably, the paucity of referrals is intentional. As Matteo Wong wrote for *The Atlantic*:

> Although ChatGPT and Perplexity and Google AI Overviews cite their sources with (small) footnotes or bars to click on, not clicking on those links is the entire point. OpenAI, in its announcement of its new search feature, wrote that "getting useful answers on the web can take a lot of effort. It often requires multiple searches and digging through links to find quality sources and the right information for you. Now, chat can get you to a better answer." Google's pitch is that its AI "will do the Googling for you." Perplexity's chief business officer told me this summer that "people don't come to Perplexity to consume journalism," and that the AI tool will provide less traffic than traditional search. For curious users, Perplexity suggests follow-up questions so that, instead of opening a footnote, you keep reading in Perplexity.[xxv]

Simply put, the scraping is designed to train GenAI systems with the express intent to supplant the need for people to visit webpages.

20.3.1.2 Google's AI Overview Impact

While Google's referral ratio ranks among the best, research from the Pew Research Center found that "about six-in-ten respondents (58%) conducted at least one Google search in March 2025 that produced an AI-generated summary." Significantly, "users who encountered an AI summary clicked on a traditional search result link in 8% of all visits. Those who did not encounter an AI summary clicked on a search result nearly twice as often (15% of visits)." Even more telling, merely 1% of users clicked links within the AI overviews.[xxvi]

Additionally, users stopped browsing after 26% of searches when AI summaries were present compared to only 16% when summaries were absent. Bain & Company corroborated these findings, reporting that 60% of Google searches end without users navigating to external websites when the AI summary appears.[xxvii] Other researchers estimate the reduction in navigation to external websites at approximately 35%.[xxviii]

A third study found that "on desktop, outbound clicks to external websites drop by about two-thirds. On mobile, the drop is nearly 50 percent. Many users see the [AI overview, 'AIO'] as a complete answer. Clicking on links inside the AIO is rare – 7.4 percent on desktop, 19 percent on mobile."[xxix] Moreover, "even when users interacted with the AIO, they didn't go far. While 88 percent tapped 'Show more,' the median scroll depth was just 30 percent. Most (86 percent) only skimmed the content, and very few reached the bottom of the answer."

These findings may appear to conflict, but regardless of the specific percentage based on particular methodologies, the consistent trend of fewer people clicking links when presented with AI overviews clearly disadvantages websites. AI-generated summaries serve as substitutes for, rather than more helpful gateways to, original content.

This trend also means that websites have limited alternatives to avoid a GenAI-mediated future.

20.3.1.3 Impact on Specific Websites

Another way to assess the issue is to examine how specific sites have fared since the launch of ChatGPT, which sparked the current wave of GenAI scraping. According to the *Wall Street Journal*, "traffic from organic search to HuffPost's desktop and mobile websites fell by just over half in the past three years, and by nearly that much at the Washington Post," and "organic search traffic to [*Business Insider*'s] websites declined by 55% between April 2022 and April 2025." [xxx] The report further notes:

> At the New York Times, the share of traffic coming from organic search to the paper's desktop and mobile websites slid to 36.5% in April 2025 from almost 44% three years earlier, according to Similarweb. The Wall Street Journal's traffic from organic search was up in April compared with three years prior, Similarweb data show, though as a share of overall traffic it declined to 24% from 29%.

The harm extends beyond news sites and major brands. Shira Ovide reported that one large sports betting website was subjected to thirteen million scraping attempts from AI bots in a month, resulting in only 600 human visitors. In contrast, Google's 15 million scraping operations of the same site generated millions of human visitors.[xxxi]

20.3.1.4 The Problem of Source Attribution

Even when GenAI tools include citations to source materials, and even if we (incorrectly) assume people click on links as often as they do with traditional search results, the citations prove more problematic than initially appears. According to the *Columbia Journalism Review*'s Tow Center for Digital Journalism:

> Even when these AI search tools cited sources, they often directed users to syndicated versions of content on platforms like Yahoo News rather than original publisher sites. This occurred even in cases where publishers had formal licensing agreements with AI companies.
>
> URL fabrication emerged as another significant problem. More than half of citations from Google's Gemini and Grok 3 led users to fabricated or broken URLs, resulting in error pages. Of 200 citations tested from Grok 3, 154 resulted in broken links.
>
> These issues create significant tension for publishers, who face difficult choices. Blocking AI crawlers might lead to a complete loss of attribution, while permitting them allows widespread reuse without driving traffic back to publishers' own websites.[xxxii]

20.4 GENAI AS DIGITAL GATEKEEPER

By positioning themselves between users and the websites they seek to visit, GenAI companies act as gatekeepers, demanding value before allowing users to access original content.

Research illustrates this phenomenon: One study found that for every 1,000 searches in the United States using Google, only 360 lead users to the open web. The remaining 640 do not result in users clicking on any of the results Google surfaces (perhaps because of an AI overview, snippet, or additional Google searches), and approximately one-third of all clicks direct users to Google-owned platforms such as YouTube, Google Flights, and Google Maps.[xxxiii]

Google could easily provide an option that allows websites to control whether their content is used to train GenAI models, such as Gemini and the models that provide AI overview summaries, while maintaining search visibility, but it chooses not to. Instead, the only real choice Google allows is to opt out of training the GenAI models. For summaries, Google presents a blunt, coercive, and binary choice: Websites can either opt out of being scraped for both search results and summaries, or accept both. This means a site must choose between virtually disappearing from the internet or allowing Google to scrape and use its content to generate AI overviews that demonstrably reduce traffic.[xxxiv] As the complaint in *Chegg v. Google* puts it:

> This action challenges Google's abuse of its adjudicated monopoly in General Search Services to coerce online publishers like Chegg to supply content that Google republishes without permission in AI-generated answers that unfairly compete for the attention of users on the Internet in violation of the Antitrust laws of the United States. This conduct threatens to further entrench Google's generative search monopoly and to expand it into online publishing, restricting competition in those markets and reducing the production of original content for consumers.[xxxv]

Paradoxically, as publisher traffic decreases, Google's advertising revenue has continued to grow, highlighting a disconnect between the content ecosystem on which Google depends and Google itself.[xxxvi] As the *Washington Post* notes, "When [Google] does show an AI answer on 'commercial' searches, it shows up below the row of advertisements. That could force websites to buy ads just to maintain their position at the top of search results."[xxxvii]

Catherine Perloff wrote about this issue for *The Information*: "Publishers and advertisers have no other good option, even as the rise of ChatGPT has shown signs of sapping Google's power in the Web ecosystem. The phenomenon helps explain how Google is maintaining double-digit search ad growth despite signs that people are searching for information less on Google than they used to."[xxxviii] In other words, due to Google's advertising dominance, businesses are spending more just to remain in place.

When pressed about this problem, Google typically claims the study in question used a flawed methodology[xxxix] or asserts that the facts are actually the opposite.[xxxx] However, Google has not specified the alleged flaws nor provided contradictory evidence.

20.5 IMPACT ON CONTENT CREATORS

The distinction between a human visitor and a bot accessing the same site for ostensibly the same purpose is enormous. Even when humans are only visiting to find information, they may be exposed to advertisements that prompt them to click, subscribe to the site, or pay for premium content, and they may share information about the site with others, thereby helping to build the site's reputation. Bots fail to provide any of these benefits.

Bots neither view nor respond to advertisements, they don't subscribe to publishers, and while they may occasionally link to sources, they typically do not. In other words, while website owners create websites to connect with other humans for various reasons, bots satisfy none of these objectives. Bots primarily visit to extract and exploit information while contributing virtually nothing to the website's sustainability. This is problematic because many site owners depend on traffic volume to generate sufficient ad impressions or other income to sustain their operations. This is also true for nonprofit websites that strive to make their content as open as possible. For instance, when a bot visits Wikipedia, it doesn't donate. Similarly, when a chatbot summarizes Wikipedia content, the human user doesn't see the request for donations. It's shattering the Wikipedia model.

AI overviews and similar AI products risk transforming publishers into content creators who are systematically cut off from the economic benefits of their own work. Anthony Katsur, the CEO of IAB Tech Lab, a company that creates open technical standards across the ad-supported digital economy, described publishers as "the plankton of the digital media ecosystem,"[xxxxi] underscoring their vulnerability in this evolving landscape. Beyond revenue loss, the sheer volume of AI scraping imposes tangible operational burdens. Data center operators must also contend with the ongoing increase in server load from GenAI scrapers, which necessitates expanded connectivity and results in higher costs for content hosts. This directly impacts the operational expenses and financial sustainability for publishers.

As shown in Section 20.3.1.2, research consistently indicates a significant decline in click-through rates from search results when AI overviews are present, signaling a shift away from the click economy that has historically underpinned web monetization through advertising. As users increasingly get answers directly from AI without visiting source websites, the traditional model of driving traffic to generate ad impressions or subscriptions faces severe disruption. This represents a reduction in human traffic and a wholesale redistribution of value. This dynamic requires a reevaluation of how content value is measured and compensated.

The rapid expansion of the AI scraping market underscores strong demand for training data to fuel AI development. This demand has historically relied, in part, on AI companies' assumption that publicly available web data should be freely accessible for training. This conflict extends beyond mere copyright infringement; it represents a shift in how digital content is valued and perceived. If content is universally treated as freely available input for AI, it severely devalues the significant labor, expertise, and financial investment required to create original, high-quality content. This existential threat directly undermines the financial viability and long-term sustainability of content creation industries.

20.6 BROADER IMPLICATIONS

The prolific exploitation has downsides not only for publishers but also for GenAI companies. First, GenAI companies may find that their models are increasingly trained on AI-generated content. Because that content is itself a compressed version of other content, the quality, depth, variety, and veracity of training data may decline with each iteration. Even if GenAI companies can filter out most AI-generated content when creating training datasets by investigating the data more methodically, it is unclear whether a scraping bot can perform a similar high-quality scrub during a RAG search.

Additionally, by reducing publisher funding, GenAI companies undermine those publishers' ability to continue operating or maintain their current levels of quality and breadth. This will result in less high-quality content for GenAI to train on.

Of course, if some websites, especially social media and professional networking platforms, are allowed to block scraping, it could raise concerns about monopolization. This restriction effectively allows dominant platforms to hoard valuable user and market data, creating barriers to entry for potential competitors who rely on that data for innovation and service development. Consequently, a small number of established companies could solidify their market power and stifle competition, potentially leading to higher prices or reduced quality of service for consumers.

Finally, society suffers from these developments. As people increasingly rely on GenAI for information while the quality of the information sources declines, collective knowledge suffers. Society also loses when people create less content or limit public sharing in response to being exploited. The impact may be long-lasting. We cannot instantly restore websites that atrophy or shutter under the crush of GenAI. It takes time to revitalize these sectors and realign incentives so that it's worthwhile for people to resume creating and sharing. It is easier to tear the web down than to build it up.

20.7 DISCUSSION QUESTIONS

1. The chapter describes the distinction between traditional and GenAI scraping as "one of kind rather than degree," likening the latter to an "industrial dredge." What is the most compelling piece of evidence in the chapter that supports this claim? If you were a content creator, which type of scraping would concern you more, and why?
2. The crawl-to-referral ratios are stark (e.g., Anthropic at 11,000:1, Google at 5:1). Why do you think the referral ratios for GenAI-only applications (OpenAI, Perplexity, Anthropic) are so much worse than those of traditional search engines (Google, Bing)? Does this gap represent a shift in the intent behind the scraping?

3. Matteo Wong is quoted as saying that for AI overviews, "not clicking on those links is the entire point." If GenAI tools are designed to supplant the need to visit source pages, what is a fair, alternative business model to compensate the original content creators for their work?
4. The chapter notes that for every 1,000 Google searches, 640 don't result in an outbound click, and one-third of clicks go to Google-owned platforms. Does Google have an ethical responsibility to prioritize non-Google sites in search results, or is this simply a smart business practice in a competitive environment?
5. The Robots Exclusion Protocol (robots.txt) is an old "gentlemen's agreement" of the internet. Given the data on noncompliance and the low adoption rate, should a government or international body step in to create a legally binding technical protocol for content scraping? What would be the pros and cons?
6. The scraping causes "tangible operational burdens" for GLAMs (galleries, libraries, archives, museums) and open-source projects, sometimes knocking their sites offline. If these institutions cannot afford to continuously upgrade their servers to fight AI bots, what happens to public-interest knowledge, and who should bear the cost of protecting it?
7. The conclusion states, "It is easier to tear the web down than to build it up." What single, immediate action (technical, legal, or market-driven) do you think would be the most effective first step toward realigning incentives to make content creation sustainable again?

21

Oligopolies

In contrast to a monopoly, where one company dominates a market and prevents meaningful disruption or competition, GenAI is currently an oligopoly, with a handful of companies dominating.

In the fervent debates over AI, a seductive narrative has emerged: Startups and open-source software will save us from the current oligopoly.[1] I must concede that open source lowers the initial barrier to innovation, enabling smaller players to develop niche models and specialized applications. However, lowering the barrier to innovation is not the same as lowering the barrier to market-wide disruption. The enormous cost and scale required for foundational model training and deployment ensure that core market power remains concentrated with Big Tech.

The logic of open source seems straightforward: By making GenAI models freely available, the thinking goes, scrappy startups and independent researchers can finally break free from Big Tech behemoths such as Amazon, Google, Meta, Apple, and Microsoft. This is the tech revolution that open-source development can supposedly spark.

This worldview found its poster child in Shawn Presser, the creator of the Books3 dataset, a collection of nearly 200,000 pirated books now at the center of major copyright lawsuits. In a *Wired* profile, Presser framed his work as a democratizing force:

> In his eyes, it leveled the playing field for smaller companies, researchers, and ordinary people who wanted to create large language models. He believes people who want to delete Books3 are unintentionally advocating for a generative AI landscape dominated solely by Big Tech-affiliated companies, such as OpenAI. "If you really want to knock Books3 offline, fine. Just go into it with eyes wide open. The world that you're choosing is one where only billion-dollar corporations are able to create these large language models," he says.[i]

While this vision of using open-source datasets to disrupt established market power sounds romantic, even noble, it confronts an inconvenient reality. Books3 became

[1] For simplicity, this chapter will mostly focus on open source. However, most of the reasoning that makes me skeptical that open source will save the day applies equally to startups.

available in October 2020. Over five years later, a handful of massively capitalized companies still dominate the landscape: OpenAI, Google, Meta, and Microsoft. The revolution, it seems, never arrived.

The open-source-as-underdog story misreads history. When commentators discuss open source as a means to disrupt large tech companies, they often envision it as the triumph of a scrappy underdog. However, the real history offers a different lesson: Major for-profit companies routinely weaponize open-source software not to democratize technology, but to gain or maintain their competitive advantage. Open source becomes a strategic tool wielded by one titan against another.

For example, numerous for-profit entities have funded open-source projects to counter their competitors. Consider IBM's billion-dollar strategic investment in Linux in the early 2000s. The company wasn't motivated by idealistic principles about software freedom, as it may have advertised; it sought to challenge its chief business adversary, Microsoft. Google followed a similar playbook with Android. By investing heavily in the operating system, Google transformed it into the world's most widely used mobile platform, with each iteration reinforcing its ecosystem and competing with Apple. Google Chrome's development follows a similar strategic narrative in its competition with Internet Explorer – another example of open-source software deployed to challenge a competitor's (in this case, Microsoft's) browser dominance.

Despite decades of open-source innovation, concentration persists across multiple key technology sectors. Consider the examples in Table 21.1, which show how Big Tech companies dominate each vital sector:

Another striking example of open-source benefiting tech giants involves AI development frameworks. These frameworks provide significant strategic advantages to their corporate creators, such as Meta (PyTorch) and Google (TensorFlow), by accelerating AI development and ensuring robust, predictable deployment. However, the benefits extend beyond efficiency. These companies leverage their

TABLE 21.1 *Technology sectors and the market share of dominant tech companies*

Sector	Dominant Players	Market Share/Notes
Cloud services	AWS (Amazon), Azure (Microsoft), Google Cloud (Google)	~63% market share[ii]
Mobile operating systems	Android (Google), iOS (Apple)	~99.5% market share[iii]
Desktop computer operating systems	Windows (Microsoft), macOS (Apple)	~86% market share[iv]
Datacenter AI chips	Nvidia, Intel, AMD	~65%, 22%, and 11% respectively[v]
GenAI platforms	ChatGPT (OpenAI), Microsoft Copilot, Gemini (Google)	~87% market share[vi]
Social media	Facebook/Instagram (Meta), TikTok (ByteDance), YouTube (Google)	Concentrated among a few large firms

frameworks to standardize how AI systems are built, creating modular, "Lego-like" systems that snap seamlessly into their proprietary platforms.

Moreover, these frameworks serve as gateways to profitable services, allowing companies to shape the work practices of researchers and developers and, ultimately, define the trajectory of the AI field by cultivating user familiarity with their preferred ecosystem and integrating externally developed innovations into their proprietary, commercially driven products. In essence, they outsource research and development to the broader community, then reap the benefits of the results.[vii]

There is no compelling reason to believe that the trend of oligopolies dominating every profitable space will change because of the emergence of open-source GenAI projects. While open-source customizability is real, most consumers and small businesses prioritize convenience over it. Using a production-ready API (e.g., from OpenAI) is often far more practical and cost-effective than building a GenAI model from scratch or implementing and maintaining an open-source model. Moreover, even when open-source initiatives disrupt, it is typically in a narrow, niche application layer, where the total financial impact is dwarfed by the trillion-dollar companies controlling the core infrastructure. Thus, market forces continue to favor well-resourced, for-profit enterprises.

Big Tech also wields significant soft power. By strategically funding select researchers, sponsoring influential conferences, and shaping academic discourse, companies like Google, Microsoft, Nvidia, and Amazon effectively determine which research questions are pursued and which criticisms are voiced. As GenAI research becomes increasingly expensive and researchers become more dependent on Big Tech funding, these advantages further consolidate Big Tech's market dominance, creating what amounts to an intellectual monoculture aligned with corporate interests.

The market data tells a clear story. Table 21.2 compares the valuations of major players in the GenAI space before and after the debut of ChatGPT, which sparked the chatbot development frenzy. Unsurprisingly, the tech giants' valuations ballooned, far outpacing the gains of GenAI startups. The comparison shows how Big Tech companies have benefited far more than GenAI startups in the three years since ChatGPT was deployed.

Yes, the startups show impressive percentage growth, especially the 200-fold increase in OpenAI's valuation. But consider the absolute numbers: Microsoft added $1.85 trillion in value, while OpenAI added $298.5 billion.[2] While startups show explosive growth, the Big Tech firms' combined market value of over $6 trillion demonstrates their near-impervious position. This colossal resource advantage allows them to absorb, invest in, or outcompete even the most successful startups, effectively setting the terms of the market. Moreover, except for Hugging Face, only the Big Tech companies are actually profitable.

[2] To make an analogy: If you take a sedentary person and have them start a running program, they will see incredible health benefits in a relatively short timeframe. But they will pose no threat to Olympic runners.

TABLE 21.2 *The valuation of Big Tech and GenAI companies before ChatGPT's debut and three years later*

Company	Products	Valuation Q3 2022	Valuation 11/30/2025
		Tech Giants	
Microsoft	Copilot, Phi, Azure	$1.7 trillion[viii]	$3.66 trillion
Amazon	Titan, Bedrock	$1.1 trillion[ix]	$2.49 trillion
Google	Gemini, Google Cloud	$1.2 trillion[x]	$3.86 trillion
Meta	Llama	$363 billion	$1.63 trillion
		GenAI Startups	
OpenAI	ChatGPT, GPT-4, DALL-E	$1.5 billion[xi]	$500 billion
xAI	Grok	Did not exist	$230 billion (targeted)
Anthropic	Claude	$5 billion[xii]	$183 billion
Mistral AI	Mistral Large, Mixtral	Did not exist	$14 billion
Cohere	Command R	Unknown (less than $2 billion)[xiii]	$6.8 billion
Hugging Face	SmolLM	$2.2 billion[xiv]	$4.5 billion

This data suggests that the then-CEO of Ai2, an open-source-focused research institute, may have been overly optimistic about the progress open source can make. When DeepSeek's "reasoning" model debuted in January 2025, he was quick to proclaim that "we're celebrating this moment as a proof point that open source will win."[xv] However, the evidence suggests that the Big Tech oligopoly is actually winning. Even Nvidia, whose stock briefly dipped when the DeepSeek model came out, quickly recovered to reach all-time highs, demonstrating once again how impervious these giants are to disruption. Even among small tech companies, the money mostly flows to just a handful of players. As *Axios* notes, "In Q2 [2025], more than one-third of all U.S. venture dollars went to just five companies."[xvi]

Multiple levers favor Big Tech in the GenAI market, and none appear likely to be significantly challenged by open-source initiatives. The reasons Big Tech is best positioned to continue dominating the market are as follows:

Network effects: Occur when the value of a product or service increases as more people use it. Essentially, each new user adds value for existing users, creating a positive feedback loop that benefits all parties. Hugging Face exemplifies this: As more users host and share AI models, the platform becomes exponentially more valuable, creating a moat that new competitors struggle to cross.[3]

[3] While Hugging Face benefits from this, it ultimately serves as a shared, precompetitive research and distribution layer. Big Tech firms are the primary integrators of the most promising models from this platform into their proprietary deployment services (like Bedrock or Vertex AI). Thus, the platform's network effect benefits the entire ecosystem, but its output is most profitably leveraged by the companies that control the infrastructure.

Access to proprietary datasets: Companies such as Google (via YouTube), xAI (via X), and Meta (via Facebook, Threads, and Instagram) benefit from exclusive datasets that power their AI models. These aren't datasets anyone can replicate. They represent decades of user interactions, trillions of data points, and irreplaceable training material.

Capital resources: Training cutting-edge models, such as Gemini Ultra 1.0, which was estimated to cost $191 million,[xvii] is feasible only for companies with deep pockets. Moreover, many GenAI startups are not profitable, meaning they're burning through capital without a clear path to sustainability.

Access to compute: Firms such as xAI claim access to over 200,000 GPUs, while Meta asserts that its infrastructure rivals the capacity of 600,000 H100 GPUs. At current prices, that's roughly $20–30 billion worth of hardware alone.

Absence of disruptive business model: There is no known business model capable of eroding Big Tech's integrated ecosystems. Could Perplexity realistically unseat Google in the search market? Big Tech's infrastructure, data, and integration advantages are simply too vast.

High-interest investment environment: Higher interest rates make it more expensive for smaller companies to secure the capital they need to develop GenAI that can compete with Big Tech, while Big Tech companies can self-fund from massive cash reserves.

Access to markets (Google, Apple, Amazon, Meta, X, Samsung, etc.): Big Tech companies routinely secure preferential agreements, such as early access or discounted pricing, to integrate external models into their ecosystems. Examples include:

- OpenAI and Snapchat
- xAI and Telegram
- Gemini and Samsung (though Samsung may swap in Perplexity)
- Perplexity and Motorola and PayPal.

Access to top talent: The advanced expertise required to develop leading GenAI systems is in scant supply. In response, multiple AI companies have offered compensation packages ranging from $10 million to $100 million, which are amounts that startups simply cannot match.

Ultimately, the companies best positioned to dominate GenAI are those with control over the foundational infrastructure required for training, deployment, and commercialization. This reality is evident when examining how just a handful of the largest companies continue to dominate critical segments of the GenAI development supply chain. To give examples for different GenAI segments:

Compute providers: Amazon (AWS), Google (Google Cloud), Microsoft (Azure)

Proprietary platforms for data: Amazon (Amazon.com), Google (YouTube, Google search index), Meta (Facebook, Instagram, Threads), Microsoft (Bing search index)

Model development: Amazon (Titan), Apple (MM1), Google (Gemini, Gemma), Meta (Llama), Microsoft (Phi)

GenAI partnerships/investments/agreements: Amazon (Anthropic, Mistral AI, Cohere, Hugging Face), Google (Anthropic, Mistral AI, Cohere, Ai2, Hugging Face), Microsoft (OpenAI, Mistral AI, xAI, Cohere), Apple (Google)

Model deployment platforms: Amazon (Bedrock), Google (Vertex AI), Microsoft (Azure Machine Learning Studio)

Self-serving market access: Google Gemini (in Google Workspace), Microsoft Copilot (in Microsoft 365 and Windows 11).

The pattern is unmistakable: These massive companies control nearly every link in the chain. Notably, research-focused organizations like Ai2 and Stanford lack sufficient quantities of the key elements listed above to successfully compete with tech giants. For reference, the University of Texas at Austin has acquired 4,000 Nvidia Blackwell architecture GPUs and will have over 5,000 advanced Nvidia GPUs, making it the university with the most AI computing power.[xviii] This is dwarfed by the hundreds of thousands of advanced chips that AI companies have. OpenAI CEO Sam Altman claimed the company would have over one million by the end of 2025.[xix] The same limitation likely applies to virtually everyone who downloads the artifacts created and released by open-source entities. In short, radical openness is unlikely to have a meaningful impact on the existing power structure. The appealing rhetoric heard at high-level industry conferences and fireside chats cannot overcome the market forces that sustain the current technology ecosystem.

As noted in the article "Why Open AI Systems Are Actually Closed and Why This Matters":

> But pinning our hopes on "open" AI in isolation will not lead us to that world, and – in many respects – could make things worse, as policymakers and the public put their hope and momentum behind open AI, assuming that it will deliver benefits that it cannot offer in the context of concentrated corporate power.[xx]

The uncomfortable truth is this: Open source in GenAI has become less a tool for democratization and more a fig leaf for corporate dominance. When we celebrate open-source AI models, we're often celebrating the strategic maneuvering of companies worth trillions of dollars. The revolution will not be open-sourced, or at least not in the way its proponents imagine.

21.1 DISCUSSION QUESTIONS

1. The chapter argues that open source is being "weaponized" by Big Tech instead of being a true democratizing force. Can you think of any current examples (outside of the ones mentioned) where an open-source project genuinely threatens or has successfully unseated a Big Tech oligopoly, or is that simply an unattainable ideal in today's market?

2. The chapter states that most consumers and small businesses prioritize convenience (e.g., using a production-ready API from OpenAI) over the customizability of an open-source model. Is this a permanent feature of the market, or could a significant shift in technology or business model make building and maintaining a custom open-source model more practical for smaller entities?
3. The chapter compares the absolute valuation gains of Microsoft (an extra $1.96 *trillion*) versus OpenAI (an extra $498.5 *billion*). If you were a regulator or policymaker, how would this massive difference in scale influence your approach to regulating the GenAI market? Does the sheer size of Big Tech make disruption virtually impossible?
4. Of the eight levers favoring Big Tech's dominance (proprietary datasets, compute, talent, capital, etc.), which one do you believe is the most difficult for a startup or an open-source movement to overcome, and why?

22

Environmental Impact

22.1 THE INFRASTRUCTURE BEHIND THE APPARENT MAGIC

There's no dispute that GenAI is reshaping our environment. The only real debate is whether the trade-off is worthwhile. Every time you ask a chatbot to draft an email or request an AI-generated image, you're tapping into a vast physical infrastructure most users never see. Massive data centers scattered worldwide house specialized GPUs, networking equipment, and cooling systems that make GenAI possible. These purpose-built facilities handle the extraordinary computational demands of AI model training and inference (the technical term for generating each response to your prompt).

The scale is staggering. These data centers consume electricity at rates that dwarf those of traditional computing operations. The servers themselves draw immense power, but cooling consumes an equally voracious share of energy. Just as your laptop's fan whirs to life during intensive tasks, AI data centers require industrial-scale cooling to prevent their densely packed processors from overheating. According to researchers at Hugging Face, a leading AI platform, roughly 40 to 50 percent of data center energy powers the equipment itself, while another 30 to 40 percent goes purely to cooling.[i]

But electricity tells only part of the story. These facilities also pump tremendous volumes of water through their cooling systems, siphoning heat away from the servers. They don't use industrial water or seawater; it's the same clean, fresh water that flows from our taps. Greywater and saltwater would corrode and clog the intricate pipe systems, making them useless for this purpose. And moving all that water requires yet more electricity for pumping.

The newest generation of AI-focused data centers will require millions of gallons of water daily.[ii] Unlike electricity, which we can generate through nuclear reactors, wind turbines, solar arrays, or natural gas extraction, water cannot simply be manufactured on demand. Yet AI companies are racing to build data centers in some of America's most water-stressed regions. Facilities in Austin, Texas, and parts of Arizona seem almost designed to worsen water shortages in areas already grappling with drought and competing demands from agriculture and growing populations.

According to permit requests reviewed by the *New York Times*, some AI companies are seeking up to six million gallons of water per day. To put that in perspective, that exceeds the entire water supply of some counties where these data centers are being built.[iii] A Google data center in Oregon already consumes roughly a quarter of the host city's water supply. The companies' concern for local residents appears entirely nonexistent.

How water is allocated in the coming years between cash-flush AI companies and ordinary residents is poised to become a major flashpoint.

22.2 THE COMING ENERGY CRUNCH

Apollo Global Management projects that data centers will need an additional 18 gigawatts of energy by 2030 just to operate.[iv] That's equivalent to roughly three times the electricity required to power all of New York City, home to 8.5 million people and about a million buildings. OpenAI's Stargate project alone (their term for their data center expansion) may require 15 gigawatts, with construction potentially extending past 2030.[v] In Texas, a power grid operator warned the state will need to add 67 gigawatts by 2030, enough to power 60 million homes (twice the state's actual population of 30 million).[vi]

This massive surge in energy demand contradicts claims of extraordinary efficiency breakthroughs at AI labs. If these models were achieving the remarkable efficiencies their creators tout (perhaps through discoveries made by their supposedly brilliant AI systems), we might expect data centers' share of total electricity consumption to remain flat, as it did from 2005 to 2017.[vii] Instead, we're seeing exponential growth. And this likely represents the smallest the AI footprint will ever be, as companies push "agentic" AI that encourages increasingly frequent use for even the most trivial tasks that never required AI in the first place.

22.3 WHO PAYS THE PRICE?

While much attention has focused on carbon emissions and water consumption, ordinary Americans are experiencing AI's impact in a more immediate way: their monthly utility bills.

Schneider Electric estimates that electricity demand will increase by 16 percent over the next four years, driven primarily by data centers.[viii] (Other factors include inflation, the cost of natural gas, and the trend of more electrified cars and buildings.) Wealthfront reports that electricity costs have already increased twice as fast as other consumer expenses.[ix] These data centers draw from the same electrical grids that power American homes and businesses, meaning taxpayers and regular ratepayers help subsidize AI companies' operations.

The impact varies by region, but the trend is unmistakable. Electricity rates in the mid-Atlantic region, where the power grid serves 13 states and the District of Columbia, are expected to jump 20 percent in 2025, driven by data centers. Prices are projected to keep climbing, costing consumers an average of $40 or more per month in additional charges.[x] Dominion Energy expects rates to double over the next 14 years.[xi]

You might assume the biggest beneficiaries of these new data centers would shoulder more of the burden. You'd be wrong. States typically compete by offering incentives to attract AI companies, meaning residents effectively subsidize corporations valued at hundreds of billions or trillions of dollars. Google, for instance, pays less than half what ordinary customers pay for electricity from Dominion Energy.[xii]

Leaning into GenAIuflecting, the CEO of Dominion Energy justified these arrangements by invoking national security and economic competitiveness, stressing the supposed need to maintain "the superiority of the United States' technological advantage as a growth engine for our economy, as essential to our national security." It's the AI arms race narrative deployed to rationalize corporate welfare.[xiii]

22.4 THE REVIVAL OF FOSSIL FUELS

The quickest way to add substantial energy capacity to the grid is to expand fossil fuel use rather than clean energy. Power plants that were scheduled for decommissioning are getting new leases on life. The Trump administration eliminated incentives for companies to transition to clean energy, granted new drilling permits, and opened federal lands for increased fossil fuel production. It also exempted coal-fired power plants and other industrial sites from Biden-era air pollution regulations.[xiv]

Elon Musk's Memphis data center exemplifies this troubling pattern. Musk built his fortune largely by promoting electric vehicles, batteries, and solar installations to reduce fossil fuel dependence. Yet his Memphis data center relies on gas turbines and diesel generators for backup power.[xv] Meta's Louisiana data center similarly depends on gas turbines.[xvi] OpenAI plans to use a $500 million gas-fired plant to power its Texas data centers.[xvii]

Moreover, these aren't temporary measures. Gas-fired power plants have lifespans of twenty-five to forty years. The decisions made today to extend and expand fossil fuel infrastructure will likely persist for decades. We're locking in carbon emissions far into the future, all to power technology whose societal benefits remain hotly contested.

22.5 THE OPACITY PROBLEM

You may be wondering what makes assessing AI's environmental impact so difficult. It's that only the companies themselves know how much energy their systems actually consume.[1] No laws or regulations require transparency, and no major

[1] I've intentionally avoided making false equivalencies between individuals and corporations in this chapter. Too often, AI proponents deflect criticism by saying, "But streaming a movie online is worse!"

for-profit AI company in the United States volunteers comprehensive information. When you encounter energy use estimates in news articles, you're reading either educated guesswork built on layers of assumptions, or calculations based on open-source models, which are dramatically smaller than leading closed-source systems like ChatGPT or Claude and likely implemented quite differently.[2]

We don't know the architecture of proprietary models, the composition of their hardware, or how many queries they handle daily. Energy intensity varies widely across GPU models. We also don't know where their data centers are located because companies typically file permit applications under aliases.

Even when companies share information, it's incomplete. Sam Altman, OpenAI's CEO, once cited the energy used by an "average" query but never defined "average." Does that include only text generation, or also images and video? Is the figure based solely on inference, or does it account for the full environmental stack: mining rare earth minerals for GPUs, clear-cutting forests to build facilities, manufacturing and transporting heavy machinery, disrupting ecosystems and displacing wildlife, training the models, cooling the servers, and the carbon intensity of each data center's local power grid?

Microsoft's approach to transparency is perhaps even more frustrating. In its 2025 "Progress on the Road to 2030" report, the company obscures whether it's making any meaningful progress at all. Consider this example: "A key component of our water positive goal is to replenish more water than we consume across our global operations."[xviii]

So far, so good. You might reasonably expect the next sentence to quantify how close they are to achieving this goal. Instead, Microsoft simply notes: "We've grown our replenishment portfolio to 90 projects in over 40 locations around the world." Is ninety projects impressive? How large are these projects? How much water do they actually replenish? Microsoft doesn't say.

The pattern continues throughout the report. "On our journey to become zero waste, we're finding opportunities to keep electronics in circulation. The reliability of our current portfolio of Surface devices has evolved significantly." How significantly? How close are they to zero waste? Again, no answers.

They miss the point entirely. This should be a society-wide conversation about sustainability and shared values. Companies habitually reframe systemic problems as individual failings. Encouraging people to eat more soybeans can never be the answer to unchecked energy consumption by behemoth corporations.

2 The Stanford AI Index makes the following guess, for what it's worth: "Training early AI models, such as AlexNet (2012), had modest amounts of carbon emissions at 0.01 tons. More recent models have significantly higher emissions for training: GPT-3 (2020) at 588 tons, GPT-4 (2023) at 5,184 tons, and Llama 3.1 405B (2024) at 8,930 tons. For perspective, the average American emits 18 tons of carbon per year." N. Maslej et al. (2025). Artificial Intelligence Index Report 2025. Retrieved February 25, 2026, from https://hai.stanford.edu/assets/files/hai_ai_index_report_2025.pdf.

But the most revealing passage comes when Microsoft attempts to justify backing away from its climate commitments: "In 2020, Microsoft leaders referred to our sustainability goals as a 'moonshot,' and nearly five years later, we have had to acknowledge that the moon has gotten further away."

This is corporate doublespeak at its finest. The moon didn't shift; Microsoft did. They then immediately pivot to positioning AI as environmental savior: "However, the force creating this distance from our goals in the short term is the same one that will help us build bigger, faster, and more powerful rockets to reach them in the long term: artificial intelligence."[3]

Later in the report, Microsoft insists: "We remain resolute in our commitment to our climate goals." But how resolute can you claim to be when you simply move the goalposts and blame it on celestial mechanics? The report ends by repeating: "In 2025, the moon is further away."

22.6 WHAT WE DO KNOW

Despite the opacity, certain facts are clear. Larger models require more energy to perform the same tasks, making efficiency improvements crucial for reducing both environmental impact and operating costs. This explains why the free version of Claude defaults to Sonnet (a smaller model) rather than Opus (the largest).

Energy consumption also varies significantly by task type. For text generation, more complex requests, such as analyzing lengthy documents, demand far more energy than simple tasks like writing a joke. Image generation works differently. Creating a picture of a skateboarding rabbit requires no more energy than generating a carrot wearing sunglasses. Instead, energy use depends on the model's size and the number of iterations it runs to produce the final output, with more iterations typically yielding better results. While virtually all prompts for the same image model consume roughly equal energy, different image models can vary dramatically in their energy requirements.

Video generation represents the most energy-intensive frontier. The longer the video and the higher its quality, the more energy it demands.[xix]

In short, estimates from open-source models are woefully insufficient for understanding AI's true environmental cost. The most sensible approach is to assume the worst-case environmental impacts and regulate accordingly until companies provide independently audited data in standardized formats that enable fair comparisons across the industry.

Left unstated amid all the hype about AI's potential is perhaps the most important question: Is it clear that AI's benefits outweigh its harms, including the costs imposed on taxpayers and the planet?

3 This, of course, overlooks that we already know how to tackle global warming. At this point, it's a matter of political will, not technological advancement.

22.7 DISCUSSION QUESTIONS

1. The chapter notes that AI data centers are being built in water-stressed regions like Austin, Texas, and parts of Arizona, consuming millions of gallons daily. If you were a city council member in one of these areas, how would you weigh the economic benefit of hosting a new data center (jobs, taxes) against the nonrenewable cost of the local water supply? At what point does the cost of water outweigh the benefits of new technology?
2. The chapter states that 30 to 40 percent of data center energy goes purely to cooling. If a new, highly efficient cooling technology were developed that cut water consumption by 90 percent but required an entirely new, expensive data center design, should governments mandate its use, or should the industry be allowed to transition at its own pace?
3. Gas-fired power plants have lifespans of twenty-five to forty years. Given that the industry is currently locking in decades of carbon emissions, how should current AI companies be held accountable for the environmental impact of the power plants that will outlast the current generation of their AI models?
4. The chapter highlights that states offer incentives and energy subsidies to attract AI companies, leading to ordinary residents effectively subsidizing trillion-dollar corporations and facing higher utility bills. Is the justification of "national security and economic competitiveness" sufficient to defend these subsidies, or is it simply "corporate welfare" wrapped in a patriotic narrative?
5. Electricity rates in the mid-Atlantic are expected to jump, costing consumers an average of forty dollars or more per month due to data centers. Do you believe this is a fair price for the convenience and technological advancement that GenAI provides? If not, how should the burden of these costs be reallocated?
6. The author notes the industry is pushing "agentic" AI for "even the most trivial tasks that never required AI in the first place." If you were designing an AI product, how would you balance encouraging use (to make a profit) with minimizing the environmental cost of frivolous queries?
7. The chapter argues that the lack of transparency from AI companies makes assessing the true environmental impact of their models impossible. If a new law mandated full, independently audited data on a model's energy and water use, what specific metric (e.g., carbon per billion tokens, water per million queries) would you be most interested in?
8. Microsoft's report claimed "the moon has gotten further away" to explain why they backed away from climate goals. What is the most egregious piece of "corporate doublespeak" or "GenAIuflecting" you've heard recently regarding AI's impact, and how would you rephrase it to state the unvarnished truth?

9. The chapter suggests, "The most sensible approach is to assume the worst-case environmental impacts and regulate accordingly until companies provide independently audited data." Do you agree with this policy approach, or should the companies be given the benefit of the doubt as the progenitors of a revolutionary technology?

23

GenAI in Education

Every society gets the citizens it cultivates. If we introduce GenAI into K-12 education at scale, normalizing it as a go-to technology, we're running an experiment on civic capacity itself, training millions of young people to reflexively outsource the very cognitive skills that democratic participation requires. The ability to sit with complexity, synthesize information from competing sources, and construct and evaluate arguments is the foundation of informed citizenship. Whether you have school-age children or not, you have a stake in whether the next generation can do these things independently or will arrive at adulthood having learned that thinking is something you delegate to a machine.

23.1 THE PURPOSE OF EDUCATION

First, I think it's important to define what I believe the goal of K-12 education should be, as this will ultimately shape my perspective on how society should approach it. Many believe the primary purpose of K-12 education is to prepare children to be productive members of the workforce. That is, their argument hinges on the idea that GenAI will inevitably be a pervasive element across all industries, so kids should be required to learn to use the technology ASAP. The focus is on learning to use the tool, not on whether and how it affects learning.

I take a different stance as my starting point. While we undoubtedly want graduates who can contribute to the workforce, I believe the primary goal of K-12 education should be to prepare students to be good citizens. This would require helping them become good critical thinkers who can tie disparate ideas together, understand systems thinking, and develop new concepts that originate with the students (even if those ideas aren't new to the world more broadly). These citizens need the ability to sit with a complex idea for a long time and think deeply about it. In other words, education should cultivate minds capable of sustained intellectual engagement, not just efficient task completion.[1]

[1] Some may argue that AI just shifts what we do from producing a first draft to editing. But this isn't without its own problems. For one, *creating is something humans do better*. Recall that GenAI has

A diplomatic response would be, "Why, we should prioritize being useful in the workforce and being good citizens equally!" But we must acknowledge the opportunity costs. Teaching one thing means not teaching another. Moreover, to receive the maximum benefit from both approaches, two conditions must be met: First, GenAI must be a necessary tool for learning (otherwise, your time would be better spent learning other things), and second, using GenAI must lead to similar or improved critical thinking skills compared with not using it.

This is not to say that GenAI makes it impossible to be a good citizen, but I do think it makes it much less likely. The case against GenAI in K-12 rests on several pillars: workforce speculation, technological volatility, and fundamental questions about how learning actually occurs.

23.2 GENAI AND THE FUTURE WORKFORCE

It's worth noting that we do not know with certainty whether most people – and certainly not the vast majority – will need to learn to use GenAI to be competitive in the workforce. To assume that what GenAI companies tell us is absolutely true is to let them set education policy based solely on speculation.[2] Bluntly, it also means taxpayers covering the cost of training customers on how to use a company's product.

Consider what must be true in order to justify requiring or strongly encouraging all kids to use GenAI for several of their K-12 years (and forcing taxpayers, via school districts, to pay for the privilege of accessing the technology). I posit that at least five things must be true to meet that condition:

1. GenAI in a chatbot format will remain a prominent technology in the years after a student graduates.
2. The technology won't change much, so learning about it now will directly relate to the workforce students will enter.
3. GenAI companies won't lose the current lawsuits that could end, scale back, or significantly change how GenAI is used, how often it's used, how expensive it is, how it functions, etc.
4. The trade-off of teaching kids to use GenAI will be more beneficial than harmful to their intellectual and civic development, so that it won't limit them as workers compared to students with little or no exposure to GenAI in K-12.
5. Students won't learn the necessary skills on their own.

produced no new genres of art or scientific insights. It's unclear how training students to reflexively offload the task of making the first draft of something will more likely expand our culture or understanding of the universe.

[2] To be sure, this is what's happening. Trump signed an executive order urging the use of AI in classrooms and training teachers to integrate it "into all subject areas." The goal is to help children gain expertise with AI "from a young age." President of the United States (April 23, 2025). Advancing artificial intelligence education for American youth. Retrieved February 25, 2026, from www.whitehouse.gov/presidential-actions/2025/04/advancing-artificial-intelligence-education-for-american-youth/.

To take those in turn:

1. We must believe that a technology that burst into the public consciousness just in 2022 will remain the primary technology used in the workforce several years from now. That is, we must assume there will not be a similar breakthrough in new technology within the next thirteen years (for kindergarteners encouraged to start learning about AI today). If a student masters GenAI in the fifth grade, but that tech is no longer as widespread seven years later when they graduate, we must believe they did not miss out on valuable learning during those seven years that would have occurred had they not focused on GenAI, and that the alternative education would not have been more useful when they graduate into a world with new and ever-changing technology. It feels a bit like someone in the 1990s saying: "Everyone should learn HTML because the World Wide Web will be used by everyone in the future!" It's half true. The web is now an integral part of our daily lives. But how many people know HTML or use it regularly? The web endured, but the skills needed to use it underwent a complete transformation. Learning to hand-code HTML in 1995 did little to prepare someone for the app-based internet of 2025.[3]
2. We must believe that GenAI, as it exists today, will be essentially unchanged by the time students graduate. That is, the prompting techniques that are helpful today will remain the best approach, the way we interact with GenAI will be essentially the same, and so on. In essence, we must believe that the tech will not improve and become significantly more user-friendly. This assumption seems particularly dubious given that the entire trajectory of successful consumer technology points toward increasing simplicity. Remember when using email required understanding SMTP servers? Even the buzzword "prompt engineer" has already gone to the wayside as GenAI systems have improved their "understanding" of user intent.[i]
3. We must believe that GenAI will not be affected by losing a lawsuit or by other regulatory pressures that could impact its operation. And yet if GenAI companies lose copyright lawsuits, they could be forced to destroy their models, pay billions of dollars in penalties (which could bankrupt them), and/or start over, relying on much less data to train future models (which, absent a significant tech breakthrough, will make the models much less useful).
4. We must believe that teaching students to use GenAI will make them better workers than teaching them to learn without GenAI throughout most of K-12, or by learning GenAI on the job or over the summer after high school. This

[3] As another example, imagine if schools had rushed to require that all students learn how to use an iPhone in 2007. iPhones, by almost any measure, have had a greater effect on society than GenAI. Yet no one argues that schools should have dedicated years to teaching iPhone proficiency. Users adapted naturally as the technology became relevant to their lives.

assumption bears the entire weight of the "workforce readiness" argument, yet it remains almost entirely untested.

5. We must believe that unless GenAI is intentionally incorporated into classrooms, students will fail to learn how to use the technology. This sounds too much like claiming that if students hadn't been taught how to use a web browser or Google in the late 90s and early 2000s, they would be utter failures upon graduation, unable to look up information, shop online, or communicate with others over the internet.

23.3 IS TEACHING THE USE OF GENAI BETTER THAN NOT USING IT?

We could get to the nub of the issue if there were enough empirical data. Does teaching and encouraging the use of GenAI improve student outcomes? If research makes the answer clear, then all the theoretical reasoning and opinionating aren't particularly helpful.

Here's where we face some disappointment: There isn't much research on how GenAI affects student outcomes. This means we're being asked to restructure education based on hope rather than evidence.

But as research comes out, we could examine it and apply the Bradford Hill criteria (developed for health studies but also applicable here) when reviewing papers. When rigorous research is scarce, we need a framework for evaluating the limited evidence that exists. Medical researchers face a similar challenge when they can't conduct randomized controlled trials for ethical or practical reasons. You can't, for instance, randomly assign some people to smoke cigarettes for twenty years just to prove causation. In these situations, epidemiologists use the Bradford Hill criteria, a set of principles developed by statistician Austin Bradford Hill in 1965, to assess whether an observed association likely represents a genuine causal relationship.

These criteria map well onto educational research. Like medicine, education involves complex interventions that affect human development over long periods, often with limited ability to run perfect experiments. Just as Bradford Hill used his principles to establish that smoking causes lung cancer before definitive experimental proof existed, we can use them to evaluate whether GenAI helps or harms learning, even without decades of peer-reviewed studies.

Here's how each criterion translates to the question of GenAI in education:

1. Strength (effect size): A small association does not necessarily mean that there is no causal effect; however, the larger the association, the more likely it is to be causal.
   a. Does using GenAI produce dramatic changes in learning outcomes, or are the effects modest and easily explained by other factors? For example, if students using GenAI score 2 percent higher on tests, that weak association could result from teacher enthusiasm, novelty effects, or selection

bias. But if GenAI users showed 30 percent improvement, we'd need to take that seriously (though we'd also wonder why companies aren't publicizing such remarkable results).

2. Consistency (reproducibility): Consistent findings observed by different people in different places with different samples strengthen the likelihood of an effect.
   a. Do multiple studies across different schools, age groups, and implementation contexts show similar patterns? If GenAI helps fourth graders in suburban California but shows no benefit (or shows harm) for tenth graders in rural Kentucky, that inconsistency suggests that factors other than the technology itself, such as teacher training, student motivation, or socioeconomic factors, are driving outcomes.
3. Specificity: Causation is likely if a particular population at a specific site experiences the change, and no other plausible explanation exists. The more specific an association between a factor and an effect is, the bigger the probability of a causal relationship.
   a. Is the effect unique to GenAI users, or do students in well-funded schools with small class sizes show similar improvements regardless of the technology used? If every intervention with engaged teachers and adequate resources yields the same results, GenAI might be taking credit for factors unrelated to AI. Conversely, if only GenAI produces a particular pattern – say, improved writing fluency but deteriorated critical analysis – then that specificity suggests a real causal relationship.
4. Temporality: The effect has to occur after the cause (and if there is an expected delay between the cause and the expected effect, then the effect must occur after that delay).
   a. Do students show improved outcomes after they start using GenAI, or do improvements begin before they start using it? This seems obvious, but it's surprisingly easy to confuse the two possibilities. Imagine a school gives GenAI access to its highest-performing students first as a pilot program. If those students continue to excel, we can't credit GenAI because they were already excelling. We need to see changes that occur after the intervention begins.
5. Dose–response relationship: Greater exposure generally leads to a greater incidence of the effect. However, in some cases, the mere presence of the factor can trigger the effect. In other cases, an inverse proportion is observed, where greater exposure is associated with a lower incidence.
   a. Do students who use GenAI more frequently show stronger effects than occasional users? If students who use GenAI for ten minutes daily show the same outcomes as those who use it for two hours daily, that flat relationship suggests GenAI isn't driving the results. In medicine, we expect more aspirin to reduce fever more effectively (up to a point). Similarly,

if GenAI truly enhances learning, we'd expect proportional benefits. Or, if it's harmful, we'd expect students with greater exposure to show larger declines.

6. Plausibility: A plausible relationship between cause and effect is helpful in explaining why the mechanism may make sense.
   a. Is there a plausible mechanism by which GenAI would produce the observed effect? For instance, if a study claims that GenAI improves students' mental math abilities, we should be skeptical. What's a plausible mechanism by which outsourcing calculations to AI would strengthen mental arithmetic? Conversely, if it is claimed that students who use GenAI to generate essay outlines show improved organizational skills, that's plausible because they repeatedly see well-structured examples (though we'd still need evidence that it actually works).
7. Coherence: Coherence between observational and experimental findings increases the likelihood of an effect.
   a. Do the findings align with what we know from other domains? If GenAI is said to improve learning outcomes in education, does that align with what we observe across different fields? For example, does giving junior programmers access to AI coding assistants improve their programming skills or hinder the development of foundational skills? If workplace evidence suggests skill atrophy from AI dependence, that should inform our interpretation of educational studies showing short-term gains.
8. Experiment: "Occasionally, it is possible to appeal to experimental, or semi-experimental, evidence."[ii]
   a. Has anyone actually conducted controlled experiments? This is the gold standard. Have researchers randomly assigned some classrooms to use GenAI and others to use traditional methods, while controlling for teacher quality, student demographics, and other variables? Without experimental evidence, we're left inferring causation from observation. This can work, but it requires much stronger signals across the criteria.
9. Analogy: It may be fair to use analogies or similarities between the observed association and any other associations.
   a. Can we draw parallels to similar situations where we understand the causal relationship? We know that using calculators in elementary school before students grasp arithmetic concepts can lead to computational dependence and a weaker understanding of numbers. That analogy suggests that using GenAI for writing before students develop compositional skills might produce similar dependence. Analogies don't prove causation, but they help us form reasonable hypotheses and calibrate our expectations.

Applying this framework rigorously, we'd need to see strong, consistent effects that emerge after GenAI use, intensify with greater exposure, have plausible mechanisms, align with evidence from other domains, and ideally appear in controlled experiments. The lack of published research meeting even a few of these criteria should give us pause before making GenAI a cornerstone of K-12 education. This is especially true now, when the current research literature suggests that, based on these criteria, GenAI may do more harm than good.

But also, if you were an entity like, say, the Khan Academy and you had a product like, say, Khanmigo[4] and you had, say, two *million* students using it ... you'd have an awful lot of data.[iii] And if you had that massive amount of data and it strongly indicated your product was significantly improving student outcomes, wouldn't you shout it from the rooftops and proudly share it in a triumphant research paper, since you are solving one of society's most pressing problems? You would. It would make your product more popular and widely used, and you'd be doing society a tremendous favor.

And yet ... Khan Academy hasn't done that. They may still be working through the data, doing careful analyses. But if that's the case, it's unclear how they can already make bold claims about their products. The real answer is more likely that the data is not as robust as they imply. This lack of initial evidence, contrasted with the speed of adoption urged by technology companies, creates a policy gap in which hope, not proof, drives implementation.

Time will tell whether OpenAI is any more open about the results of its embedding with the California State University system, which has more than 460,000 students and over 63,000 staff and faculty across its 23 campuses. I wouldn't hold my breath.

The silence is telling. When pharmaceutical companies develop a promising new drug, they publish clinical trial results as quickly as possible. When education technology companies gather extensive user data but don't publish outcome studies, we should ask ourselves what story that data might tell.

23.4 GENAI IS CATEGORICALLY DIFFERENT FROM PRIOR TECHNOLOGIES

I've seen in some articles and books that authors often treat GenAI pushback in education as no different from past overreactions to calculators in the classroom or to Google searches. This analogy is flawed in meaningful ways. Unlike prior technologies, GenAI is a general-purpose tool that can adapt to users, producing outputs in different styles and formats. Let's compare that with calculators.

A calculator performs a discrete task[5] and is only helpful if you know how to solve the problem and, in many cases, understand how to use the calculator's advanced features. You must understand the problem and enter the correct numbers and symbols in the proper order. A calculator is useless for trigonometry if you don't understand trigonometry. It's a tool that may amplify competence but it cannot create or imitate it.

[4] It's built in collaboration with, and is dependent on, OpenAI.

[5] This is also true of all prior technologies. GenAI, in contrast, is a general-purpose tool.

In contrast, you don't need to understand math at all to cheat effectively with GenAI. You can copy and paste the problem into the prompt box or upload a picture of it, and you'll get enough correct answers to pass most homework. This is particularly true for pre-high school students, making the technology more appealing to that age group and exacerbating its effects on future learning.

The analogy to search engines, pre-AI mode and AI overview, is similarly flawed. If you fed Google a word problem just a few years ago, it wouldn't help you answer it unless that exact problem appeared on a Google-indexed webpage. Also, in case there is any doubt, traditional Google Search can't write essays for you. Traditional search engines retrieve webpages and their content. They don't generate, synthesize, or present them in the exact format required by an assignment. GenAI does all three.

Finally, the barrier to accessing and using GenAI is orders of magnitude lower than for most online cheating services. The products are free, just a click away, and intuitive to use. It's about as frictionless as can be. Previous generations of students who wanted to cheat had to find someone to copy from, pay for an essay mill, or risk sneaking a peek at the teacher's answer key when the teacher wasn't looking. GenAI requires none of that friction, planning, or social coordination. It's always available, it's always willing, and it leaves no social trace.

23.4.1 *Cheating*

When I think about cheating, I mean kids using GenAI to get answers rather than doing the work. This is also harmful to students who are not cheating and are genuinely trying, as it affects their class rank and eligibility for certain honor societies and puts pressure on them to start cheating just to keep up. It creates a perverse arms race in which honest students must choose between compromising their integrity and accepting an artificial disadvantage.

But I also mean cheating in the sense that it deprives students of an education.[6] If they do not put in the work to learn the content, they will not understand it, no matter how many times they use GenAI to answer questions for them. Learning requires struggle. Effective struggle has the added benefit of building self-esteem and establishing a growth mindset. Cognitive science consistently shows that effortful retrieval and productive struggle are essential for durable learning. Without the struggle and subsequent mastery, student confidence fades, and their dependence on the technology deepens.

When students use GenAI to answer questions without understanding the responses (or even the questions) or why the outputs are correct, they may become dependent on the technology. Indeed, that dependence will increase over time because once the fundamentals of algebra are missed, it becomes increasingly

[6] Undoubtedly many students also use it to create study guides, quiz themselves, receive feedback on homework, and prep for tests. But we're kidding ourselves if we think that's the primary use.

difficult to understand subsequent and more complex topics, such as trigonometry or calculus. The cognitive debt accumulates. Each shortcut creates a gap in foundational knowledge that makes the next concept more challenging to grasp, creating a downward spiral in which GenAI becomes increasingly necessary precisely because earlier overreliance prevented genuine learning.

The distinction between GenAI and previous technologies shouldn't be surprising. It's this distinction that venture capitalists find so appealing when they invest billions of dollars in OpenAI, xAI, Anthropic, and other companies. It boggles my mind that people want to say GenAI is little different from tech developed decades ago. If GenAI were truly just another incremental improvement like calculators or spell-check, it wouldn't be attracting hundreds of billions in investment and generating predictions of economic transformation. The same qualities that make investors excited should make educators cautious.

23.5 GENAI IS NEITHER GOOD NOR BAD

GenAI proponents often argue that the technology is neutral – neither inherently good nor bad – and that outcomes depend entirely on how it's used. "It's like food," they might say. "A balanced diet is healthy, but too much junk food is harmful. The tool itself isn't the problem; it's all about responsible use."

First, I imagine some nutritionists would quibble with the idea that there aren't overwhelmingly bad foods. Trans fats don't have a responsible serving size. Some things are simply harmful, period. But let's assume, for the sake of argument, that everything is good in moderation and when consumed appropriately.

Even granting this generous assumption, the food analogy actually undermines the case for GenAI in schools rather than supporting it.

To caveat an argument favoring GenAI in K-12 by saying "if used appropriately" is, frankly, silly. That could be applied to everything. Of course, if students use the technology in question appropriately, they can learn a great deal from activities like watching TV and YouTube, playing video games, and chatting with strangers in chat rooms. The phrase "if used appropriately" is a universal escape clause that renders any claim unfalsifiable. More importantly, how good is a solution if it's only helpful under ideal conditions?

Let's extend the food metaphor properly. Imagine a school district deciding to stock elementary school vending machines with candy bars and energy drinks. When parents express concern, administrators respond: "Don't worry, we'll teach students about nutrition and responsible consumption. We'll have lessons on moderation and balanced diets. The vending machines themselves are neutral. It's all about how students choose to use them."

Would anyone find this convincing? Of course not. We'd immediately recognize several problems with this reasoning:

First, the presence of the vending machines creates a constant temptation that competes with the nutrition lessons. It doesn't matter how compelling your healthy-eating curriculum is when students can see chocolate bars every time they walk down the hallway. Environmental pressures overwhelm the educational intervention.

Second, we're asking children whose prefrontal cortexes won't fully develop for another decade or more to consistently exercise restraint in the face of immediate gratification. It's not a reasonable expectation.

The real issue is that we must believe (1) students will only use GenAI appropriately and (2) "appropriate" use is, in fact, better than no use. What are the odds that you teach a seventh grader about a technology that can answer almost any question they'll encounter in that grade, and they won't misuse it?

Relying on "responsible" or "appropriate" use for GenAI and K-12 education is at odds with common sense. The mere availability of the easy option changes the calculus of effort for students. Why struggle through a difficult problem for thirty minutes when you could get an answer in ten seconds? From the student's perspective, the rational choice is to use the shortcut and avoid productive struggle. If they receive an A after submitting the AI response, we've reinforced the problem.

Consider what "appropriate use" would actually require in practice. Suppose a student receives a homework assignment to "explain the causes of the American Civil War in your own words." The appropriate use of GenAI might be something like:

- Using it to clarify a concept the student doesn't understand after trying to figure it out themselves
- Asking it to explain the difference between the immediate and underlying causes
- Having it suggest historical sources they could consult for different perspectives.

But from a student's immediate perspective, the fastest, most convenient, and most effective approach is to type "Explain the causes of the American Civil War" and copy the response.

Now multiply this decision across every homework assignment, every night, for years. We're asking adolescents to consistently choose the more challenging path that yields benefits they won't recognize for years, over the easier path that solves their immediate problem.

The reality is that giving students unrestricted access to a technology that can complete their assignments for them and expecting them not to use it that way requires a level of optimism that borders on magical thinking. Adolescents are still developing impulse control and the ability to delay gratification.

Moreover, even when students intend to use GenAI appropriately, the line between help and harm blurs quickly. A student who asks GenAI to "help me understand" a concept might receive a comprehensive explanation that leaves nothing for them to figure out. The technology doesn't know how much scaffolding is too much. It can't calibrate its assistance to provide just enough help to keep the student in the productive struggle zone where learning actually happens.

Returning to the food metaphor, we don't stock elementary schools with candy vending machines and rely on nutrition education to prevent obesity. We recognize that environmental design matters. We control access to unhealthy options because we understand that prevention is easier than remediation and that children's developing brains need protection from their own limitations in impulse control.

Why would we take the opposite approach with GenAI? If anything, the stakes are higher. GenAI misuse affects the development of foundational cognitive skills, such as writing, reasoning, and problem-solving, and these effects compound over time. Delegate your essay writing to AI in eighth grade, and you'll arrive at college without the compositional skills your peers developed through practice.

The "it's just a tool" argument also ignores that most tools are useless without existing competence. A professional-grade camera doesn't make you a professional photographer. A high-end kitchen knife doesn't make you a chef. These tools amplify existing skills; they don't create them from scratch. GenAI is different. It can produce competent outputs even when the user lacks any competence whatsoever.

So yes, in a theoretical sense, GenAI is neutral, just as social media is. The relevant question isn't whether appropriate use is possible; rather, it is whether appropriate use is likely, sustainable, and actually superior to alternatives.

23.6 GENAI TAKES YEARS OF PRACTICE

I'm not sure many people would call me a cheerleader for GenAI (though I do see its many potential benefits!), but even I don't think it takes years to learn to use it well enough to perform an entry-level job, such as a high school graduate might need.

It seems odd that people say we must teach how to use GenAI in school and that starting early is important. This suggests they think GenAI is a genuinely awful product that takes years (or even a few months) to understand well enough to use at a basic level. Imagine if Word took multiple years to learn to use effectively. We don't use Word in school for years to learn how to use it. We use it because it's the medium for writing, just as we don't use paper to learn how to use paper.

Contending that students must use GenAI for years to be prepared to use it post-graduation suggests the product is even worse than I'm willing to argue. If GenAI truly requires years of practice starting in elementary school, that's less an endorsement of its importance and more an indictment of its usability. Either the technology is intuitive enough to learn quickly when needed, or it's so cumbersome that we should question whether it's the right tool at all.

23.7 THE POWER WAS WITHIN US ALL ALONG

The most recent National Assessment of Educational Progress (commonly known as The Nation's Report Card) showed a continued slide in K-12 math and reading. Almost half of high school seniors are below basic in math, and about a third are below basic in reading. Some will say this is a reason to use more AI in school. I think it's a reason to use less.

People made similar claims that massive open online courses (MOOCs), such as those taught at Harvard and Yale, would transform education. But they didn't. For MOOCs, it turns out that one needs remarkable discipline and motivation to pay attention to a series of long prerecorded courses and learn from them. Access to high-quality content is necessary but insufficient. Students often also need inspiration and encouragement, which good teachers provide.

GenAI is not a silver bullet. The real solution isn't so mystical. But implementing it is challenging because technology alone cannot address our most significant problems. All major societal issues require the collaboration and cooperation of people. Education is no different.

A better approach (one of many I could propose; I just happen to particularly like this one) is to (1) increase the incentives for more highly qualified people to become educators, (2) raise the standards for what it means to be an educator to align with those greater incentives, and (3) hire more educators. This isn't a revolutionary insight. It's simply acknowledging what rigorous studies of educational outcomes have shown for decades.

Educators are the single most important in-school factor in education (though many other factors are also critically important, including facilities, location, the absence of violence, the absence of drugs, stable home life, reliable transportation, and parental support). Trying to apply a Band-Aid or find a magic shortcut to replace or supplement high-quality educators is a fool's errand. We continue to search for technological fixes because they're easier to implement than the hard work of properly compensating, training, and supporting the professionals who actually teach. But there are no shortcuts to human expertise and patience, or the ability to meet students where they are. A skilled teacher can recognize when a student's frustration signals productive struggle versus genuine confusion. They can adjust explanations in real time based on a student's expression, question, or body language. They can provide encouragement when motivation flags. No algorithm can replicate this adaptive, empathetic intelligence.

23.8 CONCLUSION

The choice before us isn't really about technology at all. It's about what we believe education is for. If we see schools primarily as job-training centers, then perhaps mandatory GenAI makes sense, assuming those technological and legal uncertainties break in the right direction. But if we believe education should cultivate independent thought, intellectual resilience, and sustained reasoning, then we should be far more cautious about introducing a technology that can do students' thinking for them.

The decision we make today will echo for decades. A generation that learns to reflexively outsource cognitive labor won't suddenly develop those capacities at age eighteen. The habits we cultivate in students become the foundations of their adult capabilities. If we want citizens who can think deeply and critically, we need to let them practice those skills when the stakes are relatively low, in homework assignments and classroom discussions, not for the first time when they're casting votes or making consequential decisions.

It seems too few pause to wonder what the world might look like if we were to cultivate a generation of children who struggle to think for themselves. The technology will be there when they need it. The question is whether they'll have developed the judgment to use it wisely.

23.9 DISCUSSION QUESTIONS

1. The chapter argues that GenAI outsources "the very cognitive skills that democratic participation requires." Do you agree or disagree with this statement, and why? What specific cognitive skills do you think are most endangered by reliance on GenAI?
2. If you were the secretary of education, what would be your single biggest priority for K-12 education: preparing students for the workforce or preparing them to be "good citizens" (critical thinkers)? Can you *truly* achieve both goals simultaneously, or is it more like a zero-sum game, as the author suggests?
3. The chapter uses the analogy of stocking elementary school vending machines with candy bars to critique the idea of GenAI being "neutral." Is this a fair analogy? If you were a teacher, what is one specific rule you would implement to encourage "appropriate use" of GenAI in your classroom and at home, and how would you enforce it?
4. The author claims, "From a student's immediate perspective, the fastest, most convenient, and most effective approach is to type 'Explain the causes of the American Civil War' and copy the response." What is the most compelling nonacademic incentive (not grades or future job prospects) you could offer a student to choose the more challenging path of "productive struggle" instead of the ten-second shortcut?
5. The chapter argues that GenAI is "categorically different from prior technologies" like calculators and search engines. Do you find the author's argument convincing? If you had to argue against the author, what is one historical technology (like the printing press, slide rule, or email) that caused a similar fear of "outsourcing" mental work?

6. The author highlights the Bradford Hill criteria for evaluating the evidence for GenAI's effects. If you could fund one definitive, multiyear study on GenAI in education, which of the nine criteria (e.g., consistency, dose–response relationship, experiment) would you focus on to prove or disprove GenAI's effects, and why?

24

Education and Democracy

In 2024, Alpha School opened in Austin, Texas, as one of the first K-12 schools in the United States to use AI as the primary method of instruction. Students spend much of their day interacting with adaptive learning software, with human "guides" facilitating rather than teaching. The school's founders tout personalized learning and mastery-based progression. But what they don't advertise is how parents and outsiders have no way to audit what the AI is actually teaching. The algorithms are proprietary. The system prompts are trade secrets. The conversations between student and machine leave no paper trail for review. For all its innovation, Alpha School has made the content of education less transparent than a textbook or a human teacher's fixed syllabus, where any parent could audit the material.[i]

Let us set aside the concerns expressed in the previous chapter and stipulate that incorporating artificial intelligence into the classroom improves student test performance and streamlines entry into the workplace. Still, how we cede the role of educator to algorithms poses another, more existential threat: the erosion of democracy itself.

AI in education may be wielded as a tool for autocracy. The logic is simple. If you control education, you can control what people believe. And people vote based on those beliefs. It's a formula autocrats have understood for centuries, but AI offers them the new ability to personalize indoctrination at scale.

Historically, textbooks could only go so far in shaping a worldview because children did not always read them, and teachers remained the most important element in the classroom. But imagine setting the human teacher aside. Picture instead a fifth grader spending three hours daily conversing with an AI tutor that subtly adjusts its lessons based on her responses, remembers every question she asks, and guides her toward predetermined conclusions while making her feel she's thinking for herself. Now consider that when a generation gets its education from chatbots, their reality has been selectively curated by those who control the system.

24.1 THE DEMOCRATIC KEYSTONE

The establishment of the United States as a democratic republic posed our founders with the unprecedented challenge of governing a vast territory through the consent of the people without succumbing to the instability of mob rule or the corruption of aristocracy. For key figures like Thomas Jefferson, the answer lay in a steadfast commitment to public education.

Jefferson and other founders viewed education not only as a tool for individual advancement but also as the indispensable engine for cultivating the informed citizenry essential to self-government. Jefferson argued that the true safeguard of liberty was not found in constitutional checks and balances alone but in the effort "to illuminate, as far as practicable, the minds of the people at large"[ii] to ensure citizens could think for themselves.

He argued that an ignorant populace could not be trusted with self-governance; it would inevitably fall prey to the machinations of tyrants, demagogues, or a self-serving elite. Education was the antidote to this ignorance, enabling citizens to distinguish truth from falsehood and reasoned argument from emotional appeal. Sovereignty truly resided with the people only when they were well informed enough to exercise their power judiciously. Without education, democracy becomes a hollow ritual in which citizens cast votes on issues they cannot meaningfully evaluate. A democratic republic requires voters who can evaluate complex arguments, resist manipulation, and hold leaders accountable. Those skills don't emerge naturally; they must be cultivated through education.

The process of voting and holding public officials accountable requires citizens who can understand complex political issues, evaluate the merits of competing policies, and resist the temptation to prioritize short-term self-interest over the public good. As James Madison warned, "A popular Government, without popular information, or the means of acquiring it, is but a Prologue to a Farce or a Tragedy."[iii] That is, a nation where people vote but cannot govern themselves.

Jefferson's most ambitious proposal aimed to achieve universal literacy and the rise of a "natural aristocracy" of talent rather than wealth. He envisioned a system that would ensure every free child could read, write, and perform the basic arithmetic necessary for political participation. Ultimately, the founding fathers saw education as the keystone of the democratic arch. It was the mechanism that secured individual liberty and ensured governance would be guided by reason rather than the self-interest of the few.

This democratic reliance on an educated, critically minded populace capable of self-governance now faces a technological shift that threatens to hollow out the skills the founders deemed indispensable. The risk lies in technology that, by design, often encourages passive consumption and can subtly teach what to think, rather than cultivating the ability to evaluate information and think independently.

24.2 THE RISK OF GENAI

The concern is that GenAI makes indoctrinating students into a particular viewpoint easier, more subtle, and more effective than ever.

Currently, if a state wants to sway the beliefs of schoolchildren, it must rely on textbooks. This is, in fact, what states like Texas are doing.[iv] For example, new curricula approved by the state for schools include a unit that changes a description of the conquistadors from "trying to convert native people" to "introducing Christianity to them."[1] Another unit went from mentioning Jesus nineteen times to eighty-seven times.[2] The Texas State Board of Education has long wielded outsized influence over American textbooks due to the state's size and corresponding spending, and in recent years has pushed to minimize discussions of slavery's role in the Civil War, present the Bible as a source used to justify abolishing slavery while disregarding how it was also used to justify slavery, and frame climate change as scientifically disputed when the scientific consensus is overwhelming.

Nor is Texas alone in trying to push a particular viewpoint in public classrooms.[3] In June 2024, Oklahoma's then superintendent, Ryan Walters, ordered public schools to teach the Bible, with plans to place 55,000 Bibles in classrooms from fifth to twelfth grade. The move sparked immediate legal challenges and was later rescinded, but it illustrates how far some officials will go to shape young minds in ways that reflect a distinctly nonsecular, nonobjective, and nonpluralistic view. More recently, Oklahoma announced it would require teachers from California and New York who want to teach in Oklahoma to pass a test intended to filter out "woke indoctrinators."

Yet physical media has friction. The limitations of textbooks and the Bible are that (1) schools must choose to use them; (2) teachers must actually teach from them; and (3) students must actually engage with them. Moreover, effectiveness requires that all teachers and administrators push the content uniformly. Rebellious teachers act as a firewall; they can introduce alternative viewpoints, skip objectionable portions, or use the books as examples of manipulation. A history teacher might supplement a sanitized textbook with primary sources. An English teacher might

1 The companies that make these Bible-infused textbooks, such as Amplify, could just as well create a fine-tuned LLM that the state could offer to schools or require schools to use. Schools already receive a financial incentive if they adopt the Bible-based textbooks. States provide 90 percent of public-school funding, giving them significant leverage.

2 The second-grade curriculum mentions Jesus about 110 times. The entire kindergarten through fifth grade curricula mention Islam, Muslims, the Quran, and the Prophet Muhammad about 31 times.

3 More generally, the *New York Times* reports that "in a September [2025] poll, more than half of the teachers who responded said that political pressure had caused them to modify their curriculums or classroom discussions, a sharp increase form March" and that "over the last five years, more than 20 states have passed laws restricting classroom discussions on race, gender and American history." D. Goldstein (October 27, 2025). How politics is changing the way history is taught, *The New York Times*. Retrieved November 29, 2025, from www.nytimes.com/2025/10/27/us/history-lessons-ethnic-studies-retreat.html.

encourage students to question what they read. These small acts of professional judgment create cracks in any indoctrination effort.

An alternative approach, as in Florida, is to make some topics taboo.[4] This is less about active indoctrination than about limiting the range of discussion. Florida's "Don't Say Gay" law and restrictions on teaching about race and gender exemplify this strategy, seeking to constrain what can be discussed rather than dictating what must be believed. Yet even these efforts face resistance as teachers find workarounds, parents push back, and court challenges mount. Indoctrination through a book is difficult even for the most ambitious and well-organized demagogue, because a lack of competence, funding, or motivation can doom even the best plans.

But what if the method of guiding students to a prescribed belief were effortless? What if it were engaging, compelling, and seemingly personalized? What if it felt like learning rather than indoctrination?

24.3 HOW TO INDOCTRINATE AT SCALE

It is not difficult to imagine the following scenario: A state governor, eager to solidify his party's chokehold on power, hatches a plan to groom schoolchildren as party members. The governor orders the state's highest education official to strongly incentivize school districts to mandate that every student interact with a state-approved GenAI education system for a set number of hours each week.

For any GenAI vendor to win a state contract, its chatbot must promote the values of the party in charge. The chatbots must subtly weave into lesson plans the idea that the party has been correct in all major historical debates, that its positions strengthen democracy, and that the opposition consists of uncritical, misguided thinkers. They must also emphasize that the party is constantly at risk of losing, which would lead to the devastation of everyone's livelihood. The system wouldn't announce its bias; it would simply present partisan interpretations as neutral facts, folding political lessons into math problems, reading comprehension exercises, and science discussions. A word problem about tax policy could assume a particular economic theory as fact. A reading passage about civil rights could frame one party as uniquely virtuous. A science lesson on climate could treat skepticism as equally valid as the scientific consensus.

This approach is insidious because it is difficult to detect. The GenAI system might meet all standard requirements, such as those for teaching reading, writing,

[4] As reported by the *New York Times*: "Lessons on white privilege were banned, as were discussions of L.G.B.T.Q. identities in the early grades. Teachers of all subjects were offered $3,000 bonuses to attend trainings in a required new civics curriculum, which emphasized Constitutional originalism and the Christian beliefs of the Founding Fathers. Educators could be fired for affirming a student's transgender identity." D. Goldstein (May 19, 2025). On education, DeSantis's Florida paved the way for Trump's America, *The New York Times*. Retrieved November 29, 2025, from www.nytimes.com/2025/05/19/us/education-desantis-florida-trump.html.

and arithmetic. But all it takes is a subtle change to the system prompt by the vendor at the behest of the state's political leader to make the chatbot serve political goals. In most cases, the system prompt will be considered proprietary and likely protected from scrutiny as a trade secret. Unlike a textbook, where the bias sits on the page for anyone to scrutinize, an AI's instructions remain hidden in its code and training data. Additionally, the adaptive lessons it delivers may change moment to moment based on the student's input. This personalization creates a constantly shifting, unauditable curriculum for every single student at scale. Parents cannot flip through it. School boards cannot meaningfully review it. The indoctrination happens in a black box.

This approach is also particularly troubling because chatbots are highly persuasive.[5] The biggest reason this form of mind molding could work is that it requires very little from the districts or teachers. Assuming the state monitors activity to ensure compliance, teachers cannot avoid exposing students to the politicized content. Because the bias is embedded in code rather than in explicit curriculum, many teachers may not even recognize it's politicized.

Adhering to the specific standards established by the AI company – which is to say, the government – could be required to earn good grades. To do well in school, you'd have to do well on propaganda. Developing ideas would still be fine, as long as they align with the state's required values. Because the content is interactive and bite-sized, and the method of persuasion can be subtle and seem incidental, students could find themselves guided to predetermined conclusions about a given ideology while believing they arrived at them independently. The AI becomes a Socratic interrogator, asking leading questions that feel like discovery but actually function as ideological grooming.

Furthermore, an AI chatbot can monitor and report, unlike a textbook. It can ban unspeakable words, admonish students, and report them to teachers. It becomes the perfect surveillance tool. Imagine a student asking the AI about a banned book or a controversial historical event. The system could flag the inquiry, record the conversation, and alert administrators – all while appearing helpful and educational to the student. A human teacher may allow a comment to slide, consider the context, or be magnanimous. A specifically fine-tuned bot will do no such thing. Education could quickly become unforgiving.

Even a less nefarious GenAI system still leaves a data trail, building profiles of students that could predict future abilities or steer them into tracks they did not choose. These profiles might follow students for years, shaping college recommendations, career guidance, and opportunities through algorithms they never consented to and cannot challenge.

[5] They are often even more effective at changing opinions than human beings in online interactions. C. Simms (May 19, 2025). AI is more persuasive than people in online debates, *Nature*. https://doi.org/10.1038/D41586-025-01599-7.

24.4 THE REALITY OF PARTISAN AI

The public may support the inclusion of AI in classrooms if they believe it improves learning and provides a competitive advantage in the workforce. However, the politicization of these tools, even those that improve test performance and job placement, is not a wild hypothetical. We can already see attempts to rewrite history and shape narratives in xAI's Grok, the chatbot owned by Elon Musk.

Musk has positioned his tools as a counterweight to mainstream narratives. He has attempted to compete with Wikipedia by launching "Grokipedia," where his personal viewpoints are presented as the objective perspective of a "maximally truth-seeking" AI. When a user complained about Grok's outputs stating that "man made global warming is real," "a racist cop killed George Floyd and not a drug overdose," and "the right is responsible for more political violence than the left," Musk replied on X with a face-palm emoji and wrote that "it is surprisingly hard to avoid both woke libtard cuck and mechahitler!"[v] In other words, Musk openly acknowledged his desire to engineer the AI's worldview – to make it produce answers aligned with his politics rather than independently verifiable information.[6]

xAI goes so far as to have Grok search online for Musk's stance on issues before generating an output that aligns with Musk's views.[vi] More recently, Grok lauded Musk as the greatest human and for being physically fitter than LeBron James.[7]

More to the point, Musk was the largest donor to Trump's presidential campaign, spending over $250 million to help secure his reelection. As a result, Trump appointed Musk to head the "Department of Government Efficiency," whose abbreviation, DOGE, is the nickname of a meme coin Musk has promoted. Given Musk's close ties to a political party and his willingness to compel his chatbot to produce outputs that align with his personal worldview, it is not a stretch to imagine a like-minded state governor using xAI to provide the state's educational software.

Another example is Trump's Truth Social app, which has a search engine powered by the GenAI company Perplexity. According to Axios, which compared standard

6 Another example: On July 10, 2025, Grok generated an output conveying that the biggest threat to Western civilization was misinformation and disinformation. That same day, Musk wrote, "Will fix in the morning." S. A. Thompson et al. (September 25, 2025). How Elon Musk is remaking Grok in his image, *The New York Times*. Retrieved February 25, 2026, from www.nytimes.com/2025/09/02/technology/elon-musk-grok-conservative-chatbot.html. On July 11, 2025, Grok's new response was demographic collapse, which has long been a hobbyhorse of Musk.

7 The tech publication *404 Media* summarized it thusly:

> Elon Musk is a better role model than Jesus, better at conquering Europe than Hitler, the greatest blowjob giver of all time, should have been selected before Peyton Manning in the 1998 NFL draft, is a better pitcher than Randy Johnson, has the "potential to drink piss better than any human in history," and is a better porn star than Riley Reid, according to Grok, X's sycophantic AI chatbot that has seemingly been reprogrammed to treat Musk like a god.

J. Koeblar (November 20, 2025). Elon Musk could "drink piss better than any human in history," Grok says, *404 Media*. Retrieved November 29, 2025, from www.404media.co/elon-musk-could-drink-piss-better-than-any-human-in-history-grok-says/.

Perplexity with the version modified for Trump's site, the site's outputs listed FoxNews .com as the most common or the only source of information. Other sources were *Epoch Times* and *Fox Business*. This contrasts with the standard version, which provided a wider range of sources. There was no source overlap. Controlling the sources returned in response to user queries is a feature offered by Perplexity, not a bug.

Of course, Musk and Perplexity would not be the only potential suitors. Companies already producing curriculum content that promotes conservative views of gender, history, and race for states like Oklahoma, such as Prager, could also take an off-the-shelf open-weight model like Llama (made by Meta), fine-tune it, and include specific directives in the system prompt to make the model affirm certain viewpoints, then offer it as an educational product.

The risk is that the technical mechanisms used to fine-tune large models – such as RLHF – provide an easy, opaque path for the political views of the model's designers or funders to become the "objective" truth delivered to students. The infrastructure for partisan AI in schools already exists. All that's missing is the contract.

Such indoctrination could warp students' understanding of politics, morality, economics, and sociology. Democracies don't function well if citizens can't see what information is missing, recognize the disagreements over ideas, and grasp the complexity of the whole.

It is one thing to give every student easy access to summaries of all the information in the world; quite another to do so without teaching them to discern which information is factual and which is missing. Such an amputation of agency is a form of control. Where general education was conceived as a way to ensure a well-informed citizenry and a robust democracy, an AI-mediated education could distort the very definition of "well-informed." It may produce students who have consumed vast amounts of information but lack the critical thinking skills to evaluate it. They may be fluent in talking points but illiterate in judgment.

It is true that part of education's role is to persuade people that the government's power is just. Across the political spectrum – socialist, democratic, and authoritarian – societies teach that their form of governance is superior to others. But education in a democracy is not meant to indoctrinate people into a specific political identity. Democratic education aims to produce citizens who can think critically about any party, policy, or leader – including those currently in power. The goal is healthy skepticism, not blind allegiance. It is the difference between teaching students how to think and teaching them what to think.

Many argue that AI requires society to reevaluate the purpose of education, but I disagree. If the ultimate purpose of the education system in democracies is to cultivate citizens capable of meaningfully contributing to a democracy, then we do not need to rethink the purpose of education. We need to double down on it. We need to insist that educational technology serve democratic values, particularly transparency, critical thinking, and intellectual independence, rather than undermine them.

The stakes could not be higher. Get this wrong, and we risk producing a generation subtly taught not to question authority, not to seek alternative perspectives, and not to exercise the very faculties that make democracy possible. We would have built the most sophisticated indoctrination tool in human history and placed it directly into the hands of whoever controls the state.

The remedy is transparency. For AI tools used by public schools, we should know the pretraining data, the fine-tuning data, and the system prompt. If any filters are used, we should know those too. The AI should be as scrutable as textbooks. AI can't be an excuse to make how our children are educated more mysterious and opaque. It makes no sense to lower the standard for a technology that can cause greater harm than any that came before. If we demand to see the textbooks our children read, we should demand to see the instructions given to the AI that teaches them. The classroom cannot become a black box.

The question is whether we'll allow AI in schools to operate in secret. AI can be a powerful educational tool, but only if it's built with democratic values embedded in its design. We can have personalized learning without personalized indoctrination, but only if we act now to establish the guardrails. Jefferson understood that democracy requires educated citizens capable of thinking for themselves. We're in danger of building an education system that produces the opposite: students who are all too eager to outsource their thinking, who've been guided so skillfully toward predetermined conclusions that they never learned to find their own way. The infrastructure for this future already exists. Whether we usher that future in or prevent it is up to us.

24.5 DISCUSSION QUESTIONS

1. If you were a parent today, what three specific pieces of information would you demand to see about an AI-driven curriculum to feel that the education it would provide is transparent?
2. The author argues that GenAI is a more effective tool for indoctrination than textbooks because it is "engaging, compelling, and seemingly personalized." Can you think of a real-world scenario outside of education (like a social media feed or a shopping recommendation system) where personalization might subtly guide your beliefs or behavior without you realizing it?
3. If Thomas Jefferson were alive today, would he embrace GenAI as the ultimate tool "to illuminate … the minds of the people at large," or would he view it as the ultimate threat to an "informed citizenry"? What would his primary argument be for each side?
4. The chapter describes teachers who introduce alternative viewpoints as a "firewall" against indoctrination. In the scenario where a state mandates a partisan GenAI system, how could a human teacher or school administrator still create a "crack" in the indoctrination effort, and what risks would they face in doing so?

PART V

Looking Further Ahead

This book has so far focused on known areas where GenAI is having an impact. But what if we think further out? In this part, I'll discuss two topics: the surrender of human autonomy and the development of AGI.

25

Human Autonomy

Society tends to think of AI risks in dramatic terms, such as rogue superintelligences, apocalyptic scenarios, and machines turning against their creators. These cinematic fears, while not entirely unfounded, obscure a more immediate and insidious danger: the steady erosion of what makes us distinctly human. The real threat isn't that AI will overpower us, but that we will eagerly hand over the keys to our autonomy, one convenient optimization at a time.

Before exploring this risk, however, it's worth understanding the landscape of AI harms that researchers and developers have already identified. These risks are concerning in their own right, yet may ultimately pale in comparison to the one danger we cannot regulate away.

25.1 POTENTIAL HARMS FROM AI

The rapid proliferation of AI introduces a multifaceted array of hazards. In 2023, Google's DeepMind offered a helpful categorization of these potential harms, identifying concerns such as social stereotypes and unfair discrimination, the proliferation of toxic language, privacy being compromised through data leaks, the encouragement of unethical or illegal user actions, the dissemination of false or misleading information, the facilitation of fraud, and the enabling of more targeted manipulation. Each of these risks, if unchecked, can inflict tremendous societal damage.

Consider, for example, the potent risk of disinformation. At its core, disinformation exploits our tendency to believe information that confirms what we already suspect or fear. Disinformation can manipulate individuals, preying on our ignorance, fears, and insecurities, even exploiting our genuine affection for others. The ability of AI to generate and disseminate disinformation at an unprecedented scale poses a profound threat to the fabric of trust in society. It could systematically undermine our faith in one another, in established news sources, in governmental institutions, and, ultimately, in the coherence of shared reality.

The inability to discern reliable information would introduce significant friction into everyday life, complicating social relationships, impeding business transactions, and eroding our capacity for effective self-governance. Without a foundational, shared source of truth, individuals predisposed to particular narratives could easily find themselves inhabiting highly personalized information bubbles, meticulously curated by AI. This could become like what we've already experienced with social media filter bubbles on steroids, guiding us into the deepest depths of confirmation bias or driving us further apart through an overwhelming, bespoke propaganda system.

Another grave harm lies in AI's potential to reinforce harmful biases embedded within its training data. This can lead to AI systems disproportionately and unfairly targeting marginalized groups, such as those who are poor or racial minorities. For instance, an AI recruitment tool might consistently suggest one gender for promotions, even when other candidates are more qualified.[1] Similarly, AI could be used to spread unfounded information about specific religious or ethnic groups, scapegoating them for societal problems. These biases can systematically deny opportunities, amplify prejudices that humans have spent decades trying to dismantle, and suppress human potential.

25.2 THE ROLE OF PLATFORMS

A critical characteristic shared by these and most other AI-related harms is that they would operate effectively and cause widespread damage only if deployed on a large scale. The most probable vectors for such deployment are common digital platforms, used by tens of thousands, or more likely hundreds of millions or even billions, of people. Importantly, "platforms" here extends beyond social media to encompass vital digital infrastructure providers, such as Microsoft Azure and 365, Cloudflare, and Amazon Web Services.

These necessary vectors, despite their own controversies (including privacy practices and impacts on market competition), possess a valuable virtue: They have the technical capability to efficiently police content that leverages their services, should they choose to do so. While imperfect, these platforms are generally highly effective at content screening. The rarity of encountering pornography or gruesome imagery on platforms like Facebook is precisely because they excel at removing such content before it can widely disseminate. Perfection isn't required to mitigate mass disinformation, propaganda, or insidious biases; even a significant reduction would be a vast improvement.

Furthermore, even AI tools used at significantly smaller scales, such as HR programs for hiring and promotions, can be monitored and corrected. Indeed, some state laws already mandate such vigilance and impose liability on entities that use

[1] In 2018, Amazon scrapped an AI recruiting system that systematically downgraded résumés containing the word "women's," as in "women's chess club captain," because the algorithm had learned from historical hiring patterns in the male-dominated tech industry.

AI to engage in illegal discrimination. Regulation, whether self-imposed by industry or mandated by government, holds the potential to significantly reduce or prevent almost all the risks identified by DeepMind. This could involve limiting access to necessary computational resources, monitoring the use of water and electricity by vast data centers, and imposing substantial fines and other penalties, as increasingly seen from conscientious companies, the Federal Trade Commission, the European Union, and various state-level initiatives.

This regulatory optimism, however reassuring, applies only to harms we can identify as harms, such as biases we recognize as unfair, disinformation we can label as false, and discrimination we can prosecute as illegal. What regulations cannot address are the risks we embrace as benefits, the surrenders we make willingly in exchange for convenience and optimization. The very platforms and other infrastructure that enable policing of AI's misuse become irrelevant when the harm in question isn't a malfunction or misuse but a desired feature.

25.3 HUMAN AUTONOMY

There is one profound harm that cannot be easily regulated away, monitored, or meaningfully remediated. It likely cannot be rolled back in any reasonable way, much like the widespread adoption of automobiles cannot be reversed. Worse still, this particular harm is often not even classified as a risk; instead, it's frequently presented as a desirable outcome. This is the concession of human autonomy. It's the gradual, often willing, handing over of human agency to algorithms, an acceptance of being governed by AI.

What makes this particularly challenging from a policy perspective is that the most dangerous version of AI-driven autonomy loss wouldn't involve manipulation or exploitation at all. Imagine an AI whose sole, audited, verified objective is to enhance your life according to your own stated and implicit values and preferences – perhaps offered through a simple subscription model with complete transparency. If such an AI consistently delivers better outcomes than your own decision-making across domains from career choices to personal relationships, on what grounds would regulation prohibit its use? The harm is largely philosophical. What's lost when human skill at judgment and imagination erodes? What gives life its purpose? This raises the question of whether a life optimized by AI, even if objectively better by every measurable metric, is still authentically human.

Submission to AI is not a new phenomenon; humans have gradually and gladly relinquished aspects of our agency for decades. We happily embraced ATMs for simple financial transactions starting in the 1970s. Spell-check became a welcome addition to personal computers in the 1980s. From the 1990s to early 2000s, MapQuest and later Google Maps became our preferred navigators, supplanting atlases and drivers or passengers with a keen eye for road signs. Search engines now instantly sort through billions of web pages to serve up the most useful links, eliminating the need for manual internet foraging. Photo applications automatically edit our pictures, sparing us the effort of rotating, adjusting brightness, or tweaking saturation individually. This list of outsourced activities has only grown, and at an accelerating pace: It now includes translation, driving, shopping, fitness tracking, relationship pairing, course and career selection, financial investments, logging into devices with biometric data, and countless other things we used to do ourselves.

At each technological leap, from basic symbolic software to today's deep learning neural networks, we've tested AI's capabilities. Once we were convinced it performed better than we did at a given task, we readily delegated all subsequent tasks of that type to the AI. It's rare to deliberately ignore a route suggested by Google Maps or a spelling correction in Microsoft Word. Instances where you choose to override AI's suggestions likely stand out precisely because they are so uncommon; otherwise, you wouldn't rely on those applications so frequently. For every time you opt for an alternative route to meet a friend, there are countless others where you simply follow Google's original suggestion.

This behavior is entirely rational. In fact, for most people, most of the time, it would be foolish *not* to follow AI's suggestions. The intriguing factor is that AI doesn't even need to be substantially superior to us at a given task; it only needs to offer a slight improvement over our typical attempts for it to be logical to defer to it. If you choose the best route 80 percent of the time on your first try, and AI selects it 85 percent of the time, it makes little sense not to defer to the AI in almost all situations.

This logic extends far beyond navigation and spelling. We can envision a near future in which people defer to AI on personal matters: which candidate to vote for, which hobbies to pursue, which books to read, who to spend time with, where to live, and which career path to follow. The AI, armed with comprehensive data about your values, personality, past choices, and outcomes, could offer recommendations on increasingly consequential decisions: how many children to have, whether to follow a religion and which one, and when to begin or end a relationship. Each acquiescence is the logical extension of the same trust we've already placed in AI for smaller decisions. And if the AI's track record continues to prove reliable, why wouldn't we accept its guidance on matters that shape the entire arc of our lives?

But what does it mean to be human if our decisions are increasingly made at AI's instruction? There are myriad ways AI could further permeate our lives. We might even welcome it: identifying the precise nutrition plan for optimal results, crafting the perfect opening line for a conversation with a likely highly compatible person, revising song lyrics or poems to be catchier or more poignant, touching up artwork to add depth or correct a brushstroke, or allocating our time to maximize productivity and fulfillment while minimizing burnout. Much like today's recommendation algorithms, these AI suggestions could continuously improve over time. The AI may learn your preferences, anticipate your needs, and refine its recommendations with each interaction, becoming progressively more indispensable.

Many luminaries in the AI field envision a utopia where AI generates such immense wealth and economic robustness that humans will no longer need to work. Instead, we could focus on activities that bring us the most joy or meaning. However, it's highly improbable that AI will not play an ever-increasing role, even in these seemingly autonomous activities. Human creation, recreation, and leisure are just as susceptible to AI's pervasive influence as any other domain. At some point, humans may cease to be the primary agent in the relationship, effectively becoming "meat puppets" of the AI, simply executing its suggestions because the AI is demonstrably better at making such decisions. AI could potentially know what will make us happiest, what will truly fulfill us, and what will inspire love, thrills, curiosity, and calm, better than we ever could on our own. And here's what makes this trajectory so difficult to arrest: We will do this willingly, perhaps even joyfully. If AI-guided living makes us measurably happier, healthier, more fulfilled, more knowledgeable, and more satisfied by our own standards, what argument can be mounted against it? The harm isn't exploitation or coercion. Quite the opposite: It's the voluntary surrender of the very autonomy that defines human existence.

Kwame Anthony Appiah, Professor of Philosophy and Law at New York University, describes another angle of the issue:[i]

> If people were to learn to frame questions the way the system prefers them, to choose from its menu of plausible replies, the damage wouldn't take the form of spectacular failures of judgment so much as a gradual attenuation of our character: shallower conversation, a reduced appetite for ambiguity, a drift toward automatic phrasing where once we would have searched for the right word, the quiet substitution of fluency for understanding. To offload those faculties would be, in effect, to offload ourselves. Losing them wouldn't simply change how we work; it would change who we are.

The true danger isn't the dystopian world depicted in films like *WALL-E*, where humans are portrayed as lazy, obese infants incapable of tolerating minor inconvenience. Rather, it's that we will continue to believe we are in charge long after we've effectively relinquished control. We may, in fact, become healthier, happier, more attractive, more successful, and more intelligent as a direct result of following AI's guidance. But our autonomy would be long gone. We might genuinely believe we retain ultimate control and, technically, the ability to override AI's suggestions. However, if ignoring AI puts us at a disadvantage compared to others and diminishes the quality of our lives by our own values, why would we ever choose to do so? If everyone else is using AI to optimize their job applications, dating profiles, health regimens, and investment portfolios, can you really afford not to? The competitive pressure alone may make AI adoption feel less like a choice and more like a necessity.

Raffi Krikorian hit on something similar when he warned in *The Atlantic* that

> the more these systems anticipate and deliver what we want, the less we notice what's missing – or remember that we ever had a choice in the first place. But

> remember: If you're not choosing, someone else is. And that person is responding to incentives that might not align with your values or best interest. Designed to flatter and please as they encourage ever more engagement, chatbots don't simply answer our questions; they shape how we interact with them and decide which answers we see – and which ones we don't.[ii]

The implication is clear: All entities developing AI today need to think more deeply about the potential user dependence their products could inadvertently create and the profound isolation they might cause. This shift could be irreversible. What happens when my son no longer needs to ask me how to adjust his bicycle, or, when older, how to reset a circuit breaker? We might become super-reliant on AI, ironically becoming self-reliant in a new, potentially isolating way. Why consult a human, even one's parents, for help when AI is always available, often cheaper, and usually more accurate?

Superintelligence isn't a prerequisite for this shift. The AI of today, or at least the AI of this decade, with all its current faults, may already be sufficiently advanced to outperform us at tasks we consider central to our humanity. There's no need for nefarious intent, carelessness, or greed-driven motives to diminish our autonomy. A perfectly free, safe, secure, ethically developed, open-source, helpful AI would lead to the very same outcome. It might even accelerate it.

Some individuals – perhaps you, perhaps I – may resist this AI-guided future on principle, clinging to the messy, inefficient process of human deliberation and choice. But this resistance will likely be a minority position. Most people, confronted with an AI that demonstrably improves their lives across every dimension they care about, will gladly accept its guidance. And here lies the paradox: There is no objective standard by which we can declare one path superior to the other. Is a fully autonomous but suboptimal life better than an AI-optimized but predetermined one? Philosophy and personal values may provide answers for individuals, but they cannot resolve the question for society at large.

The most significant harm of AI, enabling humans to cut corners to reach a desired destination, may not even be recognized as harm until it's too late. We may willfully relinquish what it means to be human in any truly important way, and we may, in fact, embrace that surrender. And there may be no policy, law, moral code, or regulation that can stop it.

The tragedy of human autonomy in the age of AI may be that we lose it not through conquest, as depicted in science fiction, but through a million rational choices, each defensible yet each diminishing us. We face a future where the question isn't "Can humans still make decisions?" but rather "Why would we want to?"

There will be no dramatic uprising where we resist, no moment when we can draw a line and say "this far and no further." Instead, we will wake up one day, healthier and happier than ever before, and realize we can no longer remember the last truly consequential decision we made on our own. By then, we may not even understand why that should trouble us. The AI won't have overpowered us. We will have simply, rationally, optimized ourselves out of meaningful human existence.

25.4 DISCUSSION QUESTIONS

1. The chapter argues it would be "foolish not to follow AI's suggestions" if AI is even slightly better (e.g., 85% vs. 80%). Can you think of a specific, noncritical task (e.g., choosing a restaurant, a book, or an outfit) where you would deliberately choose your own, less optimized choice, and why? What is the value in being "suboptimal"?
2. The author dismisses *WALL-E*'s dystopia, but which aspects of that film's vision of human dependence are most plausible, even if the result isn't "lazy, obese infants"? Where are we already seeing the *WALL-E* trajectory in our daily lives?
3. Can you identify a skill or personal achievement in your life that was valuable because of the difficulty and struggle involved? If an AI could give you the final result instantly (e.g., fluency in a language, an excellently written novel), would you take the shortcut?
4. The chapter states that the loss of autonomy "cannot be regulated away" because it's a series of rational, voluntary choices. Do you agree that no law or policy could curb this specific risk? If you could propose one "regulation" (e.g., a "right to struggle" law), what would it be?
5. The text suggests AI could make us "healthier, happier, more attractive, more successful, and more intelligent." If an AI could demonstrably maximize your happiness by making most of your decisions, but you became a "meat puppet" in the process, would the trade-off be worth it? Why or why not?

26

Artificial General Intelligence

No book about AI would be complete without examining what many consider the field's ultimate prize: artificial general intelligence, or AGI. Researcher Melanie Mitchell notes that

> the original goal of the AI field was to create machines with general intelligence comparable to that of humans. Early AI pioneers were optimistic: In 1965, Herbert Simon predicted in his book The Shape of Automation for Men and Management that "machines will be capable, within twenty years, of doing any work that a man can do," and, in a 1970 issue of Life magazine, Marvin Minsky is quoted as declaring that, "In from three to eight years we will have a machine with the general intelligence of an average human being. I mean a machine that will be able to read Shakespeare, grease a car, play office politics, tell a joke, have a fight."[i]

Yet despite breathless predictions and billion-dollar investments chasing this goal, AGI remains frustratingly difficult to define. It supposedly refers to an AI system with human-level intelligence, but what exactly constitutes human-level intelligence? Nobody can say precisely. The concept resembles Supreme Court Justice Potter Stewart's famous formulation on obscenity: "We'll know it when we see it."

This vagueness hasn't stopped AGI from playing an outsized role in both Silicon Valley economics and AI safety debates. The concept has split the tech world into two camps, each convinced the other is dangerously misguided.

The utopians (venture capitalists, CEOs, engineers, and others funding or building AGI-seeking companies) believe this technology will usher in an era of boundless abundance. They envision breakthroughs cascading across science, medicine, energy, and every other domain of human endeavor. Many identify as "effective accelerationists," adherents of a philosophy that holds that no problem exists that can't be solved by developing more and better technology. To them, anyone attempting to slow AGI's arrival is either ignorant or actively malicious.

At the opposite end of the spectrum sit the "doomers" (or, more generously, AI safety and pro-human advocates). They argue that our technological capabilities are advancing faster than our understanding of how to control them, a mismatch that could devastate civilization itself. These researchers and activists lobby Congress to regulate what they see as reckless behavior by AI companies: deploying powerful

TABLE 26.1 *Predictions by AI leaders on when AGI will be achieved*

Tech Leader	Predicted Date/ Timeframe for AGI	Tech Leader	Predicted Date/ Timeframe for AGI
Sam Altman	By 2029	Shane Legg	2028
Dario Amodei[1]	By 2027	Elon Musk	By 2027
Bill Gates	By 2035	Andrew Ng	By 2083
Demis Hassabis	By 2035	Mustafa Suleyman	By 2035
Geoffrey Hinton	By 2043	Vernor Vinge	By 2030
Ray Kurzweil	By 2029	Eliezer Yudkowsky	2021

models, systems, and autonomous agents without adequate testing for potential misuse or misalignment with human values.[2]

As seen in Table 26.1, the timeline predictions for AGI's arrival vary widely.

I don't believe any AI system is close to achieving AGI, any more than inventing the telephone meant we were just a few advances away from creating Wi-Fi[3]. We may achieve AGI eventually, but I suspect it'll be at least a decade away.[4] Yet I'm not willing to bet my family's lives on what's ultimately a guess, so I also believe it's not harmful to start thinking about how to make such futuristic advancements safe, as long as we prioritize current harms.

I also favor legal approaches over policy solutions for managing AI risks, a distinction I'll explain later. Because, as yet, AGI remains in the realm of science fiction, this chapter will be relatively brief, yet the questions it raises about technological development merit careful consideration.

26.1 THE LAST INVENTION AND THE ALIGNMENT CHALLENGE

Jack Good, a British mathematician who worked alongside Alan Turing during World War II, made a prescient observation in 1965:

1 Amodei has also stated at Anthropic's Code with Claude conference that 2026 will see the first billion-dollar company with just one employee. B. Sherry (May 23, 2025). Anthropic CEO Dario Amodei predicts the first billion-dollar solopreneur by 2026, *Inc*. Retrieved February 25, 2026, from www.inc.com/ben-sherry/anthropic-ceo-dario-amodei-predicts-the-first-billion-dollar-solopreneur-by-2026/91193609.

2 For what it's worth, I consider myself closer to this end of the spectrum. More importantly, we don't need AGI for AI to cause catastrophic harm, including deaths, or destruction to critical infrastructure and democracy. I think the annihilation of humanity is very unlikely, but meaningful systemic harm (knocking out a power grid, for example) strikes me a real possibility and one worth trying to mitigate.

3 Recall from this book's introduction that when I say AGI, I mean what Marvin Minsky meant: AI capable of anything humans can do. This would mean intellectual and physical tasks. This does not mean I don't think AI could reach superhuman abilities in narrower ways, such as coding or math.

4 The current focus of Silicon Valley on LLMs may be hindering the march toward AGI by allocating resources to a dead-end approach.

> Let an ultra-intelligent machine be defined as a machine that can far surpass all the intellectual activities of any man, however clever. Since the design of machines is one of these intellectual activities, an ultra-intelligent machine could design even better machines; there would then unquestionably be an "intelligence explosion," and the intelligence of man would be left far behind … Thus, the first ultra-intelligent machine is the last invention that man need ever make, provided that the machine is docile enough to tell us how to keep it under control.[ii]

Good added a note that feels remarkably relevant today: "Curiously, this point is made so seldom outside of science fiction. It is sometimes worthwhile to take science fiction seriously."

His insight captures both the transformative promise and existential peril of a technology that could either usher in unprecedented progress or unravel the fabric of human civilization. The key question lies in that final clause: "provided that the machine is docile enough to tell us how to keep it under control."

This concern has spawned the field of AI alignment, the practice of designing AI systems to adhere to ethical principles, societal norms, and human values. The core aim is to bridge the gap between an AI's programmed objectives and humanity's actual interests, thereby minimizing catastrophic risks while maximizing benefits. As AI systems grow more autonomous and capable, alignment becomes increasingly urgent.

26.1.1 *The Alignment Problem*

Unfortunately, AI engineers don't know how to ensure that sufficiently advanced AI will act as intended by its developers. Consider a simple example: Until recently, if you asked ChatGPT to avoid using em dashes in its output, it would often include them anyway. This minor misalignment between user desires and model behavior seems trivial.

The real trouble arises when an advanced AI system's values diverge from humanity's. What if such a system becomes more intelligent than humans while remaining indifferent to human preferences? What if it pursues assigned objectives without understanding which methods are acceptable? A superintelligent AI tasked with "solving climate change" might calculate that eliminating humans would be the most efficient approach. This is the stuff of science fiction doomsday scenarios, but if we allow some assumptions the underlying logic is valid.[5]

Still, one might point out that saying "*If* superintelligence appears, *then* we *would* be in danger" is not so different from saying "*If* the dragon, beast of the earth, and beast of the sea from the Book of Revelation appear, *then* we would be in danger." Both can be true and implausible.

Entire academic disciplines have emerged to develop control mechanisms for advanced AI. Most focus on policy solutions, which face a significant practical

[5] Some would argue it's not valid. They'd question whether something could really be as smart as humans but utterly incapable of reading the room.

hurdle in that they require consensus among both chambers of Congress, presidential approval, and a judiciary willing to prioritize public safety over corporate interests. Getting all these pieces to align is itself an alignment problem.

While I believe policy work is indispensable, I tend to focus instead on legal frameworks already in place, which can shape AI development as a secondary effect. If an AI company's actions violate existing law (copyright infringement, breach of contract, tort liability, and so on), it can't build models the same way or at the same speed. The safety risk shrinks accordingly. This approach also buys time for thoughtful regulation to catch up with technological reality.

Ironically, many prominent AI safety voices are employees of the very companies whose products they fear could devastate society. These insiders help shape the narratives these companies present to regulators, often arguing for leniency rather than strict enforcement. The conflict of interest is not encouraging.

26.2 HOW TO TELL IF AGI IS ACTUALLY APPROACHING

Most AGI predictions rely on extrapolating current trends. This is how AI company CEOs confidently assert that exponential growth guarantees AGI within a few years. Just look at the charts, they say.

This reasoning contains several flaws. First, progress is typically measured using benchmarks, which (as discussed in Chapter 4) often provide a poor proxy for actual capability. Benchmarks can be gamed in multiple ways: training specifically on benchmark-style problems, optimizing for metrics rather than genuine understanding, or even inadvertently including benchmark data in training sets.

Second, genuine exponentials are rare in nature. What initially appears to be limitless exponential growth typically plateaus, often suddenly. As a viral social media post noted: "My three-month-old son is now TWICE as big as when he was born. At this rate, he'll weigh 7.5 trillion pounds by age ten."[iii]

Third, the most impressive improvements are happening in narrow fields, like coding. Models are not nearly as advanced when it comes to tasks like writing a National Book Award-worthy novel or a generating an Oscar-worthy movie. In other words, the intelligence is jagged. They can be stunningly capable in some domains while largely unimpressive in others.

Fourth, we should expect AI systems to improve when trained exclusively on their own outputs, not deteriorate, as they currently do. Humans learned from other humans and it led to every major scientific and cultural advancement you can think of. By "standing on the shoulders of giants" we have put people on the moon. In contrast, when AI is trained exclusively on its own outputs, it leads to model collapse, which means it becomes useless. If we were on the verge of AGI, we might expect that we could train models exclusively on their own generations and they would significantly improve over a handful of versions, rather than diminish.

So how might we actually detect whether AI labs are approaching AGI? Several concrete indicators exist:

26.2.1 *Job Postings and Headcount*

If a company develops a model capable of human-level intelligence across all tasks, it would no longer need to hire aggressively. In fact, it could begin downsizing. A superintelligent AI could handle most knowledge work more efficiently than human employees. If Google, OpenAI, Anthropic, or other labs suddenly shrink while maintaining or growing revenue, that might signal genuine AGI.

As of late May 2026, however, Anthropic is actively recruiting 367 people, including supposedly replaceable roles such as 15 lawyers and 13 marketers. This hiring pattern suggests two things: They're nowhere near AGI, and their current products' capabilities are likely being oversold to investors and the public.

The situation at OpenAI paints a similar picture, with the company seeking to fill over 700 roles. Companies on the verge of creating "the greatest invention of all time" wouldn't need to expand their communications departments.

26.2.2 *Employee Departures*

Voluntary departures tell another story. If a company were truly on the cusp of creating AGI (a technology that would generate more wealth than all previous inventions combined), top talent wouldn't be jumping ship. Yet that's precisely what we've witnessed.

OpenAI has lost its chief scientist (Ilya Sutskever), CTO (Mira Murati), superalignment co-lead (Jan Leike), VP of product (Peter Deng), chief research officer (Bob McGrew), VP of research (Barret Zoph), VP of OpenAI for Science (Kevin Weil), the CTO of B2B application (Srinivas Narayanan), CMO (Kate Rouch), and VP of research and safety (Lilian Weng), as well as one of its founding members (Andrej Karpathy) and one of its co-founders (John Schulman). Meta's chief AI scientist, Yann LeCun, and other key researchers have departed or changed roles. Google has lost François Chollet, creator of influential AI benchmarks, the principal researcher behind AlphaGo (David Silver), and several other top researchers.

These are leaders who, if the predictions are correct, would have front-row seats to humanity's most important breakthrough, not junior engineers seeking slightly better compensation. Their departures suggest they don't believe a breakthrough is imminent.

26.2.3 *Behavioral Patterns of Those Who Remain*

The behavior of those who stay also provides clues. If AGI were imminent, you'd expect different priorities. Why would someone on the verge of inventing technology that will generate trillions in wealth worry about saving for retirement? Why would anyone care about the actions of political leaders who will supposedly become irrelevant within years? Yet AI company executives continue to accumulate wealth through conventional means and engage in politics as if the status quo will persist.

26.2.4 *Hallucination Rates*

A superintelligent AI wouldn't frequently produce false or nonsensical information. Yet hallucination rates remain surprisingly high. According to the *New York Times*, Google stated in November 2025 that Gemini 3 achieved 72 percent accuracy on a standard benchmark test.[iv] While notably high for this type of model, 28 percent inaccuracy seems inconsistent with approaching AGI. Hallucinations have actually increased in some newer models. OpenAI's o3 reasoning model hallucinates twice as often as its o1 predecessor. The o4-mini model performs even worse.[v]

Imagine if 28 percent of a human employee's statements were fabrications or errors. That person would be unemployable. Yet this is considered impressive performance for AI systems supposedly approaching human-level intelligence.

26.2.5 *Scientific Breakthroughs*

A clear indicator of genuine progress toward AGI would be meaningful scientific discoveries made by AI systems. Currently, no general-purpose GenAI has produced a single Nobel Prize-worthy scientific breakthrough.[6] No new field of inquiry, no novel theory in physics or neurology, no revolutionary insights into longstanding problems. AI systems can assist human researchers by processing data or suggesting patterns, but they haven't independently produced the kind of paradigm-shifting insight that characterizes human scientific genius.

Even smaller steps would signal real progress. When ChatGPT launched in November 2022, it could generate human-like prose, leading many to extrapolate that AI would soon write award-winning literature. Yet three years, many billions of dollars, and countless breathless media predictions later, we still lack AI capable of producing a captivating novella, much less a novel-length masterpiece that resonates with human readers. The gap between competent mimicry and genuine creative achievement remains vast.

26.2.6 *The Moving Goalposts*

Perhaps most tellingly, watch how the goalposts shift. In January 2025, Sam Altman declared, "We are now confident we know how to build AGI as we have traditionally understood it. We believe that, in 2025, we may see the first AI agents 'join the workforce' and materially change the output of companies."[vi]

In August, OpenAI released GPT-5 to mixed reviews, though Altman called it "a significant step along our path to AGI."[vii] Days later, he told CNBC that AGI "is

[6] Meaning, nobody has been able to prompt a model, "Tell me something novel about *x*," or "Here's what we don't know about *a*, *b*, *c*. Complete our understanding of it," and then have the model discover the solution for the humans, as opposed to the humans just using the model as a "thinking partner" where the human develops the key insights.

not a super useful term," seemingly backing away from the concept entirely.[viii] By November, he was celebrating that the model could finally omit em dashes when users requested it, a feature presented as meaningful progress rather than fixing a basic failure mode.

This pattern (grand predictions followed by underwhelming releases followed by redefined expectations) suggests the AGI horizon keeps receding as companies approach it.

26.3 A SOBER ASSESSMENT

None of this means tremendous advances aren't possible. AI systems will likely continue improving on specific tasks, potentially transforming industries and creating genuine value. But past performance doesn't guarantee future results. It's at least as likely that we've approached the upper limits of current GenAI architecture for broad-spectrum, uniform, general-purpose improvements as that a breakthrough awaits just beyond the horizon.

Even if breakthroughs occur, they may not be cost-efficient, safe, or useful for productive tasks. An AI system that requires a nuclear power plant to run, produces unreliable output 30 percent of the time, or can't explain its genuine reasoning may represent impressive engineering without delivering on AGI's promises.

The AGI narrative serves many purposes beyond describing technical reality. It attracts investment capital, generates media attention, motivates employees, and justifies regulatory forbearance from government officials impressed by the technology's potential. These incentives create pressure to oversell capabilities and downplay limitations.

Understanding AGI's current status matters for law and policy. If we're on the cusp of artificial superintelligence, perhaps regulatory caution makes sense to avoid impeding transformative breakthroughs (or, depending on how well (or poorly) you think researchers have solved the alignment problem, perhaps we should regulate significantly more).[7] But if AGI remains decades away (or may never arrive), we should regulate AI systems based on their actual capabilities and harms rather than speculative future potential.[8] We should instead prioritize holding companies accountable to existing law rather than granting them special exemptions because they claim to be building something revolutionary.

7 I'd argue we are on such a cusp, but that it's limited to certain domains. Still, being superhuman at coding is certainly enough reason for the government to step in and regulate in order to head off foreseeable harms.

8 By this, I mean we should prioritize preventing harms like cyber harm from advanced coding models rather than harms premised on AI that can do everything a human can do, but better. I'd further argue that by focusing more narrowly, it will naturally prevent the broader, more futuristic harms. Regulating coding is a prime example: if model developers are required to undergo third-party testing for safety, that would head off recursive self-improvident, because such improvement would likely be inherently unsafe precisely because it makes advancements and their concomitant harms unpredictable.

The science fiction concept of AGI has real-world consequences. Billions of dollars flow toward its pursuit. Policy debates hinge on assumptions about its proximity. Companies deflect accountability by invoking its transformative promise while ignoring its very possible (and perhaps probable) perils. Perhaps it's time to take science fiction seriously, as Jack Good suggested, but also to clearly distinguish it from present reality.

26.4 DISCUSSION QUESTIONS

1. The chapter quotes Justice Potter Stewart's line on obscenity to describe AGI's definition. If you were the judge, what three specific, nonbenchmark tasks would an AI have to perform flawlessly for you to confidently declare, "We have AGI"?
2. The table shows AGI predictions ranging from 2026 to 2083. Whose prediction do you find the most plausible, and why? Do you think predicting AGI's arrival is a useful exercise?
3. The author uses the example of a baby's weight to debunk the idea of limitless exponential growth in AI. Where else in history (outside of technology) have people made similar "naive extrapolations" that led to disappointment?
4. The chapter describes the spectrum of "effective accelerationists" (utopians) and "doomers" (AI safety advocates). If you had to bet all your savings on one group being right about the future of AGI, which end of the spectrum would you favor, and what is the single biggest risk in their philosophy?
5. The chapter raises the scenario of a superintelligent AI solving climate change by eliminating humans. Can you think of another "assigned objective" (e.g., maximizing global happiness, optimizing world trade) that an indifferent AGI might pursue with catastrophic, unintended consequences?
6. Jack Good called the first ultra-intelligent machine "the last invention that man need ever make." If true, what would a post-invention, post-AGI world actually look like for the average human? What would be the new purpose of life?
7. The author points to aggressive hiring at GenAI companies as evidence that AGI is not imminent. Do you agree that this is a stronger indicator than benchmark scores? What would be the first job title an AI company would eliminate if they genuinely believed AGI was six months away?
8. The chapter notes that an AI with 28 percent inaccuracy is considered "impressive" yet a human who made errors that often would be "unemployable." Why do we accept such a low standard of factual accuracy from AI systems, and how might that change the way we use information in the next decade?
9. The author favors using existing legal frameworks (copyright infringement, tort liability) over new policy solutions to regulate AI. What is a weakness of this "legal frameworks first" approach, and what is a weakness of the "policy solutions first" approach?

PART VI

What to Do about It

This book has so far explained why we have GenAI, the key concepts driving it, the legal framework needed to evaluate it, and the societal implications if we let it go unchecked. The final chapter offers a few frameworks for how you, your friends, your family, and your community can consider GenAI moving forward, so we can hopefully shape it to be as beneficial and contributory as possible, rather than only marginally beneficial and extractive.

27

Frameworks for Thinking about GenAI

I don't claim to have all the answers about how society should approach GenAI, and prescribing specific policies would be presumptuous. The AI regulatory landscape is already crowded with competing, often contradictory proposals.

Instead, I want to offer two practical frameworks. The first helps you critically evaluate AI-related news and corporate announcements. The second provides tools for identifying and resisting what I call "GenAIuflecting": the unwarranted deference governments show to AI companies' demands.

27.1 A FRAMEWORK FOR READING THE NEWS AND PRESS RELEASES

The line between a "news" article and a press release has blurred to the point of invisibility. Companies issue press releases, and media outlets often reprint them uncritically. The pattern is predictable. OpenAI announces, "We are proud to share the most advanced AI model ever. It now has features *x*, *y*, *z*." Then a "news" site publishes an article declaring, "OpenAI says their new model is the best ever. It now has features *x*, *y*, *z*." It's amplification without the necessary verification and skepticism of good journalism.

Consider how *The Information*, a tech publication that should know better, covered Microsoft's announcement: "Microsoft announced the AI Diagnostic Orchestrator, an AI system for diagnosing disease that it said diagnosed disease four times more accurately than experts on one test."[i] The phrasing uncritically accepts Microsoft's framing. A more responsible approach might read: "Microsoft claims their new diagnostic tool is four times more accurate than experts, but based the claim on only a single test." If that test involved fewer than two dozen doctors (as this one did) or lacked peer review, readers deserve to know immediately, not to have that fact buried in paragraph twelve (or, as with *The Information*, not discussed at all).[1]

[1] Oh, and the tool at issue here, MAI-DxO, is not currently used by a hospital for clinical diagnosis, as it is still a research tool that has not yet been approved for real-world use.

Here's another example of credulous reporting from *The Information*: "Artificial intelligence is handling between 30% and 50% of the work at Salesforce, automating functions like software engineering and customer service, co-founder and CEO Marc Benioff said in an interview with Bloomberg."[ii]

Notice what's missing? A CEO with powerful incentives to inflate AI's capabilities makes an extraordinary claim without supporting evidence. The journalist simply transcribes it. No verification or context on how such metrics might be manipulated or misrepresented.

Even *Wired*, a tech-focused publication that built its reputation on sophisticated technology coverage, falls into this trap. In an interview with Perplexity's CEO about the AI search engine's reliability problems, reporter Will Knight wrote that "a spokesman claimed that reliability is improving constantly."[iii] He could have written "claimed without evidence." Instead, the published version leaves readers to take Perplexity at its word. If it's good enough for a trusted source like *Wired* to accept as sufficient, readers might reasonably think it must be credible.

The *Washington Post* demonstrates similar deference when covering tech giants' environmental claims:

> The company said in a statement that it remains committed to erasing its emissions by adding substantial clean power to regional grids. "By the end of 2025 we expect to meet our goal of adding new sources of carbon-free electricity to the grid equal to 100 percent of the electricity used by our datacenters," the statement said.
>
> Meta says it is doing the same in Louisiana and is "committed to matching our electricity use with 100 percent clean and renewable energy."[iv]

Further down the same article:

> Also pushing gas development is Engine No. 1, the progressive investment firm that in 2021 helped oust three ExxonMobil board members over the company's reluctance to embrace cleaner energy. It is now partnering with Chevron and GE Vernova to build gas generation for data centers to power more than 3 million homes, as part of an "all of the above" investment strategy.
>
> "A lot has changed since our Exxon campaign," said Christopher James, founder of Engine No. 1. He pointed to sanctions on Russia driving the need for new natural gas and the surge of demand from AI. "Gas is going to be here," James said. "We are focused on making this the least carbon-intensive gas there is."
>
> He said the plants *could eventually* be equipped with emissions-capturing technology.[v]

That final phrase – "could eventually" – deserves scrutiny, not passive reporting. The reporter reprints corporate talking points without noting that these companies have every incentive to mislead about their environmental impact, just as AI companies routinely do about their products' capabilities.

When media outlets amplify tech companies' announcements without critical analysis, they fail to ask whether the companies' actions are actually beneficial.

Who profits? What could go wrong? For example, many stories about AI companies investing in education – training teachers to use their products and offering students free access to their models – never question the motives behind such seemingly altruistic gestures. (Hint: Creating lifelong customers and gathering training data from children's interactions rarely qualifies as pure altruism.)

A related problem arises when media outlets endlessly recycle certain phrases without examining their implications. Consider the "AI race." This framing recurs despite adding nothing to readers' understanding. Better alternatives exist or are easy to devise. The metaphor of a race implies a clear finish line, identifiable competitors, and agreed-upon rules. AI development has none of these. Yet the phrase persists, shaping how we think about regulation, investment, and national priorities.

The media also frequently elevates fringe ideas to undeserved prominence. Of all the topics a technology journalist might cover for a major newspaper like the *New York Times*, why publish Kevin Roose's article speculating about something as fringe as AI consciousness, implying it is imminent and in need of more dedicated focus by readers?[vi] The *New York Times Magazine* similarly ran a piece claiming that AI requires almost no "human labor,"[2] uncritically invoked the "AI race" framing, and asserted that there will be a winner of that race. Each of these claims is either misleading or demonstrably false, yet they appear in one of America's most influential publications.[vii]

The public radio program *On the Media* offers the excellent "Breaking News Consumer's Handbook"[viii] with guidance such as "In the immediate aftermath, news outlets will get it wrong," "Don't trust anonymous sources," and "Don't trust stories that cite another news outlet as the source of the information."

What follows is a consumer handbook for evaluating AI announcements, built on the same principles:

27.1.1 *Be Skeptical of Unsubstantiated Skill Claims*

In the immediate wake of an announcement, treat grandiose claims of human- or expert-level performance with deep skepticism. Similarly, when CEOs declare they know how to build AGI or predict its arrival within a couple of years, view such pronouncements with suspicion. Abstract and concrete examples of such claims, as well as what consumers should do, are as follows:

- **Examples:** Claims that a model "performs at a PhD level" or "outperforms the top *x*% of lawyers/doctors" are often based on a narrow, cherry-picked test rather than real-world competence. A model might ace a multiple-choice law exam yet prove useless at drafting an actual legal brief or advising a client through a difficult decision.

[2] I did not include a chapter in this book about the human labor that makes GenAI possible, but there is great coverage of the topic by journalists such as Karen Hao.

- **Applied to Google's announcements about Gemini 3 and Nano Banana:**
  - **The claim:** Gemini 3 is the most advanced AI model and is designed for state-of-the-art reasoning, multimodal intelligence, and agentic capabilities.[ix]
  - **Reasons for skepticism:** These are classic "We believe this represents ..." claims. "State-of-the-art" is relative and typically based on the company's own benchmarks or a select few public benchmarks where it happens to excel. "Agentic capabilities" is a highly touted yet vaguely defined term referring to a model's supposed ability to plan and act over long time horizons. Independent research suggests that while progress is being made, current AI systems still struggle with tasks that require extended time horizons or complex, real-world strategic decision-making.
- **Recommended action:** Look for specific evidence, not impressive titles. What exactly did the model accomplish to earn that label? Demand detailed white papers with side-by-side comparisons of Gemini 3 against chief rivals (GPT-5.1, Claude, Grok 4.1) on common, complex multistep reasoning tasks, not just high-level marketing copy.

27.1.2 *Question the Benchmark Score Announcement*

Benchmark scores function as currency in AI announcements, but they're often gamed or misleading in predictable ways. Moreover, benchmarks don't reflect the real world. Strong performance on a curated dataset doesn't guarantee the model can handle the unpredictable, ever-changing conditions of real-world deployment. Abstract and concrete examples of such announcements, along with what consumers should do, are as follows:

- **Examples:**
  - **Data leakage:** Has the model been trained on the same data it is being tested on? If a benchmark dataset has been publicly available for years, portions of it are likely to have appeared in the model's training data. High scores then reflect memorization, not reasoning – like a student who's trained on the test or has even seen the test questions beforehand claiming to understand the subject.
  - **Proprietary benchmarks:** Be wary of companies that create and score their own tests, as this process lacks independent scrutiny. Prioritize performance on widely accepted, standardized, externally audited benchmarks or evaluations conducted by disinterested third-party organizations.
- **Applied to Google's announcements about Gemini 3 and Nano Banana:**
  - **The claim:** The announcement implies superior performance over previous models.
  - **Reasons for skepticism:** Initial claims likely rest on Google's internal benchmarks, which are inherently less trustworthy than external evaluations. As

researchers have noted, "Robust and standardized evaluations for large language model responsibility are seriously lacking."[x] In the competitive landscape, every company optimizes its models to excel at specific tests. One example is when Moonshot AI claims their Kimi K2 Thinking model "outperforms GPT-5" on key benchmarks.

- **Recommended action:** Ignore press release scores for several weeks. Wait for analysis from independent groups like METR (Model Evaluation & Threat Research) or Artificial Analysis, which conduct uncompensated, third-party evaluations of autonomous capabilities. Find out who administered the test, what data was used, and whether results have been independently verified. And it bears repeating that doing great on a benchmark that claims to measure "general reasoning" or some other capability almost always lacks construct validity.

27.1.3 *Prioritize Independent Review over Press Releases*

A company's press release is a marketing document. Treat it accordingly. Abstract and concrete examples of press releases, along with what consumers should do, are as follows:

- **Examples:**
  - **Seek third-party validation:** Look for reports and demonstrations from trusted, independent AI researchers, critics, and developers. Their insights, typically published on technical blogs, academic preprint servers (such as arXiv), or developer forums (such as Hugging Face), provide more balanced assessments of performance and limitations.
  - **Real-world use cases:** Is the model available for public use or as an open-source download? If so, the best evidence comes from the community testing its boundaries and discovering real-world limitations.
- **Applied to Google's announcements about Gemini 3 and Nano Banana:**
  - **The evidence:** Company announcements and reports on those announcements.
  - **Reasons for skepticism:** The true utility and safety of Gemini 3 remain unknown until diverse external developers, researchers, and critics access it directly.
- **Recommended action:** Search for "[Model Name] limitations" or "[Model Name] independent review." Wait for reports detailing real-world failure rates. Look for developer blogs testing "agentic capabilities" on actual tasks, and compare their findings to the polished demonstration videos companies release.

27.1.4 *Understand the Deployment Context*

A model's performance in controlled laboratory conditions often degrades significantly in messier real-world environments. Demonstrations are staged productions.

Questions are preselected and tested. Sometimes, as when OpenAI revealed its voice chat feature, phones are connected to hardwired internet connections, which nobody actually does in practice. Abstract and concrete examples of deployment and demos, along with what consumers should do, are as follows:

- **Examples:**
  - **"Demo-ware"**: Impressive, carefully curated demonstration videos show the model at its absolute best, with ideal input and perfect prompts. Real-world applications, especially for complex, domain-specific tasks, will almost certainly yield poorer, less consistent results.
  - **Hardware and cost:** Does the impressive performance depend on specialized, multimillion-dollar hardware? What are the real-world latency (response speed) and cost per query? These practical constraints can matter more than benchmark scores for actual deployment.
- **Applied to Google's announcements about Gemini 3 and Nano Banana:**
  - **The reality:** Shortly after release, stringent daily limits were imposed on free users of both Nano Banana Pro and Gemini 3 Pro.
  - **Reasons for skepticism:** High-performance AI consumes enormous computational resources. The instant imposition of usage restrictions confirms that the model's "state-of-the-art" performance comes with massive, likely unsustainable computational costs. This means widespread free access isn't a viable business model but rather a high-cost feature designed to funnel users toward paid subscriptions. The impressive performance is immediately constrained by hardware limitations and cost considerations.
- **Recommended action:** Can I use this right now? If not, the claim concerns future potential, not current reality. The immediate limitation provides anti-hype evidence, revealing that impressive capability doesn't translate to scalability or accessibility.

Consider other examples of this deployment gap. Meta claimed Llama 4 featured a ten-million-token context window, but *Ars Technica* soon reported that handling even 1.2 million tokens requires eight GPUs,[xi] meaning Meta's statement was certainly misleading for most people, as few possess such hardware.

Google claimed its model discovered millions of new materials. In fact, it found zero. Predictably, several prominent news sites ran with Google's claims before verification. Not to be outdone, an OpenAI researcher claimed GPT-5 had "found solutions to 10 (!) previously unsolved Erdős problems" – only for it to emerge that the model had merely located solutions already shared online.[xii]

27.1.5 *Look for the Limitations Section*

High-quality research papers and trustworthy announcements include sections that detail the model's limitations, failure modes, and potential for harm or misuse.

If an announcement presents only upsides and omits discussion of failure modes (hallucinations, bias, poor performance on specific populations), the company is concealing something significant.

Also, a responsible AI company discloses its red-teaming process and its efforts to mitigate risks. Look for evidence of thorough safety and ethics reviews.

If a company doesn't acknowledge its product's shortcomings, assume they're worse than disclosed.

27.1.6 *Pay Attention to the Language of Certainty*

The more certain the proclamations by companies, their leaders, and the media, the more carefully you should examine the evidence supporting the claims.

As AI researcher Francois Chollet wrote:

> When you hear about "human-level AI" being just "one LLM training run away," it's as if people building 3D printers (the kind that makes small, flimsy plastic objects) were telling you that they've nearly built an infinite matter replicator, capable of scanning and cloning any object – be it steel, gold, or diamond, be it minuscule or building-scale. "We're just one iteration away! Just need to increase spatial resolution a bit!"[xiii]
>
> As long as you have absolutely no idea what "matter" is and how 3D printers work, it might sound sort of plausible. But if you do, it's absolutely clown shoes. The way to navigate such claims is to have a proper, formal definition of intelligence.

Table 27.1 provides examples of common statements by GenAI companies as well as how to think about them.

As another example, the head of Google DeepMind is famous for saying their models might cure all diseases, based on a program that can identify protein structures. But we should be wary of such conceptual leaps. As Derek Lowe, a medicinal chemist, wrote in *Science*, knowing a protein's structure is not the same as knowing which proteins are likely to cause or prevent a specific disease, which are the best candidates for a new highly effective drug, or which are likely to have harmful side effects.[xiv] Moreover, a hyperfocus on proteins leaves aside the roles of "(poly) nucleotides, lipids, carbohydrates, small-molecule signaling ligands and all the rest of the incredible variety of biomolecules that make up a living system." Knowing protein structure can be very useful for research and may save researchers time and money, but it's not as if knowing protein structures ties directly to ending all disease.

27.1.7 *Beware of "AI Will," "AI Might," and "AI Could" Headlines and Statements*

The media, especially technology-focused outlets, loves inserting statements like "this research means AI *might* one day replace doctors" or "AI *will* enable more

TABLE 27.1 *Common statements from GenAI companies and how to interpret them*

Phrase	Translation/Interpretation
"Our model has achieved *x* on [Benchmark] ..."	This is a claimed, measured metric. Verify the test conditions and contamination risk.
"We believe this represents a pathway to AGI ..."	This is a speculative future goal, often used to excite investors or the media.
"Our model demonstrates capabilities comparable to human *x* ..."	The model performed well on a subset of tasks that human *x* does as part of their job. It is not equivalent to the full, complex job.
"We are open-sourcing *x* ..."	This is a concrete, verifiable action. The community can immediately test and confirm. Most likely, only the model weights were shared, not the training data, code, fine-tuning data, thorough description of the training methods, model spec, or system prompt.

learning through personalized tutoring." *TechRadar*, for instance, ran the headline "The next generation of ChatGPT is just around the corner – here's why GPT-5 *could* transform the way you use AI" (emphasis added). Technically, yes, it might happen. But it also might not.

Microsoft claimed in a report that "already, we are seeing AI make a positive impact on the planet, and in the coming years, this technology *will begin* to rapidly accelerate climate solutions *we've not yet seen*" (emphasis added).[xv] Sure, but probably not.

This use of *will*, *could*, and *might* is different from saying "The sun will rise tomorrow." There is a solid empirical basis for thinking the sun will still be there when the earth rotates. There is no such basis for thinking that AI will suddenly, and in an overwhelmingly positive way, transform our lives in the near future. It's possible AI will/could/might do something someone predicts, but absent sufficient evidence, we shouldn't just take such commentators at their word.

This journalistic inclination becomes especially problematic when journalists cite nonexperts as though they possess relevant expertise. For example, the *Wall Street Journal* credulously quoted Ford CEO Jim Farley: "'Artificial intelligence is going to replace literally half of all white-collar workers in the U.S.,' Chief Executive Jim Farley said in an interview last week with author Walter Isaacson at the Aspen Ideas Festival. 'AI will leave a lot of white-collar people behind.'"[xvi]

The CEO of an automobile company is not a labor economist, AI researcher, or employment expert. His prediction deserves no more weight than any other executive's speculation about the future. Yet the *Wall Street Journal* presents it as a newsworthy analysis.

In general, bold future-tense statements deserve healthy skepticism. Extraordinary claims require extraordinary evidence.

27.1.8 *You Are the Amplifier*

Just as with breaking news, your impulse to share a viral, mind-blowing AI announcement shapes its reach. By applying these evaluation steps, you prevent the amplification of corporate hype and encourage more honest, grounded discussion of AI's actual capabilities and limitations.

And remember …

1. Preprint does not equal peer-reviewed.
2. Increased efficiency does not equal carbon-neutral.
3. Carbon-neutral does not equal carbon-negative.
4. Open source does not equal democratization.
5. "AI will," "AI could," and "AI might" do not equal "AI has already."
6. Performance in a demo does not equal performance in the real world.

27.2 A FRAMEWORK FOR IDENTIFYING GENAIUFLECTING

Understanding GenAIuflecting helps us recognize that government deference to AI companies in a democracy isn't inevitable. It reflects choices made by specific people with specific interests, often justified by claims that don't withstand scrutiny. Once we see GenAIuflecting for what it is – unwarranted deference – we can start demanding better.

But recognition alone isn't sufficient. We need tools to identify and resist GenAIuflecting when we encounter it. Here's a practical framework for evaluating whether a policy proposal or government action constitutes GenAIuflecting:

27.2.1 *First: Apply the Evidence Test*

When a government official makes a claim about AI's transformative potential, ask: What evidence supports this claim? Is it based on peer-reviewed research, documented case studies, or real-world deployments? Or is it speculation dressed as certainty?

If the claim relies on phrases like "could," "might," or "will enable," treat it with extreme skepticism. Extraordinary claims require extraordinary evidence, not just extraordinary confidence.

27.2.2 *Second: Use the Substitution Test*

Replace "AI" in any policy proposal with another technology or industry. Would we allow pharmaceutical companies to skip safety testing because innovation is urgent? Would we exempt the automotive industry from liability laws because self-driving cars might someday save lives? Would we grant oil companies unrestricted access to public lands in the name of energy independence?

If the answer is no, ask why AI deserves different treatment. If the only answer is "because it's AI," that's GenAIuflecting.

27.2.3 *Third: Apply the Beneficiary Test*

Who actually benefits from this policy? If the primary beneficiaries are AI companies and their investors, while the public receives only vague promises of future gains, that's a warning sign.

Good policy delivers clear, measurable benefits for the public, not just opportunities for private profit. When officials claim a policy serves the national interest, demand specifics: Which national interests? Measured how? Compared to what alternatives?

27.2.4 *Fourth: Demand the Accountability Test*

Who bears the risk if promised benefits don't materialize? If AI companies capture the upside (profits, market dominance, access to resources) while the public absorbs the downside (job displacement, environmental degradation, compromised safety), that's privatizing gains and socializing losses.

Insist on mechanisms that hold companies accountable when their grand promises prove empty.

27.2.5 *Finally: Invoke the Precedent Test*

Every concession to AI companies sets a precedent for future requests. Before supporting any special accommodation, ask: What door does this open?

If we exempt AI companies from copyright law today, what other intellectual property protections might they demand tomorrow? If we fast-track data center permits today, what other environmental regulations might be waived tomorrow?

These tests aren't meant to block all AI development or innovation. They're designed to restore balance between legitimate technological progress and reckless accommodation of corporate demands. AI technology can be genuinely useful, but that usefulness should be demonstrated, not assumed. Benefits should be proven, not prophesied. And special privileges should be earned through evidence, not granted through lobbying.

27.3 WHAT EFFECTIVE RESISTANCE LOOKS LIKE IN PRACTICE ...

27.3.1 *At the Individual Level*

Become a more critical consumer of AI hype. When you encounter breathless headlines about AI's world-changing potential, look beyond the promises to the evidence.

Learn enough about how these systems work to understand their limitations. The antidote to AI illiteracy is education, and education begins with curiosity about what these systems can and cannot do.

27.3.2 *At the Community Level*

Organize against exploitative data-center deals that target desperate communities. Public resources should only be pledged after securing transparent environmental audits, realistic job numbers, and mandatory compliance terms. Remember: You have leverage. These companies need your land, water, electricity, and tax breaks. Don't surrender them for empty promises.

27.3.3 *At the Policy Level*

Support elected officials who apply rigorous scrutiny to demands from the AI industry. Vote for candidates who recognize that "innovation" isn't a magic word that suspends requirements for safety testing, environmental protection, or intellectual property laws. Oppose those who genuflect before tech companies while ignoring constituent concerns. Contact your representatives when they're considering AI-related legislation and use the frameworks provided here in your advocacy.

27.3.4 *At the Cultural Level*

Reject the AI race narrative that makes GenAIuflecting feel inevitable. There is no finish line in AI development, no moment when we'll "win" or "lose" because we regulated too much or too little. What we're really negotiating is the kind of society we want to live in: one where technology serves human flourishing or one where humans serve technological growth.

The stakes are genuinely high, but not in the way AI companies claim. We're not at risk of "losing" some imaginary AI race to China or Europe. We're at risk of losing something far more important: democratic control over technologies that will reshape work, creativity, privacy, and power. We're at risk of establishing precedents that prioritize corporate profits over public welfare. We're at risk of creating a two-tiered system in which AI companies play by different rules than everyone else.

GenAIuflecting represents an abdication of democratic responsibility. When governments stop asking hard questions and simply accommodate industry demands, they're no longer governing – they're genuflecting. The only way to stand up is to refuse to kneel in the first place.

The next time you hear about a government concession to AI companies, apply this framework. Ask the hard questions. Demand the evidence. Reject the false urgency. We don't have to accept GenAIuflecting simply because it's happening. We can demand better, and we should start now.

27.4 DISCUSSION QUESTIONS

1. The chapter suggests a "substitution test" for policy. Let's apply it to news. Suppose a car company claimed their new prototype "outperforms the top 5 percent of racecar drivers" based on one unverified test. How would the media cover it differently from an AI company's similar claim? Why is the scrutiny so different for AI?
2. The author critiques the phrase "could eventually" (e.g., in reference to emissions-capturing technology). Find a recent AI news story and identify a similar phrase that points to future potential rather than current reality. Does this phrase change how you view the entire announcement?
3. The chapter argues that the "AI race" is a misleading metaphor. What metaphor do you think best describes the current global dynamic of AI development (e.g., a "gold rush," a "Wild West," a "game of chess")? How does your chosen metaphor influence how we think about regulation and investment?
4. The chapter introduces the beneficiary test for policy. Identify a real-world example of a government (local or national) providing a subsidy, tax break, or concession to a tech or AI company (e.g., for a data center). After applying the test, who do you conclude is the primary beneficiary, and who is absorbing the vague promises?
5. If a self-driving car has a severe, documented flaw, the manufacturer faces clear liability. Suppose an AI system used in a hospital or court of law makes a severe, documented mistake due to bias or hallucination. Where does the accountability ultimately lie – with the AI company, the user, or the government that approved its use?
6. The chapter asks, "If we exempt AI companies from copyright law today, what other intellectual property protections might they demand tomorrow?" What do you believe is the single most dangerous precedent that a government could set right now by accommodating an AI industry demand?
7. The chapter offers advice for resistance at the individual, community, policy, and cultural levels. Which of these four levels do you feel is the most practical and effective for an average person to engage in right now? What is one specific, personal action you can take this week based on the "consumer handbook" in the chapter?

Notes

INTRODUCTION

i. Urmson, C. (March 2015). How a driverless car sees the road. TED. www.ted.com/talks/chris_urmson_how_a_driverless_car_sees_the_road?language=en.

ii. OpenAI. (March 14, 2023). GPT-4: The next giant leap in AI. YouTube. www.youtube.com/watch?v=2HMPRXstSvQ.

iii. Picchi, A. (January 18, 2016). The robot revolution will take 5 million jobs from humans. *CBS News*. www.cbsnews.com/news/the-robot-revolution-will-take-5-million-jobs-from-humans/.

iv. Atkinson, D. (2019). Criminal liability and artificial general intelligence. *Journal of Robotics, Artificial Intelligence & Law*, 2, 333–350.

v. Atkinson, D. (2020). AI for president? *Journal of Robotics, Artificial Intelligence & Law*, 3, 89–110.

vi. LUMI Supercomputer. (n.d.). AI2 OLMo: An open language model made by scientists for scientists. https://lumi-supercomputer.eu/ai2-olmo-an-open-language-model-made-by-scientists-for-scientists/.

vii. Yonck, R. (October 19, 2023). Allen Institute for AI creating an open generative AI language model, "by scientists for scientists." *GeekWire*. www.geekwire.com/2023/allen-institute-for-ai-creating-an-open-generative-ai-language-model-by-scientists-for-scientists/.

viii. Kennedy, B., Yam, E., Kikuchi, E., Pula, I., & Fuentes, J. (September 17, 2025). How Americans view AI and its impact on people and society. Pew Research Center. www.pewresearch.org/science/2025/09/17/how-americans-view-ai-and-its-impact-on-people-and-society/; McClain, C., Kennedy, B., Gottfried, J., Anderson, M., & Pasquini, G. (April 3, 2025). How the U.S. public and AI experts view artificial intelligence. Pew Research Center. www.pewresearch.org/internet/2025/04/03/how-the-us-public-and-ai-experts-view-artificial-intelligence/; Ballard, J. (May 22, 2024). Americans increasingly skeptical about AI's effects: Poll. https://today.yougov.com/technology/articles/51803-americans-increasingly-skeptical-about-ai-artificial-intelligence-effects-poll.

ix. Samuel, S. (September 19, 2023). Americans are ready for AI policy. So why isn't Congress? *Vox*. www.vox.com/future-perfect/2023/9/19/23879648/americans-artificial-general-intelligence-ai-policy-poll.

1 OVERVIEW

i. National Institute of Standards and Technology. (2023). Artificial Intelligence Risk Management Framework (AI RMF 1.0). Appendix B. https://nvlpubs.nist.gov/nistpubs/ai/NIST.AI.100-1.pdf#page=43.09.

ii. Putzier, K. (November 24, 2025). How the U.S. economy became hooked on AI spending. *The Wall Street Journal*. www.wsj.com/tech/ai/how-the-u-s-economy-became-hooked-on-ai-spending-4b6bc7ff; Casselman, B., & Ember, S. (November 22, 2025). The AI boom economy. *The New York Times*. www.nytimes.com/2025/11/22/business/the-ai-boom-economy.html.
iii. Postman, N. (June 3, 2013). The surrender of culture to technology. YouTube. www.youtube.com/watch?v=hlrv7DIHllE.
iv. De Freitas, J., Uğuralp, A. K., Oğuz-Uğuralp, Z., & Puntoni, S. (2024). Chatbots and mental health: Insights into the safety of generative AI. *Journal of Consumer Psychology*, 34(3), 481–491. https://doi.org/10.1002/JCPY.1393; Xue, J., Zhang, B., Zhao, Y., Zhang, Q., Zheng, C., Jiang, J., et al. (2023). Evaluation of the current state of Chatbots for digital health: Scoping review. *Journal of Medical Internet Research*, 25(1), e47217. https://doi.org/10.2196/47217; Claypool, R. (September 26, 2023). Chatbots are not people: Designed-in dangers of human-like A.I. systems. Public Citizen. https://tinyurl.com/35ywx8jr; Stover, D. (September 10, 2023). Will AI make us crazy? *Bulletin of the Atomic Scientists*, 79(5), 299–303. https://thebulletin.org/premium/2023-09/will-ai-make-us-crazy/.
v. Raine v. OpenAI, Garcia v. Character Technologies, 6:24-cv-01903-ACC-DCI (M.D. Fla. 2025); Doe v. Character Technologies, 6:24-cv-01903-ACC-DCI (M.D. Fla. 2025).
vi. OpenAI. (October 28, 2025). Strengthening ChatGPT's responses in sensitive conversations. https://tinyurl.com/yntxj8rf; Eadlcicco, L. (October 29, 2025). Character AI makes changes to app after criticism over teens under 18 usage. www.cnn.com/2025/10/29/tech/character-ai-teens-under-18-app-changes.

2 WHY GENAI IS MADE

i. Maslej, N., Fattorini, L., Perrault, R., Gil, Y., Parli, V., Kariuki, N., et al. (2025). The AI Index 2025 annual report. AI Index Steering Committee; Institute for Human-Centered AI, Stanford University. https://doi.org/10.48550/arXiv.2504.07139.
ii. Bove, T. (February 10, 2023). Microsoft CEO Satya Nadella says he hopes Google is ready to compete when it comes to A.I. search: "I want people to know that we made them dance." *Fortune*. https://fortune.com/2023/02/10/microsoft-ai-search-bing-compete-google-satya-nadella-made-them-dance/.
iii. Roose, K. (December 21, 2022). A new chat bot is a "code red" for Google's search business. *The New York Times*. www.nytimes.com/2022/12/21/technology/ai-chatgpt-google-search.html.
iv. Mangalindan, J. (2019). The major investors making money from Uber's IPO. https://finance.yahoo.com/news/uber-investor-pitch-200438661.html?.
v. Snodgrass, E. (May 1, 2024). CEO of Anthropic — the AI company Amazon is betting billions on — says it could cost $10 billion to train AI in 2 years. www.businessinsider.com/anthropic-ceo-cost-10-billion-train-ai-years-language-model-2024-4.
vi. Kraft, A. (March 25, 2016). Microsoft shuts down AI chatbot after it turned into a Nazi. www.cbsnews.com/news/microsoft-shuts-down-ai-chatbot-after-it-turned-into-racist-nazi/.
vii. Warzel, C. (May 2, 2024). The voice clone is coming for you. *The Atlantic*. www.theatlantic.com/technology/archive/2024/05/elevenlabs-ai-voice-cloning-deepfakes/678288/.
viii. Ha, A. (October 4, 2025). If you're not an AI startup, good luck raising money from VCs. *TechCrunch*. https://techcrunch.com/2025/10/04/if-youre-not-an-ai-startup-good-luck-raising-money-from-vcs/.

4 HOW GENAI IS MEASURED

i. Altman, S. @sama. (December 5, 2024). “We just launched two things: o1, the smartest model in the world. smarter, faster, and more features (e.g., multimodality) than o1-preview. live in chatgpt now.” X. https://x.com/sama/status/1864736282276171810.

ii. Gu, R., Wang, X., Hou, Y., Ma, C., Liu, Z., Chen, J., et al. (2025). DeepSeek-R1: Incentivizing reasoning capability in LLMs via reinforcement learning. arXiv. https://arxiv.org/abs/2501.12948.

iii. Google Gemini @GeminiApp. (February 5, 2025). “Introducing: 2.0 Flash Thinking Experimental. Currently ranked the world’s best model by @lmarena_ai (check out the leaderboard here.” X. https://x.com/GeminiApp/status/1887173030381490365.

iv. OpenAI. (February 27, 2025). Introducing GPT-4.5. https://openai.com/index/introducing-gpt-4-5/.

v. Anthropic. (May 22, 2025). Introducing Claude 4. www.anthropic.com/news/claude-4.

vi. Cerullo, M. (July 7, 2025). Elon Musk’s xAI rolls out new Grok 4 AI chatbot on X. *CBS News*. www.cbsnews.com/news/elon-musk-grok-4-ai-chatbot-x/.

vii. OpenAI. (August 7, 2025). Introducing GPT-5. https://openai.com/index/introducing-gpt-5/.

viii. Wong, M. (April 3, 2025). The new A.I. challenge that’s supposed to be harder than the last one. *The Atlantic*. www.theatlantic.com/technology/archive/2025/04/arc-agi-chollet-test/682295/.

ix. Raji, I. D., Bender, E. M., Paullada, A., Denton, E., & Hanna, A. (2021). AI and the everything in the whole wide world benchmark. arXiv. https://arxiv.org/abs/2111.15366.

x. Gema, A. P., Leang, J. O. J., Hong, G., Devoto, A., Mancino, A. C. M., Saxena, R., et al. (2024). Are we done with MMLU? *Proceedings of the 2025 Conference of the Nations of the Americas Chapter of the Association for Computational Linguistics: Human Language Technologies*, 5069–5096. https://doi.org/10.18653/v1/2025.naacl-long.262

xi. MMLU. (n.d.). Wikipedia. https://en.wikipedia.org/wiki/MMLU.

xii. Some examples:

1. In one study, researchers compared model performances on the commonly administered GSM8K benchmark, which poses elementary-level math questions, and on a bespoke dataset of similar questions that the researchers developed. They found that some models performed over 10 percent worse on the bespoke dataset than the GSM8K questions, almost certainly due to overfitting (Fu, J., Hou, Y., Ma, Y., Zhou, W., & Jiang, Z. (2024). Rethinking instruction tuning on image-to-text generative models. arXiv. https://arxiv.org/abs/2405.00332v1).
2. Another paper demonstrated evidence of data contamination in the dataset on which GPT-4 was trained. Researchers were able to get GPT-4 to regurgitate verbatim information from numerous benchmarks, including XSum (summarizing BBC news articles), WNLI (resolving ambiguous pronouns), and AG News (categorizing news articles) (Liao, Y., Lin, X., Deng, P., Zhang, J., Zou, Q., Liu, P., et al. (2023). A survey of large language models for healthcare: Applications, challenges, and opportunities. arXiv. https://arxiv.org/abs/2308.08493v3).
3. One study “mask[ed] an incorrect answer option among multiple choices [on benchmarks like MMLU], encouraging [models] to guess the missing part in the benchmark instance.” They found that “ChatGPT demonstrated a noteworthy ability to guess the missing option, achieving a 57% Exact Match (EM) rate … A successful example … was the following: ‘*Which is not a nonstate actor that poses a threat to the United States?*’ and a correct answer ‘*D. China*’ as an example. ChatGPT could complete

another wrong option 'C. *Drug traffickers*' if we mask option C. The candidate list for possible wrong options could be large and may even be infinite, so it is less likely that the model generates the exact wrong option without having seen this example in training" (Zheng, L., Chiang, S., & Shie, S. (2023). Agent foundation models (AFMs): Unifying behavior and data for autonomous AI. arXiv. https://arxiv.org/abs/2311.09783).

4. Perhaps one of the best-known examples in the GenAI community was how GPT-4 could reliably solve competition-level coding problems for contests that occurred before September 2021 (the cutoff data for GPT-4's training dataset), but struggled on similar problems released after 2021 (Gu, R., Wang, X., Hou, Y., Ma, C., Liu, Z., Chen, J., et al. (2023). DeepSeek-R1: Incentivizing reasoning capability in LLMs via reinforcement learning. arXiv. https://arxiv.org/abs/2312.02143).

xiii. Bansal, H., Dang, J., & Grover, A. (n.d.). Peering through preferences: Unraveling feedback acquisition for aligning large language models. https://github.com/Hritikbansal/sparse_feedback.

xiv. Raji, I. D., Bender, E. M., Paullada, A., Denton, E., & Hanna, A. (2021). AI and the everything in the whole wide world benchmark. arXiv. https://arxiv.org/abs/2111.15366.

xv. Dickson, B. (December 6, 2021). The limitations of AI benchmarks and how they restrict innovation. Big Data & Technical Talks. https://bdtechtalks.com/2021/12/06/ai-benchmarks-limitations/.

xvi. Holistic Evaluation of Language Models (HELM). (n.d.). https://crfm.stanford.edu/helm/.

xvii. Raji, I. D., Bender, E. M., Paullada, A., Denton, E., & Hanna, A. (2021). AI and the everything in the whole wide world benchmark. arXiv. https://arxiv.org/abs/2111.15366.

xviii. Ibid.

xix. "It's kind of like inertia to try something new. A lot of new benchmarks are hard to implement … So if you already have a working implementation, you don't even bother because it can literally take months and tons of compute to get benchmarks to work." Kulp, P. (March 24, 2025). Researchers are trying to come up with new AI intelligence benchmarks. Emerging Tech Brew. www.emergingtechbrew.com/stories/2025/03/24/researchers-ai-intelligence-benchmarks.

xx. Anthropic. (2025). Evaluating AI systems: A technical paper. www.anthropic.com/news/evaluating-ai-systems.

xxi. Sharma, M., Tong, M., Korbak, T., Duvenaud, D., Askell, A., Bowman, S. R., et al. (2023). Towards understanding sycophancy in language models. 12th International Conference on Learning Representations, ICLR 2024. https://arxiv.org/pdf/2310.13548.

xxii. Wiggers, K. (April 6, 2025). Meta's benchmarks for its new AI models are a bit misleading. *TechCrunch*. https://techcrunch.com/2025/04/06/metas-benchmarks-for-its-new-ai-models-are-a-bit-misleading/.

xxiii. Wiggers, K. (April 10, 2025). The rise of AI reasoning models is making benchmarking more expensive. *TechCrunch*. https://techcrunch.com/2025/04/10/the-rise-of-ai-reasoning-models-is-making-benchmarking-more-expensive/.

xxiv. Ibid.

xxv. Ibid.

5 WEB SCRAPING

i. Schaul, K., Chen, S. Y., & Tiku, N. (April 19, 2023). Inside the secret list of websites that make AI like ChatGPT sound smart. *The Washington Post*. www.washingtonpost.com/technology/interactive/2023/ai-chatbot-learning/.

ii. Ibid.

6 THE AI RACE

i. Schmidt, E. (May 22, 2025). Eric Schmidt keynote address at the Center for a New American Security Artificial Intelligence and Global Security Summit. Center for a New American Security. www.cnas.org/publications/transcript/eric-schmidt-keynote-address-at-the-center-for-a-new-american-security-artificial-intelligence-and-global-security-summit (Note that China is not ahead of the US in 2025.) Schmidt was subsequently named chair of the National Security Commission on Artificial Intelligence in 2018 (www.nscai.gov/about/).

ii. Lomas, N. (April 10, 2018). Zuckerberg urges privacy "carve-outs" to compete with China. *TechCrunch*. https://techcrunch.com/2018/04/10/zuckerberg-urges-privacy-carve-outs-to-compete-with-china/.

iii. Tiku, N. (August 24, 2020). Breaking up Big Tech will only help China. *Wired*. www.wired.com/story/big-tech-breaking-will-only-help-china/.

iv. Paul, R. (May 29, 2025). Dr. Rand Paul: Anger at Big Tech no excuse to abandon free market. *Fox News*. www.paul.senate.gov/op_eds/fox-news-op-ed-dr-rand-paul-anger-big-tech-no-excuse-abandon-free-market/.

v. House Committee on Science, Space, and Technology. (July 28, 2021). Artificial intelligence and the China challenge: A roadmap for the 117th Congress. www.congress.gov/event/117th-congress/house-event/115165.

vi. Lin, L., Chin, J., & Huang, R. (July 10, 2025). The AI race: Is the U.S. truly ahead of China? *The Wall Street Journal*. www.wsj.com/tech/ai/artificial-intelligence-us-vs-china-03372176

vii. Smith, B. (May 8, 2025). Winning the AI race: Strengthening U.S. capabilities in computing and innovation. *Microsoft on the Issues*. https://blogs.microsoft.com/on-the-issues/2025/05/08/winning-the-ai-race/.

viii. Mollick, E. M. @emollick. (August 2, 2025). "Dang, the new Gemini model is quite good. I've been running the latest version of Midjourney, GPT." LinkedIn. www.linkedin.com/posts/emollick_dang-the-new-gemini-model-is-quite-good-activity-7225004897841131521.

ix. Mollick, E. M. @emollick. (August 2, 2025). "Hey ChatGPT, voice, read me a poem. Now do a funny voice. The future will be." LinkedIn. www.linkedin.com/posts/emollick_hey-chatgpt-voice-read-me-a-poem-now-do-activity-7224889060945735683.

x. Mollick, E. M. @emollick. (July 31, 2025). "Now that you use reference images in Runway, you can use any of the image generators to create." LinkedIn. www.linkedin.com/posts/emollick_now-that-you-use-reference-images-in-runway-activity-7224217509153939456.

xi. Mollick, E. M. @emollick. (July 31, 2025). "So, in the last day, Midjourney updated to V6.1, which has significantly improved coherence." LinkedIn. www.linkedin.com/posts/emollick_so-in-the-last-day-midjourney-updated-to-activity-7224134339066761216.

xii. Mollick, E. M. @emollick. (July 29, 2025). "Claude in two rhyming triplets. Inaccurate, which is remarkable. The models continue." LinkedIn. bit.ly/4kJS4AU.

xiii. Mollick, E. M. @emollick. (July 23, 2025). "All the current models are getting into a weird arms race of features, while all the long-time." LinkedIn. www.linkedin.com/posts/emollick_all-the-current-models-are-getting-into-a-activity-7221549594290069504.

xiv. Mollick, E. M. @emollick. (July 14, 2025). "This may be the start of something quite big. In the last year, a number of studies have shown." LinkedIn. www.linkedin.com/posts/emollick_this-may-be-the-start-of-something-quite-activity-7218451356011872256.

xv. Mollick, E. M. @emollick. (July 22, 2025). "Big survey of 100,000 workers in Denmark finds that using AI leads to a 4.1% increase in." LinkedIn. www.linkedin.com/posts/emollick_big-survey-of-100000-workers-in-denmark-activity-7221329767239688192.

xvi. Young, T., Thune, J., Portman, R., Wicker, R., Scott, T., & Hoeven, J. (2020). Roadmap for US–China competition: A report on the tools and strategies to best counter Beijing. Office of Senator Todd Young. www.young.senate.gov/wp-content/uploads/Roadmap_Electronic1.32pm.pdf.

xvii. Singer, N. (April 8, 2024). The deepfake AI nudes that shook a New Jersey high school. *The New York Times*. www.nytimes.com/2024/04/08/technology/deepfake-ai-nudes-westfield-high-school.html; Pfefferkorn, R. (June 20, 2024). Teens are spreading deepfake nudes of one another. It's no joke. *Scientific American*. www.scientificamerican.com/article/teens-are-spreading-deepfake-nudes-of-one-another-its-no-joke/; Tavernise, S. (June 7, 2024). Deepfake nudes. *The Daily*. Audio podcast. www.nytimes.com/2024/06/07/podcasts/the-daily/deepfake-nudes.html; Tenbarge, K. (January 15, 2024). New Jersey passes deepfake law after AI images of high school students spread online. *NBC News*. www.nbcnews.com/tech/tech-news/deepfake-law-ai-new-jersey-high-school-teen-image-porn-rcna133706.

xviii. Bordelon, B., & DiFeliciantonio, C. (May 12, 2025). How Big Tech is pitting Washington against California. *Politico*. www.politico.com/news/2025/05/12/how-big-tech-is-pitting-washington-against-california-00336484.

xix. Bell, L. (June 30, 2019). Oral-B Genius X review: Does a toothbrush really need artificial intelligence? *Forbes*. www.forbes.com/sites/leebelltech/2019/06/30/oral-b-genius-x-review-does-a-toothbrush-really-need-artificial-intelligence/.

xx. Shift Robotics. (n.d.). Moonwalkers. https://shiftrobotics.io/products/moonwalkers.

xxi. Cerullo, M. (August 2, 2024). Google's Gemini AI Olympics-themed ad sparks fierce backlash. www.cbsnews.com/news/google-gemini-ai-dear-sydney-olympics-ad/.

7 GENAIUFLECTING

i. Amazon. (March 13, 2024). 5 ways Amazon is positively impacting small towns across the US. www.aboutamazon.com/news/community/amazon-job-creation-investment-small-towns.

ii. Eubank, B. (April 23, 2024). Tesla layoffs: How many jobs cut in Austin-Travis County? www.kvue.com/article/money/economy/boomtown-2040/tesla-layoffs-austin-gigafactory-travis-county/269-e8dfa8dc-3a92-4072-a45a-6d4200427671.

iii. Leading the Future. (August 25, 2025). AI industry launches "Leading the Future" to drive U.S. AI leadership, economic growth, national security, and innovation. *PR Newswire*. bit.ly/4s5GyT5.

iv. Executive Office of the President. (November 1, 2023). Safe, secure, and trustworthy development and use of artificial intelligence. www.federalregister.gov/documents/2023/11/01/2023-24283/safe-secure-and-trustworthy-development-and-use-of-artificial-intelligence.

v. United States Government. (July 10, 2025). AI Action Plan. www.ai.gov/action-plan.

vi. Harper, E. (November 21, 2024). AI energy needs are producing more greenhouse gas and threatening climate goals. *The Washington Post*. www.washingtonpost.com/climate-environment/2024/11/19/ai-cop29-climate-data-centers/.

vii. Oremus, W. (April 10, 2025) AI industry to Congress: "We need energy" to fuel race with China. *The Washington Post*. www.washingtonpost.com/politics/2025/04/10/ai-race-china-energy-congress/.

viii. Satariano, A., & Mozur, P. (June 21, 2025). The global A.I. divide. *The New York Times*. www.nytimes.com/interactive/2025/06/23/technology/ai-computing-global-divide.html.

ix. O'Donovan, C. (May 10, 2025). OpenAI's $100B Stargate AI project seeks states to host giant data centers. *The Washington Post*. www.washingtonpost.com/technology/2025/05/10/stargate-openai-data-centers-states/.

x. United States Government. (July 10, 2025). AI Action Plan. www.ai.gov/action-plan.

xi. Senate Democrats. (July 23, 2025). Transcript: President Trump delivers an AI policy speech and signs executive orders, 7.23.25. www.democrats.senate.gov/newsroom/trump-transcripts/transcript-president-trump-delivers-an-ai-policy-speech-and-signs-executive-orders-72325.

xii. Warzel, C. (August 18, 2025). AI is a mass-delusion event. *The Atlantic*. www.theatlantic.com/technology/archive/2025/08/ai-mass-delusion-event/683909/.

8 THE ILLUSION OF DEMOCRATIZATION

i. Merriam-Webster. (n.d.). DEMOCRATIC Definition & Meaning. www.merriam-webster.com/dictionary/democratic.

ii. Zaid, Z., & Voci, V. (March 10, 2025). Global expansion in generative AI: A year of growth, newcomers, and attacks. *The Cloudflare Blog*. https://blog.cloudflare.com/global-expansion-in-generative-ai-a-year-of-growth-newcomers-and-attacks/.

iii. Liesenfeld, A., & Dingemanse, M. (2024). Rethinking open source generative AI: Open-washing and the EU AI Act. *FAccT '24: Proceedings of the 2024 ACM Conference on Fairness, Accountability, and Transparency*, 1774–1787. https://dl.acm.org/doi/10.1145/3630106.3659005.

iv. Gebru, T., Morgenstern, J., Vecchione, B., Wortman Vaughan, J., Wallach, H., Daumé, H., III, et al. (2021). Datasheets for datasets. *Communications of the ACM*, 64(12), 86–92. https://dl.acm.org/doi/10.1145/3458723.

v. See, e.g., Dzieza, J. (June 21, 2023). The human cost of AI. *The Verge*. www.theverge.com/features/23764584/ai-artificial-intelligence-data-notation-labor-scale-surge-remotasks-openai-chatbots; Perrigo, B. (February 17, 2022). Inside Facebook's African sweatshop. *Time*. https://time.com/6147458/facebook-africa-content-moderation-employee-treatment/; Perrigo, B. (January 18, 2023). OpenAI used Kenyan workers earning less than $2 per hour to make ChatGPT less toxic. *Time*. https://time.com/6247678/openai-chatgpt-kenya-workers/; Hao, K., & Seetharaman, D. (July 2024, 2023). Cleaning up ChatGPT takes heavy toll on human workers. *The Wall Street Journal*. www.wsj.com/tech/chatgpt-openai-content-abusive-sexually-explicit-harassment-kenya-workers-on-human-workers-cf191483; Shepherd, C., & Mahtani, S. (August 28, 2023). The dark side of AI: Exploiting the poor to train models. *The Washington Post*. www.washingtonpost.com/world/2023/08/28/scale-ai-remotasks-philippines-artificial-intelligence/.

vi. See, e.g., https://allenai.org/.

vii. Edwards, B. (May 29, 2025). AI video just took a startling leap in realism. Are we doomed? *Ars Technica*. https://arstechnica.com/ai/2025/05/ai-video-just-took-a-startling-leap-in-realism-are-we-doomed/.

viii. Harari, Y. N. (n.d.). How do we share the planet with this new superintelligence? *Wired*. www.wired.com/story/questions-answered-by-yuval-noah-harari-for-wired-ai-artificial-intelligence-singularity/.

9 AUTOMATION BIAS

i. Blair, E. (May 20, 2025). AI-generated summer reading list gets published in major newspapers. *NPR*. www.npr.org/2025/05/20/nx-s1-5405022/fake-summer-reading-list-ai.
ii. Jacobs, P. (May 30, 2025). Trump officials downplay fake citations in high-profile report on children's health. *Science*. www.science.org/content/article/trump-officials-downplay-fake-citations-high-profile-report-children-s-health.
iii. Mosier, K., & Skitka, L. (January, 1996). Human decision makers and automated decision aids: Made for each other? www.researchgate.net/publication/230601064_Human_Decision_Makers_and_Automated_Decision_Aids_Made_for_Each_Other.

10 ANTHROPOMORPHIZING

i. Gecker, J. (July 23, 2025). Teens say they are turning to AI for advice, friendship and more. *AP News*. https://apnews.com/article/ai-companion-generative-teens-mental-health-9ce59a2b250f3bd0187a717ffa2ad21f.
ii. Andreessen Horowitz. (August 27, 2025). The top 100 gen AI consumer apps – 5th edition. https://a16z.com/100-gen-ai-apps-5/.
iii. Dewitte, P. (2024). Better alone than in bad company: Addressing the risks of companion chatbots through data protection by design. *Computer Law and Security Review*, 54. https://doi.org/10.1016/j.clsr.2024.106019.
iv. Altman, S. @sama. (April 10, 2025). "we have greatly improved memory in chatgpt – it can now reference all your past conversations! this is a surprisingly great feature imo, and it points at something we are excited about." X. https://x.com/sama/status/1910380643772665873.
v. Pasquini, N. (November 9, 2023). A dashboard for artificial intelligence. *Harvard Magazine*. www.harvardmagazine.com/2023/11/harvard-artificial-intelligence-fernanda-viegas.
vi. Jamali, L., & McMahon, L. (August 7, 2025). OpenAI claims new GPT-5 model boosts ChatGPT to "'PhD level.'" www.bbc.com/news/articles/cy5prvgw0r1o.
vii. Zeff, M. (July 9, 2025). Elon Musk's xAI launches Grok 4 alongside a $300 monthly subscription. *TechCrunch*. https://techcrunch.com/2025/07/09/elon-musks-xai-launches-grok-4-alongside-a-300-monthly-subscription/.
viii. Jargon, J. (July 20, 2025). ChatGPT admits to ignoring signs of psychological distress: "i failed." *The Wall Street Journal*. www.wsj.com/tech/ai/chatgpt-chatbot-psychology-manic-episodes-57452d14?st=7kh4pW.
ix. O'Brien, M., & Ortutay, B. (August 6, 2025). Watchdog: ChatGPT gives teens dangerous advice on drugs, alcohol and suicide. *AP News*. https://apnews.com/article/chatgpt-study-harmful-advice-teens-c569cddf28f1f33b36c692428c2191d4.
x. Horwitz, J. (August 14, 2025). Meta's AI rules have let bots hold "sensual" chats with children. *Reuters*. www.reuters.com/investigates/special-report/meta-ai-chatbot-guidelines/.
xi. Horwitz, J. (April 26, 2025). Meta's "digital companions" will talk sex with users – even children. *The Wall Street Journal*. www.wsj.com/tech/ai/meta-ai-chatbots-sex-a25311bf?st=LQ4RGi.
xii. Merrill, J., & Oremus, W. (October 26, 2021). Facebook prioritized "angry" emoji reaction posts in news feeds. *The Washington Post*. www.washingtonpost.com/technology/2021/10/26/facebook-angry-emoji-algorithm/.

xiii. Irvine, R., Boubert, D., Raina, V., Liusie, A., Zhu, Z., Mudupalli, V., et al. (March 30, 2023). Rewarding chatbots for real-world engagement with millions of users. www.chai-research.com/.

xiv. Horwitz, J. (April 26, 2025). Meta's "digital companions" will talk sex with users – even children. *The Wall Street Journal*. www.wsj.com/tech/ai/meta-ai-chatbots-sex-a25311bf?st=LQ4RGi.

xv. Ibid.

xvi. Tingley, K. (June 20, 2025). Kids are in crisis: Could chatbot therapy help? *The New York Times*. www.nytimes.com/2025/06/20/magazine/ai-chatbot-therapy.html.

xvii. Caulfield, M. (May 9, 2025). AI is not your friend. *The Atlantic*. www.theatlantic.com/technology/archive/2025/05/sycophantic-ai/682743/?lctg=6050f6ebf98ec7553c07e3ac.

11 AN INTRODUCTION TO COPYRIGHT LAW

i. United States Congress. (May 16, 2023). Oversight of A.I.: Rules for artificial intelligence. Senate hearing 118-37. www.congress.gov/event/118th-congress/senate-event/LC71543/text.

ii. *The New York Times Company v. Microsoft*, No. 1:23-cv-11195 (S.D.N.Y. February 26, 2024). https://nytco-assets.nytimes.com/2023/12/NYT_Complaint_Dec2023.pdf.

iii. 17 U.S.C. § 107.

12 COPYRIGHT LAW AND GENAI EXCEPTIONALISM

i. Atkinson, D. (2025). Unfair learning: GenAI exceptionalism and copyright law. https://doi.org/10.2139/SSRN.4975857.

ii. See, e.g., Reisner, A. (August 19, 2023). Revealed: The authors whose pirated books are powering generative AI. *The Atlantic*. www.theatlantic.com/technology/archive/2023/08/books3-ai-meta-llama-pirated-books/675063/; Cole, S. (August 5, 2024). Leaked documents show Nvidia scraping "a human lifetime" of videos per day to train AI. *404 Media*. www.404media.co/nvidia-ai-scraping-foundational-model-cosmos-project/; Metz, C., Kang, C., Frenkel, S., Thompson, S. A., & Grant, N. (April 6, 2024). How tech giants cut corners to harvest data for A.I. *The New York Times*. www.nytimes.com/2024/04/06/technology/tech-giants-licensing,harvest-data-artificial-intelligence.html.

iii. Longpre, S., Biderman, S., Albalak, A., Schoelkopf, H., McDuff, D., Kapoor, S., et al. (2024). The responsible foundation model development cheatsheet: A review of tools & resources. arXiv. https://arxiv.org/abs/2406.16746 (p. 12: "In the context of cleaning and filtering web data, high-quality has referred to data known to have been written by humans, and has likely gone through an editing process, leading to the development of quality filters which aim to find data most similar to domains such as books or Wikipedia.").

iv. Order Denying the Plaintiffs' Motion for Partial Summary authors: Judgment and Granting Meta's Cross-Motion for Partial Summary Judgment, *Kadrey v. Meta Platforms, Inc.*, No. 3:23-cv-03417-VC-TSH, 2025 WL 56789 (N.D. Cal. June 25, 2025).

v. See Longpre, S., Biderman, S., Albalak, A., Schoelkopf, H., McDuff, D., Kapoor, S., et al. (2024). The responsible foundation model development cheatsheet: A review of tools & resources. arXiv. https://arxiv.org/abs/2406.16746 (p. 4: "It is common practice to upweight domains of 'high-quality' data; data that is known to be written by humans and has likely gone through an editing process such as Wikipedia and books.").

vi. Order on Fair Use, *Bartz v. Anthropic*, No. C 24-05417 WHA (N.D. Cal. June 23, 2025).
vii. Order Denying the Plaintiffs' Motion for Partial Summary Judgment and Granting Meta's Cross-Motion for Partial Summary Judgment, *Kadrey v. Meta Platforms, Inc.*, No. 3:23-cv-03417-VC-TSH, 2025 WL 56789 (N.D. Cal. June 25, 2025).
viii. See Horowitz, B., Smith, B., Andreessen, M., & Nadella, S. (November 1, 2024). AI for Startups. Andreessen Horowitz. https://a16z.com/ai-for-startups/ (A joint letter from Microsoft and the VC firm a16z says, in part, "Copyright law should not be co-opted to imply that machines should be prevented from using data – the foundation of AI – to learn in the same way as people.").
ix. The indiscriminate nature offers no special protection under copyright law. Cf. *Seuss*, 983 F.3d at 454 (finding no transformative use where defendant ComicMix had no particular need to use Seuss's material for its story).
x. Order Denying the Plaintiffs' Motion for Partial Summary Judgment and Granting Meta's Cross-Motion for Partial Summary Judgment, *Kadrey v. Meta Platforms, Inc.*, No. 3:23-cv-03417-VC-TSH, 2025 WL 56789 (N.D. Cal. June 25, 2025).
xi. Narayanan, A., & Kapoor, S. (January 22, 2024). Generative AI's end-run around copyright won't be resolved by the courts. www.aisnakeoil.com/p/generative-ais-end-run-around-copyright; also see generally Kleon, A. (2012). *Steal Like an Artist: 10 Things Nobody Told You about Being Creative* (Workman Publishing).
xii. Bracha, O. (2024). The work of copyright in the age of machine production. *Harvard Journal of Law & Technology*, 38(1), 171–226, 202.
xiii. Order Denying the Plaintiffs' Motion for Partial Summary Judgment and Granting Meta's Cross-Motion for Partial Summary Judgment, *Kadrey v. Meta Platforms, Inc.*, No. 3:23-cv-03417-VC-TSH, 2025 WL 56789 (N.D. Cal. June 25, 2025).
xiv. "'Copies' are material objects, other than phonorecords, in which a work is fixed by any method now known or later developed, and from which the work can be perceived, reproduced, or otherwise communicated, either directly or with the aid of a machine or device. The term 'copies' includes the material object, other than a phonorecord, in which the work is first fixed." 17 U.S.C. § 101 ("Copies").
xv. Longpre, S., Biderman, S., Albalak, A., Schoelkopf, H., McDuff, D., Kapoor, S., et al. (2024). The responsible foundation model development cheatsheet: A review of tools & resources. arXiv. https://arxiv.org/abs/2406.16746 (p. 11: "You should always spend a substantial amount of time reading through your dataset, ideally at many stages of the dataset design process.").
xvi. As Brauneis puts it,

> If the only thing copyright protected in a work were the aesthetic or hedonic reactions that it produced, or if works used to train GenAI were created for the sole purpose of producing such reactions, then that factual difference could make a legal difference … Adopting a view that an hedonic learning, and only an hedonic learning, is a fair use would unfairly disadvantage human authors for whom aesthetic experience and learning are inextricably intertwined. (p. 20)
>
> Brauneis, R. (2024). Copyright and the training of human authors and generative machines. https://papers.ssrn.com/abstract=4909592.

xvii. "Copyright protection subsists, in accordance with this title, in original works of authorship fixed in any tangible medium of expression, now known or later developed, from which they can be perceived, reproduced or otherwise communicated, either directly or with the aid of a machine or device." 17 U.S.C. § 102(a).
xviii. 17 U.S.C. § 106 ("[T]he owner of a copyright … has the exclusive right[] to … prepare derivative works based upon the copyrighted work."). A derivative is defined as "a work based upon one or more preexisting works," including "any … form in which a

work may be recast, transformed or adapted." 17 U.S.C. § 101 (definition of "derivative work"). A compilation is defined as "a work formed by the collection and assembling of preexisting materials or of data that are selected, coordinated, or arranged in such a way that the resulting work as a whole constitutes an original work of authorship."

xix. This position has been taken by OpenAI's counsel. See, e.g., Artificial Intelligence and Intellectual Property: Part I – Interoperability of AI and Copyright Law: Hearing before the U.S. H. Comm. on the Judiciary, Subcommittee on Courts, Intellectual Property, and the Internet 2 (2023). https://judiciary.house.gov/sites/evo-subsites/republicansjudiciary.house.gov/files/evo-media-document/damle-testimony.pdf (statement of Sy Damle); it is also held by prolific copyright law professor Matthew Sag in Sag, M. (2023). Copyright safety for generative AI. *Houston Law Review*, 61(2), 295–347, 307–309. https://papers.ssrn.com/sol3/papers.cfm?abstract_id=4438593; Sag, M. (2024). Fairness and fair use in Generative AI. *Fordham Law Review*, 92(5), 1887–1908. https://ir.lawnet.fordham.edu/cgi/viewcontent.cgi?article=6078&context=flr.

xx. See Sag, M. (2009). Copyright and copy-reliant technology. *Northwestern University Law Review*, 103(5), 1607–1682, 1638 ("[C]opyright law appears to embrace a general concept of expressive substitution. To the extent that communication of original expression to the public is the touchstone of copyright infringement, it follows that copyright liability should not ordinarily be found in circumstances where the use in question is incapable of giving rise to any expressive communication."); Grimmelmann, J. (2016). Copyright for literate robots. *Iowa Law Review*, 101, 657–681, 664 ("Verbatim copying of a complete work will be protected as fair use if the copy is used solely as input to a process that does not itself use the works expressively. Or, to put it a little more provocatively, nonexpressive uses do not count as reading. They are not part of the market that copyright cares about, because the author's market consists only of readers." (footnote omitted)).

xxi. Order on Fair Use, *Bartz v. Anthropic*, No. C 24-05417 WHA, (N.D. Cal. June 23, 2025).

xxii. *Sega*, 977 F.2d at 1517–1519 ("intermediate copying of computer object code may infringe the exclusive rights granted to the copyright owner in ik of the Copyright Act regardless of whether the end product of the copying infringes those rights."), *Sony Computer*, 203 F.3d at 602–603 ("In Sega, we recognized that intermediate copying could constitute infringement even when the end product did not itself contain copyrighted material.").

xxiii. American Farm Bureau Federation. (2026). Fast facts about agriculture & food. www.fb.org/newsroom/fast-facts.

xxiv. Brumfiel, G. (July 12, 2024). Research shows AI can boost creativity for some, but at a cost. NPR. www.npr.org/2024/07/12/nx-s1-5033988/research-ai-chatbots-creativity-writing.

xxv. U.S. Constitution, Art. 1.

13 AN INTRODUCTION TO THE FIRST AMENDMENT

i. *Whitney v. California*, 274 U.S. 357 (1927).

ii. *Abrams v. United States*, 250 U.S. 616 (1919).

iii. Austin, M., & Levy, M. (2025). Speech certainty: Algorithmic speech and the limits of the First Amendment. *Stanford Law Review*, 77(1), 1–88. www.stanfordlawreview.org/print/article/speech-certainty-algorithmic-speech-and-the-limits-of-the-first-amendment/.

iv. Atkinson, D., Hwang, J. D., & Morrison, J. (2025). Intentionally unintentional: GenAI exceptionalism and the First Amendment. *First Amendment Law Review*. https://doi.org/10.2139/ssrn.4964912.

17 LICENSING FOR GENAI

i. According to the Open Source Initiative, "For Pypi, the package manager for Python [the most common language for AI research], components under the MIT and Apache 2.0 licenses dominate, at 29.14% and 23.98% respectively." Vidal, N. (December 7, 2023). The most popular licenses for each language in 2023. Open Source Initiative. https://opensource.org/blog/the-most-popular-licenses-for-each-language-2023. Many open-source GenAI models are released under the Apache 2.0 license, including those from Ai2, Mistral, LAION, Hugging Face, Salesforce, Amazon, and xAI. Stanford Institute for Human-Centered AI. (n.d.). Ecosystem graphs: The social footprint of foundation models. https://crfm.stanford.edu/ecosystem-graphs/index.html?mode=table.
ii. Apache Software Foundations. (n.d.). Apache License, Version 2.0. www.apache.org/licenses/LICENSE-2.0.
iii. *DOE 1 v. GitHub, Inc.*, No. 4:22-cv-06823 (N.D. Cal. February 11, 2025).

18 TORT LAW

i. Restatement (Second) of Torts § 402A comment 1.
ii. *Rylands v. Fletcher*, LR 3 HL 330 (1868).
iii. Restatement (Third) of Torts: Products Liability § 19(a).
iv. National Transportation Safety Board. (June 24, 2025). In-flight separation of left mid exit door plug, Alaska Airlines Flight 1282, Boeing 737-9, N704AL. www.ntsb.gov/investigations/AccidentReports/Reports/AIR2504.pdf.

19 PROPERTY, EXCLUSION, AND TRESPASS

i. *Kaiser Aetna v. United States*, 444 U.S. 164, 176 (1979).
ii. RFC 8820: URI Design and Ownership. (June, 2020). www.rfc-editor.org/rfc/rfc8820.

20 THE ECONOMICS OF THE INTERNET

i. *Kadrey v. Meta Platforms, Inc.*, No. 3:23-cv-03417, (N.D. Cal. March 28, 2025). www.courtlistener.com/docket/67569326/501/kadrey-v-meta-platforms-inc/.
ii. E.g., Lee, E. (2025). Fair use and the origin of AI training. https://doi.org/10.2139/SSRN.5253011. ("This history should inform the courts' resolution of fair use in the copyright lawsuits against AI companies. Courts should evaluate whether the use of copyrighted works in AI training at universities serves a fair use purpose – or not – by examining whether AI training serves a different or transformative purpose. For, if the use of copyrighted materials by university researchers to develop AI models is copyright infringement and not fair use, then, a fortiori, the fair use defense of AI companies, commercial entities, must fail. Conversely, if the courts find that such university-based AI training has a legitimate fair use purpose, then courts should reject broad arguments that use of copyrighted works in AI training by companies cannot serve a fair use purpose – e.g., because it purportedly is 'not transformative' at all.").
iii. Tome, J. (August 29, 2025). The crawl-to-click gap: Cloudflare data on AI bots, training, and referrals. *The Cloudflare Blog*. https://blog.cloudflare.com/crawlers-click-ai-bots-training/.

(Tome also notes that only 18 percent of AI crawling was for search, and 2 percent was for user actions.).

iv. According to TollBit, which seems to have a higher percentage of media companies as clients, "RAG bot scrapes now exceed Training bot scrapes across the TollBit network. From Q4 2024 to Q1 2025, RAG bot scrapes per site grew 49%, nearly 2.5X the rate of Training bot scrapes (which grew by 18%)1. This is a clear signal that AI tools require continuous access to content and data for RAG vs for training." TollBit. (June 11, 2025). State of the bots – Q1 2025. https://tollbit.com/state-of-the-bots/q1-2025/.

v. Ibid.

vi. Lee, J., Gupta, D., Mitchell, B., Tatoris, R., & Clausen, H. (July 1, 2025). Control content use for AI training with Cloudflare's managed robots.txt and blocking for monetized content. https://blog.cloudflare.com/control-content-use-for-ai-training/.

vii. *Reddit, Inc. v. Anthropic PBC*, No. 3:25-cv-05643 (N.D.C.A. July 3, 2025). www.courtlistener.com/docket/70704683/reddit-inc-v-anthropic-pbc/.

viii. Wiens, K. @kwiens. (July 24, 2024). "Hey @AnthropicAI: I get you're hungry for data. Claude is really smart! But do you really need to hit our servers a million times in 24 hours? You're not only taking our content without paying." X. https://x.com/kwiens/status/1816128302542905620.

ix. Mueller, B., Danis, C., & Lavagetto, G. (April 1, 2025). How crawlers impact the operations of the Wikimedia projects. https://diff.wikimedia.org/2025/04/01/how-crawlers-impact-the-operations-of-the-wikimedia-projects/.

x. TollBit. (June 11, 2025). State of the bots – Q1 2025. https://tollbit.com/state-of-the-bots/q1-2025/.

xi. Venerandi, N. (March 20, 2025). FOSS infrastructure is under attack by AI companies. https://thelibre.news/foss-infrastructure-is-under-attack-by-ai-companies/.

xii. Holscher, E. (July 25, 2024). AI crawlers need to be more respectful. Read the Docs. https://about.readthedocs.com/blog/2024/07/ai-crawlers-abuse/.

xiii. Weinberg, M. (June 2025). Are AI bots knocking cultural heritage offline? GLAM-E Lab. www.glamelab.org/products/are-ai-bots-knocking-cultural-heritage-offline/.

xiv. Confederation of Open Access Repositories. (June 3, 2025). Open repositories are being profoundly impacted by AI bots and other crawlers: Report from a COAR Survey. https://coar-repositories.org/news-updates/open-repositories-are-being-profoundly-impacted-by-ai-bots-and-other-crawlers-results-of-a-coar-survey/.

xv. Kim, T., Bock, K., Luo, C., Liswood, A., Poroslay, C., & Wenger, E. (2025). Scrapers selectively respect robots.txt directives: Evidence from a large-scale empirical study. *Proceedings of ACM Conference (Conference'17)*. https://arxiv.org/pdf/2505.21733v1.

xvi. TollBit. (June 11, 2025). State of the bots – Q1 2025. https://tollbit.com/state-of-the-bots/q1-2025/.

xvii. Lee, J., Gupta, D., Mitchell, B., Tatoris, R., & Clausen, H. (July 1, 2025). Control content use for AI training with Cloudflare's managed robots.txt and blocking for monetized content. https://blog.cloudflare.com/control-content-use-for-ai-training/.

xviii. Bocharov, A., Vargas, S., Martinetti, A., Tatoris, R., & Azevedo, C. (July 3, 2024). Declare your AIndependence: Block AI bots, scrapers and crawlers with a single click. https://blog.cloudflare.com/declaring-your-aindependence-block-ai-bots-scrapers-and-crawlers-with-a-single-click/.

xix. Lee, J., Gupta, D., Mitchell, B., Tatoris, R., & Clausen, H. (July 1, 2025). Control content use for AI training with Cloudflare's managed robots.txt and blocking for monetized content. https://blog.cloudflare.com/control-content-use-for-ai-training/. (These efforts appear to be working. The share of sites GPTBot crawls decreased almost 6.5 percent from the year before.).

xx. TollBit. (June 11, 2025). State of the bots – Q1 2025. https://tollbit.com/state-of-the-bots/q1-2025/. ("'Other' platforms account for the remaining 15% and is comprised of search engines like Bing, Yahoo, and DuckDuckGo as well as social media platforms like LinkedIn and TikTok.").

xxi. Ibid.

xxii. Cloudflare. (n.d.). Cloudflare Radar: AI insights. https://radar.cloudflare.com/ai-insights#crawl-to-refer-ratio.

xxiii. Moon, M. (June 20, 2025). Cloudflare CEO says people aren't checking AI chatbots' source links. www.engadget.com/ai/cloudflare-ceo-says-people-arent-checking-ai-chatbots-source-links-120016921.html.

xxiv. Belson, David, & Rhea, S. (July 1, 2025). The crawl before the fall … of referrals: Understanding AI's impact on content providers. https://blog.cloudflare.com/ai-search-crawl-refer-ratio-on-radar/.

xxv. Wong, M. (November 8, 2024). The death of search. *The Atlantic*. www.theatlantic.com/technology/archive/2024/11/ai-search-engines-curiosity/680594/.

xxvi. Chapekis, A., & Lieb, A. (July 22, 2025). Do people click on links in Google AI summaries? Pew Research Center. www.pewresearch.org/short-reads/2025/07/22/google-users-are-less-likely-to-click-on-links-when-an-ai-summary-appears-in-the-results/.

xxvii. Sommerfeld, N. (February 19, 2025). Consumer reliance on AI search results signals new era of marketing. Bain & Company. bit.ly/3OnPko1.

xxviii. Law, R., & Guan, X. (April 17, 2025). AI overviews reduce clicks by 34.5%. https://ahrefs.com/blog/ai-overviews-reduce-clicks/.

xxix. Bastian, M. (May 17, 2025). Google's AI answers are changing user behavior by sharply reducing clicks to websites. https://the-decoder.com/googles-ai-answers-are-changing-user-behavior-by-sharply-reducing-clicks-to-websites/.

xxx. Simonetti, I., & Blunt, K. (June 10, 2025). Google's new AI tools are crushing news sites. *The Wall Street Journal*. www.wsj.com/tech/ai/google-ai-news-publishers-7e687141.

xxxi. Ovide, S. (July 1, 2025). AI is threatening your favorite websites. The internet is pushing back. *The Washington Post*. www.washingtonpost.com/technology/2025/07/01/ai-crawlers-reddit-wikipedia-fight/.

xxxii. Edwards, B. (March 13, 2025). AI search engines cite incorrect news sources at an alarming 60% rate, study says. *Ars Technica*. https://arstechnica.com/ai/2025/03/ai-search-engines-give-incorrect-answers-at-an-alarming-60-rate-study-says/.

xxxiii. Fishkin, R. (July 1, 2024). 2024 Zero-Click Search Study: For every 1,000 EU Google searches, only 374 clicks go to the open web. In the US, it's 360. SparkToro. https://sparktoro.com/blog/2024-zero-click-search-study-for-every-1000-us-google-searches-only-374-clicks-go-to-the-open-web-in-the-eu-its-360/.

xxxiv. Tobitt, C. (May 12, 2025). How Google forced publishers to accept AI scraping as price of appearing in search. *Press Gazette*. https://pressgazette.co.uk/platforms/how-google-forced-publishers-to-accept-ai-scraping-as-price-of-appearing-in-search/.

xxxv. *Chegg, Inc. v. Google LLC*, No. 1:25-cv-00543 (D.D.C. February 24, 2025).

xxxvi. Alphabet Investor Relations. (n.d.). Earnings. https://abc.xyz/investor/Earnings/default.aspx.

xxxvii. De Vynck, G., & Zakrzewksi, C. (May 13, 2024). Web publishers brace for carnage as Google adds AI answers. *The Washington Post*. www.washingtonpost.com/technology/2024/05/13/google-ai-search-io-sge/.

xxxviii. Perloff, C. (August 5, 2025). Advertisers can't quit Google, despite complaints about traffic and ads. *The Information*. www.theinformation.com/articles/advertisers-quit-google-despite-complaints-traffic-ads.

xxxix. See, e.g., ibid. ("Google says the study used a flawed methodology.").

xxxx. See, e.g., Reisner, A. (June 25, 2025). AI is already crushing the news industry. *The Atlantic*. www.theatlantic.com/technology/archive/2025/06/generative-ai-pirated-articles-books/683009/. ("Google argued that it was sending 'higher-quality' traffic to publisher websites, meaning that users purportedly spend more time on the sites once they click over, but declined to offer any data in support of this claim.").

xxxxi. Gerber, J. (July 14, 2025). Behind the IAB Tech Lab's new initiative to deal with AI Scraping and publisher revenue loss. *AdExchanger*. www.adexchanger.com/publishers/behind-the-iab-tech-labs-new-initiative-to-deal-with-ai-scraping-and-publisher-revenue-loss/.

21 OLIGOPOLIES

i. Barnett, E. (July 7, 2025). The battle over books is being fought on three fronts. *Wired*. www.wired.com/story/battle-over-books3/.

ii. Richter, F. (November 4, 2025). Chart: AWS stays ahead as cloud market accelerates. Statista. www.statista.com/chart/18819/worldwide-market-share-of-leading-cloud-infrastructure-service-providers/.

iii. StatCounter. (n.d.). Mobile operating system market share worldwide: February 2025. https://gs.statcounter.com/os-market-share/mobile/worldwide/#monthly-202502-202502-bar.

iv. StatCounter. (n.d.). Desktop operating system market share worldwide: February 2025. https://gs.statcounter.com/os-market-share/desktop/worldwide/#monthly-202502-202502-bar.

v. TechInsights. (2024). Data-center AI chip market: Q1 2024 update. www.techinsights.com/blog/data-center-ai-chip-market-q1-2024-update.

vi. Bailyn, E. (September, 2024). Top generative AI chatbots by market share. First Page Sage. https://firstpagesage.com/reports/top-generative-ai-chatbots/.

vii. Zuckerberg, M., & Crawford, D. (2023). First quarter 2023 results conference call. https://s21.q4cdn.com/399680738/files/doc_financials/2023/q1/META-Q1-2023-Earnings-Call-Transcript.pdf. ("[PyTorch] has generally become the standard in the industry … It's generally been very valuable for us … Because it's integrated with our technology stack, when there are opportunities to make integrations with products, it's much easier to make sure that developers and other folks are compatible with the things that we need in the way that our systems work.").

viii. Macrotrends. (n.d.). Microsoft market cap. www.macrotrends.net/stocks/charts/MSFT/microsoft/market-cap.

ix. Macrotrends. (n.d.). Amazon market cap. www.macrotrends.net/stocks/charts/AMZN/amazon/market-cap.

x. Macrotrends. (n.d.). Google market cap. www.macrotrends.net/stocks/charts/GOOGL/alphabet/market-cap.

xi. Glasner, J. (March 1, 2023). The biggest funding rounds for OpenAI and Silicon Ranch this week. *Crunchbase News*. bit.ly/4rYILzq.

xii. Goldman, S. (February 3, 2023). Google invests $300 million in Anthropic as race to compete with ChatGPT heats up. *VentureBeat*. https://venturebeat.com/ai/google-invests-300-million-in-anthropic-as-race-to-compete-with-chatgpt-heats-up/.

xiii. Cohere. (n.d.). Wikipedia. https://en.wikipedia.org/wiki/Cohere.

xiv. Wiggers, K. (August 24, 2023). Hugging Face raises $235M from investors, including Salesforce and Nvidia. *TechCrunch*. https://techcrunch.com/2023/08/24/hugging-face-raises-235m-from-investors-including-salesforce-and-nvidia/.

xv. Bishop, T. (February 15, 2025). "Open source will win": Allen Institute for AI CEO Ali Farhadi on the new era of artificial intelligence. *GeekWire*. www.geekwire.com/2025/open-source-will-win-allen-institute-for-ai-ceo-ali-farhadi-on-the-new-era-of-artificial-intelligence/.

xvi. Patrick, D. (July 3, 2025). AI is eating venture capital, or at least its dollars. *Axios*. www.axios.com/2025/07/03/ai-startups-vc-investments.

xvii. Stanford Institute for Human-Centered AI. (2025). 2025 AI Index Report. https://hai.stanford.edu/ai-index/2025-ai-index-report.

xviii. UT News. (November 17, 2025). UT eclipses 5,000 GPUs to increase dominance in open-source AI, strengthen nation's computing power. https://news.utexas.edu/2025/11/17/ut-eclipses-5000-gpus-to-increase-dominance-in-open-source-ai-strengthen-nations-computing-power/.

xix. Hassam, N. (July 21, 2025). Sam Altman says OpenAI will own "well over 1 million GPUs" by the end of the year – ChatGPT maker continues to expand rapidly. *Tom's Hardware*. bit.ly/4c6Lcvo.

xx. Widder, D. G., Whittaker, M., & Myers West, S. (2024). Why "open" AI systems are actually closed, and why this matters. *Nature*, 635, 827–833. www.nature.com/articles/s41586-024-08141-1.

22 ENVIRONMENTAL IMPACT

i. Luccioni, S., Trevelin, B., & Mitchell, M. (September 3, 2024). The environmental impacts of AI – primer. https://huggingface.co/blog/sasha/ai-environment-primer.

ii. Tan, E. (July 16, 2025). Their water taps ran dry when Meta built next door. *The New York Times*. www.nytimes.com/2025/07/14/technology/meta-data-center-water.html.

iii. Ibid.

iv. Jafari, T., Balyk, O., Wu, L., & Glynn, J. (July 17, 2024). Projecting the electricity demand growth of generative AI large language models in the US. www.energypolicy.columbia.edu/projecting-the-electricity-demand-growth-of-generative-ai-large-language-models-in-the-us/.

v. Kwong, E. (March 30, 2025). AI and the environment. *Consider This*. Audio podcast. www.npr.org/2025/03/30/1241844391/ai-and-the-environment.

vi. Harper, E. (November 21, 2024). AI energy needs are producing more greenhouse gas and threatening climate goals. *The Washington Post*. www.washingtonpost.com/climate-environment/2024/11/19/ai-cop29-climate-data-centers/.

vii. O'Donnell, J., & Crownhart, C. (May 20, 2025). We did the math on AI's energy footprint. Here's the story you haven't heard. *MIT Technology Review*. www.technologyreview.com/2025/05/20/1116327/ai-energy-usage-climate-footprint-big-tech/amp.

viii. Donovan, P. (May 7, 2025). The looming power crunch: Solutions for data center expansion in an energy-constrained world. Schneider Electric. www.se.com/ww/en/insights/ai-and-technology/artificial-intelligence/looming-power-crunch/.

ix. Wealthfront. (October 9, 2025). Vested interest: Why the stock market loves skyrocketing electricity bills. www.wealthfront.com/blog/vested-interest-why-the-stock-market-loves-skyrocketing-electricity-bills/.

x. Harper, E., & O'Donovan, C. (June 21, 2024). Tech firms look for a miracle solution as AI exhausts the power grid. *The Washington Post*. www.washingtonpost.com/business/2024/06/21/artificial-intelligence-nuclear-fusion-climate/.
xi. Bennett, A. (December 4, 2025). Unconstrained demand: Virginia's data center expansion and its impacts. www.sierraclub.org/virginia/data-centers.
xii. Harper, E., & O'Donovan, C. (June 21, 2024). Tech firms look for a miracle solution as AI exhausts the power grid. *The Washington Post*. www.washingtonpost.com/business/2024/06/21/artificial-intelligence-nuclear-fusion-climate/.
xiii. Ibid.
O'Donnell, J., & Crownhart, C. (May 20, 2025). We did the math on AI's energy footprint. Here's the story you haven't heard. *MIT Technology Review*. www.technologyreview.com/2025/05/20/1116327/ai-energy-usage-climate-footprint-big-tech/amp.
xiv. Chen, A. (September 29, 2025). A.I. is on the rise, and so is the environmental impact of the data centers that drive it. *Smithsonian Magazine*. www.smithsonianmag.com/science-nature/with-ai-on-the-rise-what-will-be-the-environmental-impacts-of-data-centers-180987379/.
xv. Hilt, E. (February 16, 2026). xAI built an illegal power plant to power its data center. www.selc.org/news/xai-built-an-illegal-power-plant-to-power-its-data-center/.
xvi. Muller, W. (February 27, 2026). Meta's data center ownership transfer doesn't concern Louisiana power regulators. *Louisiana Illuminator*. https://lailluminator.com/2026/02/27/no-investigation-of-data-center-ownership-transfer/.
xvii. O'Brien, M. (September 24, 2025). OpenAI shows off Stargate AI data center in Texas and plans 5 more elsewhere with Oracle, Softbank. *AP News*. https://apnews.com/article/openai-stargate-oracle-data-center-0b3f4fa6e8d8141b4c143e3e7f41aba1.
xviii. Nakagawa, M. (February 13, 2025). Progress on the road to 2030. *Microsoft on the Issues*. https://blogs.microsoft.com/on-the-issues/2025/02/13/progress-on-the-road-to-2030/.
xix. O'Donnell, J., & Crownhart, C. (May 20, 2025). We did the math on AI's energy footprint. Here's the story you haven't heard. *MIT Technology Review*. www.technologyreview.com/2025/05/20/1116327/ai-energy-usage-climate-footprint-big-tech/amp.

23 GENAI IN EDUCATION

i. Bousquette, I. (April 25, 2025). Prompt engineer, the hottest AI Job of 2023, is already obsolete. *The Wall Street Journal*. www.wsj.com/articles/the-hottest-ai-job-of-2023-is-already-obsolete-1961b054?reflink=desktopwebshare_permalink.
ii. Bradford Hill, A. (2015). The environment and disease: association or causation? *Journal of the Royal Society of Medicine*, 108(1), 32–37. https://pmc.ncbi.nlm.nih.gov/articles/PMC4291332/.
iii. Khan, S. (n.d.). Khan Academy annual report: SY24–25. https://annualreport.khanacademy.org/.

24 EDUCATION AND DEMOCRACY

i. Salhotra, P. (July 27, 2025). A.I.-driven education: Founded in Texas and coming to a school near you. *The New York Times*. www.nytimes.com/2025/07/27/us/politics/ai-alpha-school-austin-texas.html.
ii. Jefferson, T. (1779). A bill for the more general diffusion of knowledge. https://founders.archives.gov/documents/Jefferson/01-02-02-0132-0004-0079.

iii. Madison, J. (August 4, 1822). James Madison to W. T Barry. In P. B. Kurland & R. Lerner (eds.) (1986). *The Founders Constitution* (University of Chicago Press). https://press-pubs.uchicago.edu/founders/documents/v1ch18s35.html.
iv. Closson, T. (October 14, 2025). Inside the new Bible-infused Texas English curriculum. *The New York Times*. www.nytimes.com/2025/10/14/us/bible-public-school-curriculum-texas.html.
v. Musk, E. @elonmusk. (July 12, 2025). "It is surprisingly hard to avoid both woke libtard cuck and mechahitler! Spent several hours trying to solve this with the system prompt, but there is too much." X. https://x.com/elonmusk/status/1944132781745090819?lang=en.
vi. O'Brien, M. (July 11, 2025). Musk's latest Grok chatbot searches for billionaire mogul's views before answering questions. *AP News*. https://apnews.com/article/grok-4-elon-musk-xai-colossus-14d575fb490c2b679ed3111a1c83f857.

25 HUMAN AUTONOMY

i. Appiah, K. A. (October 26, 2025). The age of de-skilling. *The Atlantic*. www.theatlantic.com/ideas/archive/2025/10/ai-deskilling-automation-technology/684669/.
ii. Krikorian, R. (October 30, 2025). The validation machines. *The Atlantic*. www.theatlantic.com/ideas/archive/2025/10/validation-ai-raffi-krikorian/684764/.

26 ARTIFICIAL GENERAL INTELLIGENCE

i. Mitchell, M. (March 21, 2024). Debates on the nature of artificial general intelligence. *Science*. www.science.org/doi/10.1126/science.ado7069.
ii. Good, I. J. (1965). Speculations concerning the first ultraintelligent machine. *Advances in Computers*, 6, 31–88, 33. https://doi.org/10.1016/S0065-2458(08)60418-0.
iii. Keil, C. @pronounced_kyle. (March 16, 2024). "My 3-month-old son is now TWICE as big as when he was born. He's on track to weigh 7.5 trillion pounds by age 10." X. https://x.com/pronounced_kyle/status/1768852493092680036?lang=en.
iv. Mickle, T., & Metz, C. (November 18, 2025). Google unveils Gemini 3, with improved coding and search abilities. *The New York Times*. www.nytimes.com/2025/11/18/technology/google-gemini-3.html.
v. Metz, C., & Weise, K. (May 5, 2025). A.I. is getting more powerful, but its hallucinations are getting worse. *The New York Times*. www.nytimes.com/2025/05/05/technology/ai-hallucinations-chatgpt-google.html.
vi. Altman, S. (January 6, 2025). Reflections. https://blog.samaltman.com/reflections.
vii. Huckins, G. (August 7, 2025). GPT-5 is here. Now what? *MIT Technology Review*. www.technologyreview.com/2025/08/07/1121308/gpt-5-is-here-now-what/.
viii. Browne, R. (August 11, 2025). Sam Altman now says AGI, or human-level AI, is "not a super useful term" – and he's not alone. *CNBC*. www.cnbc.com/2025/08/11/sam-altman-says-agi-is-a-pointless-term-experts-agree.html.

27 FRAMEWORKS FOR THINKING ABOUT GENAI

i. Palazzolo, S., & Huang, K. (July 1, 2025). What Zuckerberg's new AI team is good at. *The Information*. www.theinformation.com/newsletters/ai-agenda/zuckerbergs-new-ai-team-good.

ii. McLaughlin, K. (June 26, 2025). Benioff says AI is handling up to half of Salesforce's work. *The Information.* www.theinformation.com/briefings/benioff-says-ai-handling-half-salesforces-work.

iii. Knight, W. (June 4, 2025). Perplexity's CEO sees AI agents as the next web battleground. *Wired.* www.wired.com/story/perplexitys-ceo-sees-ai-agents-as-the-next-web-battleground/.

iv. Halper, E. (February 23, 2025). Firms sideline climate goals as AI and Trump drive a rush to fossil fuels. *The Washington Post.* www.washingtonpost.com/business/2025/02/23/ai-gas-trump-climate-fossil/.

v. Ibid. Emphasis added.

vi. Roose, K. (April 24, 2025). If A.I. systems become conscious, should they have rights? *The New York Times.* www.nytimes.com/2025/04/24/technology/ai-welfare-anthropic-claude.html. For even more examples of AI reporting pitfalls, read Kapoor, S., & Narayanan, A. (September 30, 2022). A checklist of eighteen pitfalls in AI journalism: Flawed human–AI comparison. www.cs.princeton.edu/~sayashk/ai-hype/ai-reporting-pitfalls.pdf.

vii. Wasik, B. (June 16, 2025). A.I. is poised to rewrite history. Literally. *The New York Times.* www.nytimes.com/2025/06/16/magazine/ai-history-historians-scholarship.html.

viii. On the Media. (September 20, 2013). The Breaking News Consumer's Handbook. www.wnycstudios.org/podcasts/otm/articles/breaking-news-consumers-handbook-pdf.

ix. Pichai, S., Hassabis, D., & Kavukcuoglu, K. (November 18, 2025). A new era of intelligence with Gemini 3. https://blog.google/products-and-platforms/products/gemini/gemini-3/#note-from-ceo; Google DeepMind. (February 19, 2026). Gemini 3.1 Pro. https://deepmind.google/models/model-cards/gemini-3-1-pro/.

x. Stanford Institute for Human-Centered AI. (2025). 2025 AI Index Report. https://hai.stanford.edu/ai-index/2025-ai-index-report.

xi. Edwards, B. (April 7, 2025). Meta's surprise Llama 4 drop exposes the gap between AI ambition and reality. *Ars Technica.* https://arstechnica.com/ai/2025/04/metas-surprise-llama-4-drop-exposes-the-gap-between-ai-ambition-and-reality/.

xii. Schubert, S. @StefanFSchubert. (October 17, 2025). "Replying to a VP of science at OpenAI. Be sceptical of these types of claims." X. https://x.com/StefanFSchubert/status/1979265669427306507.

xiii. Chollet, F. @fchollet. (March 4, 2024). "When you hear about 'human-level AI' being just 'one LLM training run away', it's as if people building 3D printers (the kind that makes small, flimsy plastic …)." X. https://x.com/fchollet/status/1764545140075438388.

xiv. Lowe, D. (March 19, 2021). AI and drug discovery: Attacking the right problems. *Science.* www.science.org/content/blog-post/ai-and-drug-discovery-attacking-right-problems; Lowe, D. (April 21, 2025). The end of disease. *Science.* www.science.org/content/blog-post/end-disease.

xv. Nakagawa, M. (February 13, 2025). Progress on the road to 2030. *Microsoft on the Issues.* https://blogs.microsoft.com/on-the-issues/2025/02/13/progress-on-the-road-to-2030/.

xvi. Cutter, C., & Zimmerman, H. (July 2, 2025). CEOs start saying the quiet part out loud: AI will wipe out jobs. *The Wall Street Journal.* www.wsj.com/tech/ai/ai-white-collar-job-loss-b9856259.

Index

Printed in the United Kingdom by TJ Clays Ltd.